SANCTUARY

by
Terry Moore

I don't know what fabric lies beneath the life we live, but on the other side of our mortal pain is a place of sanctuary.

-Katchoo

STRANGERS IN PARADISE: SANCTUARY

First Edition: November 1999
ISBN 1-892597-09-8

Printed in Canada by Quebecor Printing, Montreal

Published by
Abstract Studio, Inc.
P. O. Box 271487
Houston, Texas 77277

CONTENTS

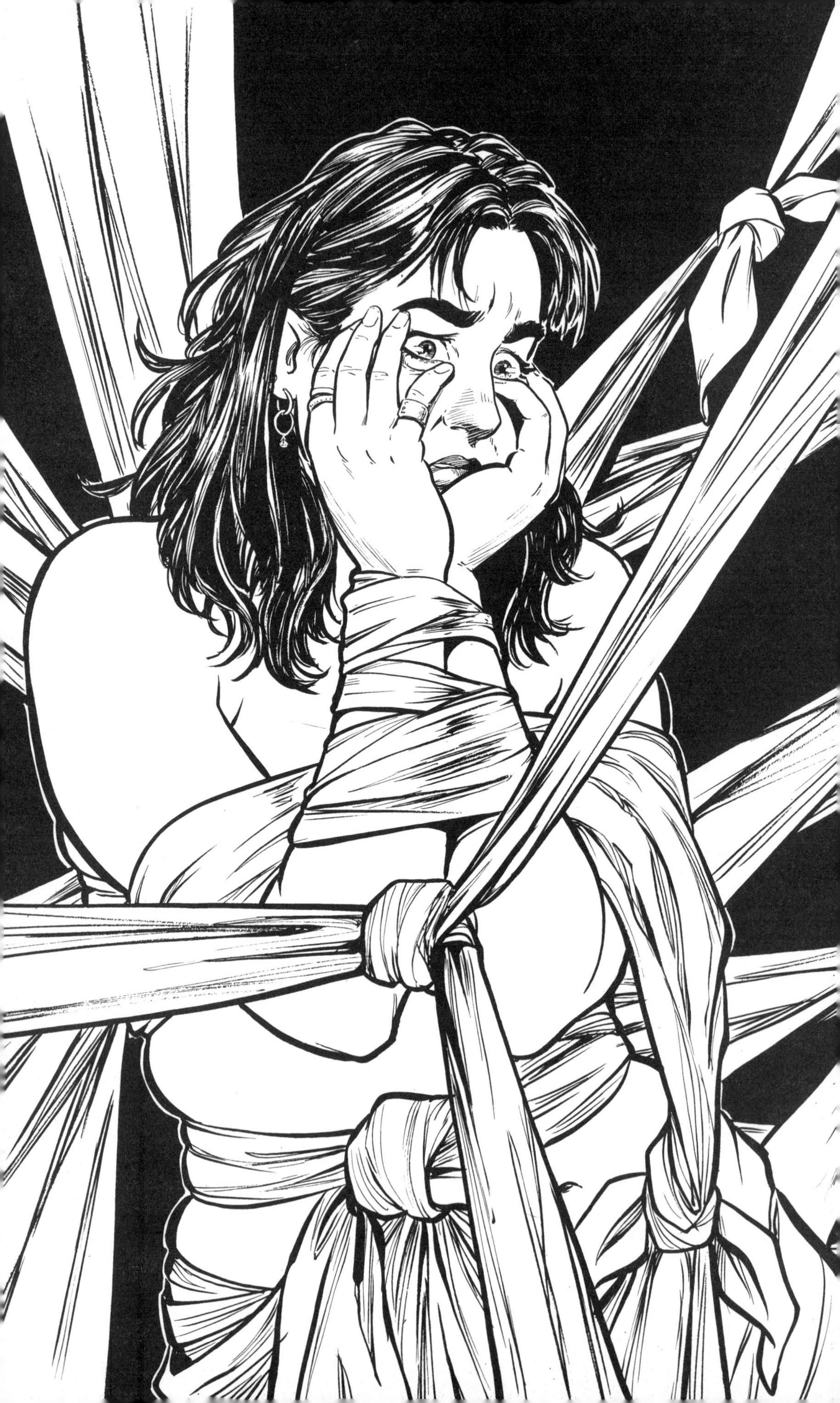

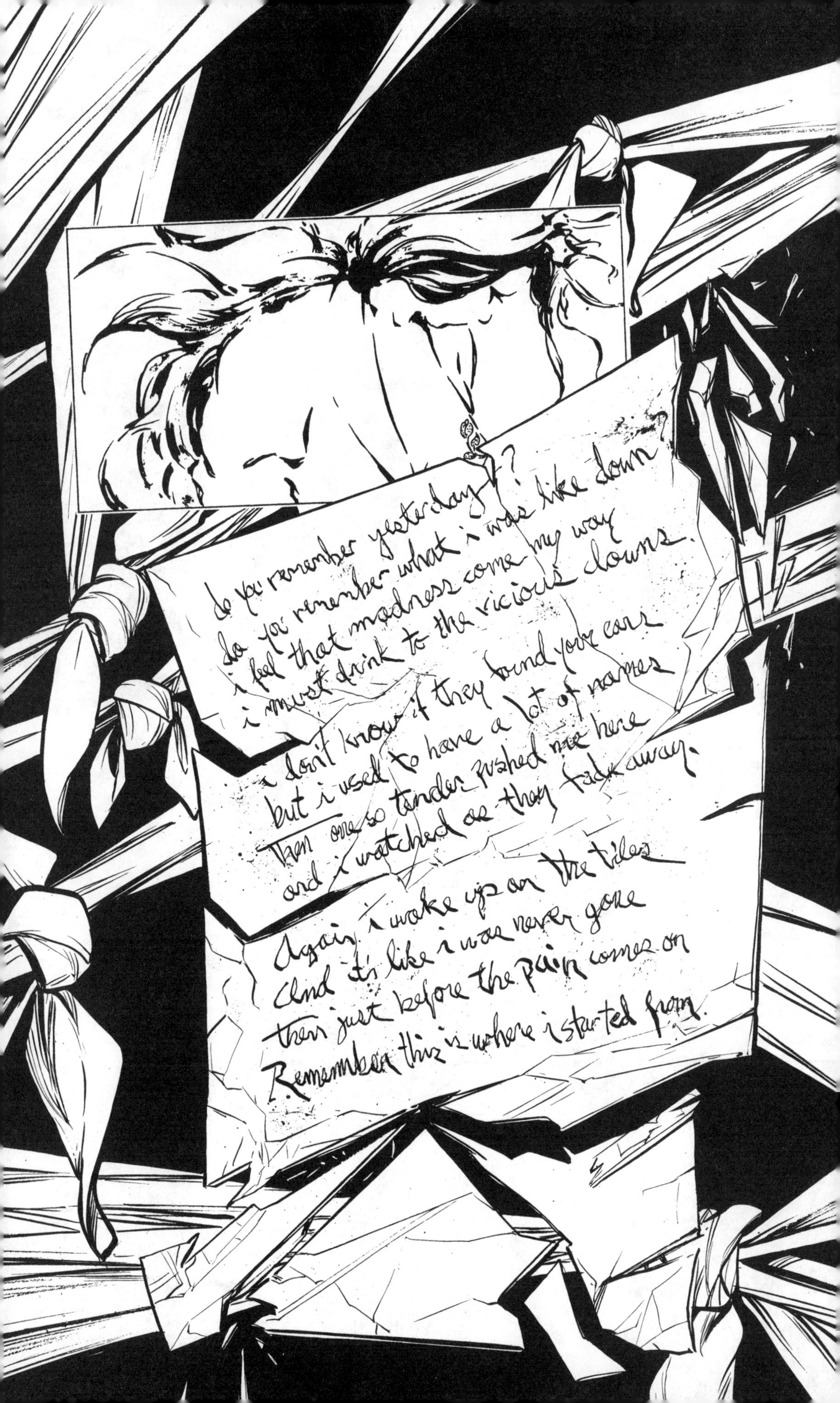
do you remember yesterday?
do you remember what i was like down
i feel that madness come my way
i must drink to the vicious clowns.
i don't know if they found your cars
but i used to have a lot of names
Then one so tender pushed me here
and i watched as they took away;
Again i wake up on the tiles
And it's like i was never gone
then just before the pain comes on
Remember this is where i started from.

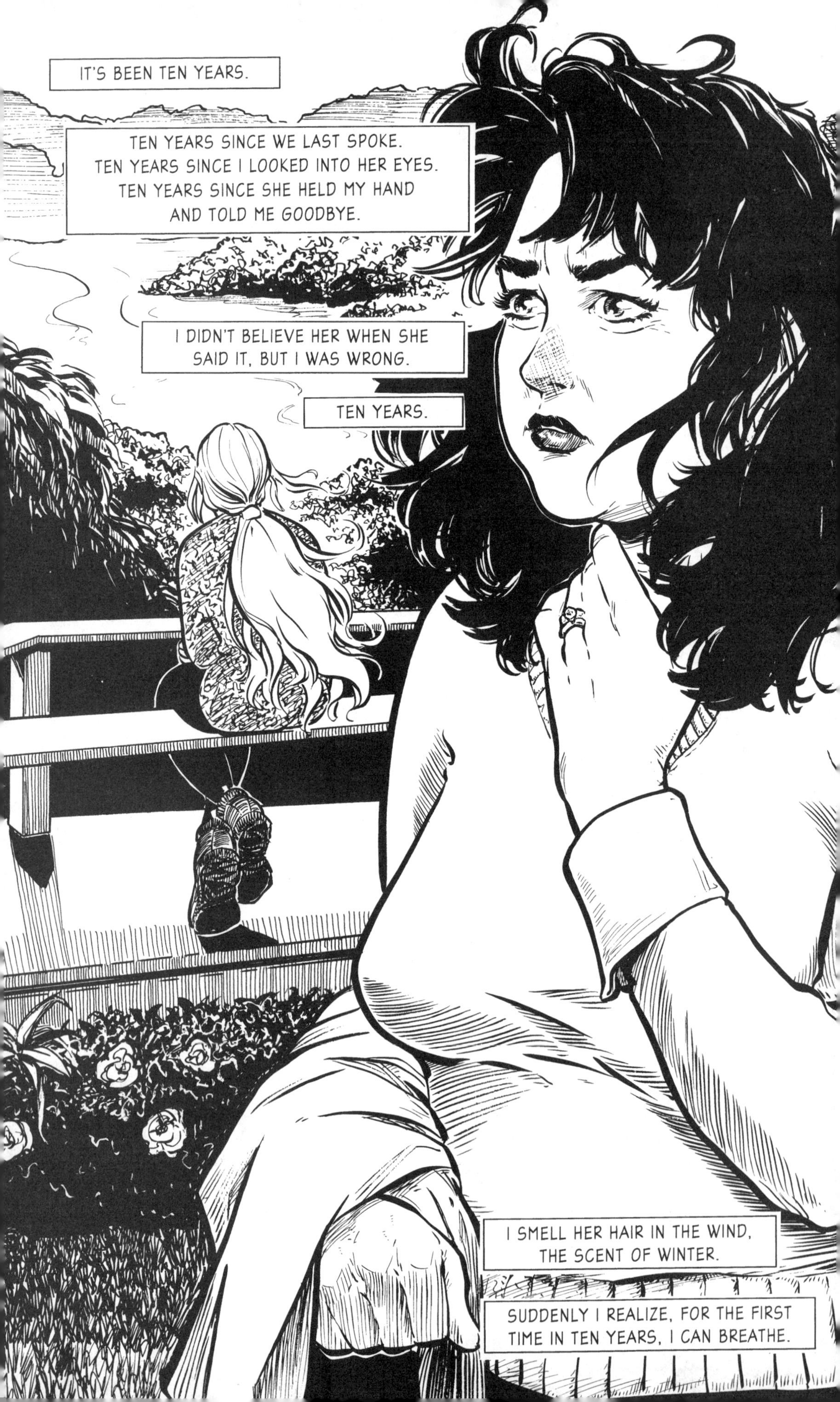
IT'S BEEN TEN YEARS.
TEN YEARS SINCE WE LAST SPOKE. TEN YEARS SINCE I LOOKED INTO HER EYES. TEN YEARS SINCE SHE HELD MY HAND AND TOLD ME GOODBYE.
I DIDN'T BELIEVE HER WHEN SHE SAID IT, BUT I WAS WRONG.
TEN YEARS.
I SMELL HER HAIR IN THE WIND, THE SCENT OF WINTER.
SUDDENLY I REALIZE, FOR THE FIRST TIME IN TEN YEARS, I CAN BREATHE.

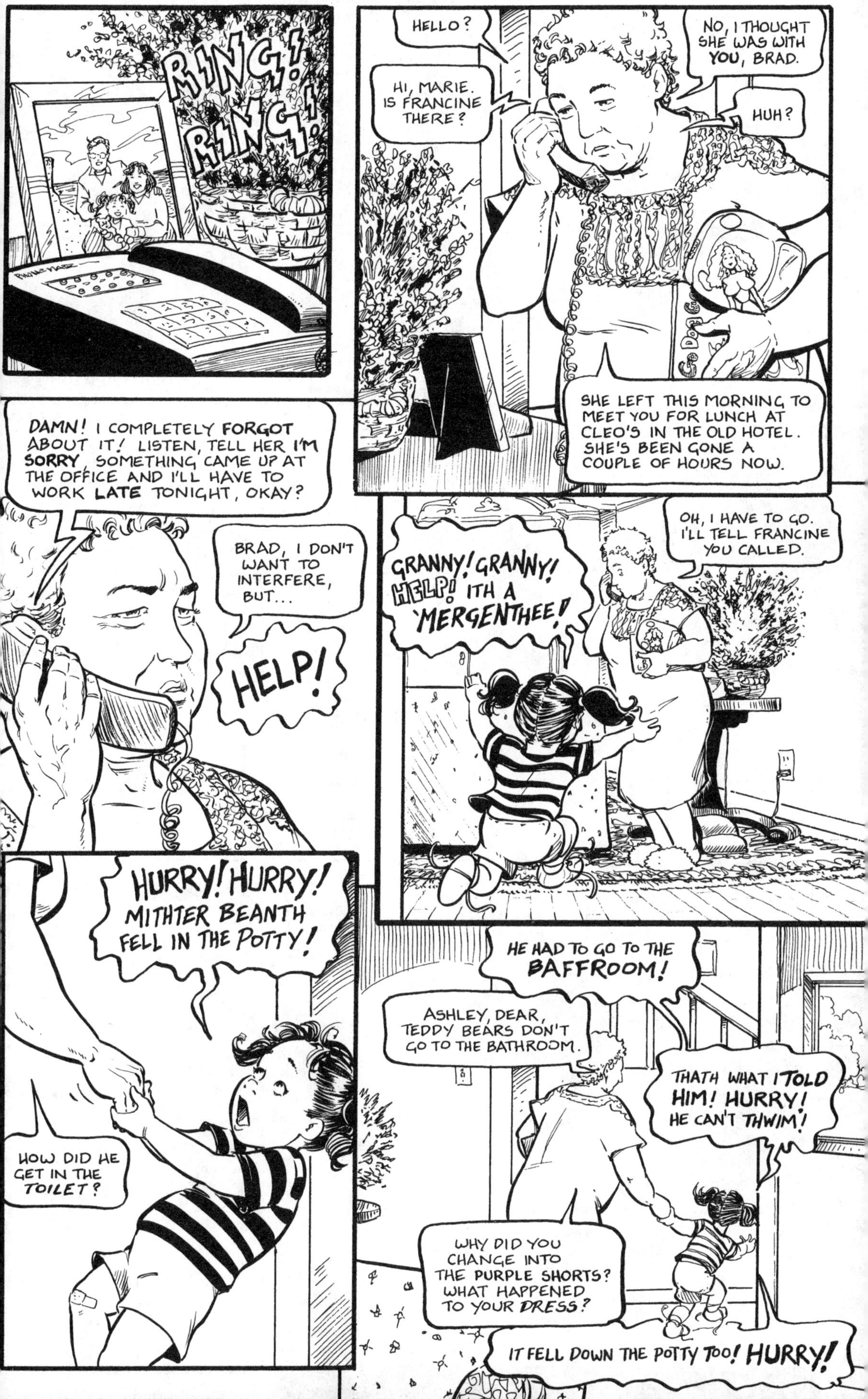
RING! RING!
HELLO?
HI, MARIE. IS FRANCINE THERE?
NO, I THOUGHT SHE WAS WITH YOU, BRAD.
HUH?
SHE LEFT THIS MORNING TO MEET YOU FOR LUNCH AT CLEO'S IN THE OLD HOTEL. SHE'S BEEN GONE A COUPLE OF HOURS NOW.
DAMN! I COMPLETELY FORGOT ABOUT IT! LISTEN, TELL HER I'M SORRY. SOMETHING CAME UP AT THE OFFICE AND I'LL HAVE TO WORK LATE TONIGHT, OKAY?
BRAD, I DON'T WANT TO INTERFERE, BUT...
HELP!
GRANNY! GRANNY! HELP! ITH A 'MERGENTHEE!
OH, I HAVE TO GO. I'LL TELL FRANCINE YOU CALLED.
HURRY! HURRY! MITHTER BEANTH FELL IN THE POTTY!
HOW DID HE GET IN THE TOILET?
HE HAD TO GO TO THE BAFFROOM!
ASHLEY, DEAR, TEDDY BEARS DON'T GO TO THE BATHROOM.
THATH WHAT I TOLD HIM! HURRY! HE CAN'T THWIM!
WHY DID YOU CHANGE INTO THE PURPLE SHORTS? WHAT HAPPENED TO YOUR DRESS?
IT FELL DOWN THE POTTY TOO! HURRY!

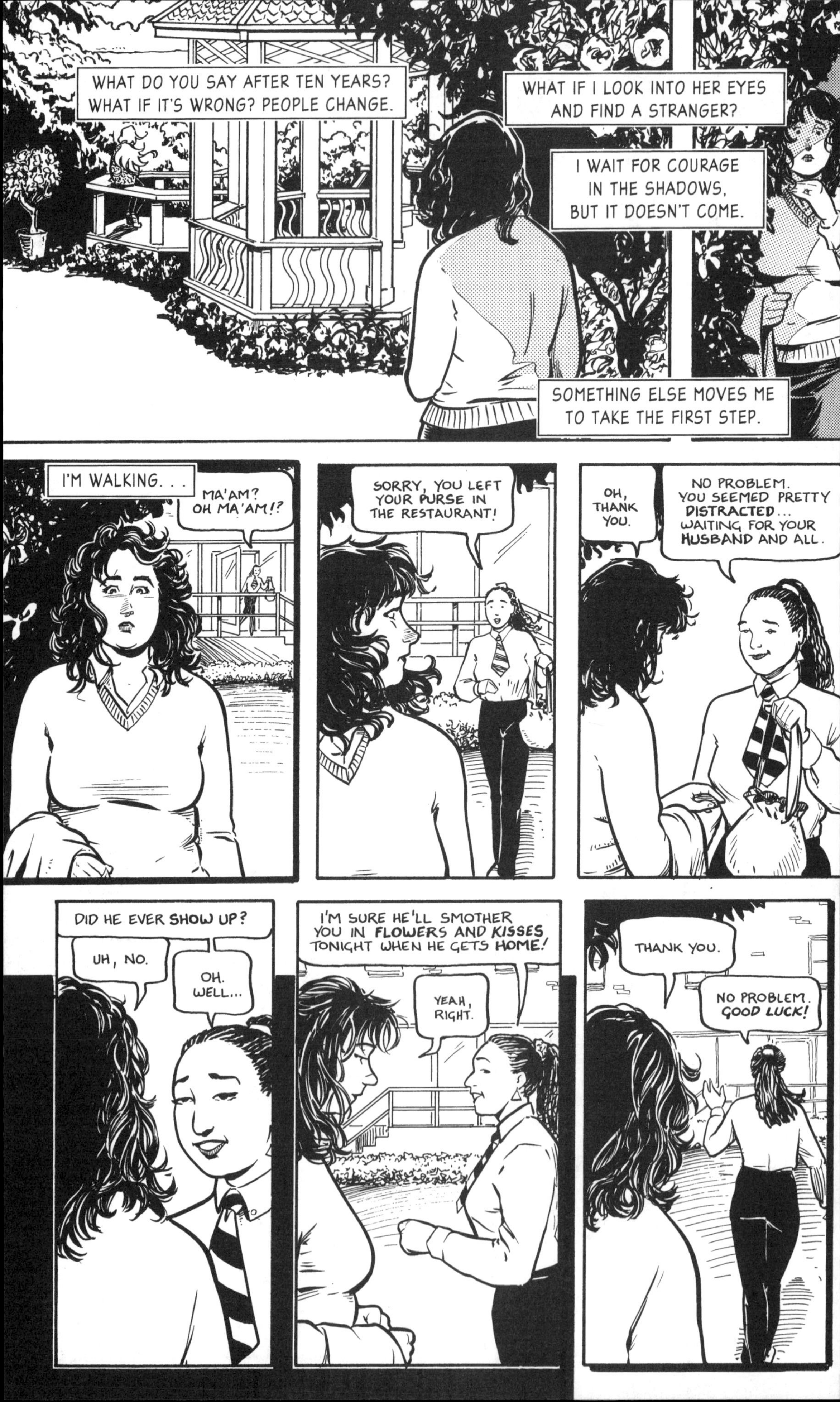
WHAT DO YOU SAY AFTER TEN YEARS? WHAT IF IT'S WRONG? PEOPLE CHANGE.
WHAT IF I LOOK INTO HER EYES AND FIND A STRANGER?
I WAIT FOR COURAGE IN THE SHADOWS, BUT IT DOESN'T COME.
SOMETHING ELSE MOVES ME TO TAKE THE FIRST STEP.
I'M WALKING. . .
MA'AM? OH MA'AM!?
SORRY, YOU LEFT YOUR PURSE IN THE RESTAURANT!
OH, THANK YOU.
NO PROBLEM. YOU SEEMED PRETTY DISTRACTED... WAITING FOR YOUR HUSBAND AND ALL.
DID HE EVER SHOW UP?
UH, NO.
OH. WELL...
I'M SURE HE'LL SMOTHER YOU IN FLOWERS AND KISSES TONIGHT WHEN HE GETS HOME!
YEAH, RIGHT.
THANK YOU.
NO PROBLEM. GOOD LUCK!

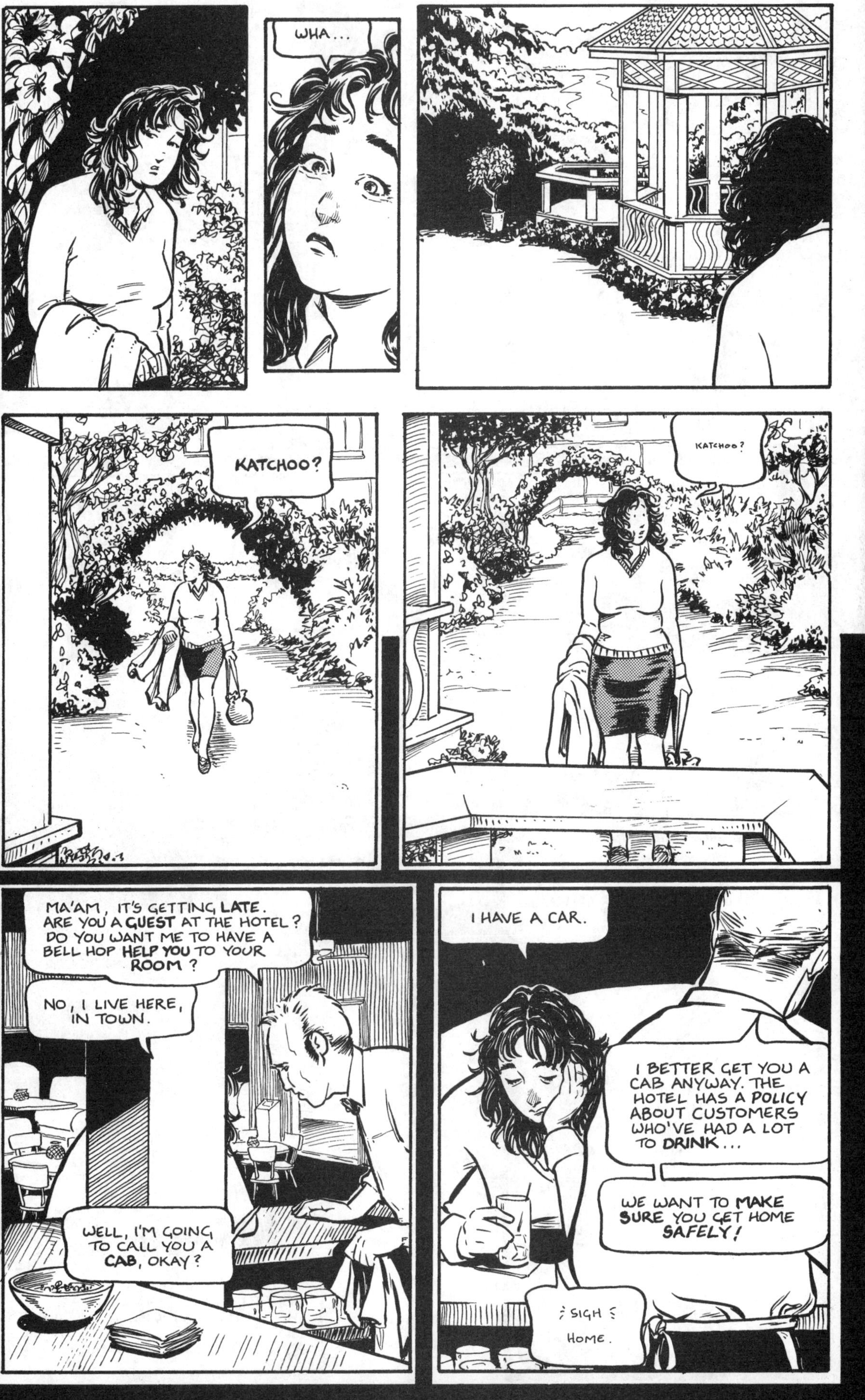
WHA...
KATCHOO?
KATCHOO?
MA'AM, IT'S GETTING LATE. ARE YOU A GUEST AT THE HOTEL? DO YOU WANT ME TO HAVE A BELL HOP HELP YOU TO YOUR ROOM?
NO, I LIVE HERE, IN TOWN.
WELL, I'M GOING TO CALL YOU A CAB, OKAY?
I HAVE A CAR.
I BETTER GET YOU A CAB ANYWAY. THE HOTEL HAS A POLICY ABOUT CUSTOMERS WHO'VE HAD A LOT TO DRINK...
WE WANT TO MAKE SURE YOU GET HOME SAFELY!
SIGH
HOME.

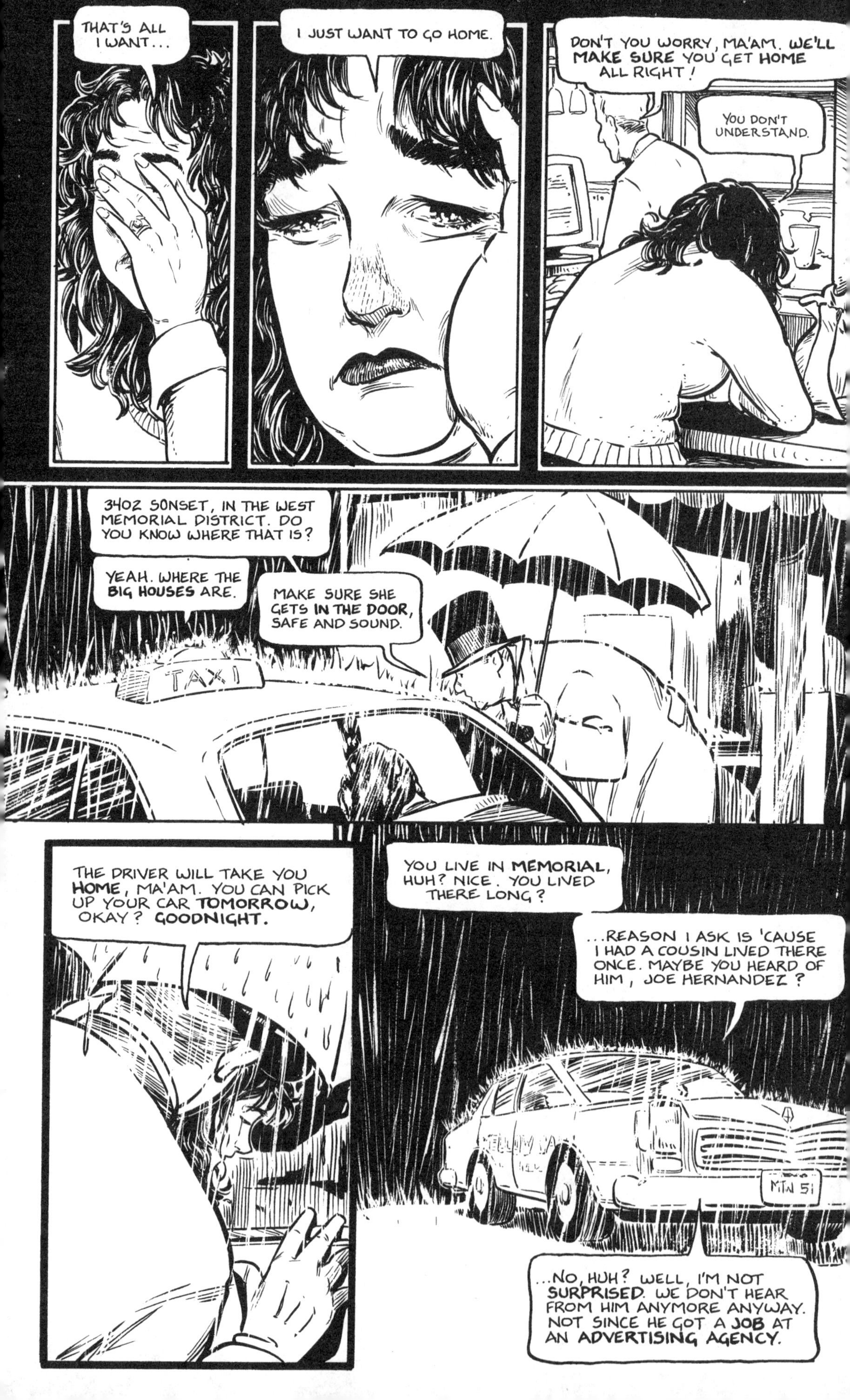
THAT'S ALL I WANT...
I JUST WANT TO GO HOME.
DON'T YOU WORRY, MA'AM. WE'LL MAKE SURE YOU GET HOME ALL RIGHT!
YOU DON'T UNDERSTAND.
3402 SONSET, IN THE WEST MEMORIAL DISTRICT. DO YOU KNOW WHERE THAT IS?
YEAH. WHERE THE BIG HOUSES ARE.
MAKE SURE SHE GETS IN THE DOOR, SAFE AND SOUND.
TAXI
THE DRIVER WILL TAKE YOU HOME, MA'AM. YOU CAN PICK UP YOUR CAR TOMORROW, OKAY? GOODNIGHT.
YOU LIVE IN MEMORIAL, HUH? NICE. YOU LIVED THERE LONG?
...REASON I ASK IS 'CAUSE I HAD A COUSIN LIVED THERE ONCE. MAYBE YOU HEARD OF HIM, JOE HERNANDEZ?
MTW 51
...NO, HUH? WELL, I'M NOT SURPRISED. WE DON'T HEAR FROM HIM ANYMORE ANYWAY. NOT SINCE HE GOT A JOB AT AN ADVERTISING AGENCY.

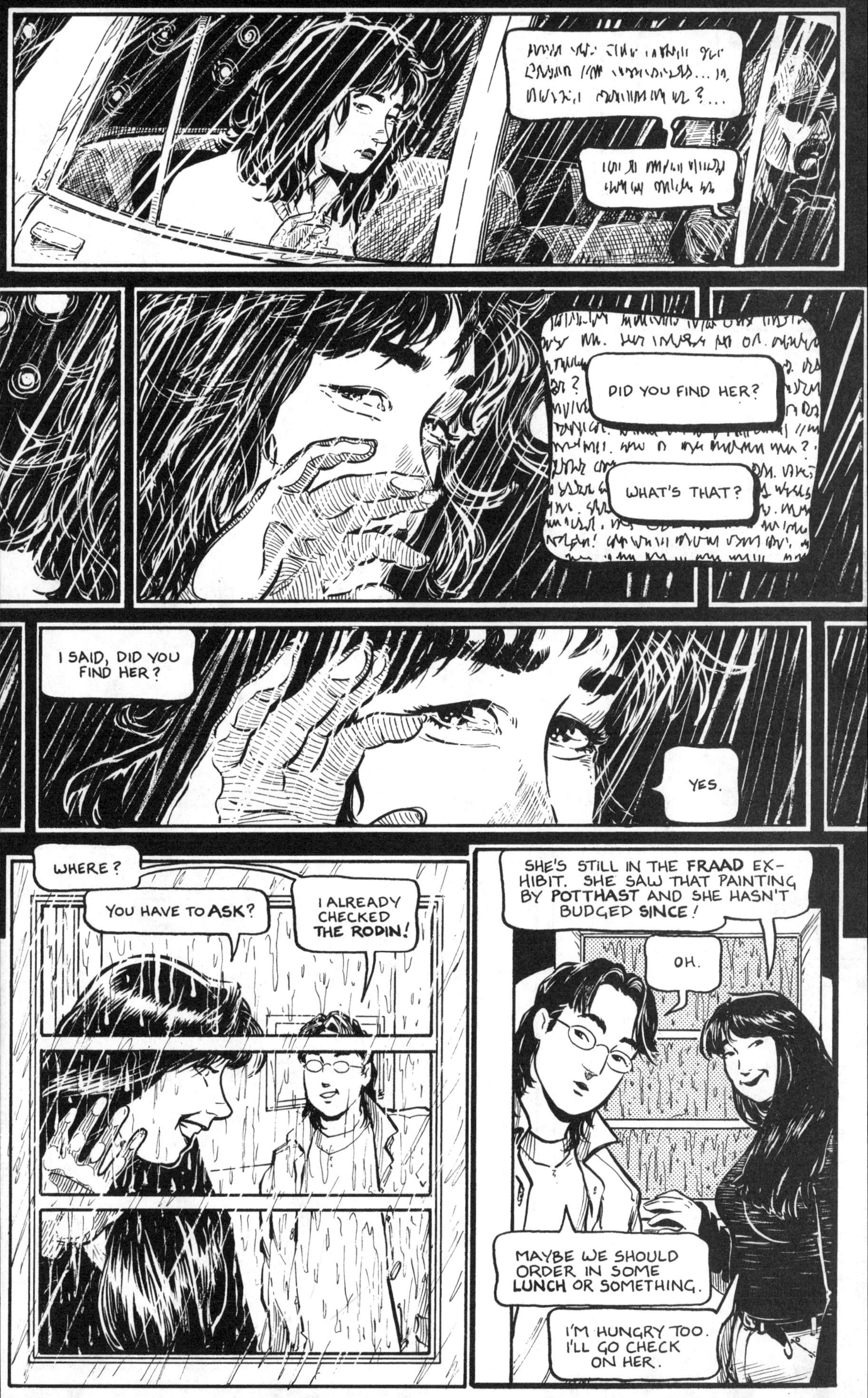
DID YOU FIND HER?
WHAT'S THAT?
I SAID, DID YOU FIND HER?
YES.
WHERE?
YOU HAVE TO ASK?
I ALREADY CHECKED THE RODIN!
SHE'S STILL IN THE FRAAD EXHIBIT. SHE SAW THAT PAINTING BY POTTHAST AND SHE HASN'T BUDGED SINCE!
OH.
MAYBE WE SHOULD ORDER IN SOME LUNCH OR SOMETHING.
I'M HUNGRY TOO. I'LL GO CHECK ON HER.

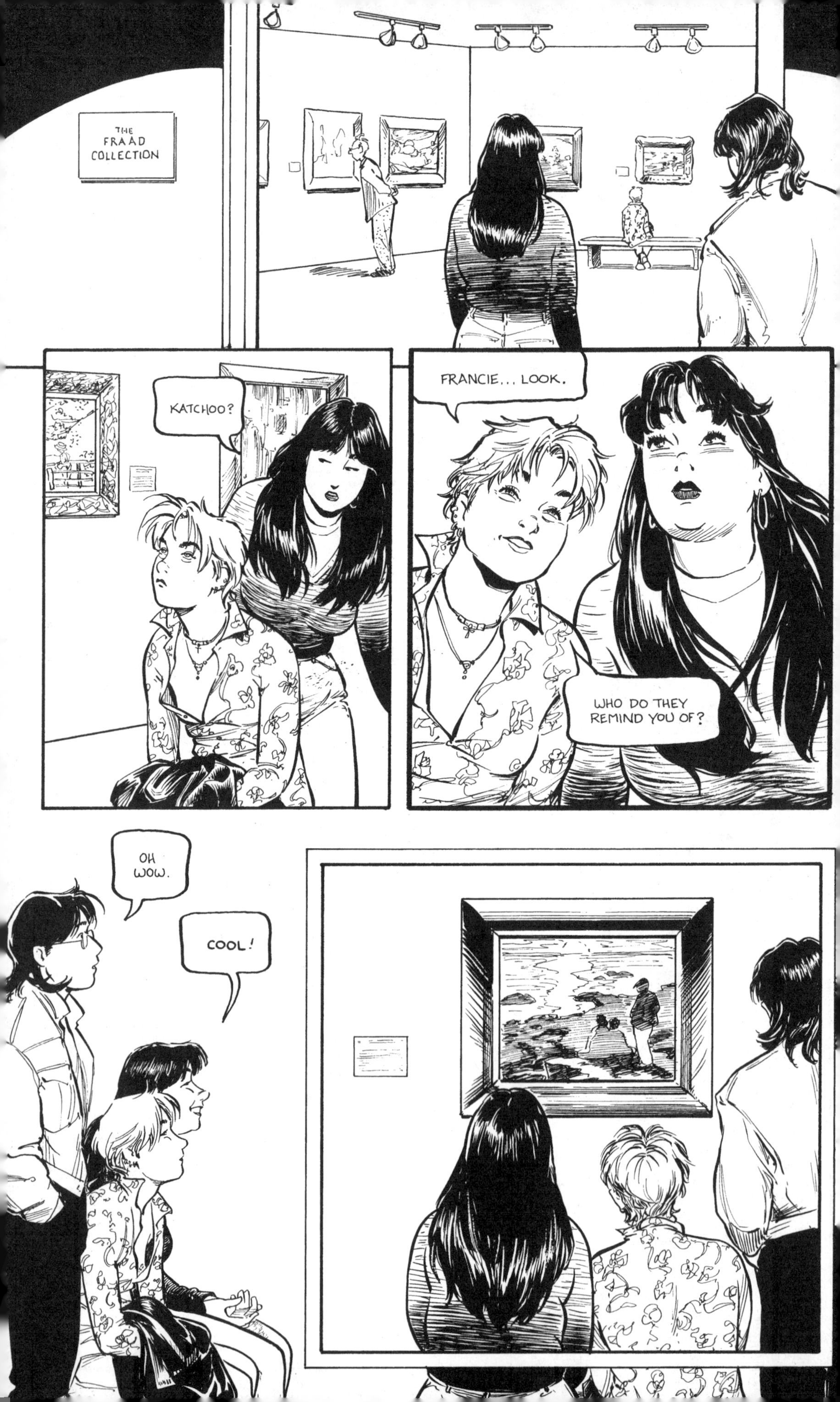
THE FRAAD COLLECTION
KATCHOO?
FRANCIE... LOOK.
WHO DO THEY REMIND YOU OF?
OH WOW.
COOL!

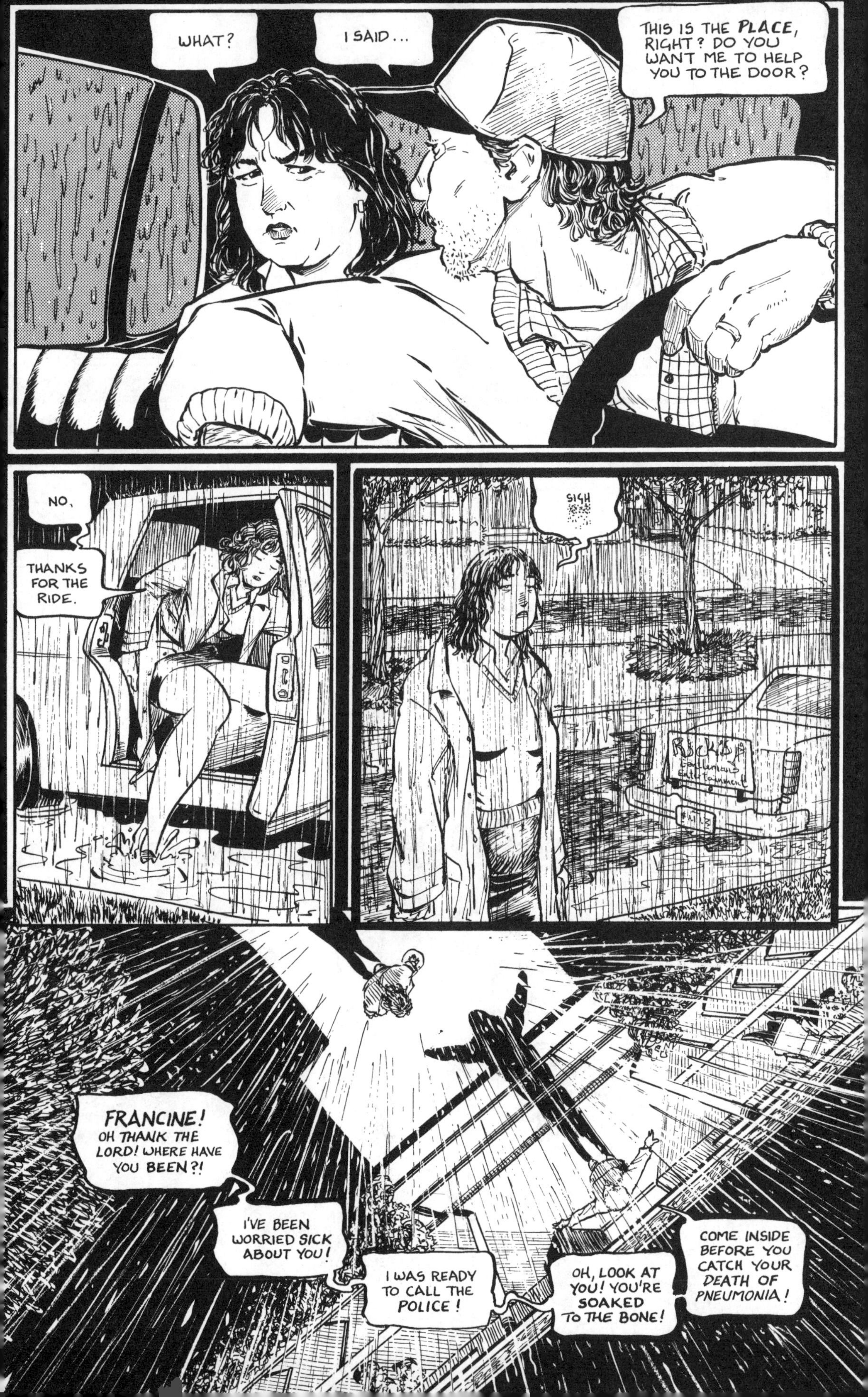
WHAT?
I SAID...
THIS IS THE PLACE, RIGHT? DO YOU WANT ME TO HELP YOU TO THE DOOR?
NO,
THANKS FOR THE RIDE.
SIGH
FRANCINE! OH THANK THE LORD! WHERE HAVE YOU BEEN?!
I'VE BEEN WORRIED SICK ABOUT YOU!
I WAS READY TO CALL THE POLICE!
OH, LOOK AT YOU! YOU'RE SOAKED TO THE BONE!
COME INSIDE BEFORE YOU CATCH YOUR DEATH OF PNEUMONIA!

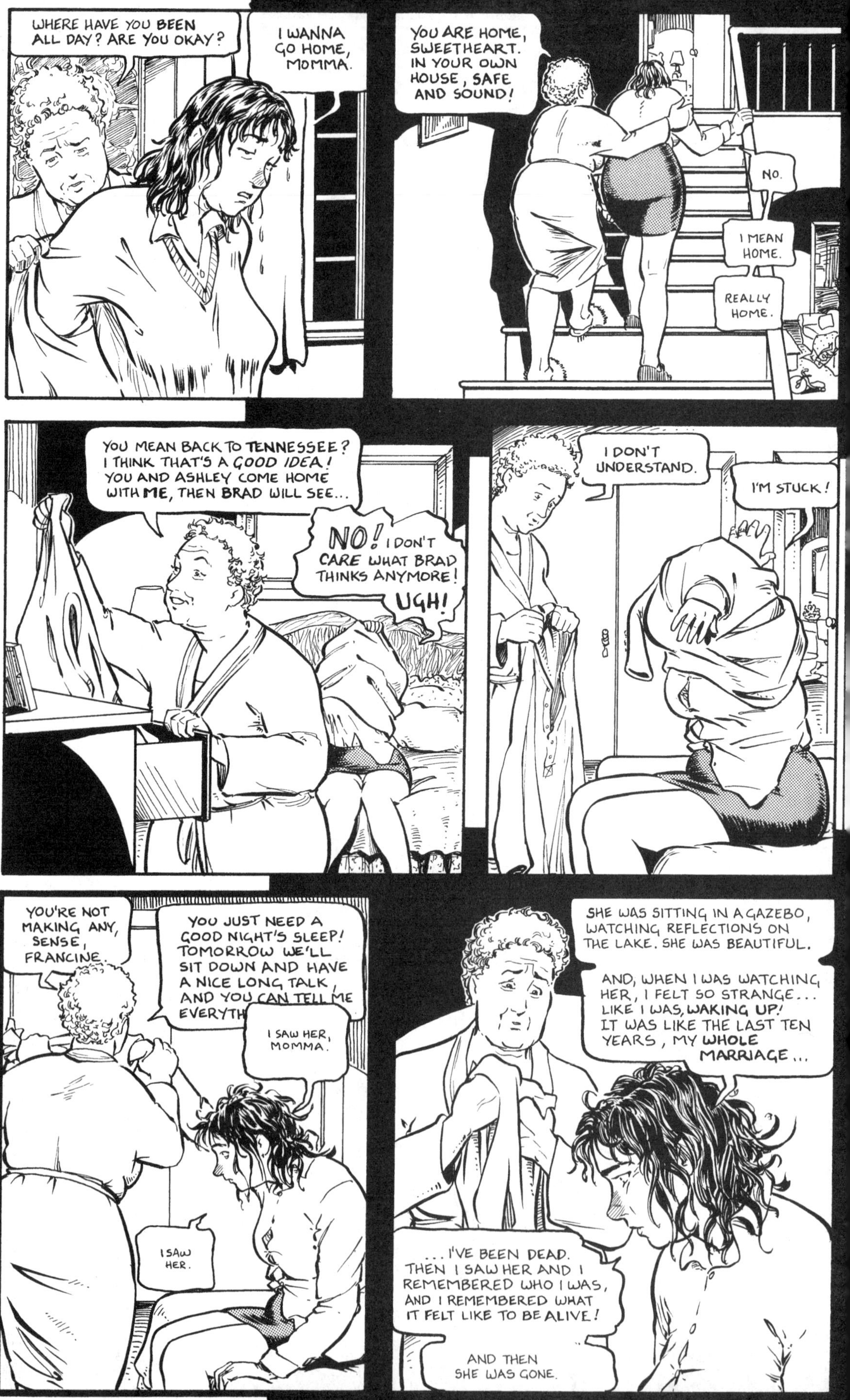
WHERE HAVE YOU BEEN ALL DAY? ARE YOU OKAY?
I WANNA GO HOME, MOMMA.
YOU ARE HOME, SWEETHEART. IN YOUR OWN HOUSE, SAFE AND SOUND!
NO.
I MEAN HOME.
REALLY HOME.
YOU MEAN BACK TO TENNESSEE? I THINK THAT'S A GOOD IDEA! YOU AND ASHLEY COME HOME WITH ME, THEN BRAD WILL SEE...
NO! I DON'T CARE WHAT BRAD THINKS ANYMORE!
UGH!
I DON'T UNDERSTAND.
I'M STUCK!
YOU'RE NOT MAKING ANY SENSE, FRANCINE.
YOU JUST NEED A GOOD NIGHT'S SLEEP! TOMORROW WE'LL SIT DOWN AND HAVE A NICE LONG TALK, AND YOU CAN TELL ME EVERYTH
I SAW HER, MOMMA.
I SAW HER.
SHE WAS SITTING IN A GAZEBO, WATCHING REFLECTIONS ON THE LAKE. SHE WAS BEAUTIFUL.
AND, WHEN I WAS WATCHING HER, I FELT SO STRANGE... LIKE I WAS, WAKING UP! IT WAS LIKE THE LAST TEN YEARS, MY WHOLE MARRIAGE...
...I'VE BEEN DEAD. THEN I SAW HER AND I REMEMBERED WHO I WAS, AND I REMEMBERED WHAT IT FELT LIKE TO BE ALIVE!
AND THEN SHE WAS GONE.

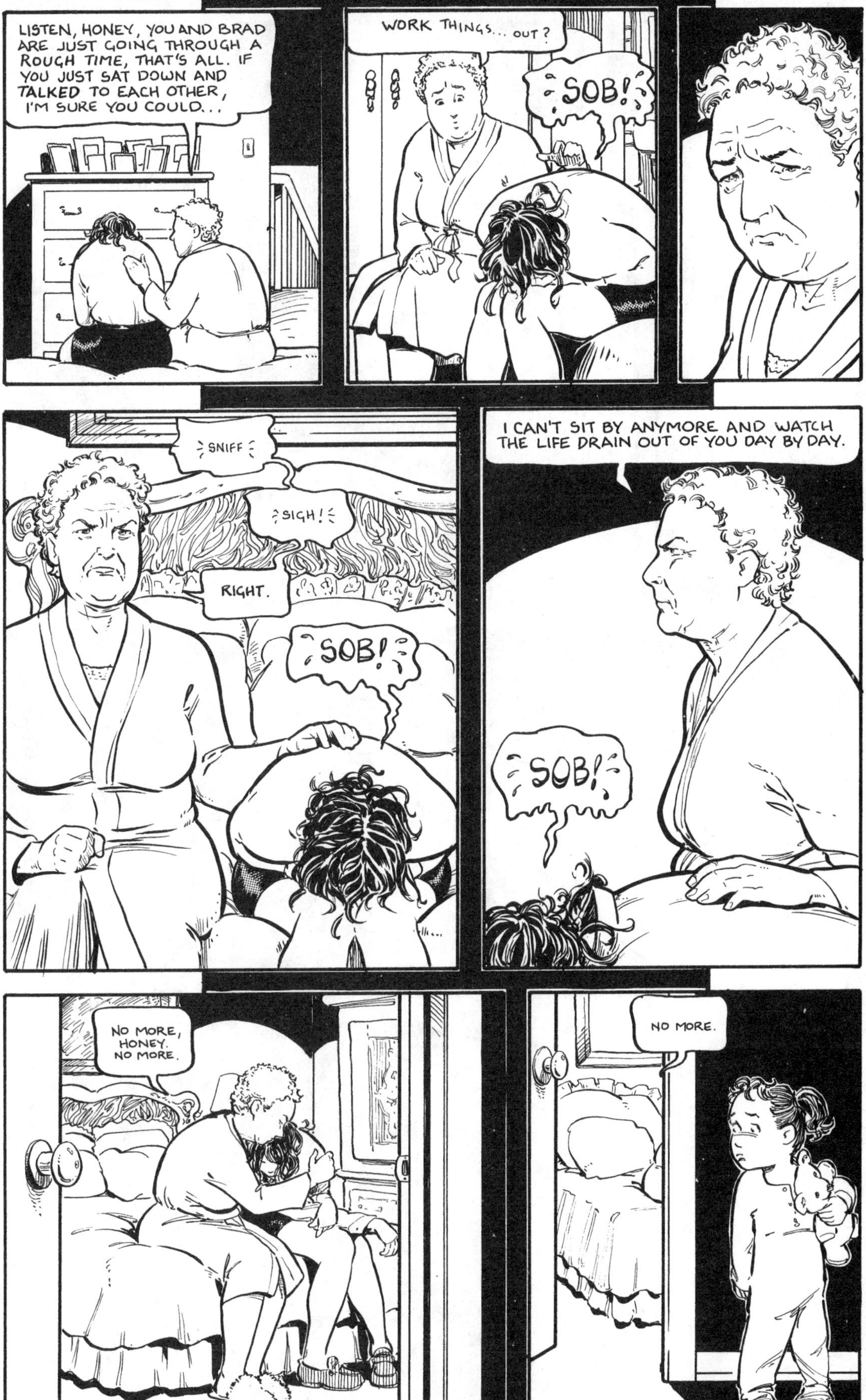
LISTEN, HONEY, YOU AND BRAD ARE JUST GOING THROUGH A ROUGH TIME, THAT'S ALL. IF YOU JUST SAT DOWN AND TALKED TO EACH OTHER, I'M SURE YOU COULD...
WORK THINGS... OUT?
SOB!
SNIFF
SIGH!
RIGHT.
SOB!
I CAN'T SIT BY ANYMORE AND WATCH THE LIFE DRAIN OUT OF YOU DAY BY DAY.
SOB!
NO MORE, HONEY. NO MORE.
NO MORE.

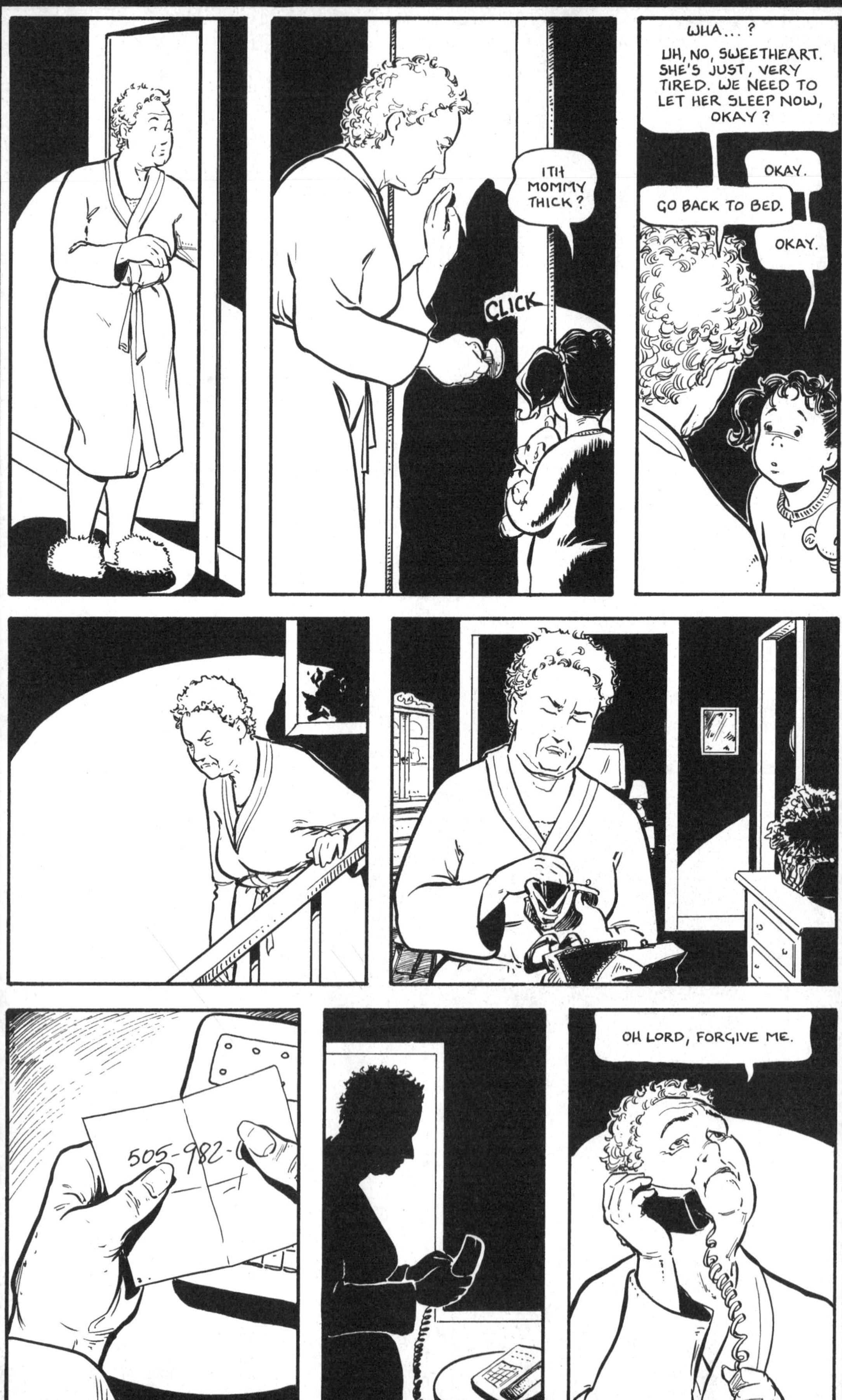
ITH MOMMY THICK?
CLICK
WHA...?
UH, NO, SWEETHEART. SHE'S JUST, VERY TIRED. WE NEED TO LET HER SLEEP NOW, OKAY?
OKAY.
GO BACK TO BED.
OKAY.
505-982-
OH LORD, FORGIVE ME.

NOW I LAY ME DOWN TO SLEEP

Now I lay me down to sleep

To close my eyes

To find my dreams.

If I do they'll let me stay

So mommy don't you cry, okay?

If by dawn my eyes won't rise

You'll know I'm home and safe inside.

So now I lay me down to sleep

If I wake up

In tears I'll be.

Again another day I'll face

'Til I can close my eyes and say,

Now I lay me down to sleep

To close my eyes

To find my dreams.

If I do they'll let me stay

So mommy don't you cry, okay?

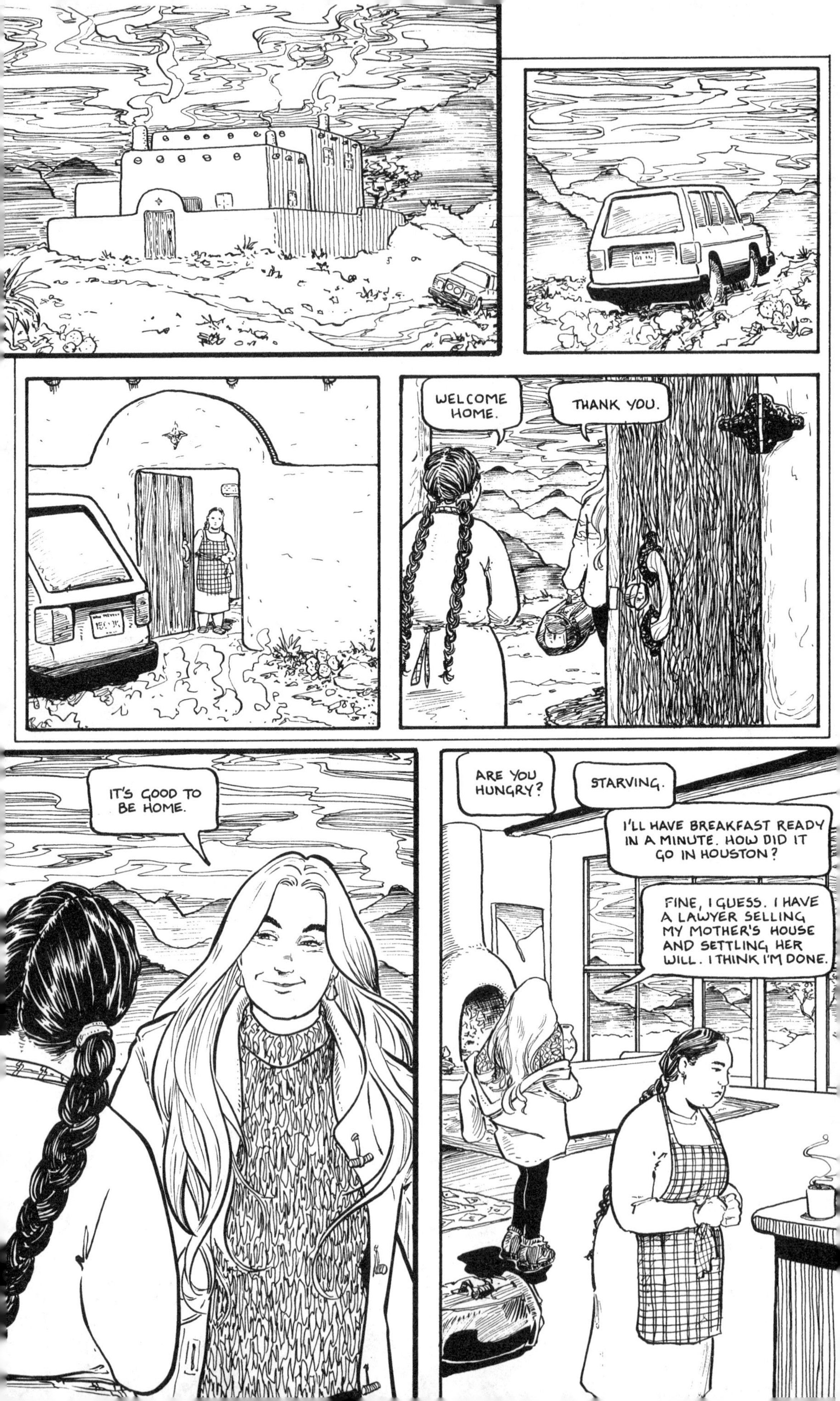
WELCOME HOME.
THANK YOU.
IT'S GOOD TO BE HOME.
ARE YOU HUNGRY?
STARVING.
I'LL HAVE BREAKFAST READY IN A MINUTE. HOW DID IT GO IN HOUSTON?
FINE, I GUESS. I HAVE A LAWYER SELLING MY MOTHER'S HOUSE AND SETTLING HER WILL. I THINK I'M DONE.

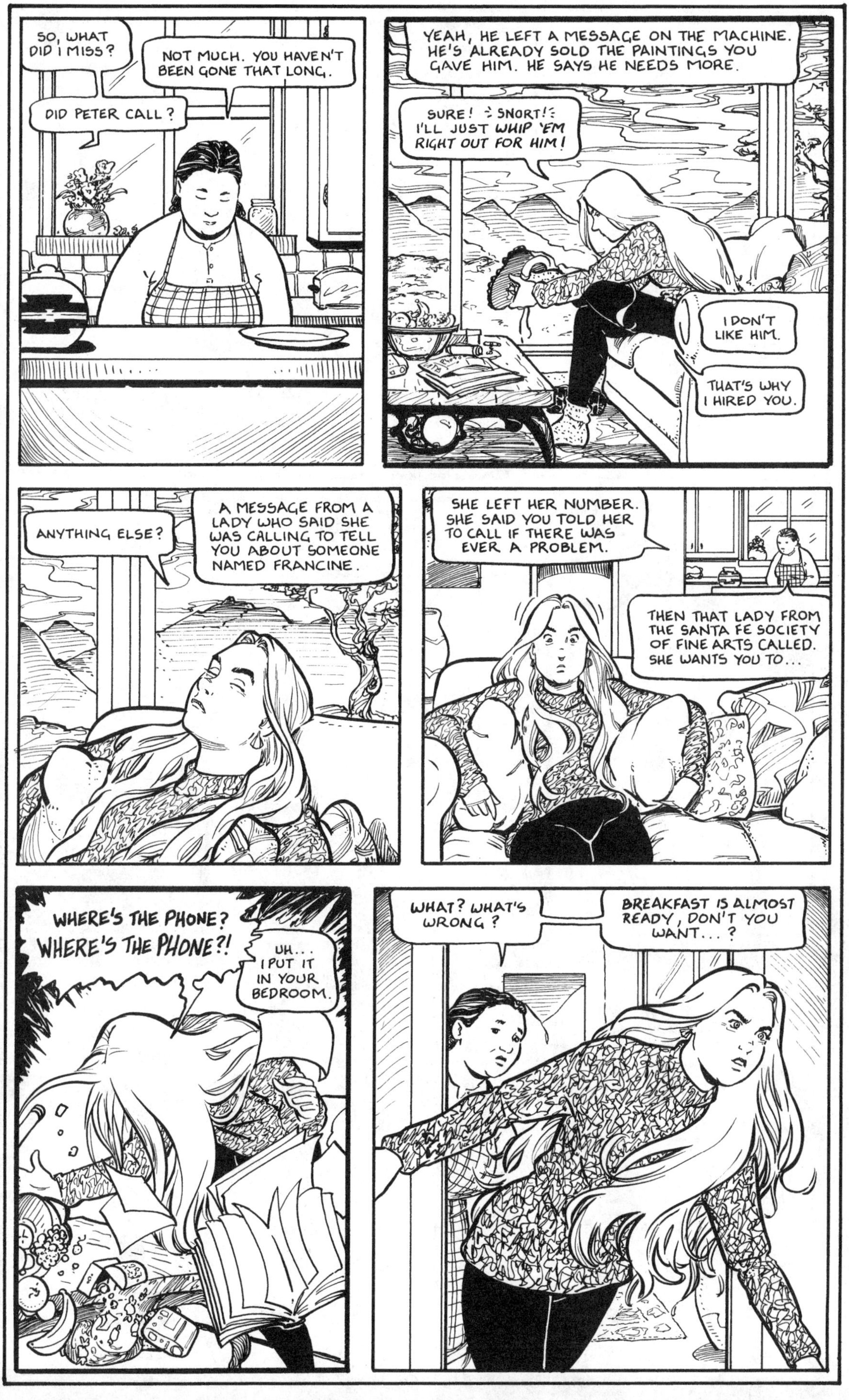

SO, WHAT DID I MISS?
NOT MUCH. YOU HAVEN'T BEEN GONE THAT LONG.
DID PETER CALL?
YEAH, HE LEFT A MESSAGE ON THE MACHINE. HE'S ALREADY SOLD THE PAINTINGS YOU GAVE HIM. HE SAYS HE NEEDS MORE.
SURE! SNORT! I'LL JUST WHIP 'EM RIGHT OUT FOR HIM!
I DON'T LIKE HIM.
THAT'S WHY I HIRED YOU.
ANYTHING ELSE?
A MESSAGE FROM A LADY WHO SAID SHE WAS CALLING TO TELL YOU ABOUT SOMEONE NAMED FRANCINE.
SHE LEFT HER NUMBER. SHE SAID YOU TOLD HER TO CALL IF THERE WAS EVER A PROBLEM.
THEN THAT LADY FROM THE SANTA FE SOCIETY OF FINE ARTS CALLED. SHE WANTS YOU TO...
WHERE'S THE PHONE? WHERE'S THE PHONE?!
UH... I PUT IT IN YOUR BEDROOM.
WHAT? WHAT'S WRONG?
BREAKFAST IS ALMOST READY, DON'T YOU WANT...?

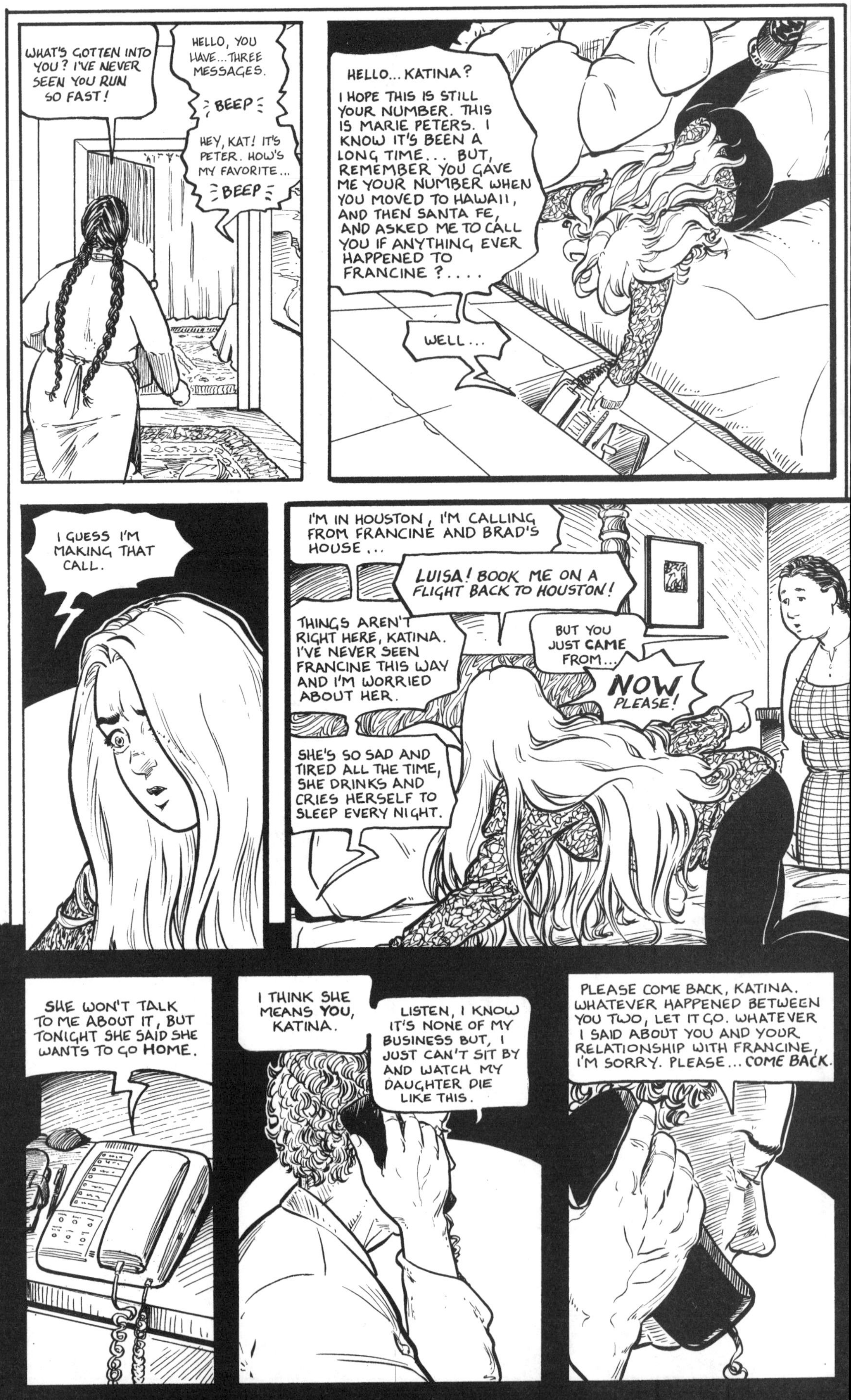

WHAT'S GOTTEN INTO YOU? I'VE NEVER SEEN YOU RUN SO FAST!
HELLO, YOU HAVE... THREE MESSAGES.
BEEP
HEY, KAT! IT'S PETER. HOW'S MY FAVORITE...
BEEP
HELLO... KATINA?
I HOPE THIS IS STILL YOUR NUMBER. THIS IS MARIE PETERS. I KNOW IT'S BEEN A LONG TIME... BUT, REMEMBER YOU GAVE ME YOUR NUMBER WHEN YOU MOVED TO HAWAII, AND THEN SANTA FE, AND ASKED ME TO CALL YOU IF ANYTHING EVER HAPPENED TO FRANCINE?....
WELL...
I GUESS I'M MAKING THAT CALL.
I'M IN HOUSTON, I'M CALLING FROM FRANCINE AND BRAD'S HOUSE...
LUISA! BOOK ME ON A FLIGHT BACK TO HOUSTON!
THINGS AREN'T RIGHT HERE, KATINA. I'VE NEVER SEEN FRANCINE THIS WAY AND I'M WORRIED ABOUT HER.
BUT YOU JUST CAME FROM...
NOW PLEASE!
SHE'S SO SAD AND TIRED ALL THE TIME, SHE DRINKS AND CRIES HERSELF TO SLEEP EVERY NIGHT.
SHE WON'T TALK TO ME ABOUT IT, BUT TONIGHT SHE SAID SHE WANTS TO GO HOME.
I THINK SHE MEANS YOU, KATINA.
LISTEN, I KNOW IT'S NONE OF MY BUSINESS BUT, I JUST CAN'T SIT BY AND WATCH MY DAUGHTER DIE LIKE THIS.
PLEASE COME BACK, KATINA. WHATEVER HAPPENED BETWEEN YOU TWO, LET IT GO. WHATEVER I SAID ABOUT YOU AND YOUR RELATIONSHIP WITH FRANCINE, I'M SORRY. PLEASE... COME BACK.

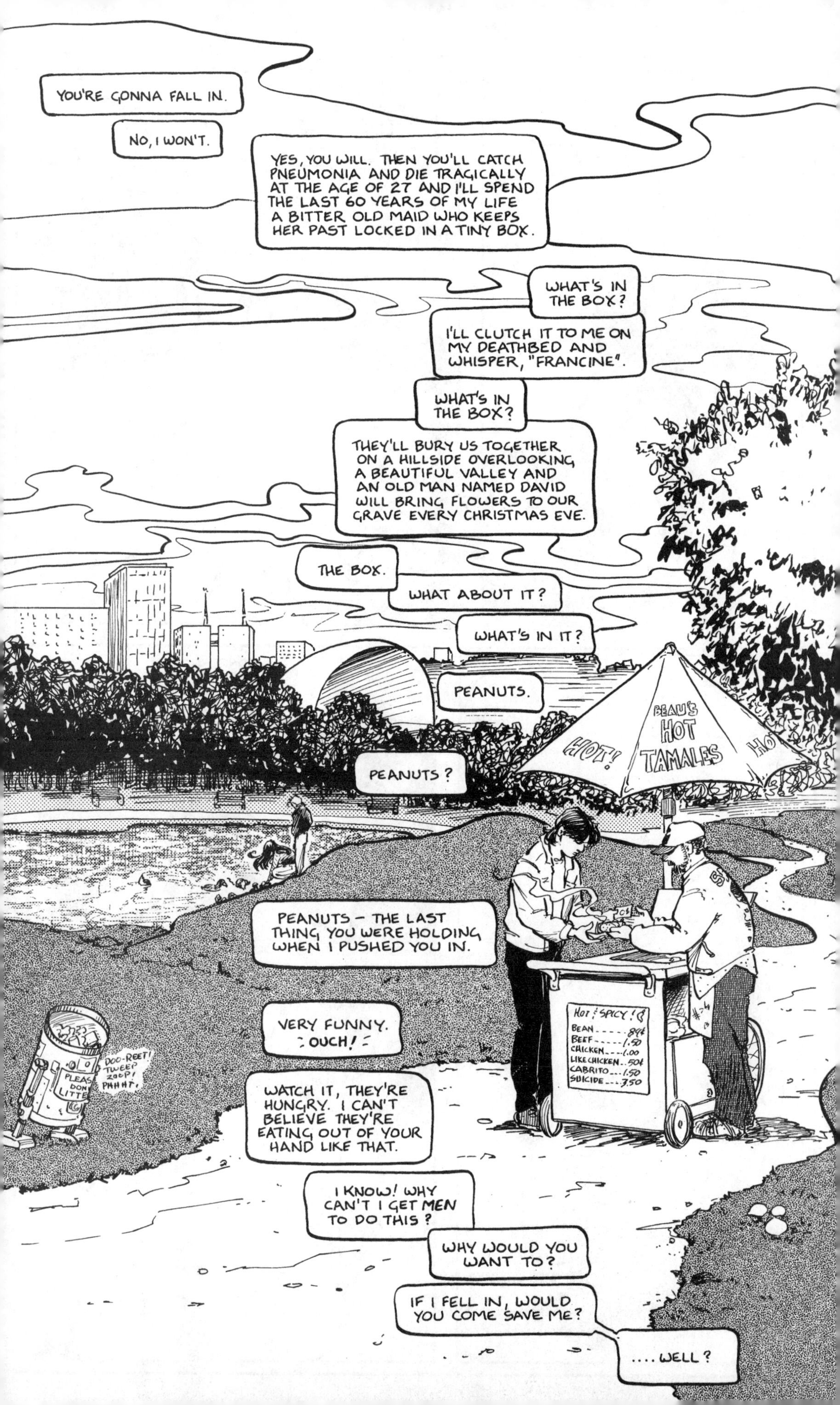

YOU'RE GONNA FALL IN.
NO, I WON'T.
YES, YOU WILL. THEN YOU'LL CATCH PNEUMONIA AND DIE TRAGICALLY AT THE AGE OF 27 AND I'LL SPEND THE LAST 60 YEARS OF MY LIFE A BITTER OLD MAID WHO KEEPS HER PAST LOCKED IN A TINY BOX.
WHAT'S IN THE BOX?
I'LL CLUTCH IT TO ME ON MY DEATHBED AND WHISPER, "FRANCINE".
WHAT'S IN THE BOX?
THEY'LL BURY US TOGETHER ON A HILLSIDE OVERLOOKING A BEAUTIFUL VALLEY AND AN OLD MAN NAMED DAVID WILL BRING FLOWERS TO OUR GRAVE EVERY CHRISTMAS EVE.
THE BOX.
WHAT ABOUT IT?
WHAT'S IN IT?
PEANUTS.
BEAU'S HOT TAMALES
HOT!
PEANUTS?
PEANUTS – THE LAST THING YOU WERE HOLDING WHEN I PUSHED YOU IN.
HOT & SPICY!
BEAN 89¢
BEEF 1.50
CHICKEN 1.00
LIKE CHICKEN 50¢
CABRITO 1.50
SUICIDE 3.50
VERY FUNNY. OUCH!
DOO-REET! TWEEP ZOOP! PHHHT.
WATCH IT, THEY'RE HUNGRY. I CAN'T BELIEVE THEY'RE EATING OUT OF YOUR HAND LIKE THAT.
I KNOW! WHY CAN'T I GET MEN TO DO THIS?
WHY WOULD YOU WANT TO?
IF I FELL IN, WOULD YOU COME SAVE ME?
....WELL?

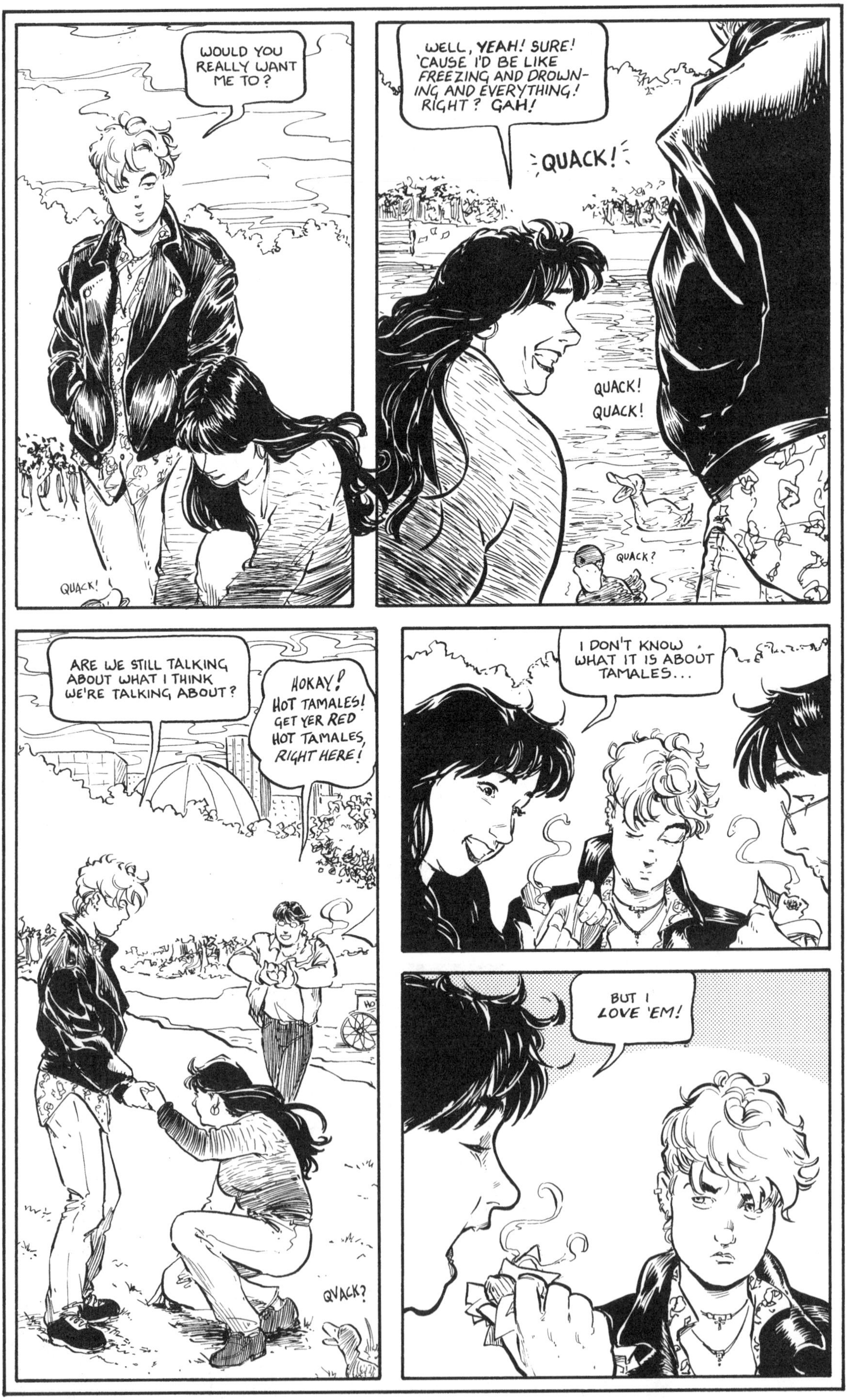
WOULD YOU REALLY WANT ME TO?
WELL, YEAH! SURE! 'CAUSE I'D BE LIKE FREEZING AND DROWNING AND EVERYTHING! RIGHT? GAH!
QUACK!
QUACK! QUACK!
QUACK?
QUACK!
ARE WE STILL TALKING ABOUT WHAT I THINK WE'RE TALKING ABOUT?
HOKAY! HOT TAMALES! GET YER RED HOT TAMALES, RIGHT HERE!
QVACK?
I DON'T KNOW WHAT IT IS ABOUT TAMALES...
BUT I LOVE 'EM!

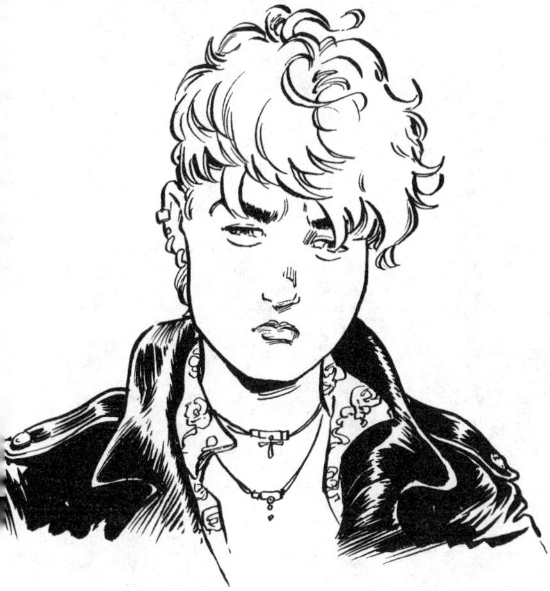

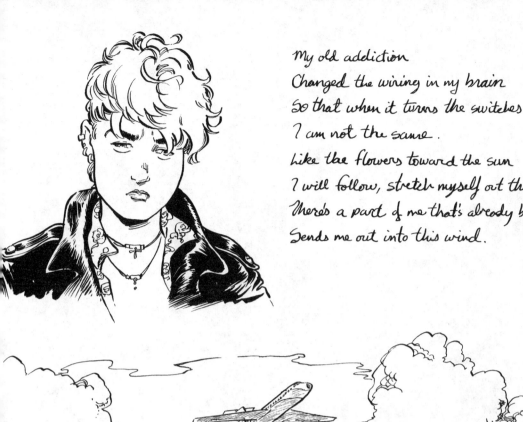

My old addiction
Changed the wiring in my brain
So that when it turns the switches
I am not the same.
Like the flowers toward the sun
I will follow, stretch myself out thin.
There's a part of me that's already buried
Sends me out into this wind.

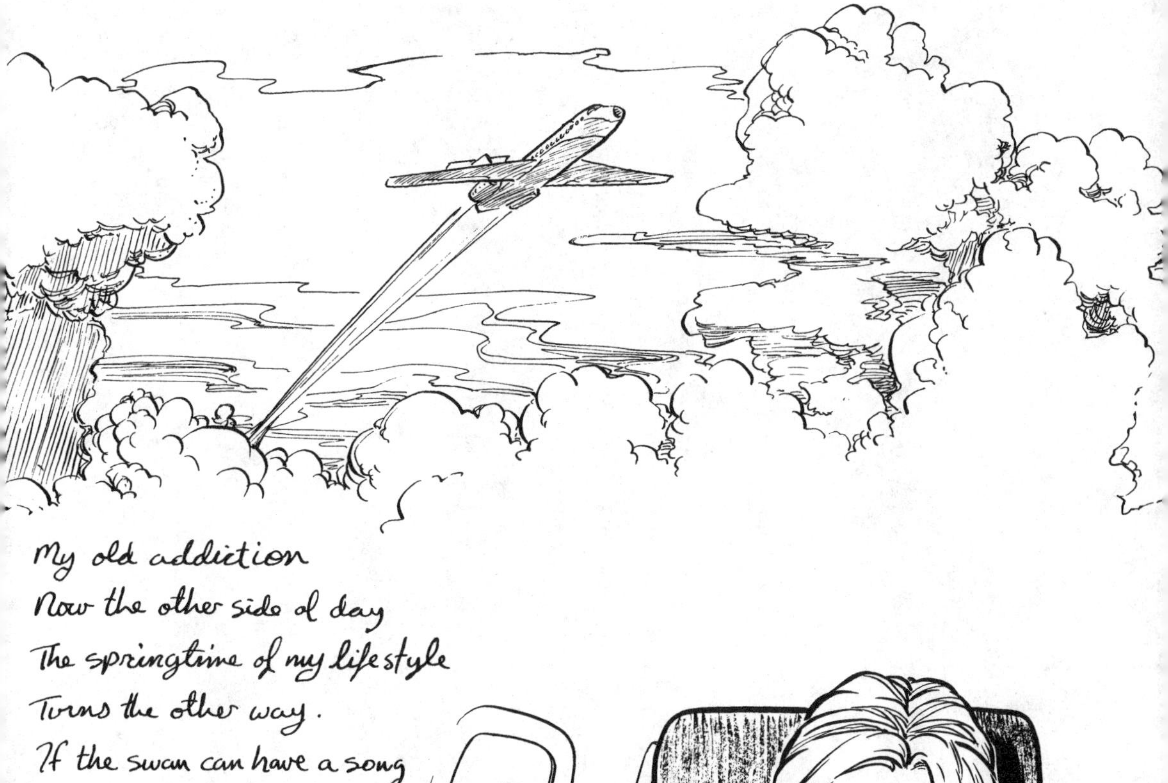

My old addiction
Now the other side of day
The springtime of my lifestyle
Turns the other way.
If the swan can have a song
Then I think I know that tune
But the page is only scroll
And I am gone
This afternoon.
The page is only scroll
And I am gone...
this afternoon.

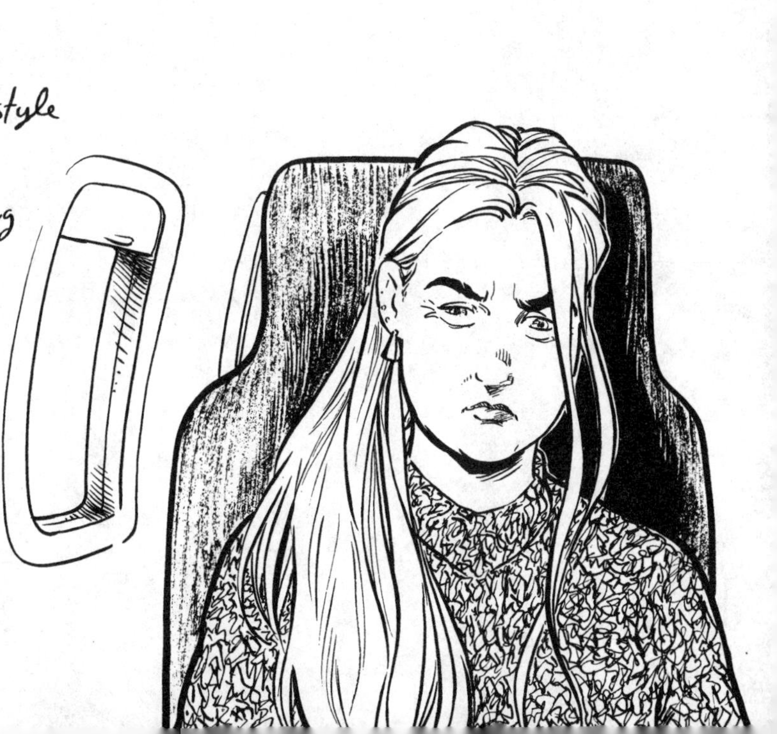

There is a place for us, so far away.
But it's closer than it was yesterday.

-Common Sense

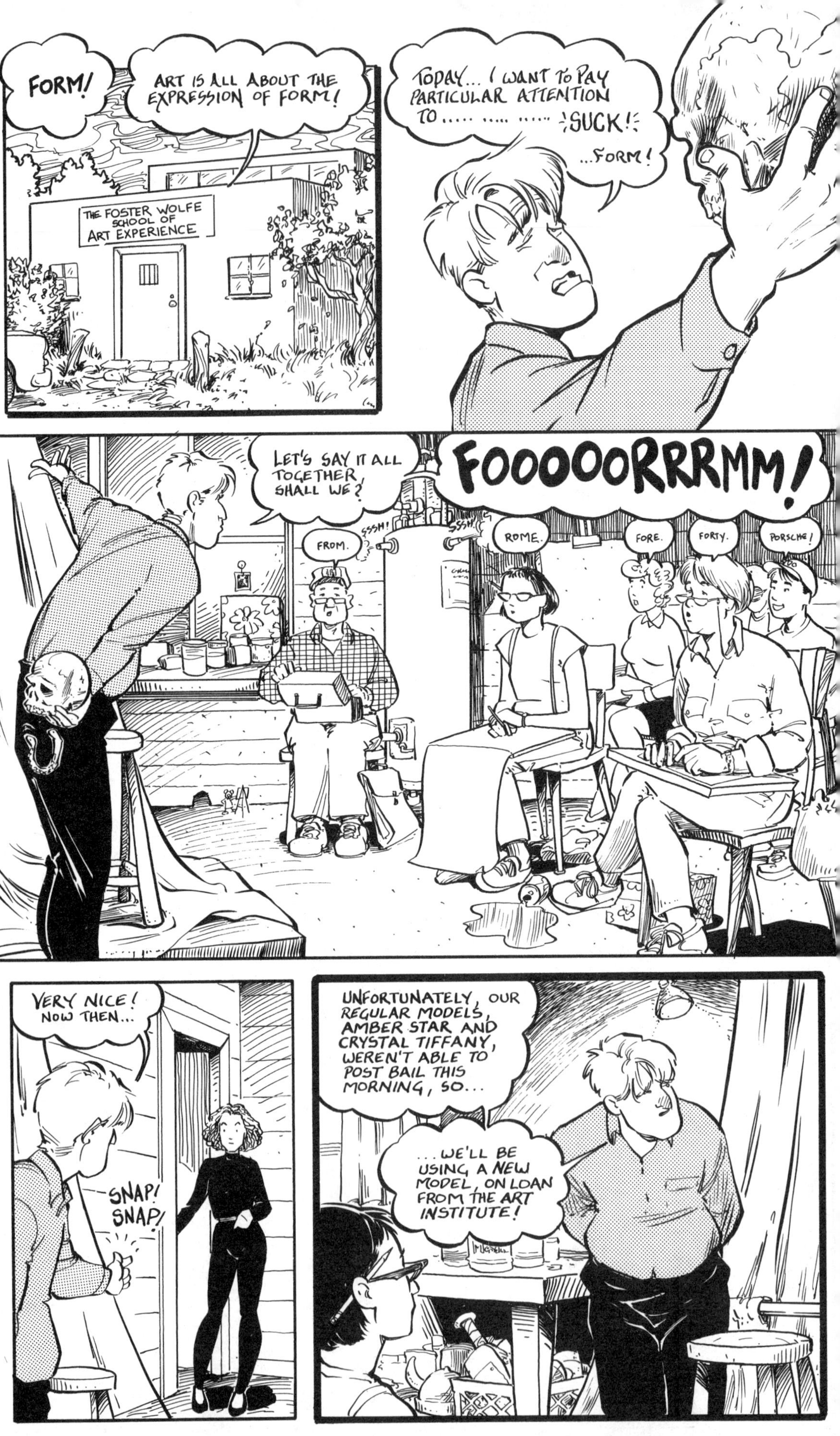
FORM!
ART IS ALL ABOUT THE EXPRESSION OF FORM!
THE FOSTER WOLFE SCHOOL OF ART EXPERIENCE
TODAY... I WANT TO PAY PARTICULAR ATTENTION TO..... .... SUCK!
...FORM!
LET'S SAY IT ALL TOGETHER, SHALL WE?
FOOOOORRRMM!
FROM.
SSSH!
SSSH!
ROME.
FORE.
FORTY.
PORSCHE!
VERY NICE! NOW THEN...
SNAP! SNAP!
UNFORTUNATELY, OUR REGULAR MODELS, AMBER STAR AND CRYSTAL TIFFANY, WEREN'T ABLE TO POST BAIL THIS MORNING, SO...
...WE'LL BE USING A NEW MODEL, ON LOAN FROM THE ART INSTITUTE!

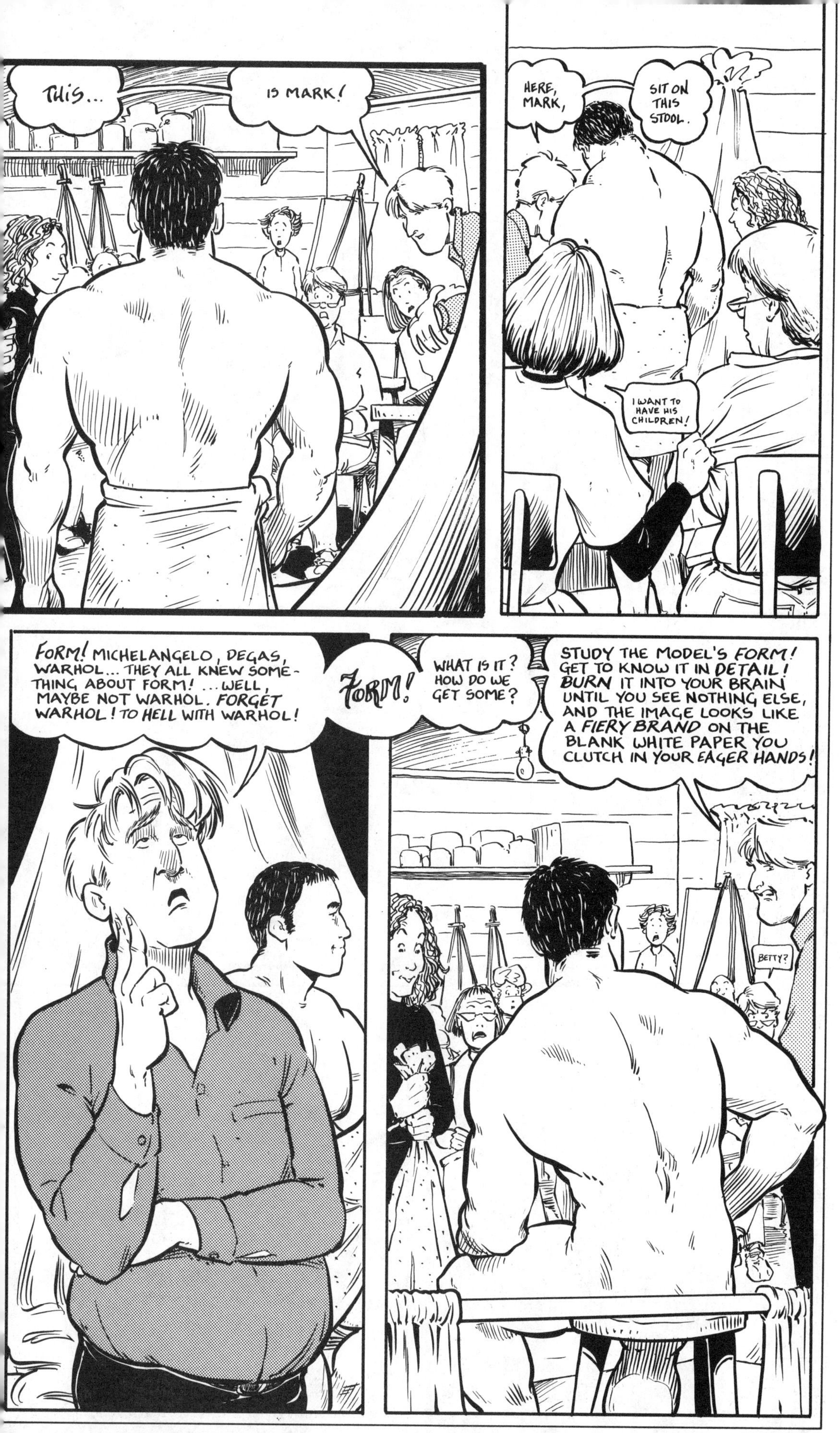
THIS...
IS MARK!
HERE, MARK,
SIT ON THIS STOOL.
I WANT TO HAVE HIS CHILDREN!
FORM! MICHELANGELO, DEGAS, WARHOL... THEY ALL KNEW SOMETHING ABOUT FORM! ...WELL, MAYBE NOT WARHOL. FORGET WARHOL! TO HELL WITH WARHOL!
FORM!
WHAT IS IT? HOW DO WE GET SOME?
STUDY THE MODEL'S FORM! GET TO KNOW IT IN DETAIL! BURN IT INTO YOUR BRAIN UNTIL YOU SEE NOTHING ELSE, AND THE IMAGE LOOKS LIKE A FIERY BRAND ON THE BLANK WHITE PAPER YOU CLUTCH IN YOUR EAGER HANDS!
BETTY?

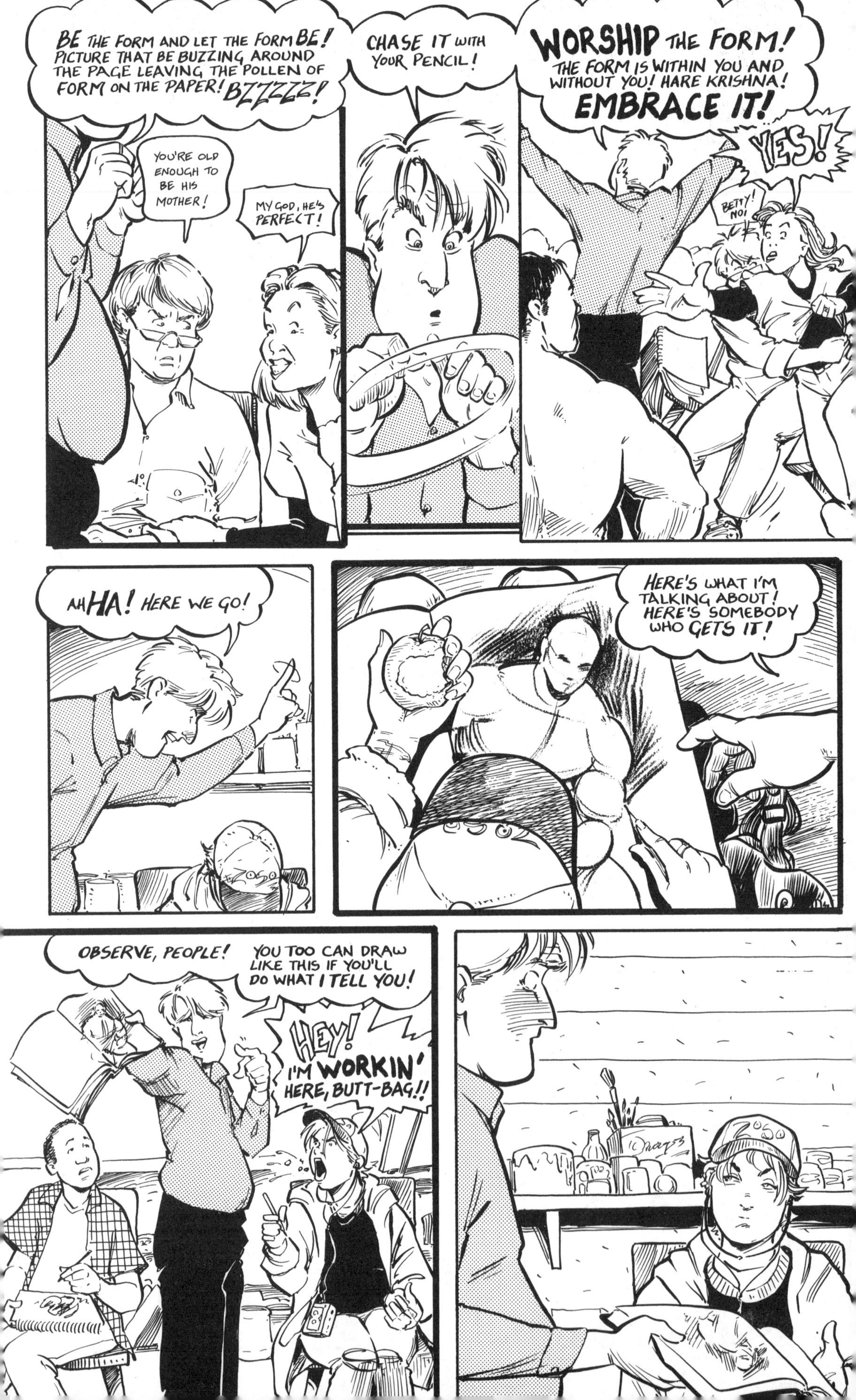
BE THE FORM AND LET THE FORM BE! PICTURE THAT BE BUZZING AROUND THE PAGE LEAVING THE POLLEN OF FORM ON THE PAPER! BZZZZZ!
YOU'RE OLD ENOUGH TO BE HIS MOTHER!
MY GOD, HE'S PERFECT!
CHASE IT WITH YOUR PENCIL!
WORSHIP THE FORM! THE FORM IS WITHIN YOU AND WITHOUT YOU! HARE KRISHNA! EMBRACE IT!
YES!
BETTY! NO!
AH HA! HERE WE GO!
HERE'S WHAT I'M TALKING ABOUT! HERE'S SOMEBODY WHO GETS IT!
OBSERVE, PEOPLE!
YOU TOO CAN DRAW LIKE THIS IF YOU'LL DO WHAT I TELL YOU!
HEY! I'M WORKIN' HERE, BUTT-BAG!!

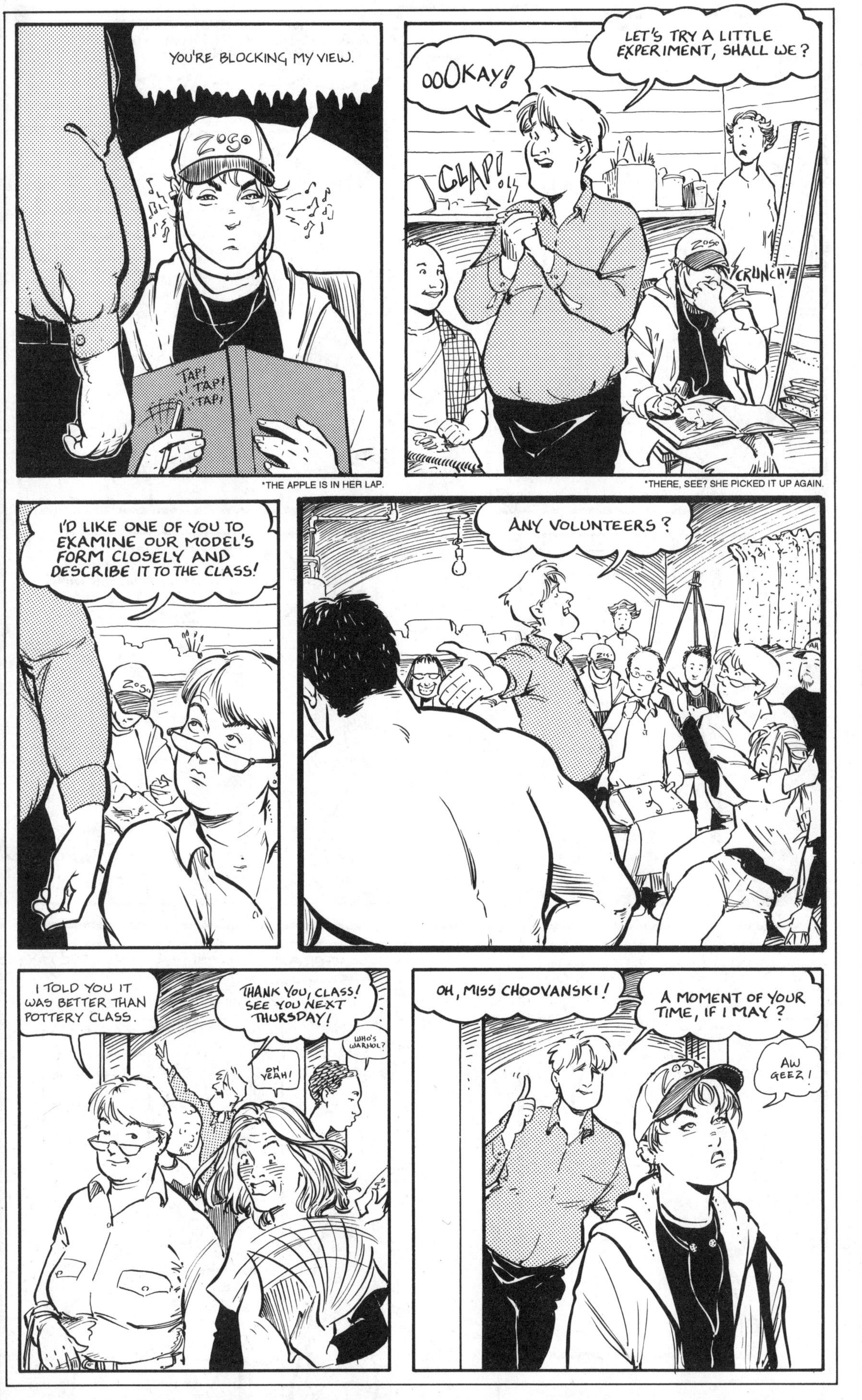
YOU'RE BLOCKING MY VIEW.
TAP! TAP! TAP!
OOOKAY!
LET'S TRY A LITTLE EXPERIMENT, SHALL WE?
CLAP!
CRUNCH!
I'D LIKE ONE OF YOU TO EXAMINE OUR MODEL'S FORM CLOSELY AND DESCRIBE IT TO THE CLASS!
ANY VOLUNTEERS?
I TOLD YOU IT WAS BETTER THAN POTTERY CLASS.
THANK YOU, CLASS! SEE YOU NEXT THURSDAY!
OH YEAH!
WHO'S WARHOL?
OH, MISS CHOOVANSKI!
A MOMENT OF YOUR TIME, IF I MAY?
AW GEEZ!

*THE APPLE IS IN HER LAP.

*THERE, SEE? SHE PICKED IT UP AGAIN.

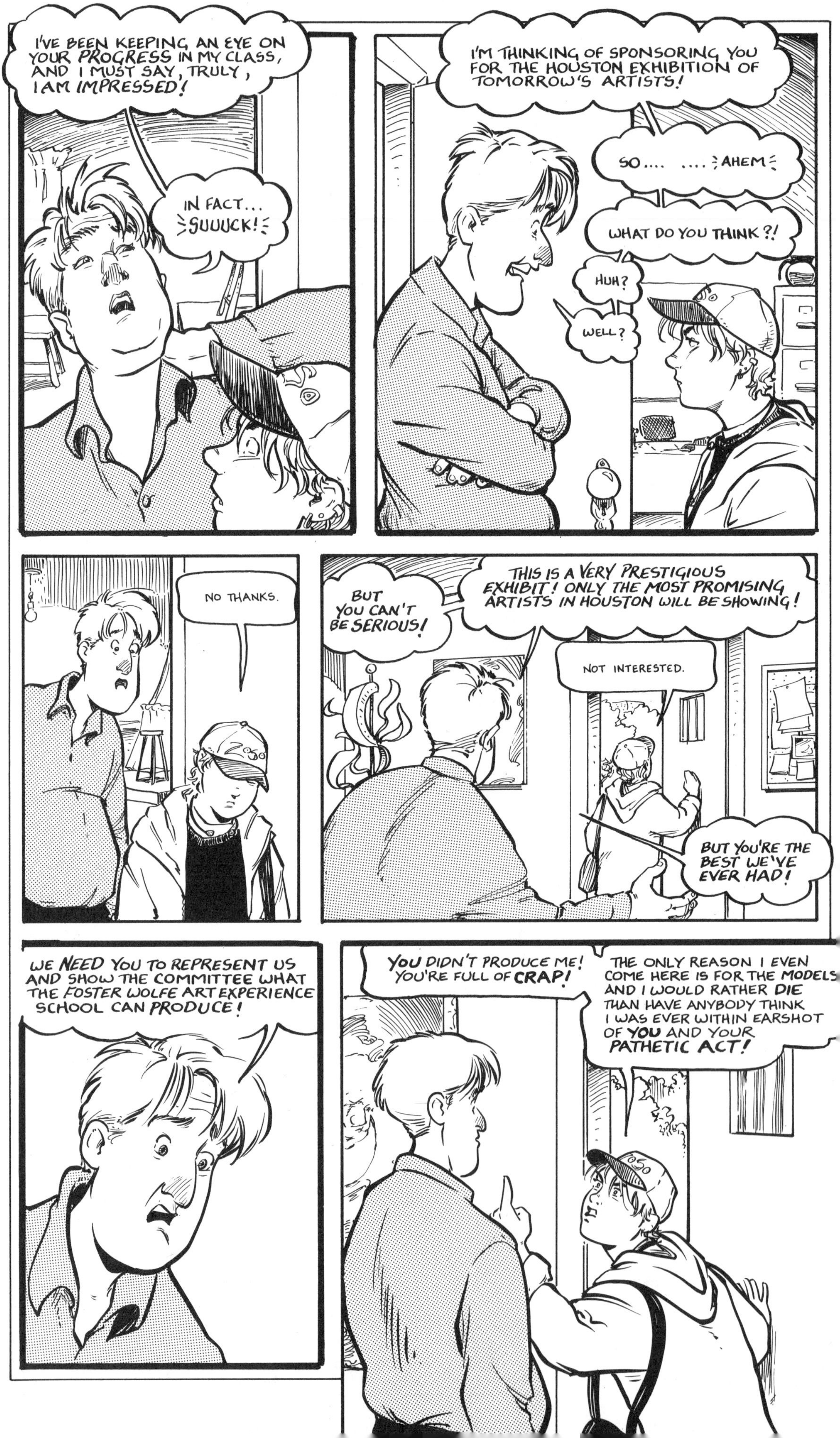

I'VE BEEN KEEPING AN EYE ON YOUR PROGRESS IN MY CLASS, AND I MUST SAY, TRULY, I AM IMPRESSED!
IN FACT... SUUUCK!
I'M THINKING OF SPONSORING YOU FOR THE HOUSTON EXHIBITION OF TOMORROW'S ARTISTS!
SO.... ....AHEM
WHAT DO YOU THINK?!
HUH?
WELL?
NO THANKS.
BUT YOU CAN'T BE SERIOUS!
THIS IS A VERY PRESTIGIOUS EXHIBIT! ONLY THE MOST PROMISING ARTISTS IN HOUSTON WILL BE SHOWING!
NOT INTERESTED.
BUT YOU'RE THE BEST WE'VE EVER HAD!
WE NEED YOU TO REPRESENT US AND SHOW THE COMMITTEE WHAT THE FOSTER WOLFE ART EXPERIENCE SCHOOL CAN PRODUCE!
YOU DIDN'T PRODUCE ME! YOU'RE FULL OF CRAP!
THE ONLY REASON I EVEN COME HERE IS FOR THE MODELS AND I WOULD RATHER DIE THAN HAVE ANYBODY THINK I WAS EVER WITHIN EARSHOT OF YOU AND YOUR PATHETIC ACT!

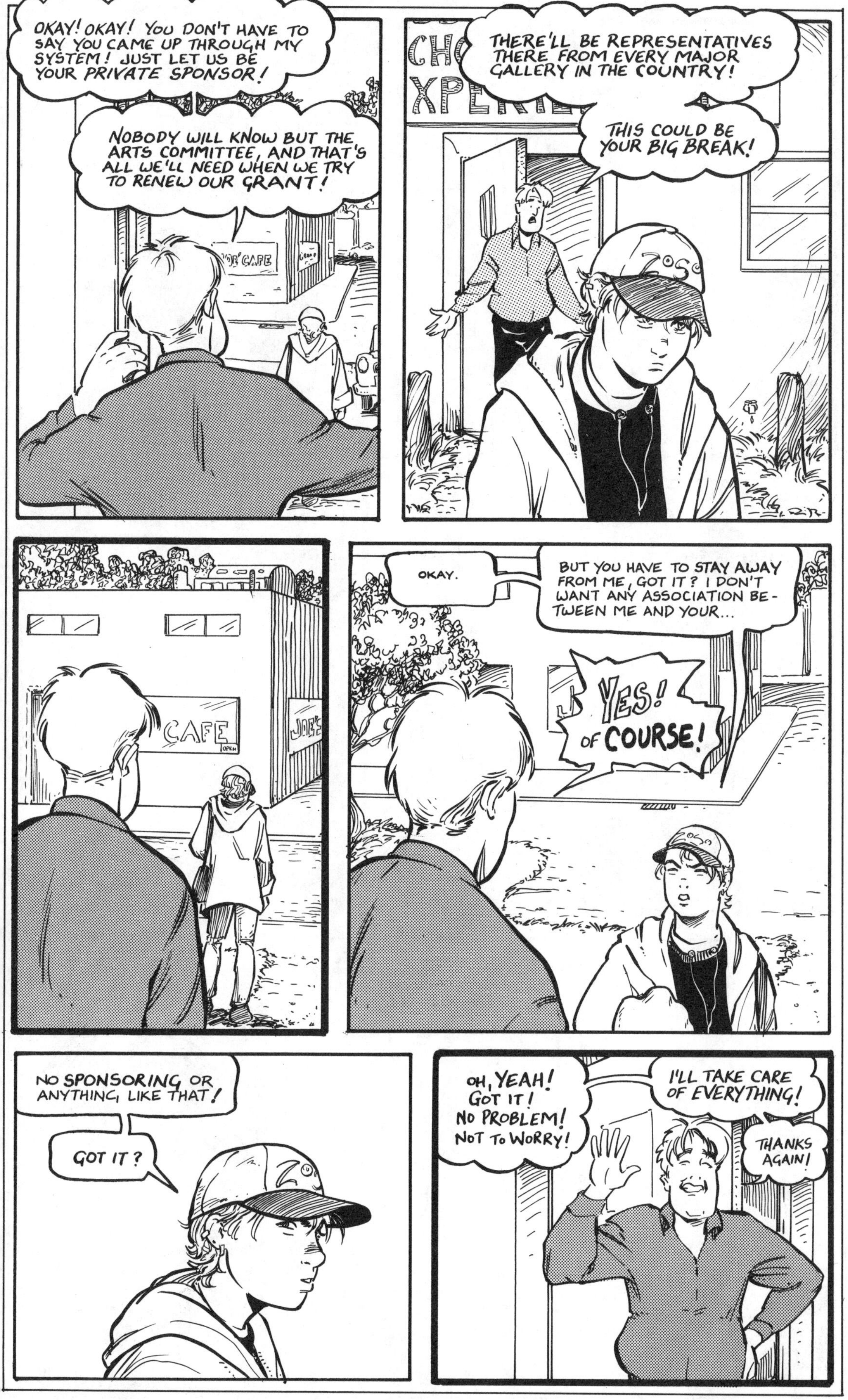
OKAY! OKAY! YOU DON'T HAVE TO SAY YOU CAME UP THROUGH MY SYSTEM! JUST LET US BE YOUR PRIVATE SPONSOR!
NOBODY WILL KNOW BUT THE ARTS COMMITTEE, AND THAT'S ALL WE'LL NEED WHEN WE TRY TO RENEW OUR GRANT!
JOE'S CAFE
THERE'LL BE REPRESENTATIVES THERE FROM EVERY MAJOR GALLERY IN THE COUNTRY!
THIS COULD BE YOUR BIG BREAK!
CAFE
OPEN
JOE'S
OKAY.
BUT YOU HAVE TO STAY AWAY FROM ME, GOT IT? I DON'T WANT ANY ASSOCIATION BE-TWEEN ME AND YOUR...
YES! OF COURSE!
NO SPONSORING OR ANYTHING LIKE THAT!
GOT IT?
OH, YEAH! GOT IT! NO PROBLEM! NOT TO WORRY!
I'LL TAKE CARE OF EVERYTHING!
THANKS AGAIN!

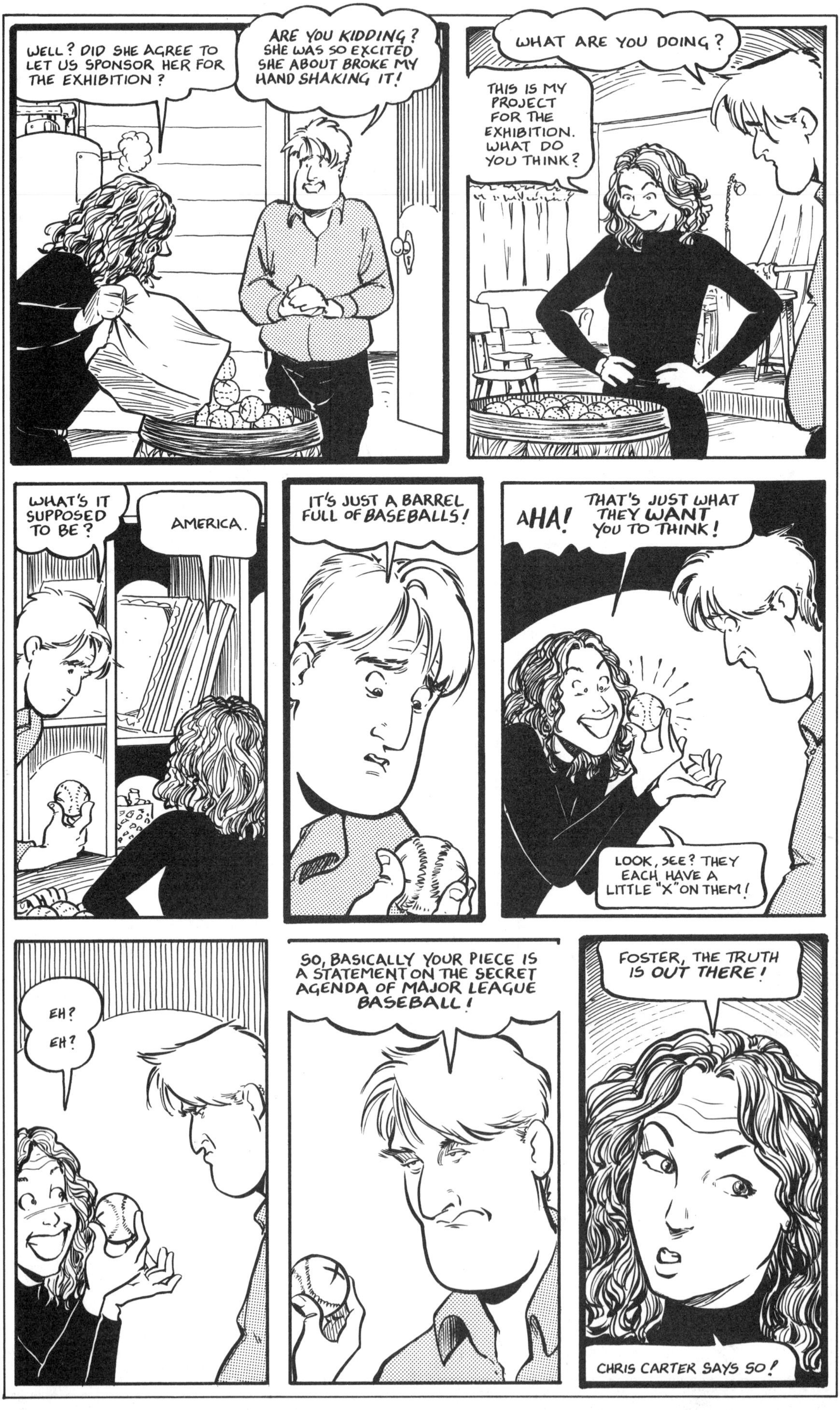
WELL? DID SHE AGREE TO LET US SPONSOR HER FOR THE EXHIBITION?
ARE YOU KIDDING? SHE WAS SO EXCITED SHE ABOUT BROKE MY HAND SHAKING IT!
WHAT ARE YOU DOING?
THIS IS MY PROJECT FOR THE EXHIBITION. WHAT DO YOU THINK?
WHAT'S IT SUPPOSED TO BE?
AMERICA.
IT'S JUST A BARREL FULL OF BASEBALLS!
AHA!
THAT'S JUST WHAT THEY WANT YOU TO THINK!
LOOK, SEE? THEY EACH HAVE A LITTLE "X" ON THEM!
EH?
EH?
SO, BASICALLY YOUR PIECE IS A STATEMENT ON THE SECRET AGENDA OF MAJOR LEAGUE BASEBALL!
FOSTER, THE TRUTH IS OUT THERE!
CHRIS CARTER SAYS SO!

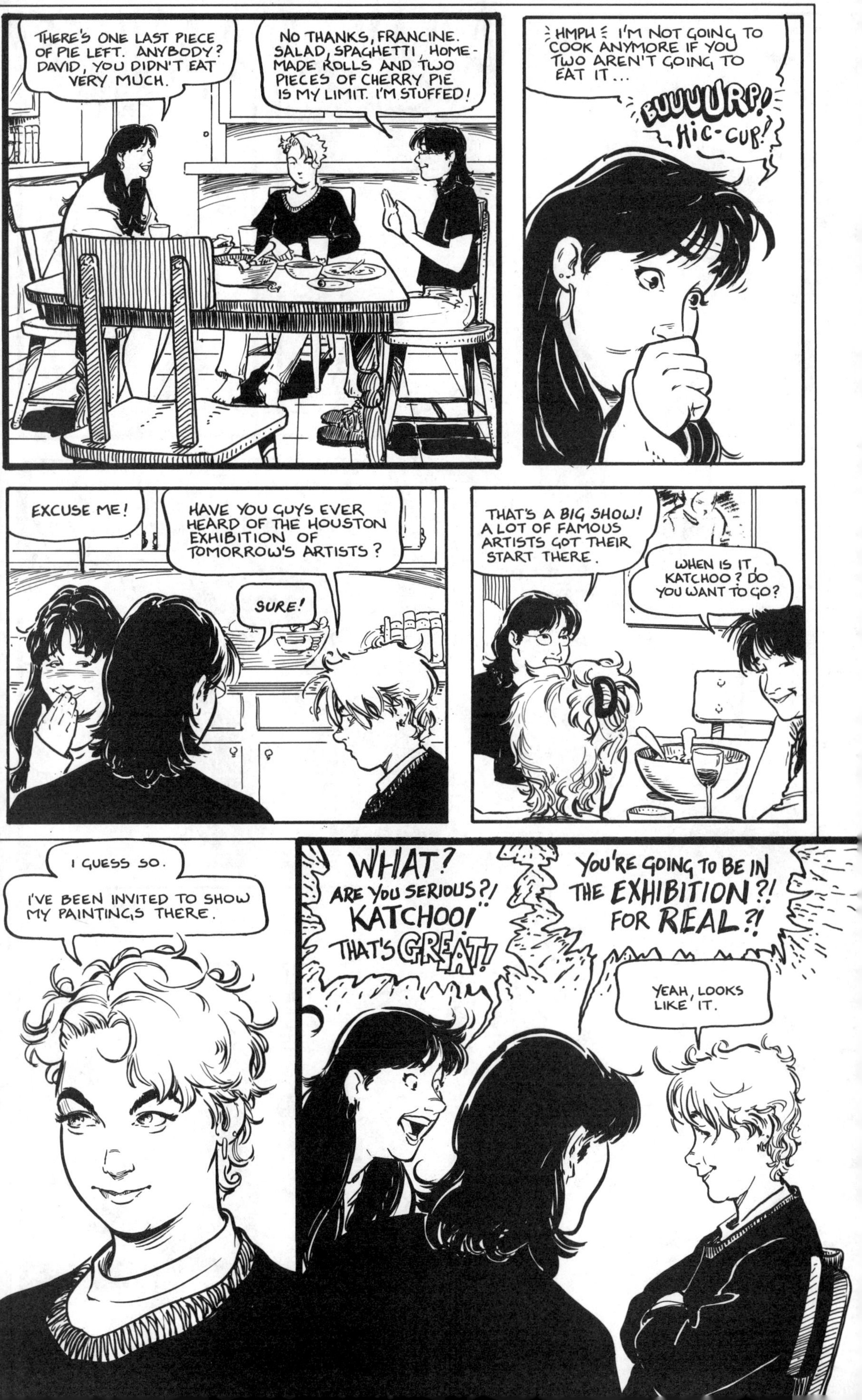

THERE'S ONE LAST PIECE OF PIE LEFT. ANYBODY? DAVID, YOU DIDN'T EAT VERY MUCH.
NO THANKS, FRANCINE. SALAD, SPAGHETTI, HOME-MADE ROLLS AND TWO PIECES OF CHERRY PIE IS MY LIMIT. I'M STUFFED!
HMPH I'M NOT GOING TO COOK ANYMORE IF YOU TWO AREN'T GOING TO EAT IT...
BUUUURP!
HIC-CUP!
EXCUSE ME!
HAVE YOU GUYS EVER HEARD OF THE HOUSTON EXHIBITION OF TOMORROW'S ARTISTS?
SURE!
THAT'S A BIG SHOW! A LOT OF FAMOUS ARTISTS GOT THEIR START THERE.
WHEN IS IT, KATCHOO? DO YOU WANT TO GO?
I GUESS SO.
I'VE BEEN INVITED TO SHOW MY PAINTINGS THERE.
WHAT? ARE YOU SERIOUS?! KATCHOO! THAT'S GREAT!
YOU'RE GOING TO BE IN THE EXHIBITION?! FOR REAL?!
YEAH, LOOKS LIKE IT.

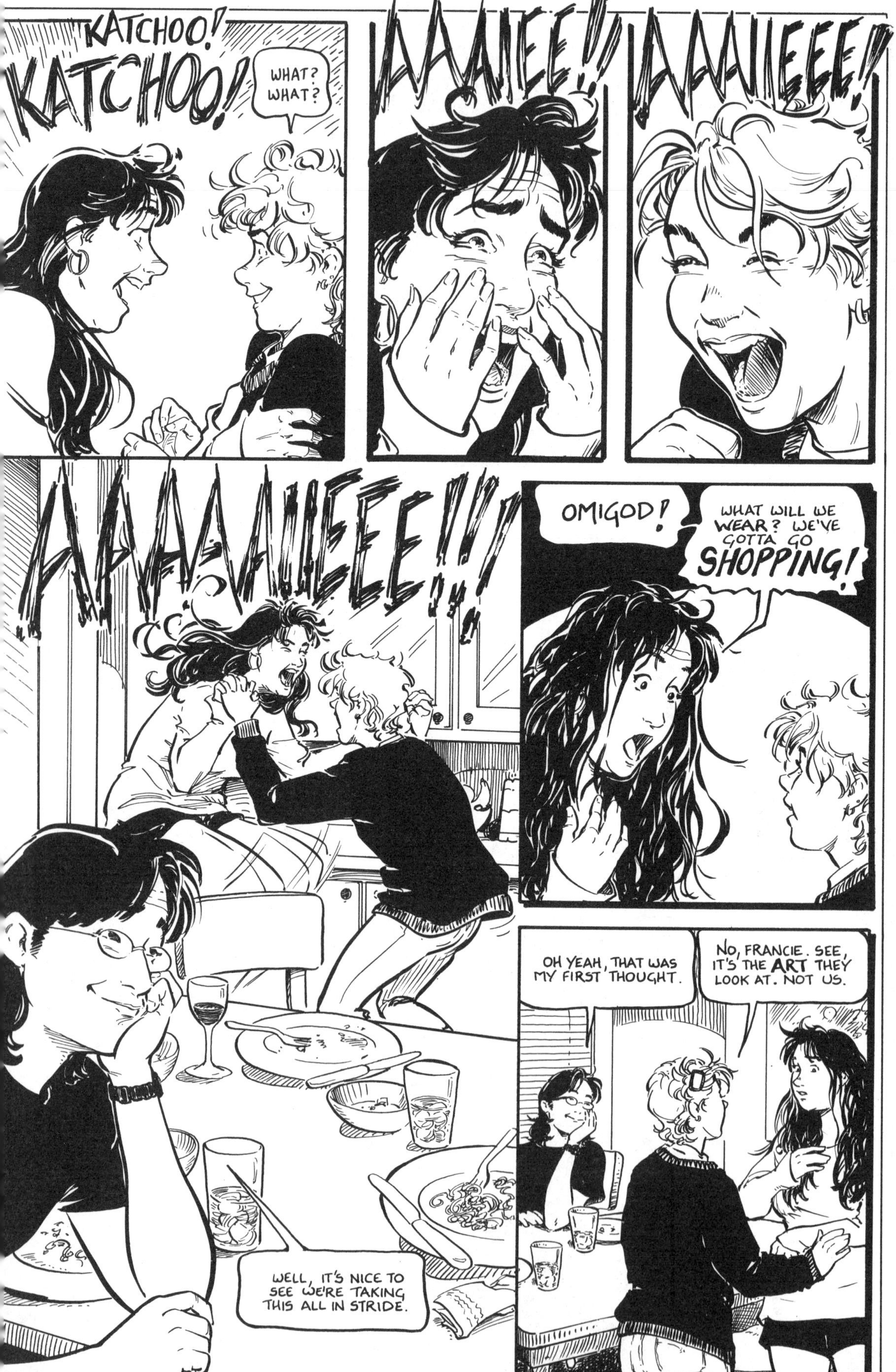
KATCHOO!
KATCHOO!
WHAT? WHAT?
AAAIEE!!
AAAIIEEE!!
AAAAAIIEEE!!!
OMIGOD!
WHAT WILL WE WEAR? WE'VE GOTTA GO SHOPPING!
WELL, IT'S NICE TO SEE WE'RE TAKING THIS ALL IN STRIDE.
OH YEAH, THAT WAS MY FIRST THOUGHT.
NO, FRANCIE. SEE, IT'S THE ART THEY LOOK AT. NOT US.

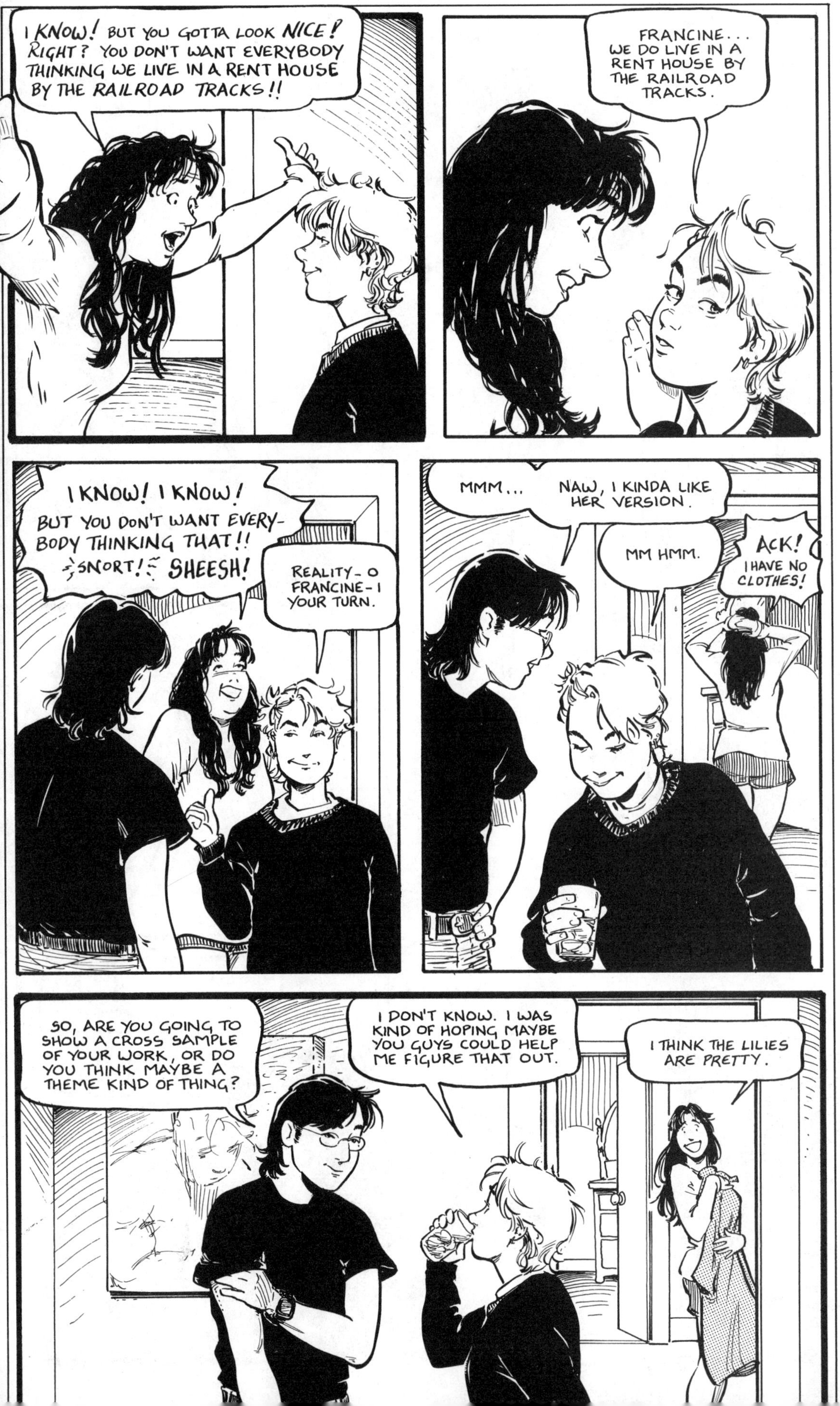

I KNOW! BUT YOU GOTTA LOOK NICE! RIGHT? YOU DON'T WANT EVERYBODY THINKING WE LIVE IN A RENT HOUSE BY THE RAILROAD TRACKS!!
FRANCINE... WE DO LIVE IN A RENT HOUSE BY THE RAILROAD TRACKS.
I KNOW! I KNOW! BUT YOU DON'T WANT EVERYBODY THINKING THAT!! SNORT! SHEESH!
REALITY-0 FRANCINE-1 YOUR TURN.
MMM...
NAW, I KINDA LIKE HER VERSION.
MM HMM.
ACK! I HAVE NO CLOTHES!
SO, ARE YOU GOING TO SHOW A CROSS SAMPLE OF YOUR WORK, OR DO YOU THINK MAYBE A THEME KIND OF THING?
I DON'T KNOW. I WAS KIND OF HOPING MAYBE YOU GUYS COULD HELP ME FIGURE THAT OUT.
I THINK THE LILIES ARE PRETTY.

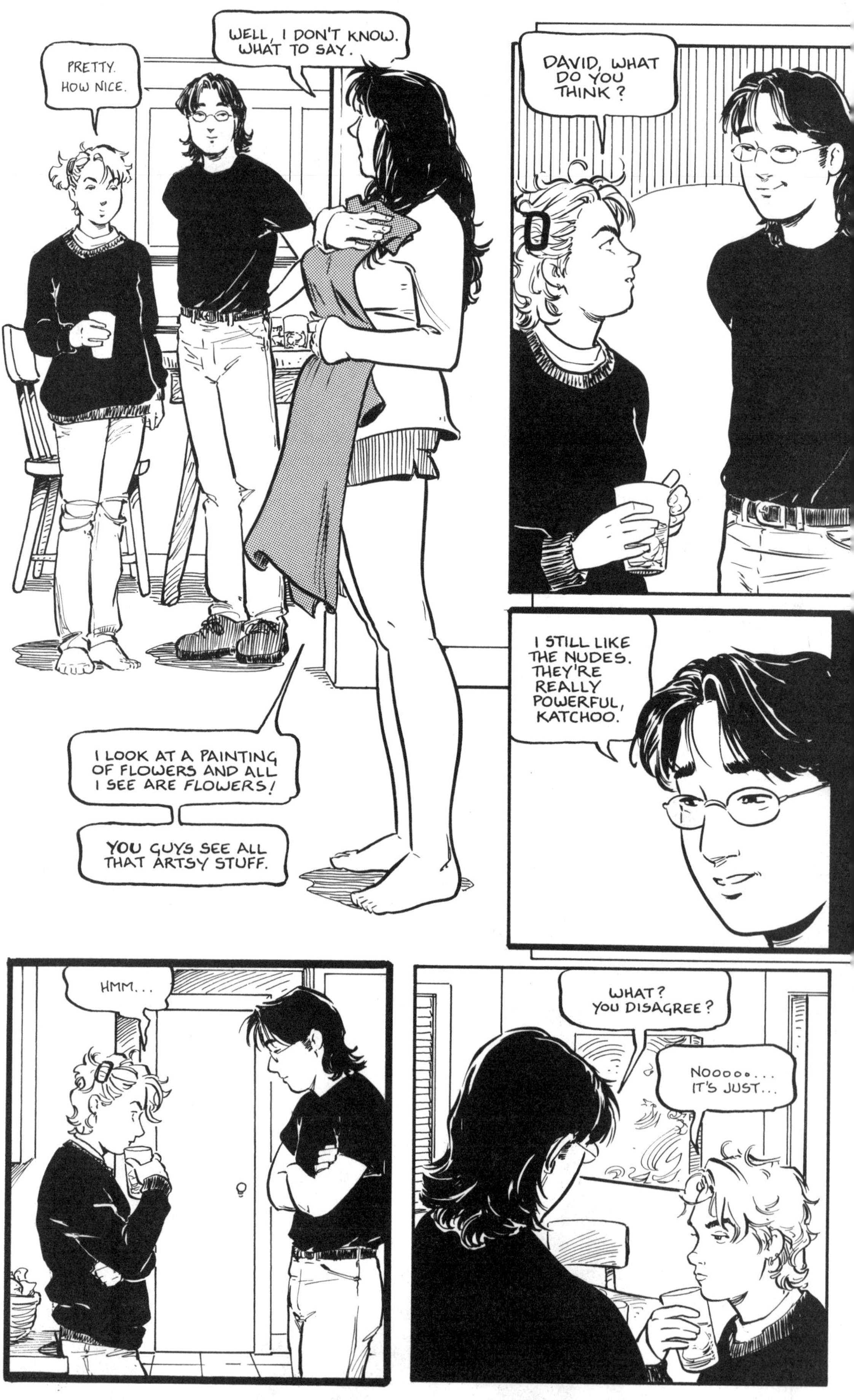
PRETTY. HOW NICE.
WELL, I DON'T KNOW. WHAT TO SAY.
I LOOK AT A PAINTING OF FLOWERS AND ALL I SEE ARE FLOWERS!
YOU GUYS SEE ALL THAT ARTSY STUFF.
DAVID, WHAT DO YOU THINK?
I STILL LIKE THE NUDES. THEY'RE REALLY POWERFUL, KATCHOO.
HMM...
WHAT? YOU DISAGREE?
Nooooo... IT'S JUST...

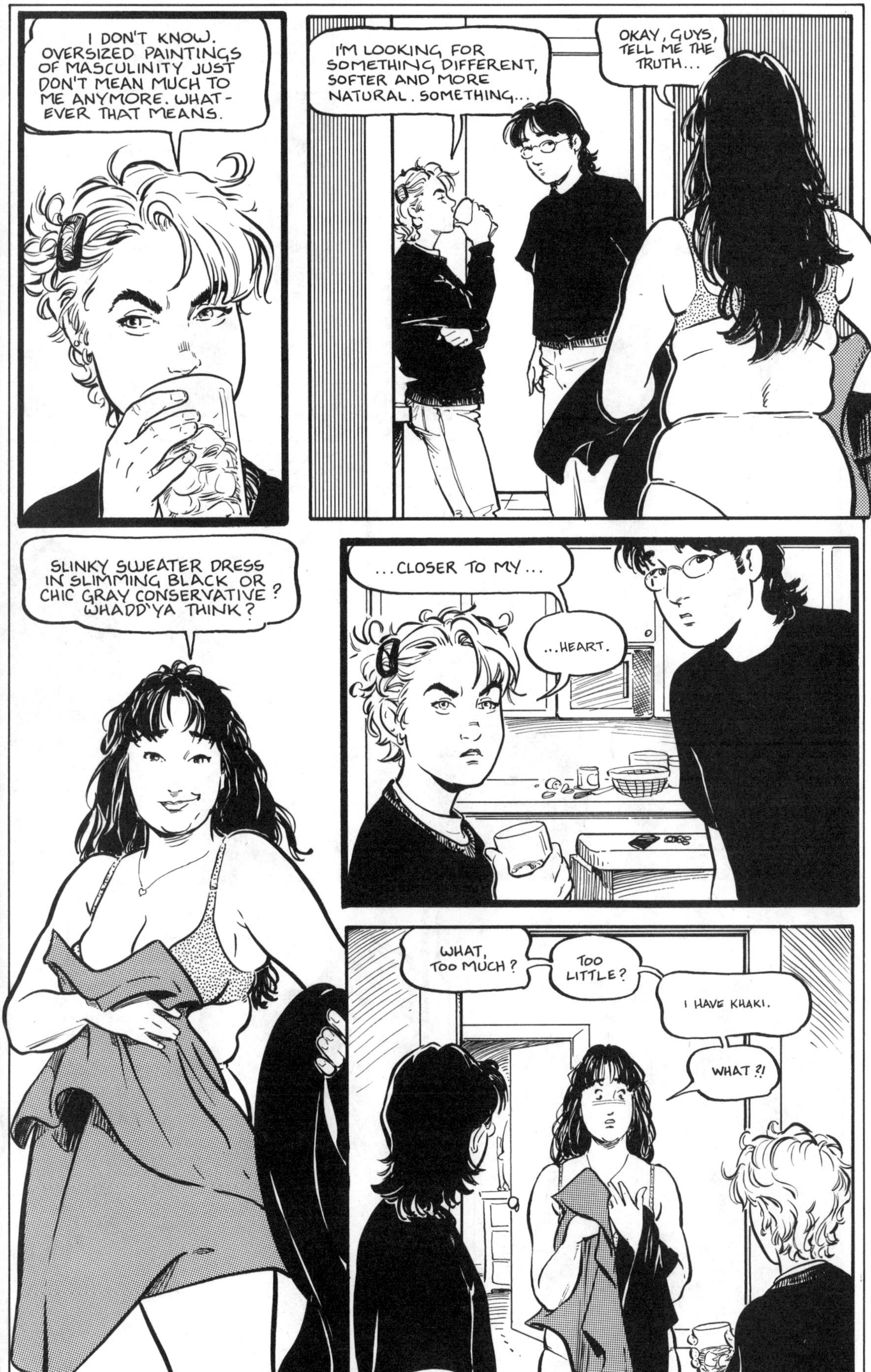
I DON'T KNOW. OVERSIZED PAINTINGS OF MASCULINITY JUST DON'T MEAN MUCH TO ME ANYMORE. WHAT-EVER THAT MEANS.
I'M LOOKING FOR SOMETHING DIFFERENT, SOFTER AND MORE NATURAL. SOMETHING...
OKAY, GUYS, TELL ME THE TRUTH...
SLINKY SWEATER DRESS IN SLIMMING BLACK OR CHIC GRAY CONSERVATIVE? WHADD'YA THINK?
...CLOSER TO MY...
...HEART.
WHAT, TOO MUCH?
TOO LITTLE?
I HAVE KHAKI.
WHAT?!

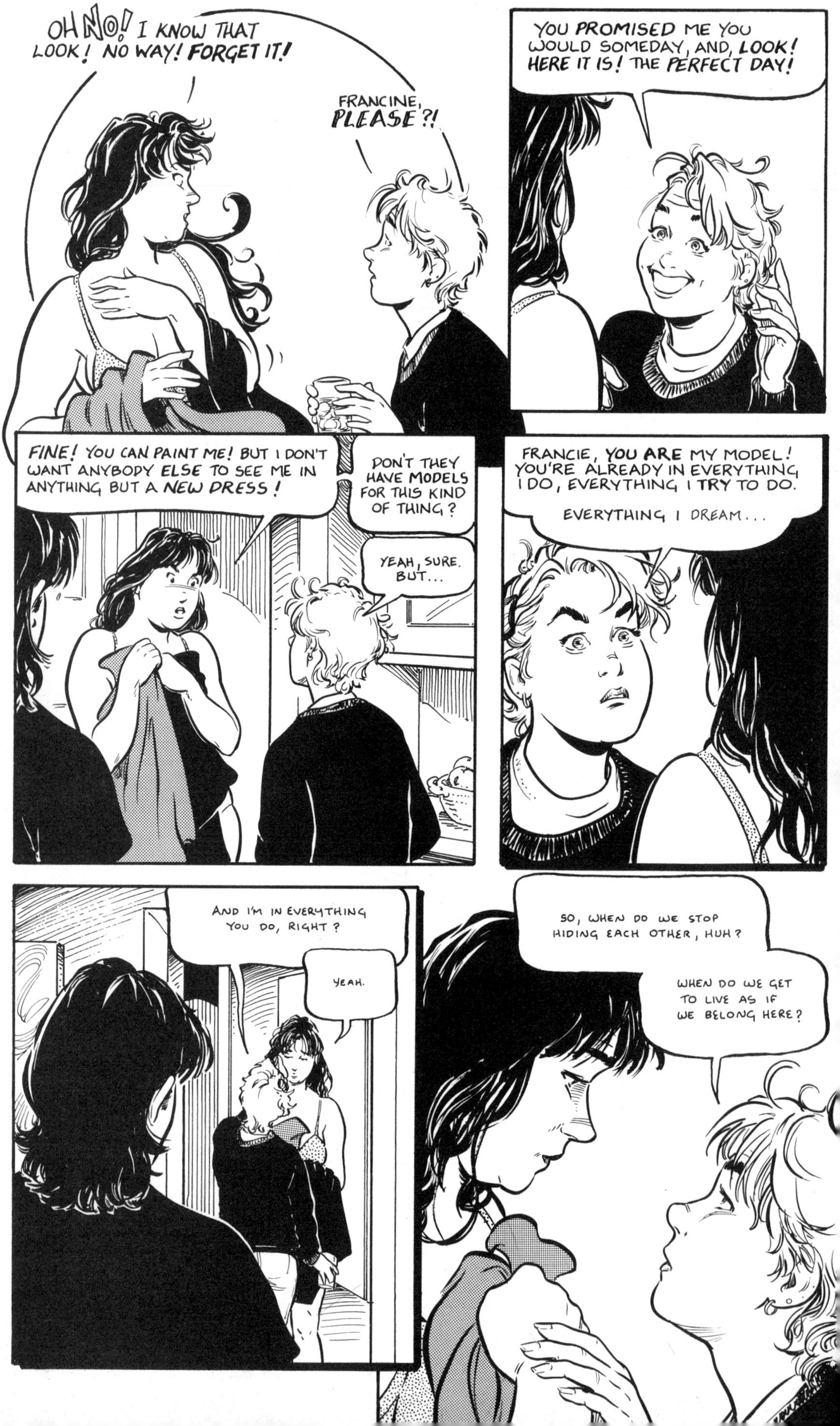

OH NO! I KNOW THAT LOOK! NO WAY! FORGET IT!
FRANCINE, PLEASE?!
YOU PROMISED ME YOU WOULD SOMEDAY, AND, LOOK! HERE IT IS! THE PERFECT DAY!
FINE! YOU CAN PAINT ME! BUT I DON'T WANT ANYBODY ELSE TO SEE ME IN ANYTHING BUT A NEW DRESS!
DON'T THEY HAVE MODELS FOR THIS KIND OF THING?
YEAH, SURE. BUT...
FRANCIE, YOU ARE MY MODEL! YOU'RE ALREADY IN EVERYTHING I DO, EVERYTHING I TRY TO DO.
EVERYTHING I DREAM...
AND I'M IN EVERYTHING YOU DO, RIGHT?
YEAH.
SO, WHEN DO WE STOP HIDING EACH OTHER, HUH?
WHEN DO WE GET TO LIVE AS IF WE BELONG HERE?

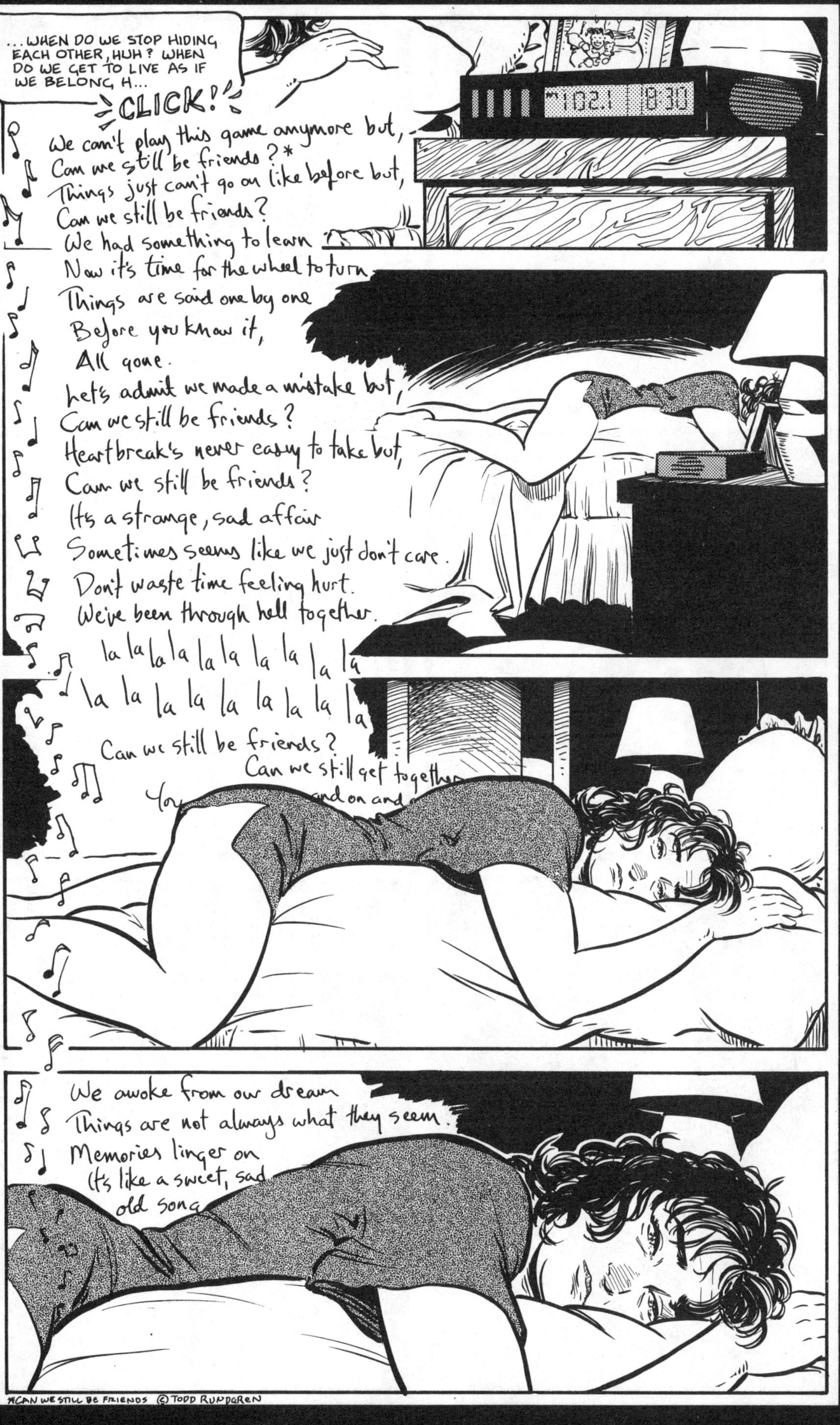

...WHEN DO WE STOP HIDING EACH OTHER, HUH? WHEN DO WE GET TO LIVE AS IF WE BELONG H...
CLICK!
102.1 18:30
We can't play this game anymore but,
Can we still be friends?*
Things just can't go on like before but,
Can we still be friends?
We had something to learn
Now it's time for the wheel to turn
Things are said one by one
Before you know it,
All gone.
Let's admit we made a mistake but,
Can we still be friends?
Heartbreak's never easy to take but,
Can we still be friends?
It's a strange, sad affair
Sometimes seems like we just don't care.
Don't waste time feeling hurt.
We've been through hell together.
la la la la la la la la la la
la la la la la la la la la la
Can we still be friends?
Can we still get togethe
You
and on and
We awoke from our dream
Things are not always what they seem.
Memories linger on
It's like a sweet, sad old song

*CAN WE STILL BE FRIENDS © TODD RUNDGREN

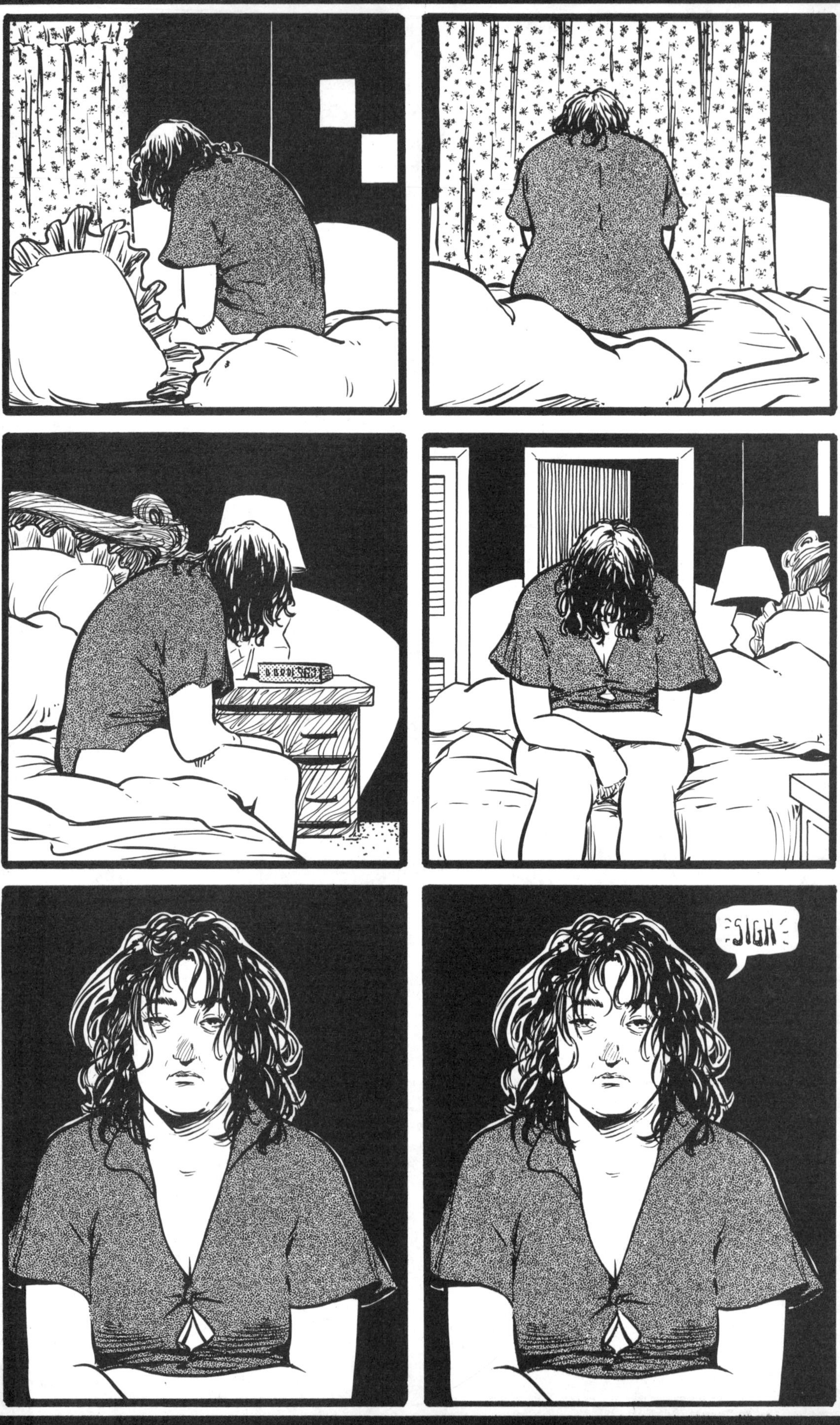
SIGH

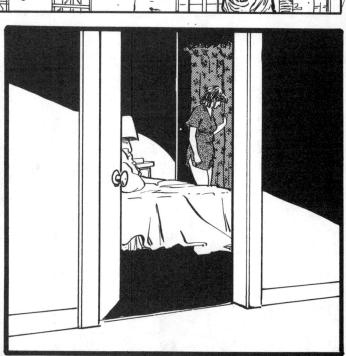

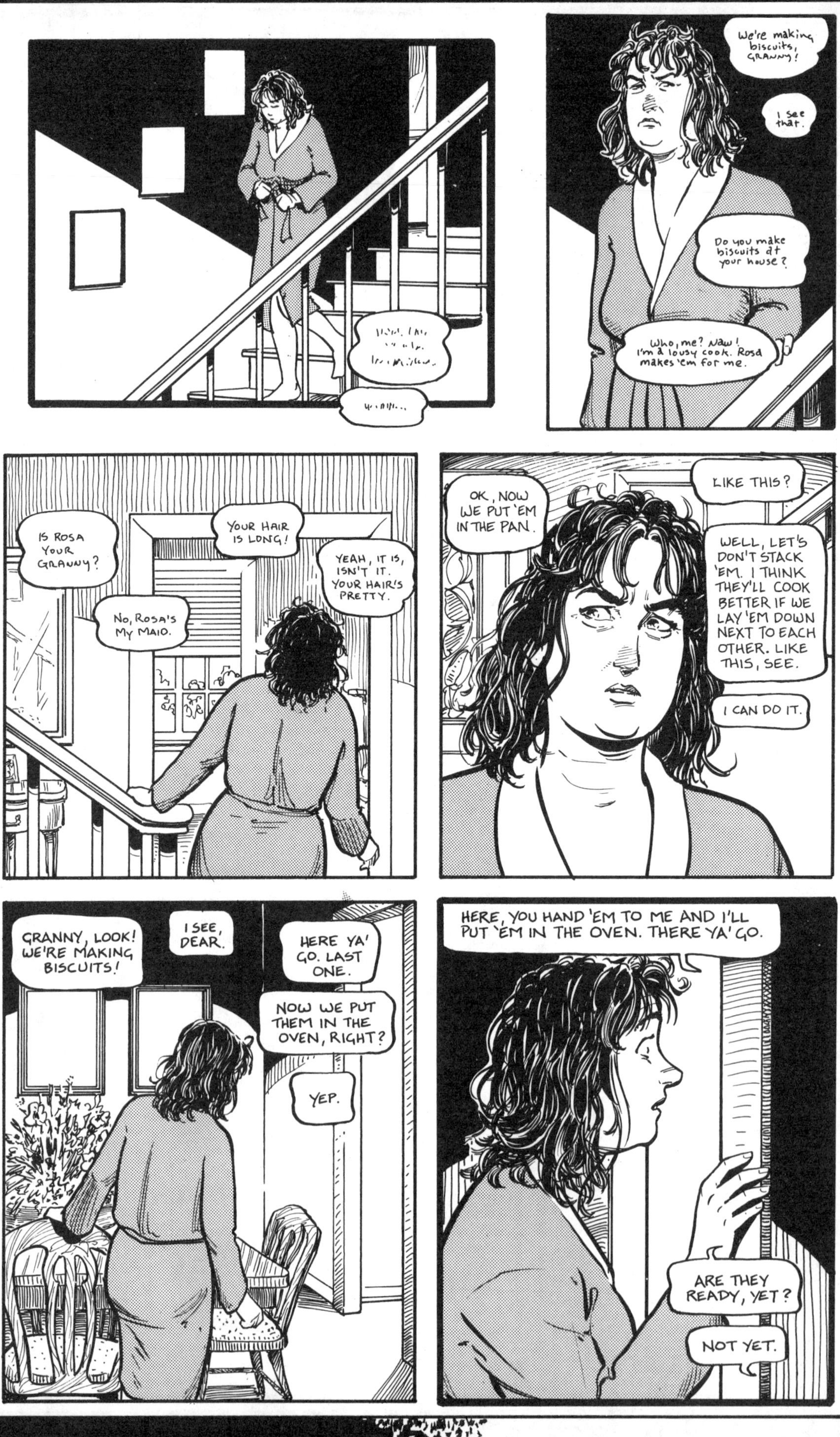

We're making biscuits, GRANNY!
I see that.
Do you make biscuits at your house?
Who, me? Naw! I'm a lousy cook. Rosa makes 'em for me.
IS ROSA YOUR GRANNY?
YOUR HAIR IS LONG!
YEAH, IT IS, ISN'T IT. YOUR HAIR'S PRETTY.
No, ROSA'S MY MAID.
OK, NOW WE PUT 'EM IN THE PAN.
LIKE THIS?
WELL, LET'S DON'T STACK 'EM. I THINK THEY'LL COOK BETTER IF WE LAY 'EM DOWN NEXT TO EACH OTHER. LIKE THIS, SEE.
I CAN DO IT.
GRANNY, LOOK! WE'RE MAKING BISCUITS!
I SEE, DEAR.
HERE YA' GO. LAST ONE.
NOW WE PUT THEM IN THE OVEN, RIGHT?
YEP.
HERE, YOU HAND 'EM TO ME AND I'LL PUT 'EM IN THE OVEN. THERE YA' GO.
ARE THEY READY, YET?
NOT YET.

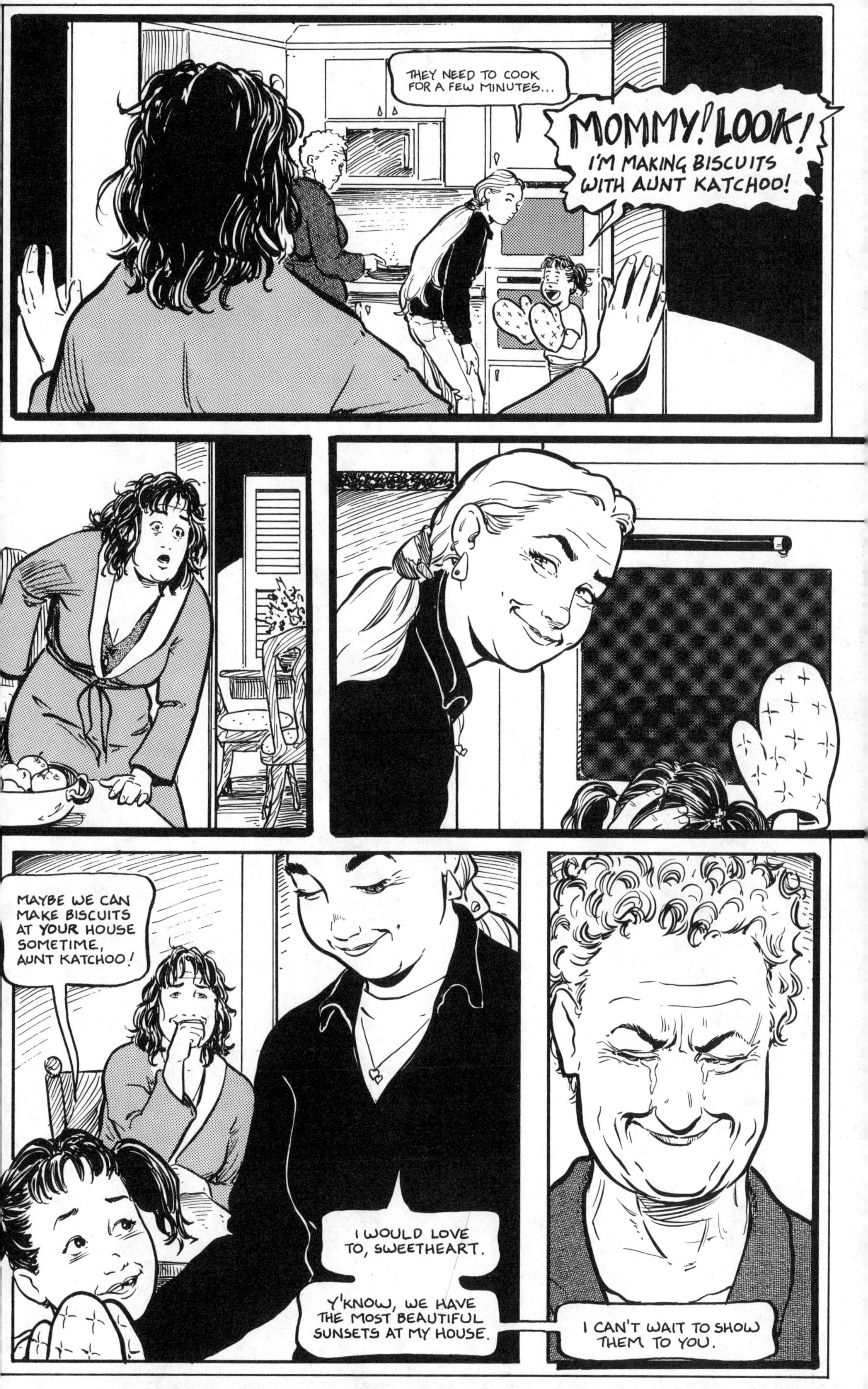
THEY NEED TO COOK FOR A FEW MINUTES...
MOMMY! LOOK! I'M MAKING BISCUITS WITH AUNT KATCHOO!
MAYBE WE CAN MAKE BISCUITS AT YOUR HOUSE SOMETIME, AUNT KATCHOO!
I WOULD LOVE TO, SWEETHEART.
Y'KNOW, WE HAVE THE MOST BEAUTIFUL SUNSETS AT MY HOUSE.
I CAN'T WAIT TO SHOW THEM TO YOU.

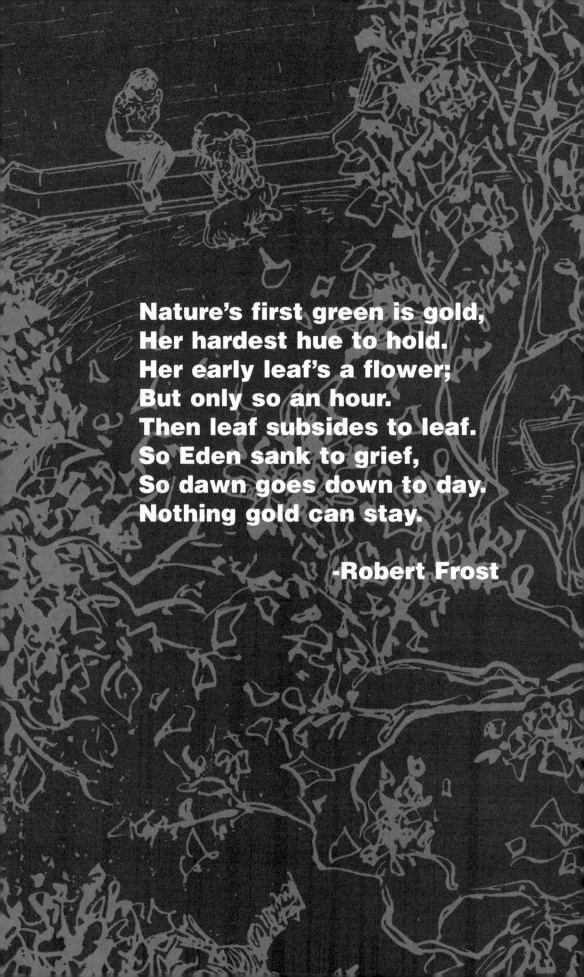

Nature's first green is gold,
Her hardest hue to hold.
Her early leaf's a flower;
But only so an hour.
Then leaf subsides to leaf.
So Eden sank to grief,
So dawn goes down to day.
Nothing gold can stay.

-Robert Frost

So softly and tenderly, I pull you
to my heart.
                    You never thought
                         to cover up.

But something's wrong, I feel
so rushed.
                    The air you breathe,
                         it's not enough.

Now whatever will ever become
of me?
                    Elegant waste and chivalry.

Will I dream my life along?
                    Or wake to find your
                         timing gone.

Will I dream of wonderous things?
                    Things that only God
                         has seen.

Or will I grow to love this world?
                    And only see the
                         man machine.

Yet, here I stand, against the wall.
                    Afraid to breathe.
                    Afraid you'll fall.

That's when you come and hold me
tight. Tell me. . .
                    Everything will be alright.

So softly and tenderly I pull you to
my heart.
                    You never thought to cover up.

But something's wrong, I feel so
rushed.
                    The air we breathe. . .

It's not enough.

WHEN I WAS THIRTEEN I WATCHED A CLASSMATE DIE ON THE CONCRETE BESIDE A SCHOOL BUS. IN THE NOISE AND PLAY OF PUSHING CHILDREN THE LITTLE BOY HAD BEEN THRUST BEFORE THE APPROACHING BUS AND RUN OVER. WAITING FOR THE AMBULANCE, WE STOOD AROUND HIM LIKE A WALL OF LIFE AND WATCHED HIM DIE.

AT FIRST HE GROANED AND COULDN'T MOVE, HIS EYES SHUT TIGHT. BUT AS THE CROWD RECALLED THE HORRIFIC MOMENT AGAIN AND AGAIN FROM VARIOUS POINTS OF VIEW, THE BOY GREW SILENT. HE OPENED HIS EYES AND LOOKED BEYOND OUR SILHOUETTES TO WATCH THE SUN WITH A PEACEFUL CALM. THEN I REALIZED HE NO LONGER SAW THE SKY OR FELT THE AUTUMN BREEZE, NOR DID HE FEEL ANY PAIN OR HEAR THE SOUND OF TEACHERS CRYING.

I DON'T KNOW WHAT FABRIC LIES BENEATH THE LIFE WE LIVE, BUT ON THE OTHER SIDE OF OUR MORTAL PAIN IS A PLACE OF SANCTUARY. I KNOW BECAUSE I STOOD BESIDE A LITTLE BOY AND WATCHED HIM FIND IT ONCE.

YEARS LATER, I HELD EMMA'S HAND UNTIL SHE FOUND SANCTUARY IN THE SNOW FALLING OUTSIDE HER WINDOW. THEN I FOUND IT IN THE BACKSEAT OF A SPEEDING POLICE CAR, UNDER FRANCINE'S TEARS.

I GUESS THAT'S WHY I CAME BACK. THERE'S SOMETHING MORE IMPORTANT THAN THE WORK WE DO AND THE ROLES WE PLAY. THERE'S SOMETHING MORE THAN HOW WE MOVE OR WHERE. THERE'S SOMETHING ABOUT WHO WE TOUCH AND WHY, AND IT MATTERS MORE THAN WE CAN UNDERSTAND OR PERHAPS REMEMBER.

SO, IT DOESN'T MATTER WHAT HAPPENED OR WHAT WAS SAID THAT AWFUL SUMMER TEN YEARS BEFORE, IF FRANCINE NEEDS ME I'LL BE HERE FOR HER, TO HOLD HER HAND AND LET HER KNOW SHE'S NOT ALONE. I OWE HER THAT MUCH, DON'T YOU SEE? IN HER EYES I FOUND SANCTUARY. AND NOW, WHEN LIFE IS SHADOWS IN THE SUN, FRANCINE LOOKS FOR IT, TOO. BUT ISN'T IT IRONIC SHE LOOKS TO ME FOR SOMETHING I SAW IN HER ALL ALONG?

I DON'T KNOW, MAYBE SANCTUARY ISN'T REALLY FOUND IN THE SUN OR SNOW OR A LOVED ONE'S TEARS. MAYBE, WHEN THE MOMENT'S RIGHT THESE THINGS MERELY CATCH A REFLECTION OF OUR OWN SOUL AND REMIND US OF WHO WE REALLY ARE AND THAT HOME IS NEVER ALL THAT FAR AWAY — JUST BEYOND THE SILHOUETTES THAT DARK THE SUN.

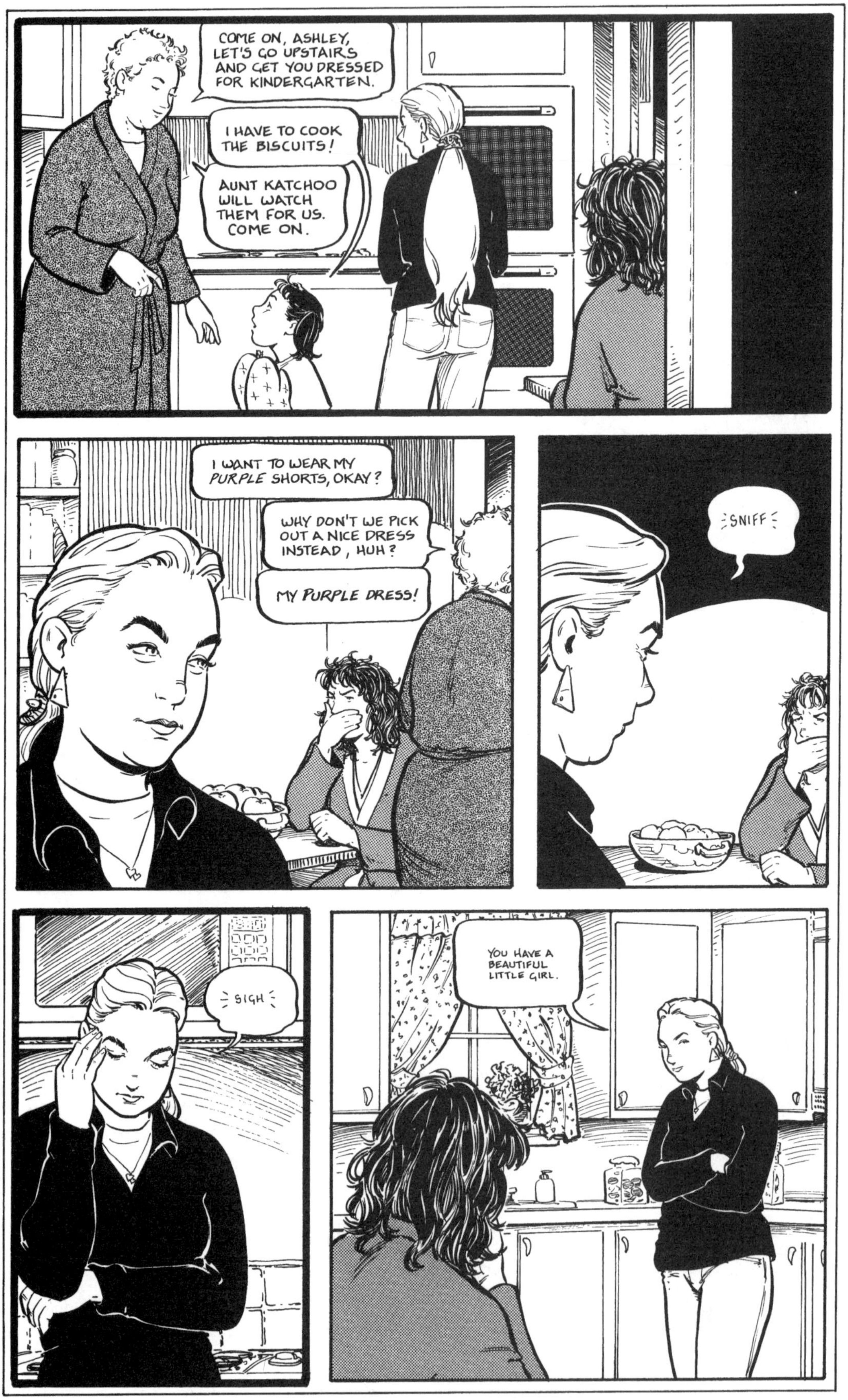

COME ON, ASHLEY, LET'S GO UPSTAIRS AND GET YOU DRESSED FOR KINDERGARTEN.
I HAVE TO COOK THE BISCUITS!
AUNT KATCHOO WILL WATCH THEM FOR US. COME ON.
I WANT TO WEAR MY *PURPLE* SHORTS, OKAY?
WHY DON'T WE PICK OUT A NICE DRESS INSTEAD, HUH?
MY *PURPLE* DRESS!
SNIFF
SIGH
YOU HAVE A BEAUTIFUL LITTLE GIRL.

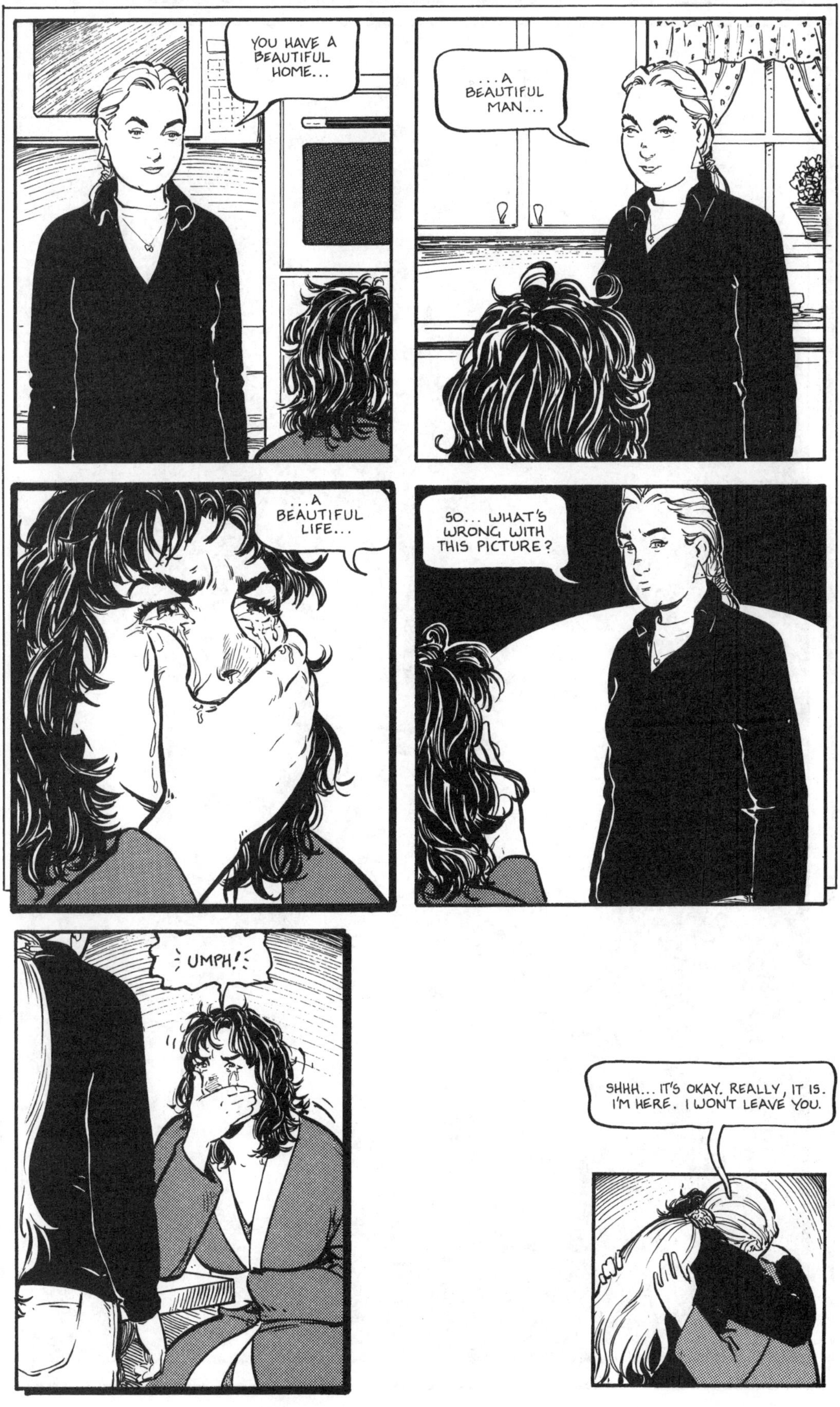
YOU HAVE A BEAUTIFUL HOME...
...A BEAUTIFUL MAN...
...A BEAUTIFUL LIFE...
SO... WHAT'S WRONG WITH THIS PICTURE?
UMPH!
SHHH... IT'S OKAY. REALLY, IT IS. I'M HERE. I WON'T LEAVE YOU.

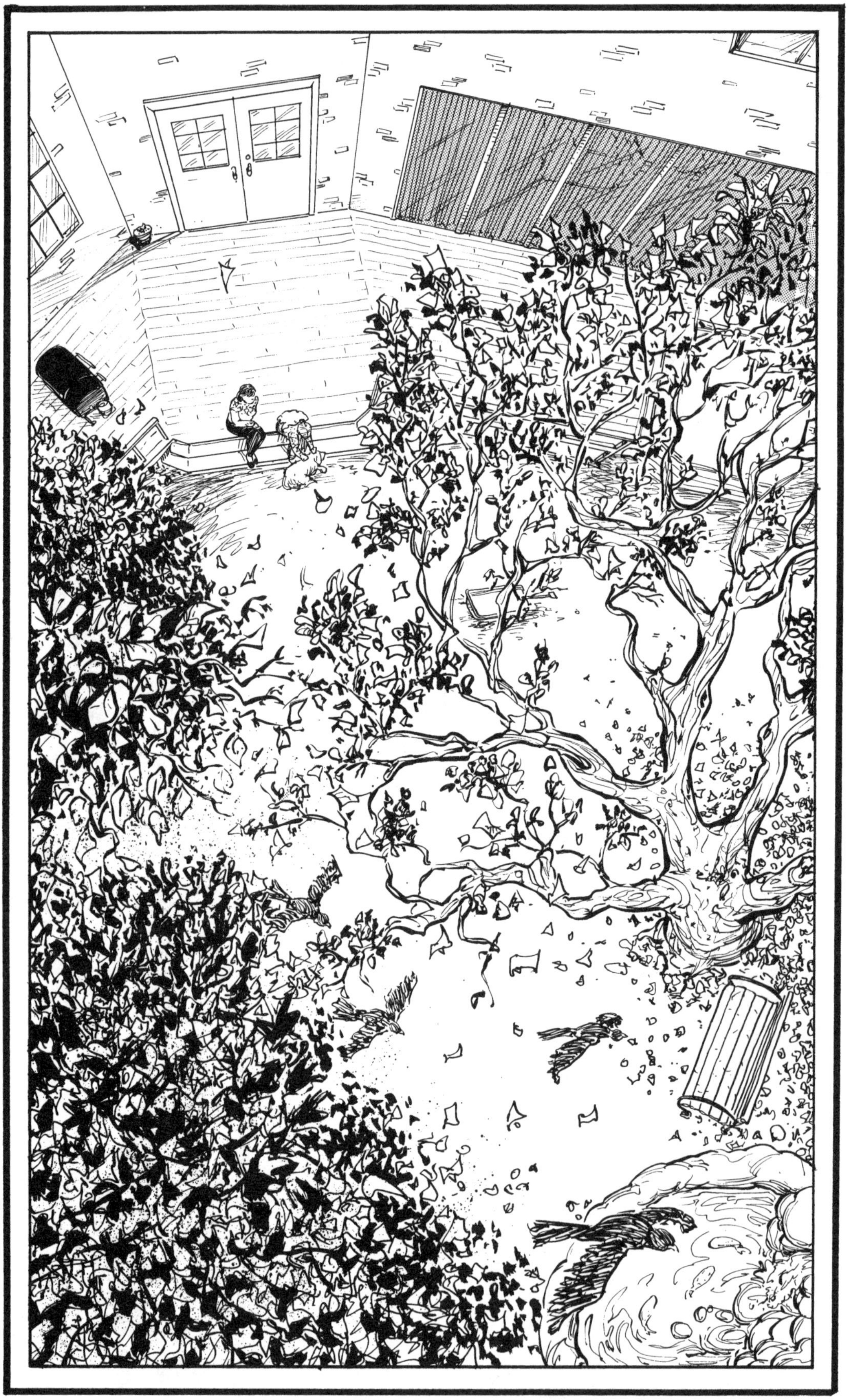

Katchoo pulled the rubber ball from Mikey's mouth and tossed it into the yard again, sending the golden retriever scampering through the autumn leaves in pursuit. It was a rare day in Houston, cool and crisp. Finally, the sky had lost its summer pale and recovered a brilliant blue. Katchoo was used to the beauty, she saw it every day in the mountains. But she had lived in Houston once and she understood the novelty of a pretty day for the locals.

The back door opened and Francine stepped out onto the deck that Brad built the year they moved in. She sat down beside Katchoo and raised a hand to shade her eyes from the sunlight. They exchanged smiles. Katchoo noted with sadness that her friend looked too old for her age. Despite the fact that she had spent the last hour bathing, shampooing, putting on makeup and a fashionable outfit, nothing could hide the lines of heartbreak on Francine's face. Her eyes, once chocolate brown and glimmering, looked dull and tired to Katchoo earlier this morning. Only now, as she smiled, did they begin to show signs of life.

"Feeling better?" Katchoo asked.

"Oh yeah. It's amazing what a shower and clean clothes will do for you, isn't it?" Francine replied. "I'm sorry I looked so ragged this morning. I didn't sleep well last night."

"No need to explain. Pretty sweater."

"Thank you," Francine smiled, picking a piece of lint from her chest. Katchoo noted the cascade of wrinkles this produced around Francine's jaw. "I got this in Santa Fe."

"Oh really? When were you in Santa Fe?"

"Brad and I went skiing there last Christmas."

"Did you stay in town?"

"Yeah, we stayed right by the plaza, downtown. One of those beautiful old places, you know? Very elegant, with all this south-western charm. They served tea in the lobby every afternoon."

"Oh, the Hotel St. Francis?" said Katchoo.

"Yes. that's the one. And at night we walked along this street lined with candles. . ."

"Yeah, Canyon Road. They line the walls and houses with lumi-

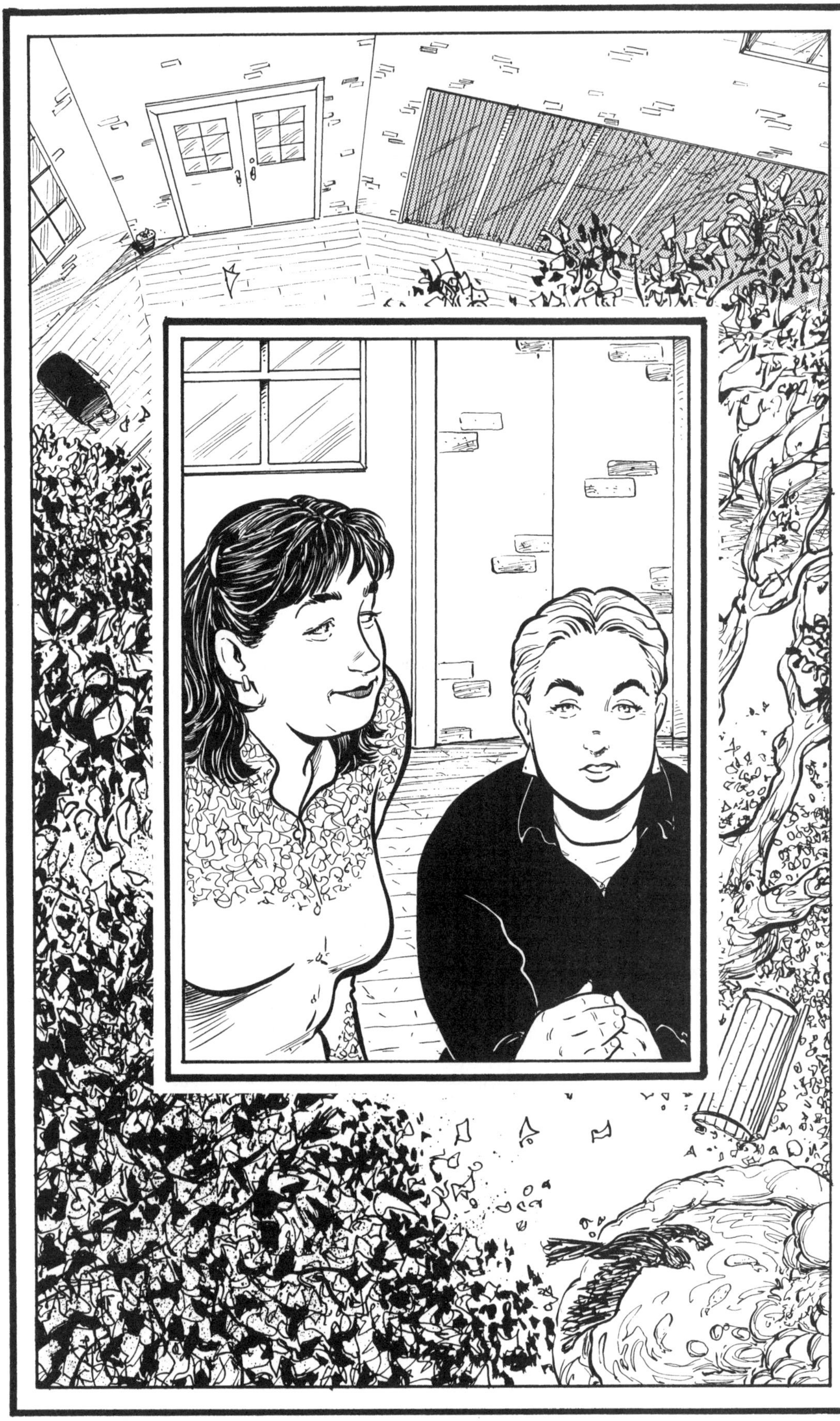

narias for the holidays. It's beautiful, isn't it?"

"Yes! You've been there?" Francine asked.

"I live just north of Santa Fe, about forty five minutes away, in the mountains," Katchoo smiled.

Francine's eyebrows shot up in surprise. "I didn't know that!" she exclaimed. "To think I was so close! All this time I thought you were living in Hawaii."

"I was. I lived there six years. But I sold the house and moved about four years ago."

Mikey bumped Katchoo's hands with the ball, demanding another round of the game. Katchoo dutifully pried the slippery wet prize from the dog's mouth and tossed it across the yard into the bushes along the back fence. Mikey disappeared into the landscape, his tail waving goodbye.

"I lived in New York for awhile after that," Katchoo continued. "Had a nice little apartment on the upper east side. Then I took a trip to New Mexico and found this place in the mountains and I thought, this is it, y'know? This is where I belong."

Francine smiled at the concept.

"I've been there ever since," Katchoo sighed.

Mikey returned, happy and out of breath. He laid down in a bare spot beside the steps and watched the yard with satisfaction, confident that it was safe from any further attacks by the rubber nemesis that remained incarcerated between his teeth.

Francine realized she was staring at Katchoo. She blinked and looked away. The neighbors cat sat perched on the fence nearby, watching snowbirds gather in the trees. Watching and waiting. Francine had spent countless afternoons on these steps watching the world spin beneath the sun. Then, just when it had felt like it was going to spin out of control. . . instinctively, she turned to make sure Katchoo was still there.

Katchoo stroked Mikey's coat, lulling him to sleep. All was right with the world.

"I thought I saw you a couple of days ago," Francine said softly, "In the gazebo behind the Ridley Hotel."

"Really? I was there. I had to come to town last weekend to take

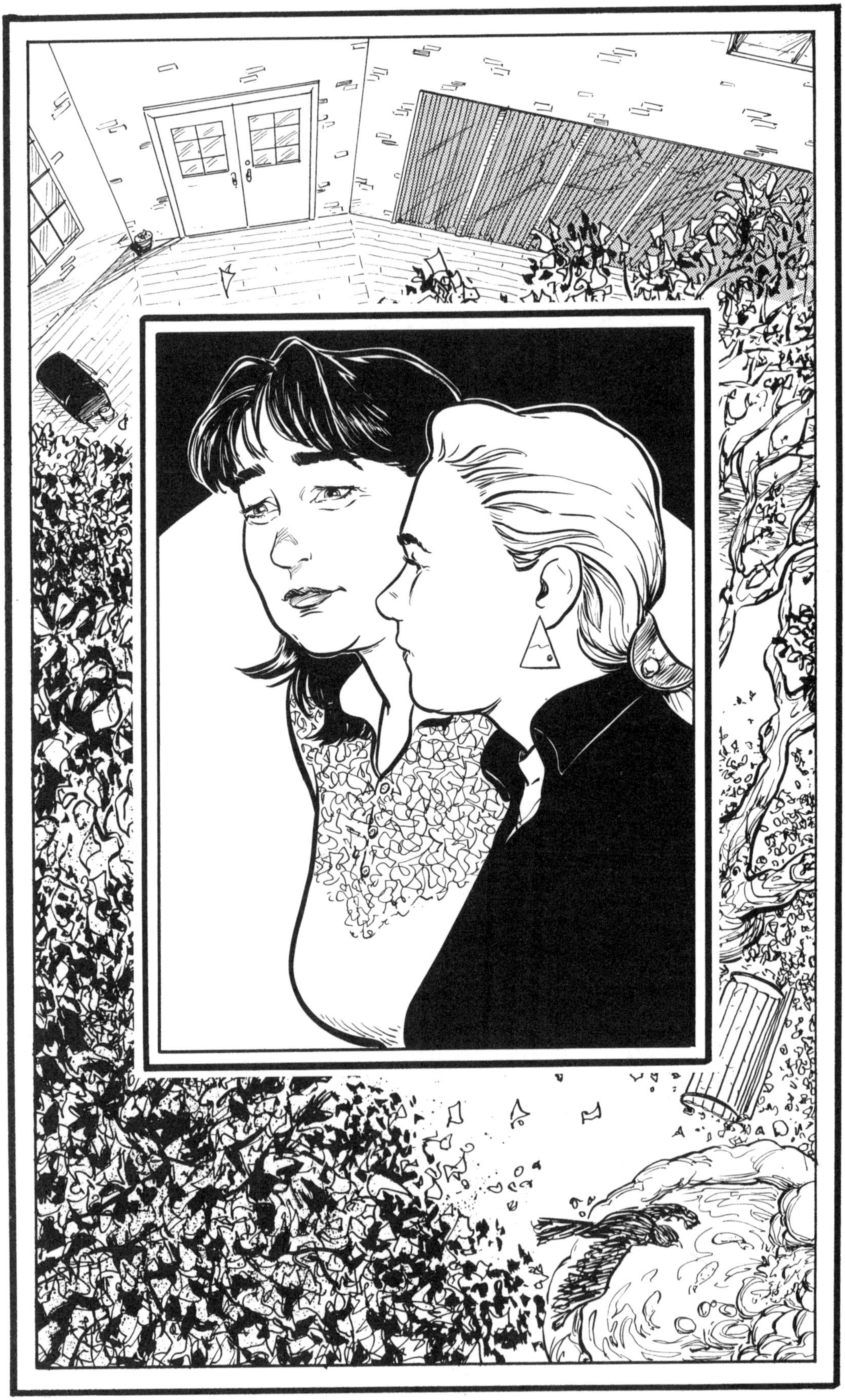

care of some business. Why didn't you say something?"

"I was going to, but I got held up, and then you were gone."

"It must have been when I was checking out. I went to look at the lake before I caught a cab."

"I was beginning to wonder if I just imagined it. You know, wishful thinking."

"No," Katchoo said, her smile dropping slightly. "My mother died last week. I had to come take care of the arrangements and all that."

"Oh, Katchoo, I'm so sorry!"

"It's okay, really. We weren't that close, y'know. I paid for her care, but that's about it. She made her choice a long time ago."

They sat in silence for awhile, watching a squirrel pick through dinner in the grass. Finally, Francine asked the question that had been on her mind all morning.

"So, after all this time, going on what, ten years. . .?"

"Ten years, two months, three weeks and a day," Katchoo replied.

Francine smiled, "Ooookay. So, after ten years, two months, three weeks. . . "

"And a day."

"And a day. After all that, I find you in my kitchen. How did I get so lucky all of a sudden?"

"Your mother called me," replied Katchoo with a wry smile.

"My *mother?*"

"Can you believe it?" Katchoo giggled, "I've been giving her my numbers all these years, y'know, in case of emergency."

Francine shook her head in wonder, "She never said a word."

"I thought she was just throwing 'em away."

Francine looked at Katchoo in amazement, allowing this new bit of information to soak in. All the time she had felt so isolated, so impossibly out of contact, Katchoo had been just a phone call away. A call her mother finally made for her.

"I've missed you, Katina," Francine said.

"I've missed you too, Francie," Katchoo smiled. The time seemed right. Katchoo cleared her throat nervously. "Listen,

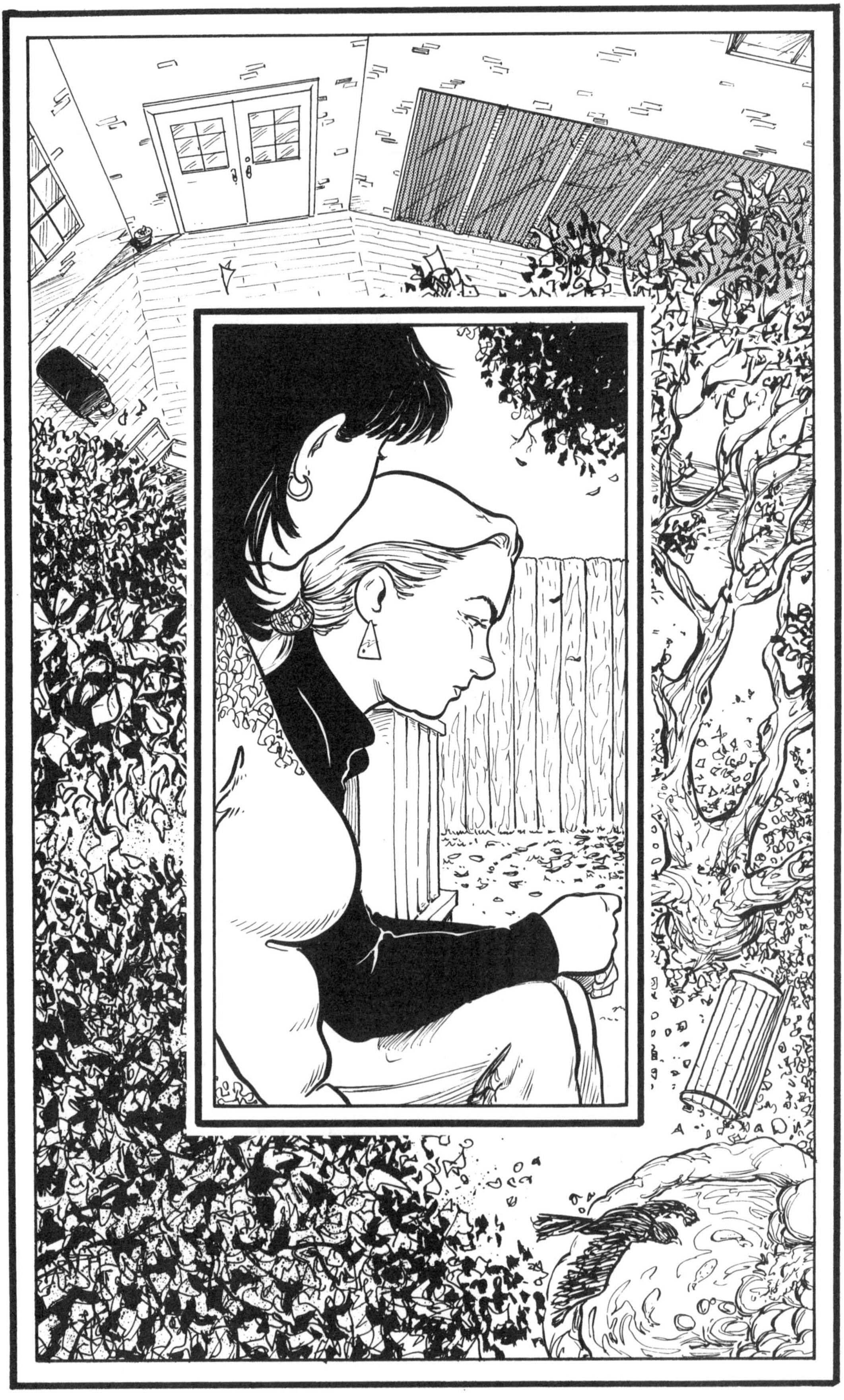

Francine. . ."

"You haven't said a word about David!" Francine interrupted. "How is he? Did you two go to Hawaii and get married like you said you would? You know, I've always tried to picture you guys living there in your beach house with these great tans and all."

Katchoo picked up a twig and pulled at the fragile buds hanging on the stem.

"It's a lot easier to picture you two in Santa Fe, though. David's always been a jean-jacket kind of guy, know what I mean? Gosh, I can't wait to see him! Oh god, can you imagine, the three of us back together again?"

Katchoo picked at the twig in silence, methodically stripping the outer bark. Francine frowned. She saw the muscles in Katchoo's jaw tighten.

"I'm sorry, did I say something wrong?"

Katchoo sighed and looked as if she were about to reply but thought better of it, avoiding eye contact.

"Katchoo, David is alright, isn't he? You guys did get married and all that, right? I mean, I just assumed. . ."

"Yeah, we were married. We had the ceremony on the cliffs near Hana. We lived in the house there," Katchoo sighed. "That was the happiest time of my life. I thought I was going to spend the rest of my life there, in Hawaii. . . with David. "

"What happened?"

Katchoo took a deep breath and let it out slowly. She felt her eyes burning and swore harshly to herself. Control. Control. Francine waited. She wanted an answer now. Katchoo could feel her watching. Eyes down, her thoughts raced.

"Katchoo?" Francine whispered, the color draining from her face.

Katchoo dropped the last bit of twig onto the miniature pyramid of twig bits between her boots. Everything had been so perfect once, the three of them against the world. Then one day they woke up and it was gone. Just gone. Like a singer losing his voice or an actor losing his timing. Nothing gold can stay, someone once wrote, and Katchoo knew the day it slipped away.

MY FOOT'S ASLEEP.

YOU'RE WHINING AGAIN.

I CAN'T FEEL MY FOOT. IS IT STILL THERE? CAN YOU SEE IT? IT'S NOT BLUE OR ANYTHING, IS IT?

FRANCINE, I SWEAR YOU'RE SO HIGH MAINTENANCE! ALL YOU HAVE TO DO IS SIT THERE. LOOK AT ME, I HAVE TO STAND AND MOVE MY ARM.

HOW MUCH LONGER?

WE JUST STARTED! I HAVEN'T EVEN FINISHED THE CHARCOAL SKETCH.

DID YOU HEAR THAT? WAS THAT THE DOOR?

WOULD YOU RELAX? GAH! NOBODY'S GOING TO WALK IN ON US. DAVID'S AT SCHOOL, THE FRONT DOOR'S LOCKED, THE BACK DOOR'S LOCKED. . .

I WISH I HADN'T EATEN BREAKFAST. I LOOK FAT, DON'T I?

YOU DON'T LOOK FAT. YOU LOOK MARVELOUS. SIMPLY MARVELOUS.

SHUT UP.

I WILL IF YOU WILL.

ALRIGHT, FINE.

FINE.

FINE.

ALRIGHT THEN.

STOP IT, I'LL LOSE MY POSE.

OKAY, WAIT. WAIT. I JUST NEED TO GET YOUR FACE HERE. HOLD STILL, JUST. . .

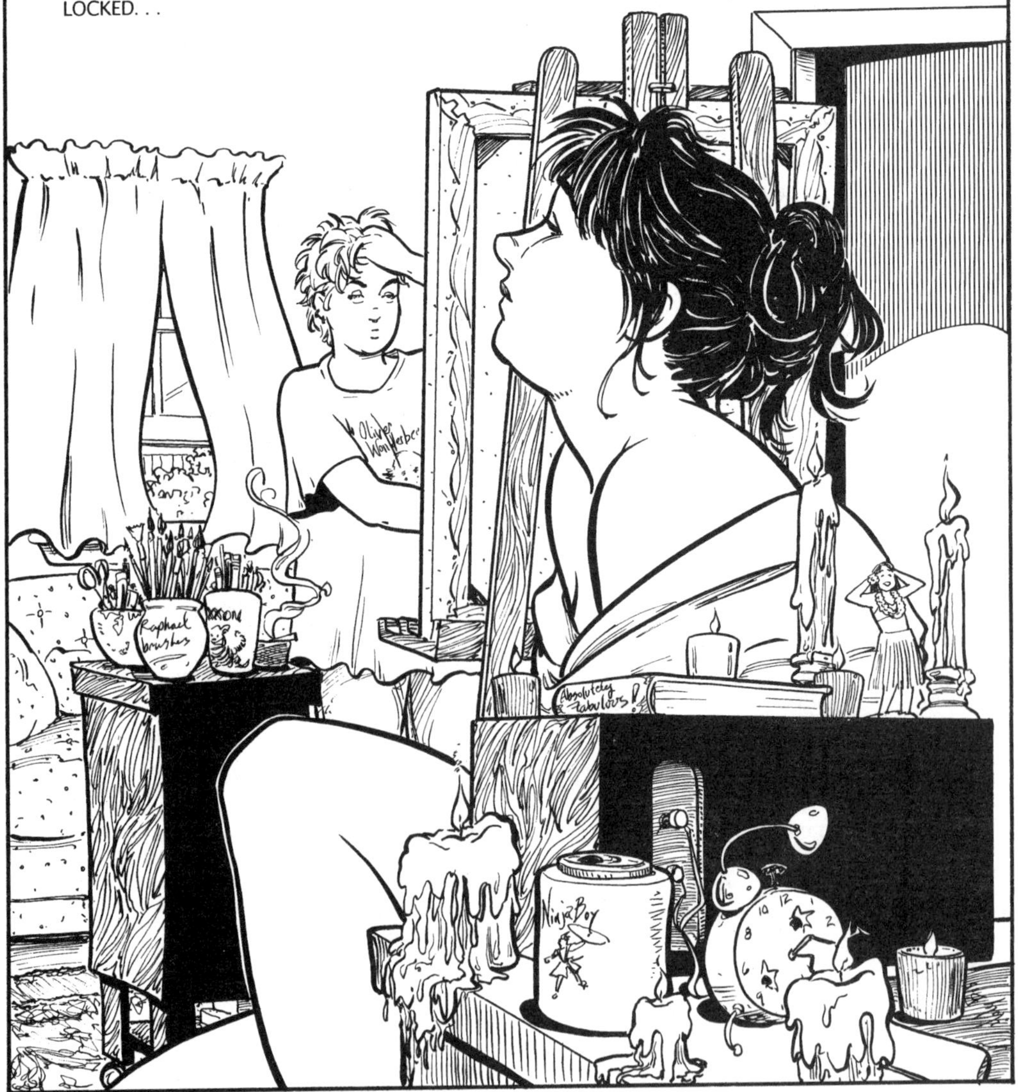
Raphael brushes
Absolutely Fabulous
Ninja Boy

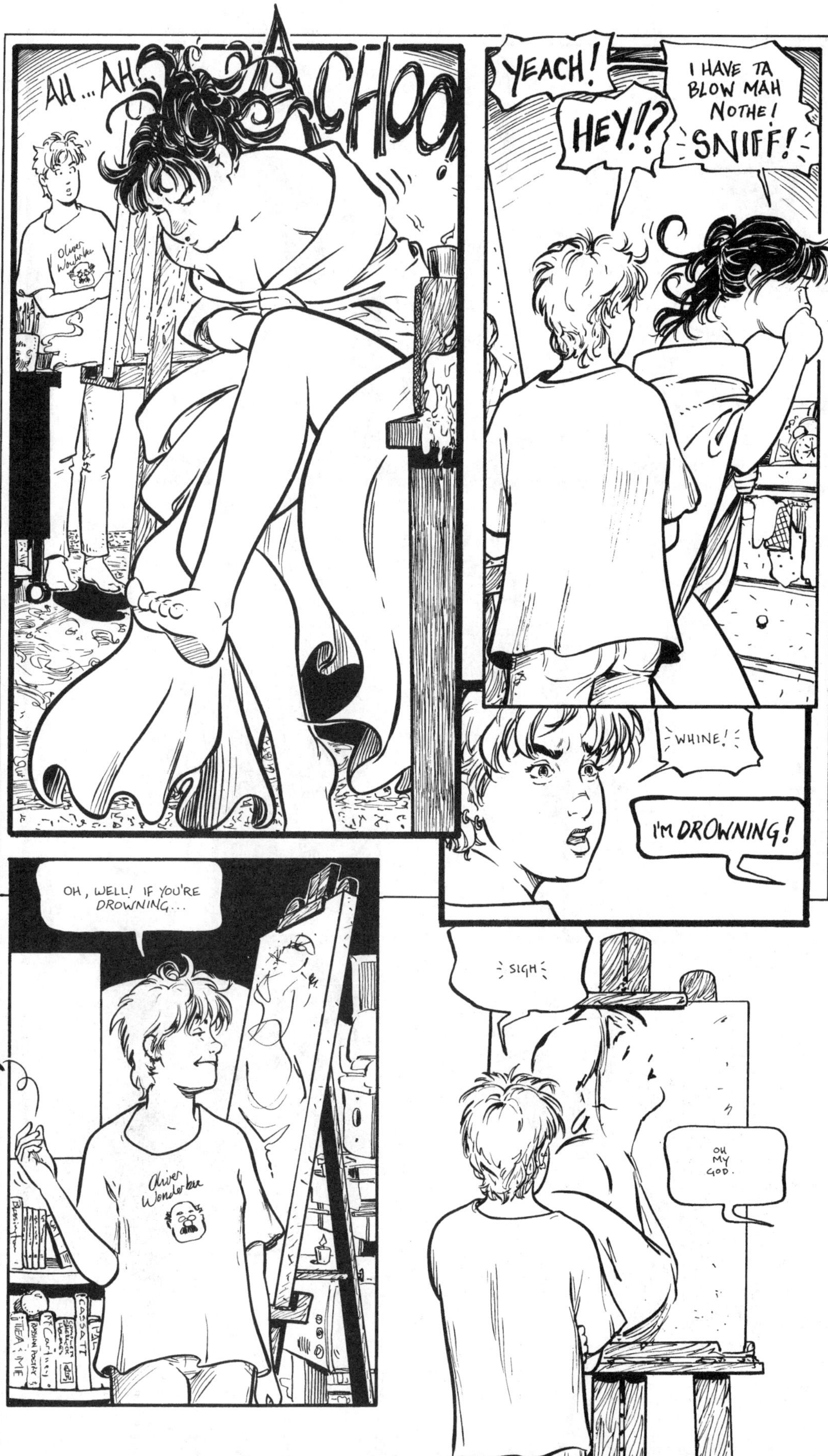
AH...AH!
ACHOO!
YEACH!
HEY!?
I HAVE TA BLOW MAH NOTHE! SNIFF!
WHINE!
I'M DROWNING!
OH, WELL! IF YOU'RE DROWNING...
SIGH
OH MY GOD.

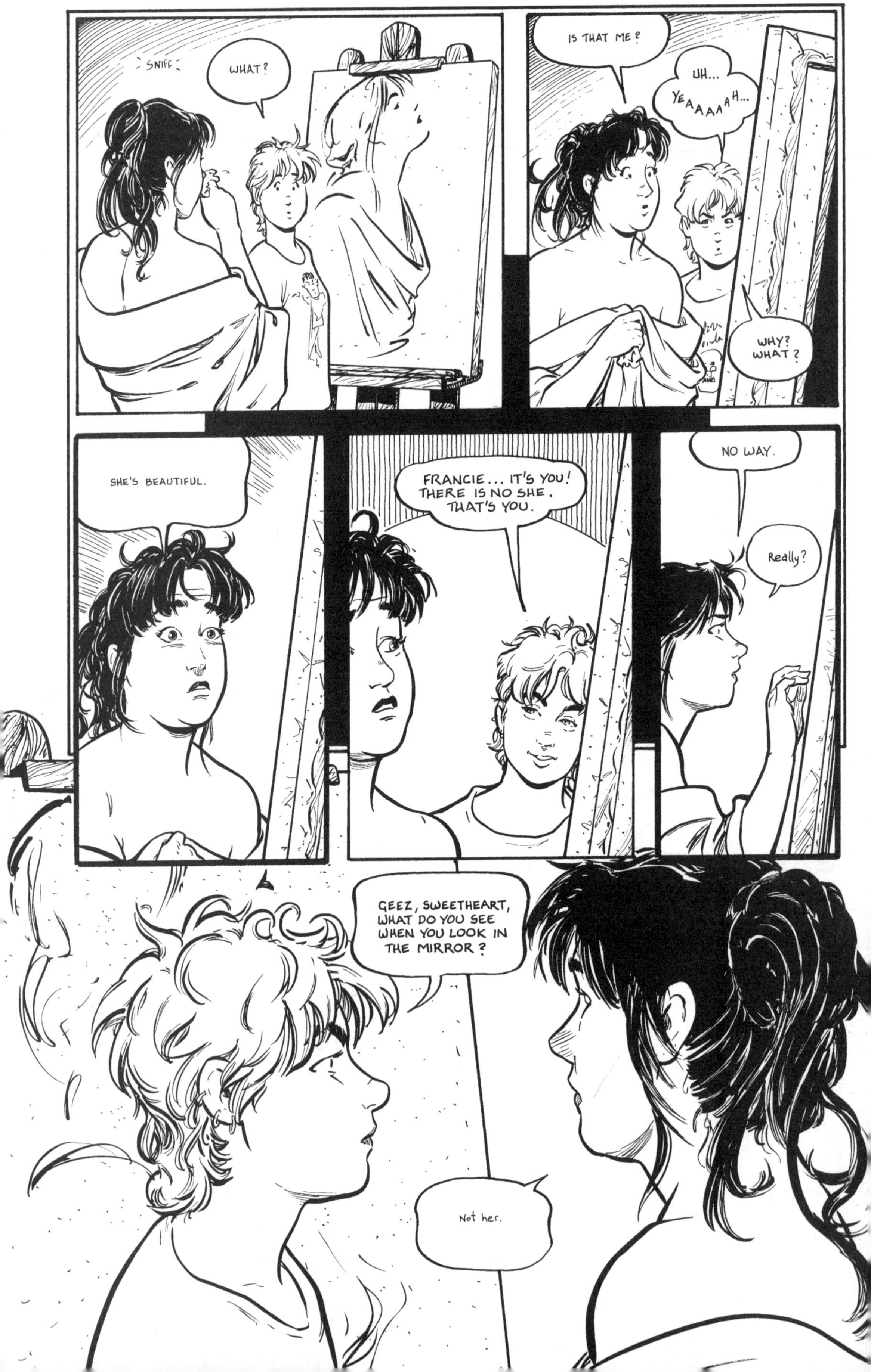
SNIFF
WHAT?
IS THAT ME?
UH... YEAAAAAAH...
WHY? WHAT?
SHE'S BEAUTIFUL.
FRANCIE... IT'S YOU! THERE IS NO SHE. THAT'S YOU.
NO WAY.
Really?
GEEZ, SWEETHEART, WHAT DO YOU SEE WHEN YOU LOOK IN THE MIRROR?
Not her.

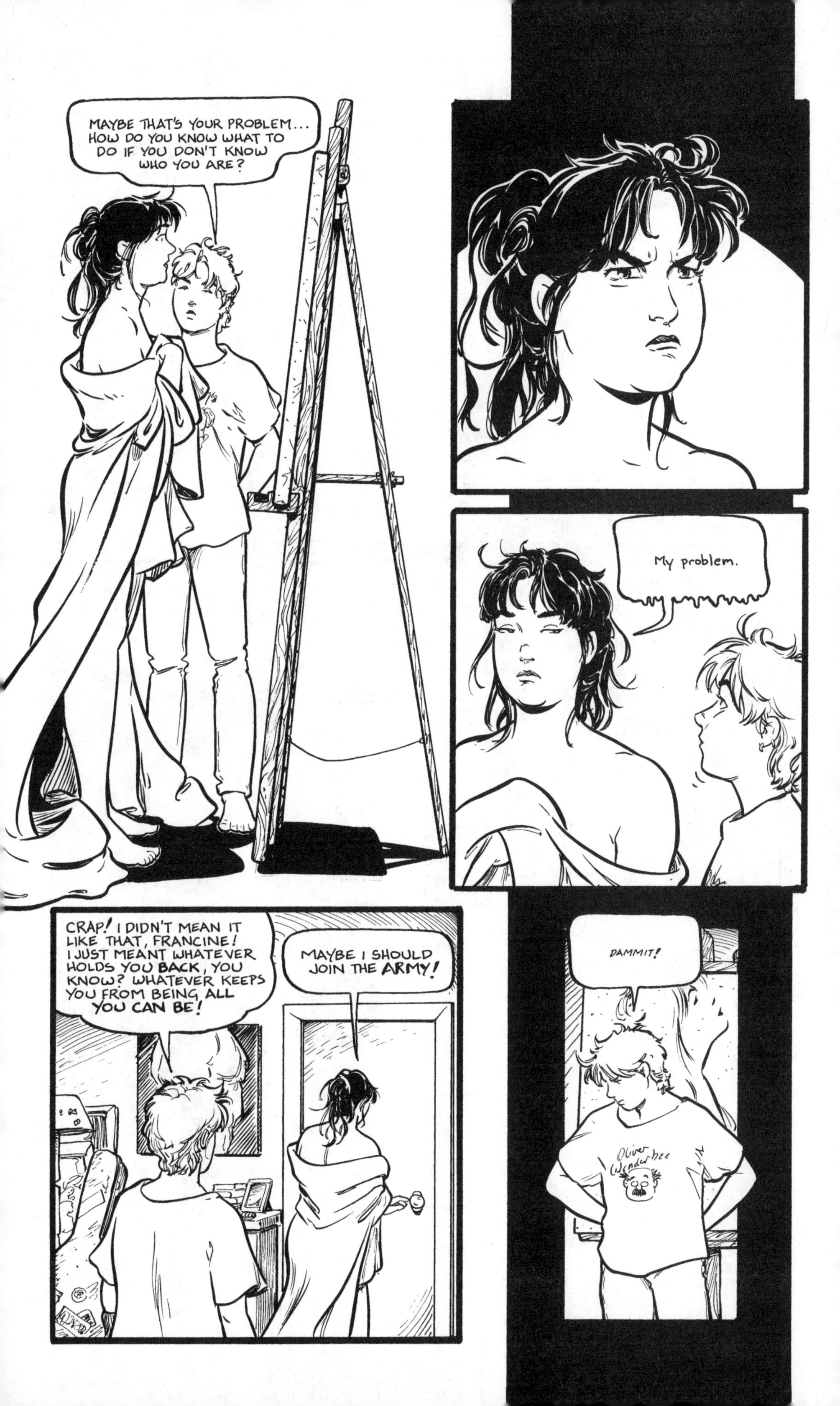
MAYBE THAT'S YOUR PROBLEM... HOW DO YOU KNOW WHAT TO DO IF YOU DON'T KNOW WHO YOU ARE?
My problem.
CRAP! I DIDN'T MEAN IT LIKE THAT, FRANCINE! I JUST MEANT WHATEVER HOLDS YOU BACK, YOU KNOW? WHATEVER KEEPS YOU FROM BEING ALL YOU CAN BE!
MAYBE I SHOULD JOIN THE ARMY!
DAMMIT!
Oliver Wenderbee

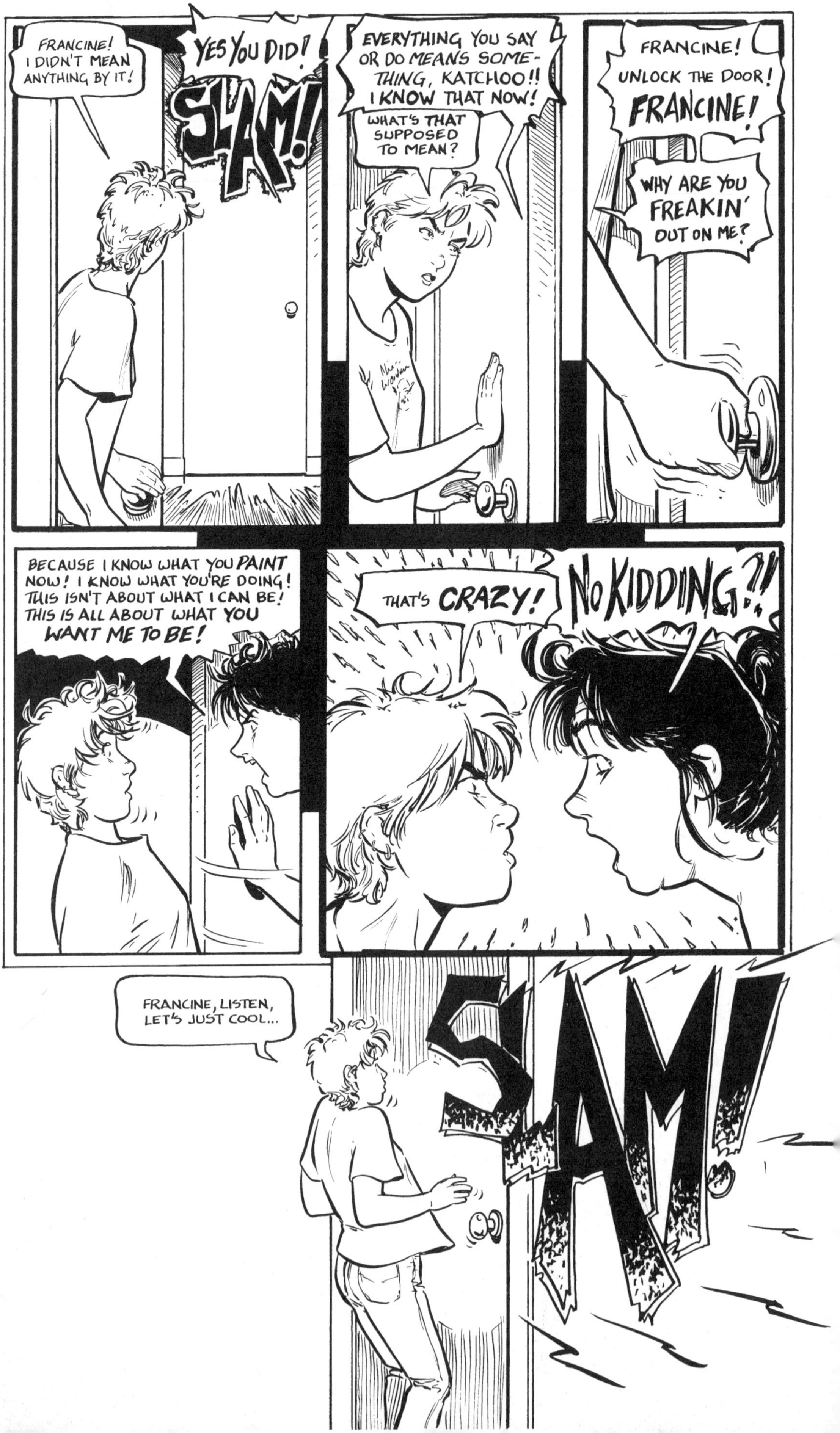

FRANCINE! I DIDN'T MEAN ANYTHING BY IT!
YES YOU DID!
SLAM!
EVERYTHING YOU SAY OR DO MEANS SOMETHING, KATCHOO!! I KNOW THAT NOW!
WHAT'S THAT SUPPOSED TO MEAN?
FRANCINE! UNLOCK THE DOOR! FRANCINE!
WHY ARE YOU FREAKIN' OUT ON ME?
BECAUSE I KNOW WHAT YOU PAINT NOW! I KNOW WHAT YOU'RE DOING! THIS ISN'T ABOUT WHAT I CAN BE! THIS IS ALL ABOUT WHAT YOU WANT ME TO BE!
THAT'S CRAZY!
NO KIDDING?!
FRANCINE, LISTEN, LET'S JUST COOL...
SLAM!

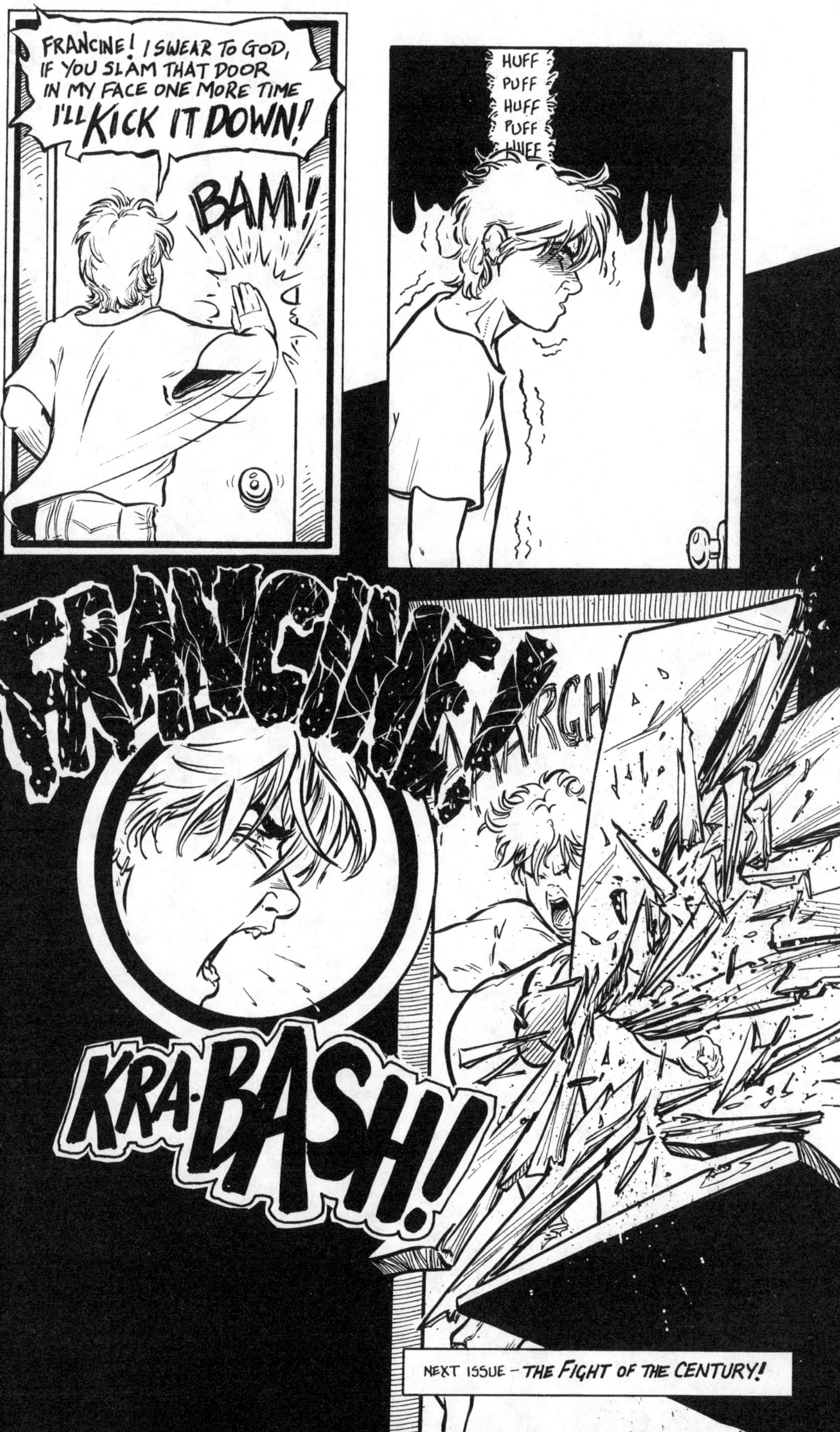
FRANCINE! I SWEAR TO GOD, IF YOU SLAM THAT DOOR IN MY FACE ONE MORE TIME I'LL KICK IT DOWN!
BAM!
HUFF PUFF HUFF PUFF HUFF
FRANCINE!
ARGH
KRA-BASH!
NEXT ISSUE - THE FIGHT OF THE CENTURY!

Let me see, I won't be denied.
Talk to me and justify it.
Let me see, don't try to hide it;
Talk to me and justify it,
Let me see, I won't be denied.
Talk to me and justify it.
Let me see, don't try to hide it;
Talk to me and justify it,
Let me see, I won't be denied.

In your life I will call you to sea,
The Winter Queen sings low.
Winter years come.

See the hearts winter claims
In frozen war.
You can't get warm.
Winter years come.

Talk to me and justify it.
Let me see, don't try to hide it;
Talk to me and justify it,
Let me see, I won't be denied.
Talk to me and justify it.
Let me see, don't try to hide it;
Talk to me and justify it,
Let me see, I won't be denied.
Talk to me and justify it.
Let me see, don't try to hide it;
Talk to me and justify it,
Let me see, I won't be denied.

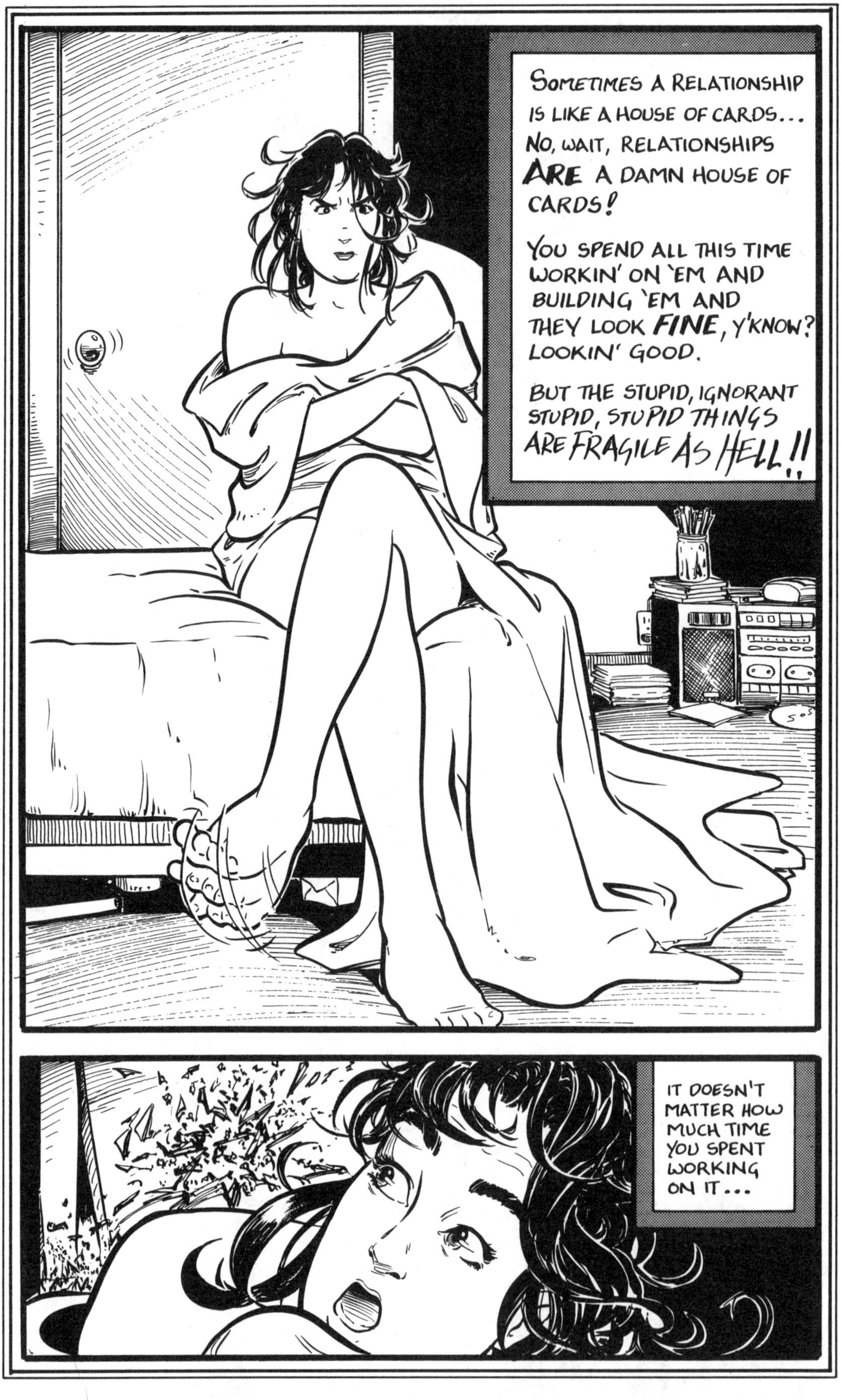
Sometimes a relationship is like a house of cards... No, wait, relationships ARE a damn house of cards!
You spend all this time workin' on 'em and building 'em and they look FINE, y'know? Lookin' good.
But the stupid, ignorant stupid, stupid things are FRAGILE AS HELL!!
It doesn't matter how much time you spent working on it...

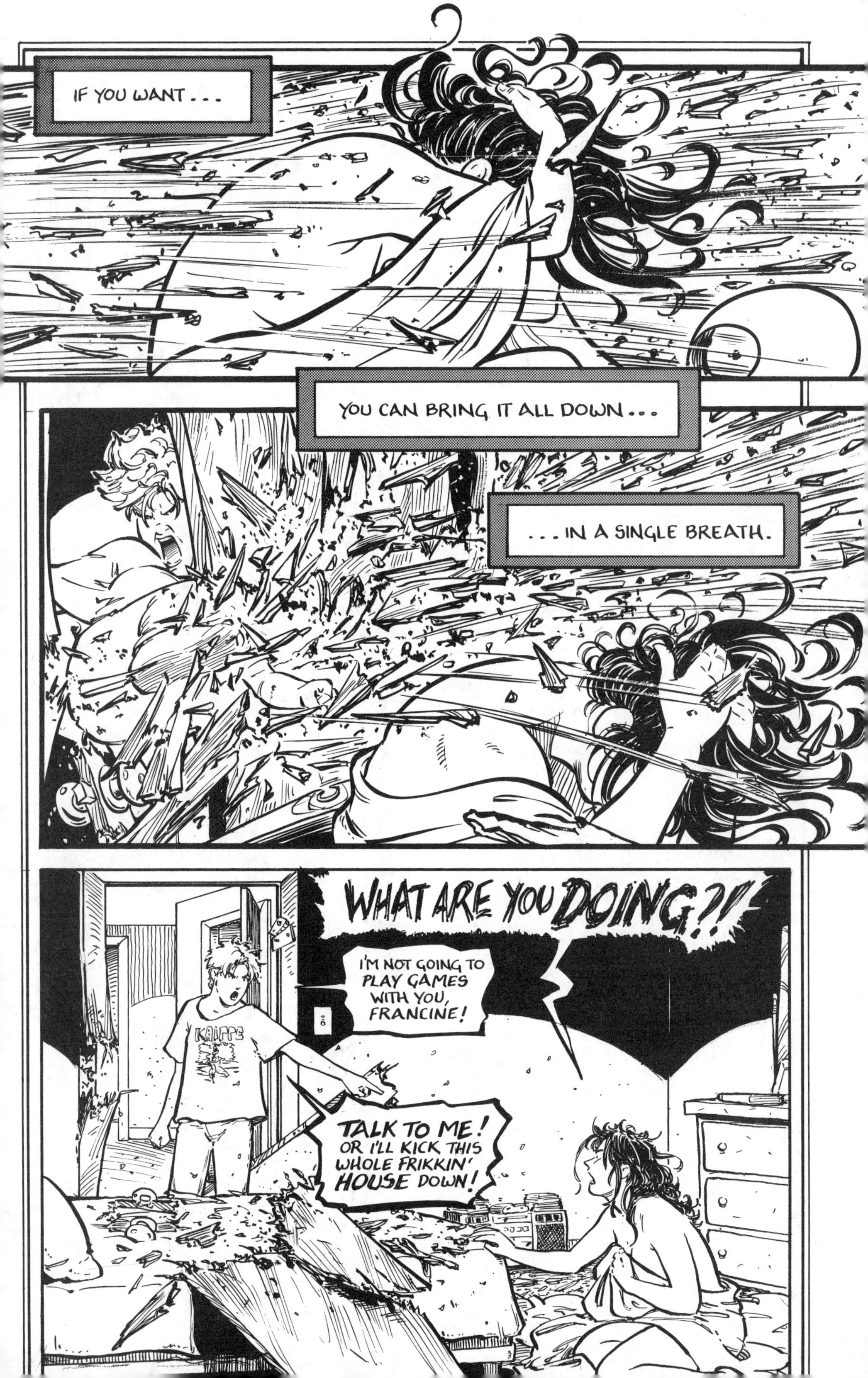
IF YOU WANT . . .
YOU CAN BRING IT ALL DOWN . . .
. . . IN A SINGLE BREATH.
WHAT ARE YOU DOING?!
I'M NOT GOING TO PLAY GAMES WITH YOU, FRANCINE!
TALK TO ME! OR I'LL KICK THIS WHOLE FRIKKIN' HOUSE DOWN!

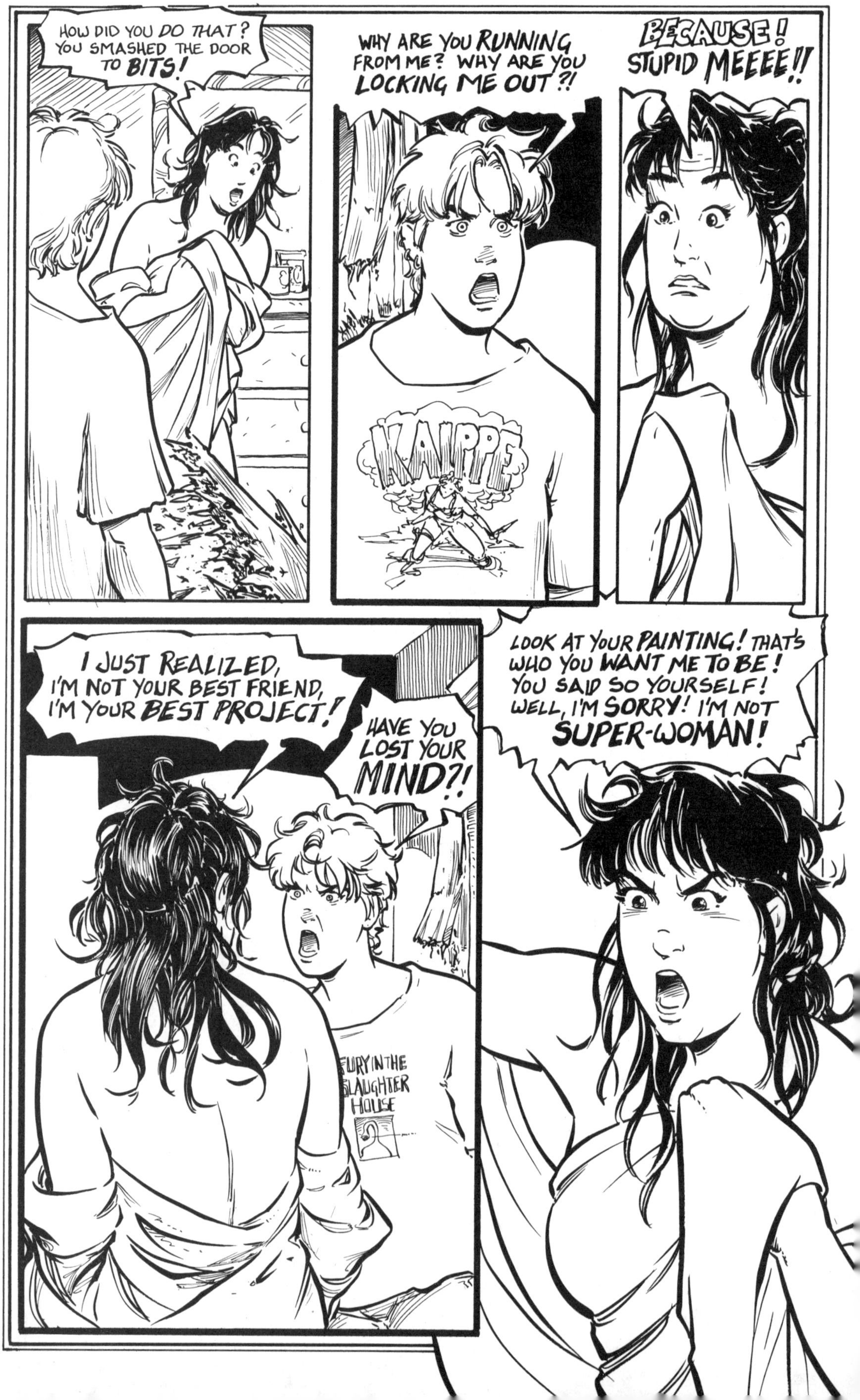

HOW DID YOU DO THAT? YOU SMASHED THE DOOR TO BITS!
WHY ARE YOU RUNNING FROM ME? WHY ARE YOU LOCKING ME OUT?!
BECAUSE! STUPID MEEEE!!
NAIPPE
I JUST REALIZED, I'M NOT YOUR BEST FRIEND, I'M YOUR BEST PROJECT!
HAVE YOU LOST YOUR MIND?!
LOOK AT YOUR PAINTING! THAT'S WHO YOU WANT ME TO BE! YOU SAID SO YOURSELF! WELL, I'M SORRY! I'M NOT SUPER-WOMAN!
FURY IN THE SLAUGHTER HOUSE

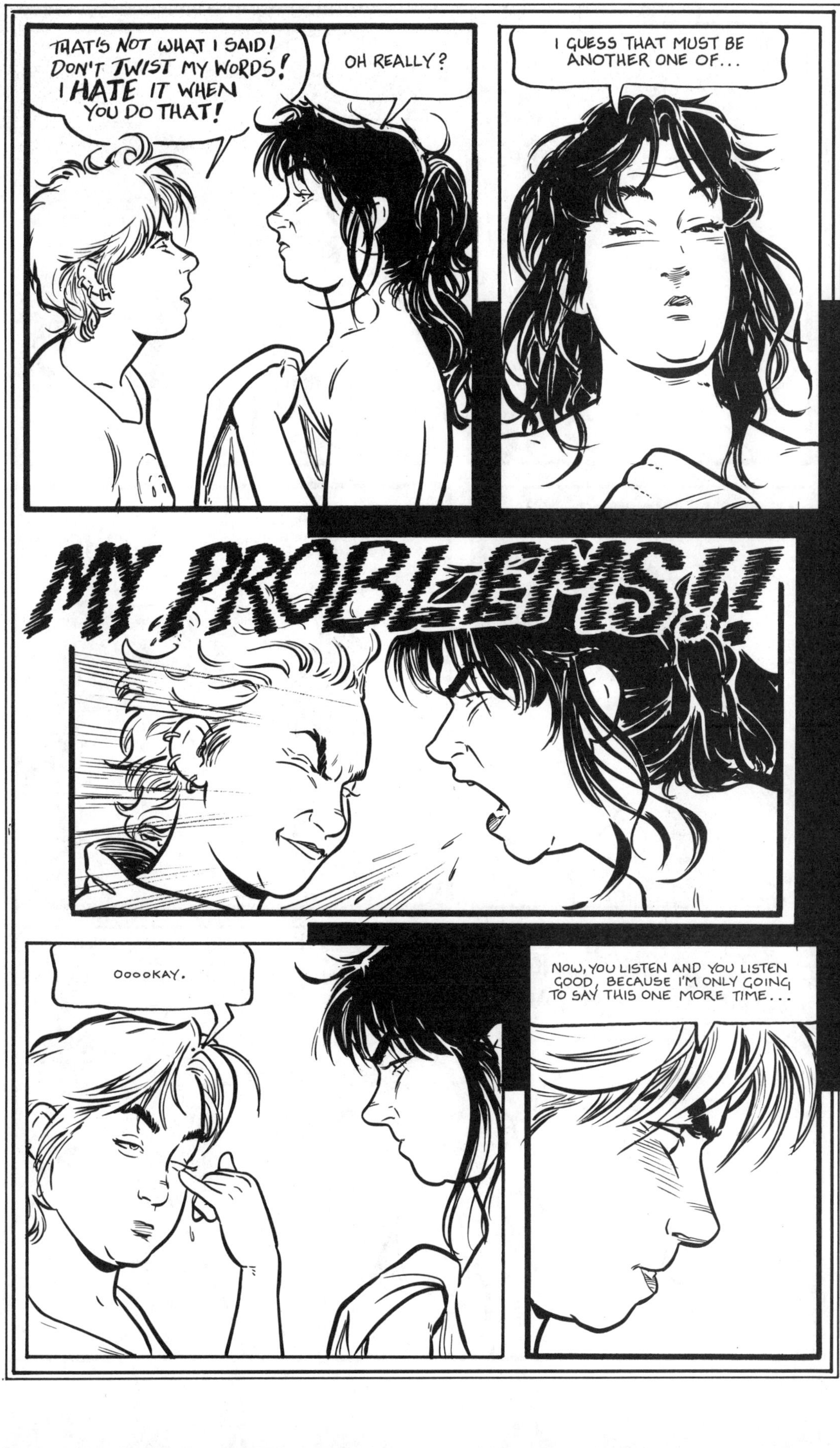
THAT'S NOT WHAT I SAID! DON'T TWIST MY WORDS! I HATE IT WHEN YOU DO THAT!
OH REALLY?
I GUESS THAT MUST BE ANOTHER ONE OF...
MY PROBLEMS!!
OOOOKAY.
NOW, YOU LISTEN AND YOU LISTEN GOOD, BECAUSE I'M ONLY GOING TO SAY THIS ONE MORE TIME...

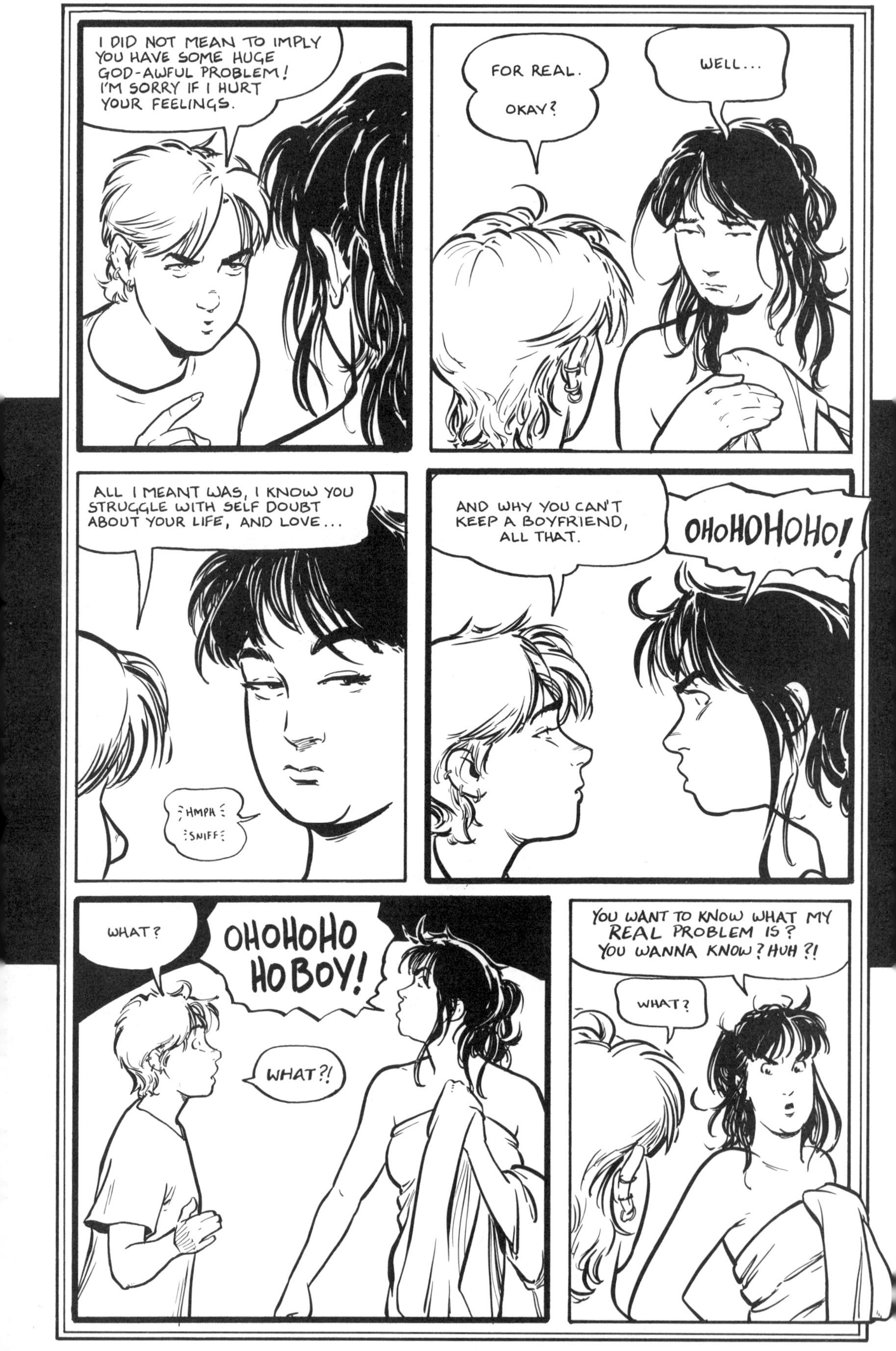
I DID NOT MEAN TO IMPLY YOU HAVE SOME HUGE GOD-AWFUL PROBLEM! I'M SORRY IF I HURT YOUR FEELINGS.
FOR REAL. OKAY?
WELL...
ALL I MEANT WAS, I KNOW YOU STRUGGLE WITH SELF DOUBT ABOUT YOUR LIFE, AND LOVE...
HMPH SNIFF
AND WHY YOU CAN'T KEEP A BOYFRIEND, ALL THAT.
OHOHOHOHO!
WHAT?
OHOHOHO HOBOY!
WHAT?!
YOU WANT TO KNOW WHAT MY REAL PROBLEM IS? YOU WANNA KNOW? HUH?!
WHAT?

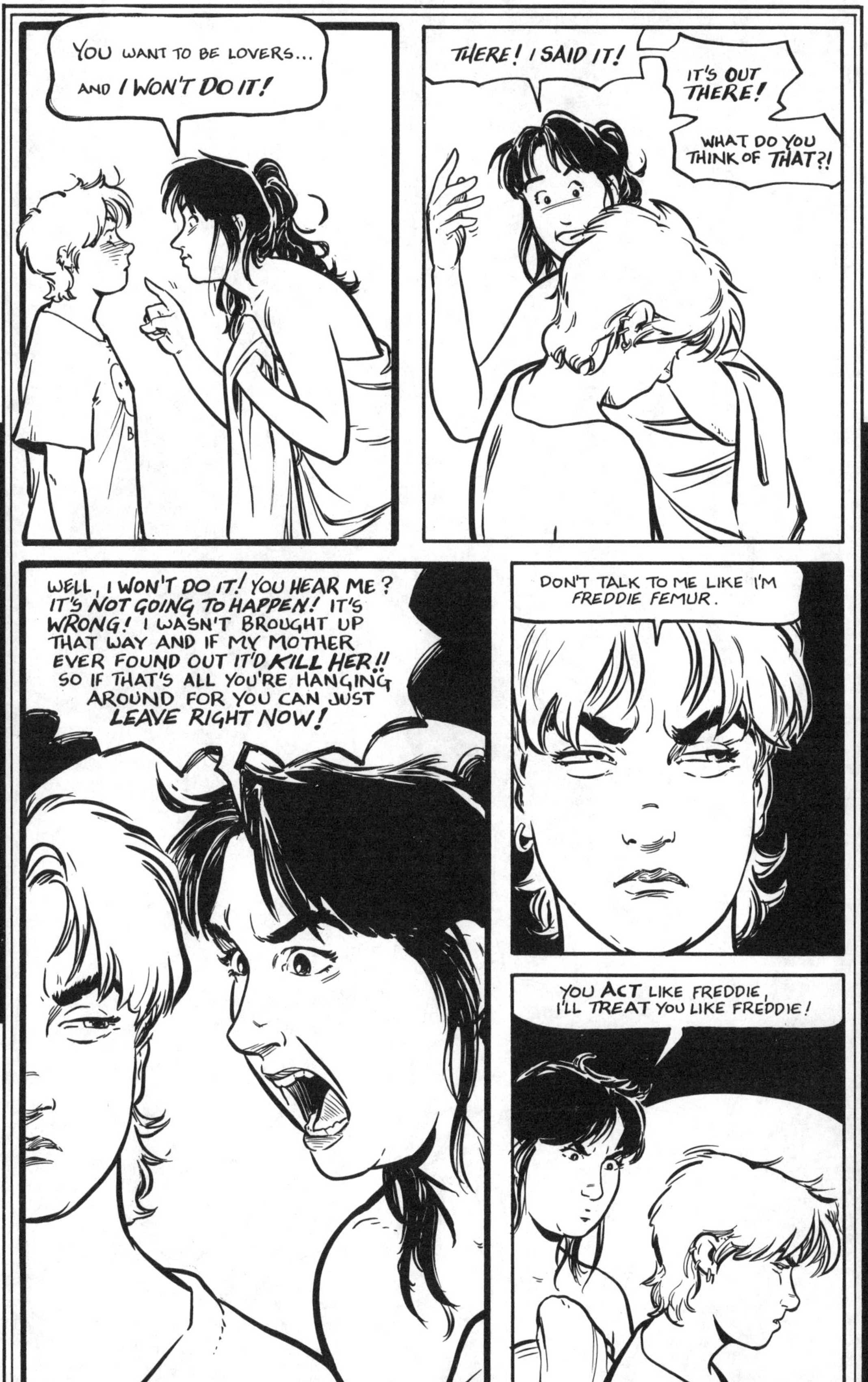
YOU WANT TO BE LOVERS... AND I WON'T DO IT!
THERE! I SAID IT!
IT'S OUT THERE!
WHAT DO YOU THINK OF THAT?!
WELL, I WON'T DO IT! YOU HEAR ME? IT'S NOT GOING TO HAPPEN! IT'S WRONG! I WASN'T BROUGHT UP THAT WAY AND IF MY MOTHER EVER FOUND OUT IT'D KILL HER!! SO IF THAT'S ALL YOU'RE HANGING AROUND FOR YOU CAN JUST LEAVE RIGHT NOW!
DON'T TALK TO ME LIKE I'M FREDDIE FEMUR.
YOU ACT LIKE FREDDIE, I'LL TREAT YOU LIKE FREDDIE!

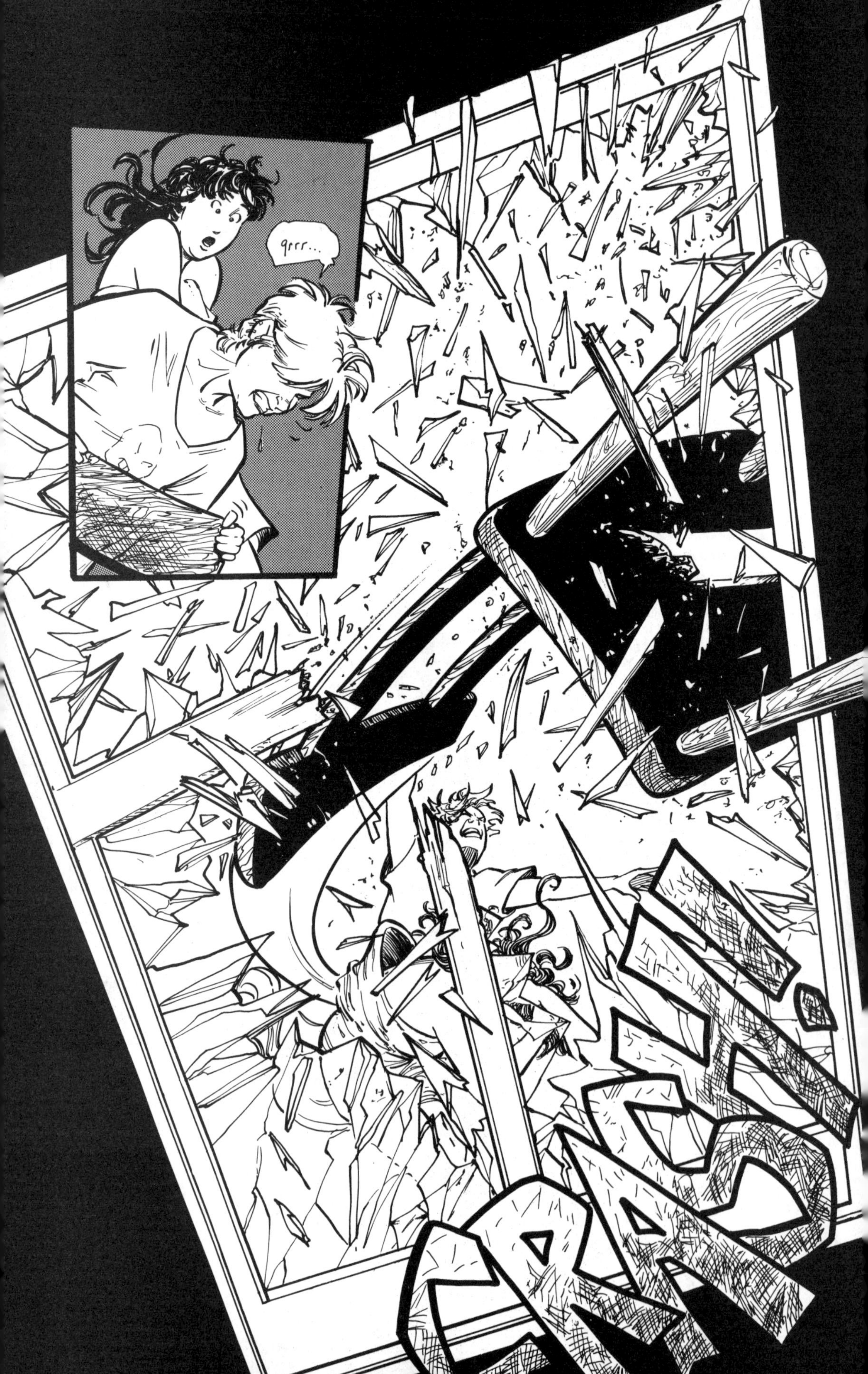
grrr...
CRASH!

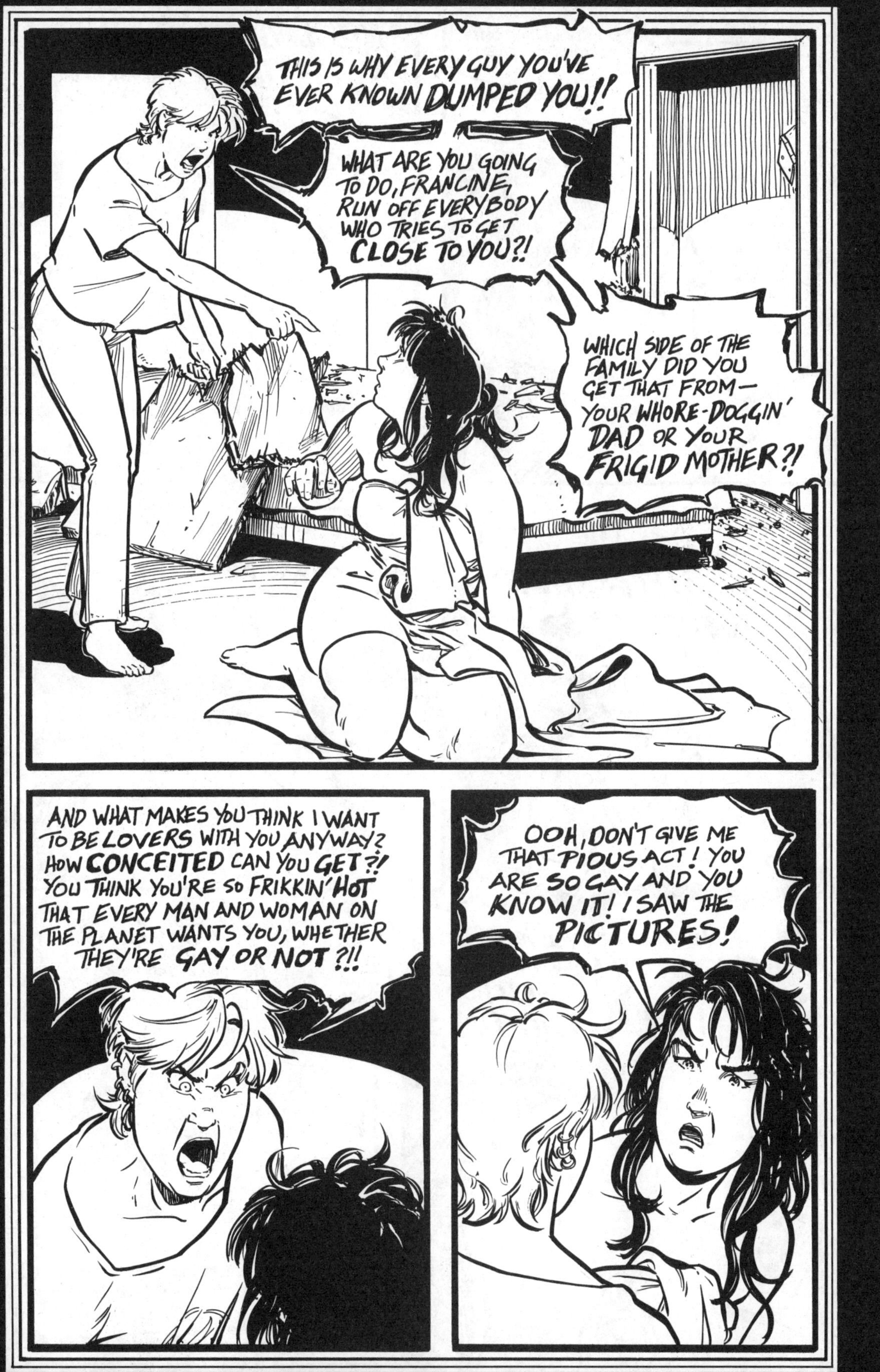
THIS IS WHY EVERY GUY YOU'VE EVER KNOWN DUMPED YOU!!
WHAT ARE YOU GOING TO DO, FRANCINE, RUN OFF EVERYBODY WHO TRIES TO GET CLOSE TO YOU?!
WHICH SIDE OF THE FAMILY DID YOU GET THAT FROM— YOUR WHORE-DOGGIN' DAD OR YOUR FRIGID MOTHER?!
AND WHAT MAKES YOU THINK I WANT TO BE LOVERS WITH YOU ANYWAY? HOW CONCEITED CAN YOU GET?! YOU THINK YOU'RE SO FRIKKIN' HOT THAT EVERY MAN AND WOMAN ON THE PLANET WANTS YOU, WHETHER THEY'RE GAY OR NOT?!!
OOH, DON'T GIVE ME THAT PIOUS ACT! YOU ARE SO GAY AND YOU KNOW IT! I SAW THE PICTURES!

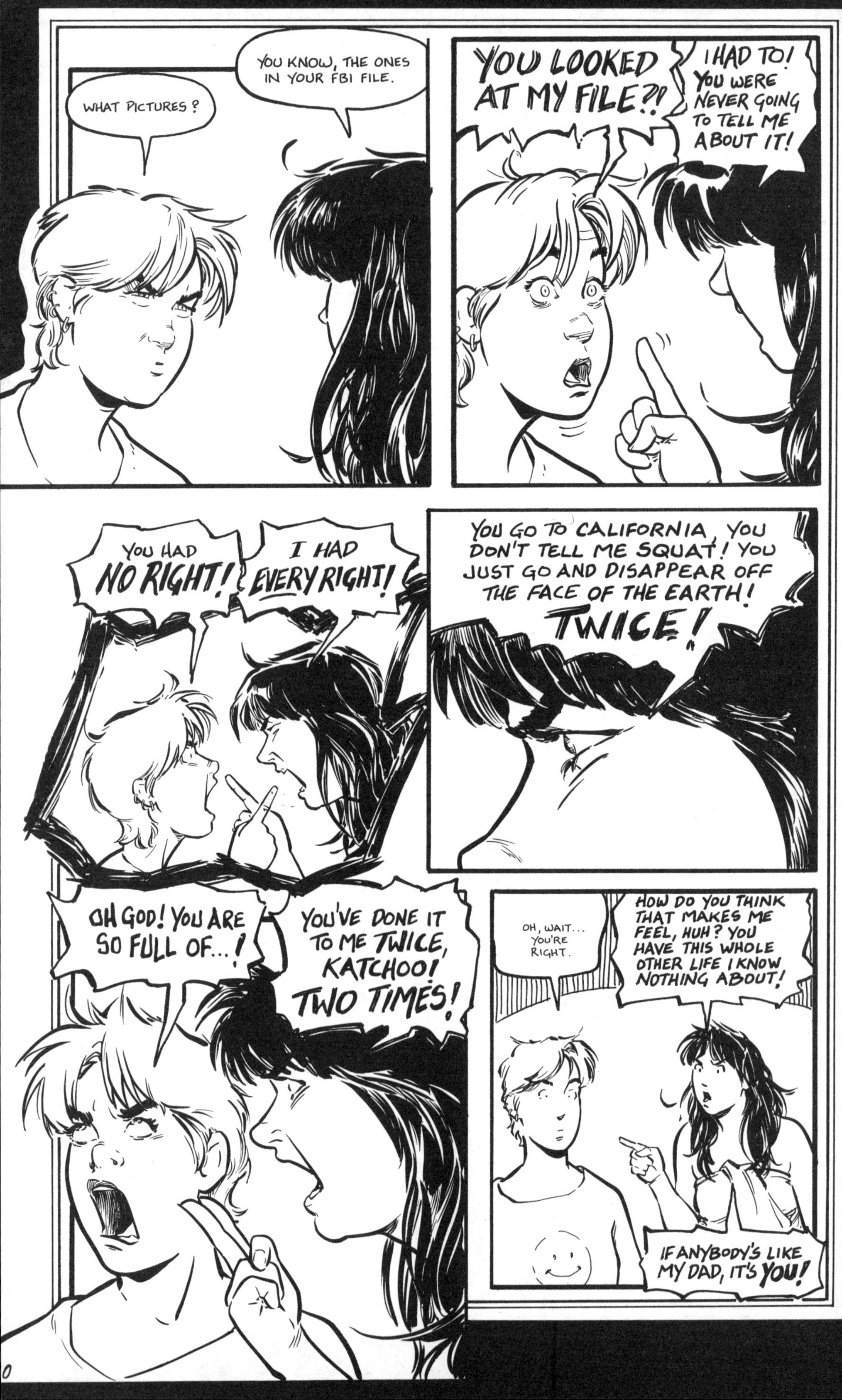

WHAT PICTURES ?
YOU KNOW, THE ONES IN YOUR FBI FILE.
YOU LOOKED AT MY FILE?!
I HAD TO! YOU WERE NEVER GOING TO TELL ME ABOUT IT!
YOU HAD NO RIGHT!
I HAD EVERY RIGHT!
YOU GO TO CALIFORNIA, YOU DON'T TELL ME SQUAT! YOU JUST GO AND DISAPPEAR OFF THE FACE OF THE EARTH! TWICE!
OH GOD! YOU ARE SO FULL OF...!
YOU'VE DONE IT TO ME TWICE, KATCHOO! TWO TIMES!
OH, WAIT... YOU'RE RIGHT.
HOW DO YOU THINK THAT MAKES ME FEEL, HUH? YOU HAVE THIS WHOLE OTHER LIFE I KNOW NOTHING ABOUT!
IF ANYBODY'S LIKE MY DAD, IT'S YOU!

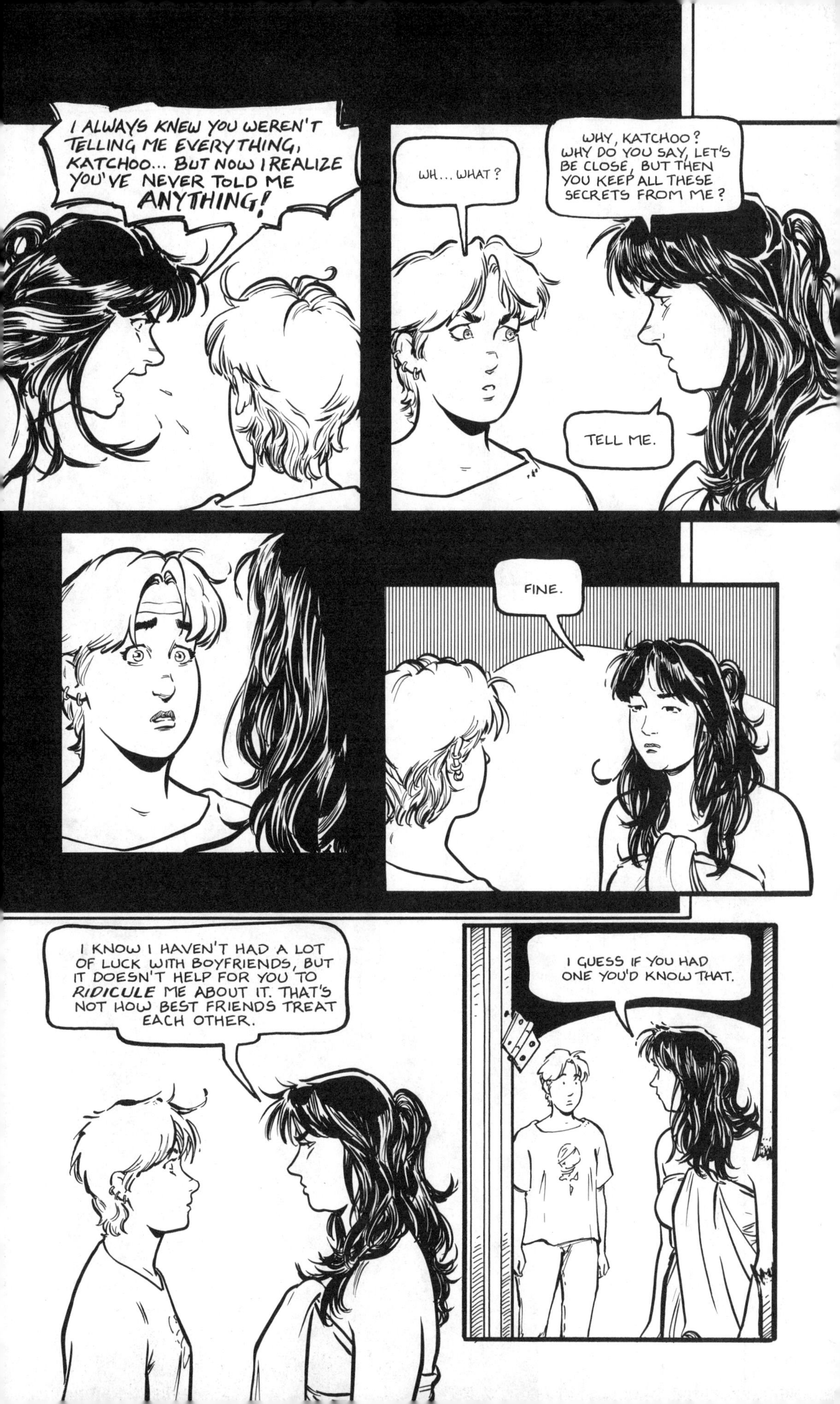
I ALWAYS KNEW YOU WEREN'T TELLING ME EVERYTHING, KATCHOO... BUT NOW I REALIZE YOU'VE NEVER TOLD ME ANYTHING!
WH... WHAT?
WHY, KATCHOO? WHY DO YOU SAY, LET'S BE CLOSE, BUT THEN YOU KEEP ALL THESE SECRETS FROM ME?
TELL ME.
FINE.
I KNOW I HAVEN'T HAD A LOT OF LUCK WITH BOYFRIENDS, BUT IT DOESN'T HELP FOR YOU TO RIDICULE ME ABOUT IT. THAT'S NOT HOW BEST FRIENDS TREAT EACH OTHER.
I GUESS IF YOU HAD ONE YOU'D KNOW THAT.

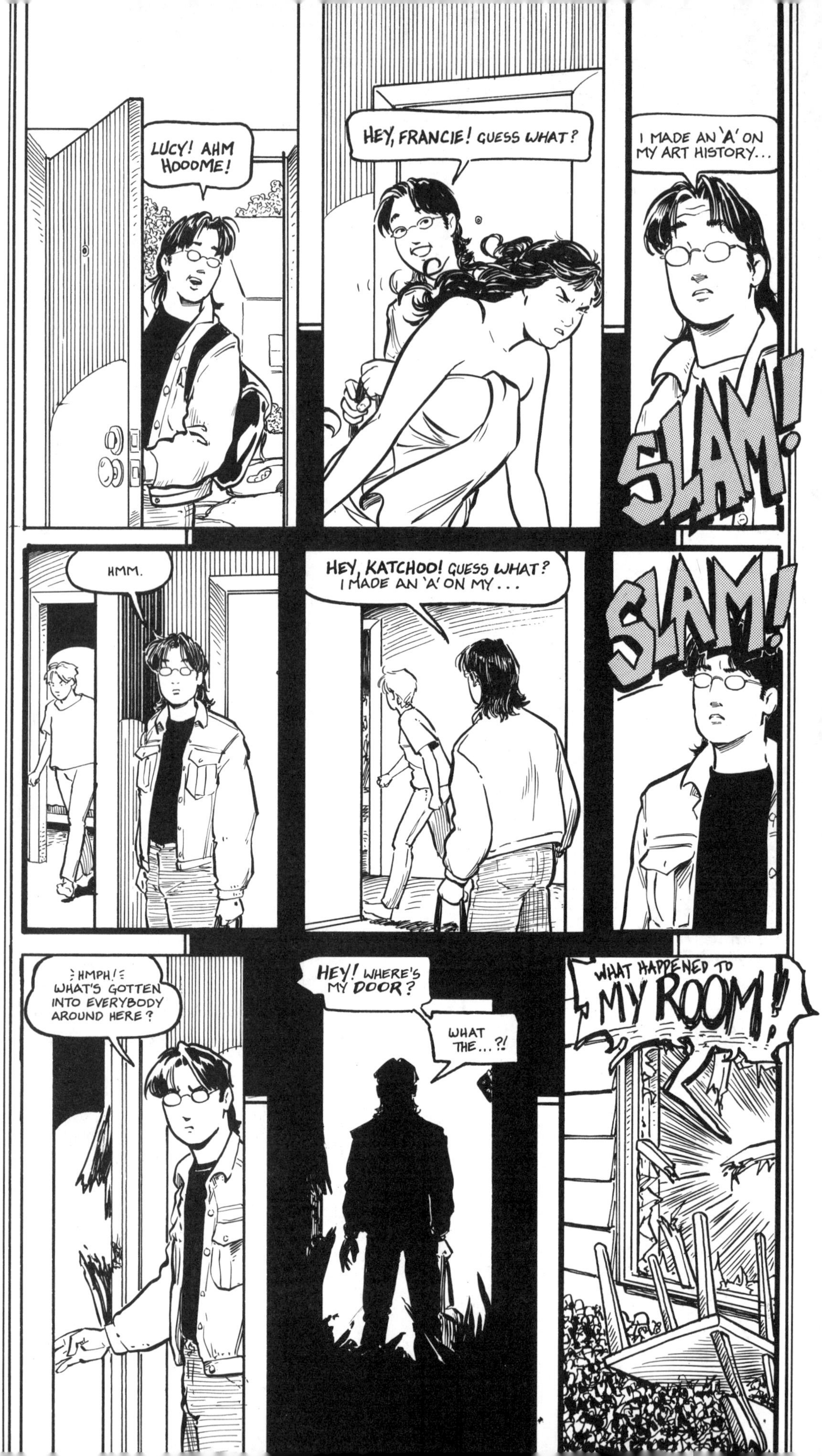

LUCY! AHM HOOOME!
HEY, FRANCIE! GUESS WHAT?
I MADE AN 'A' ON MY ART HISTORY...
SLAM!
HMM.
HEY, KATCHOO! GUESS WHAT? I MADE AN 'A' ON MY...
SLAM!
HMPH! WHAT'S GOTTEN INTO EVERYBODY AROUND HERE?
HEY! WHERE'S MY DOOR?
WHAT THE...?!
WHAT HAPPENED TO MY ROOM!

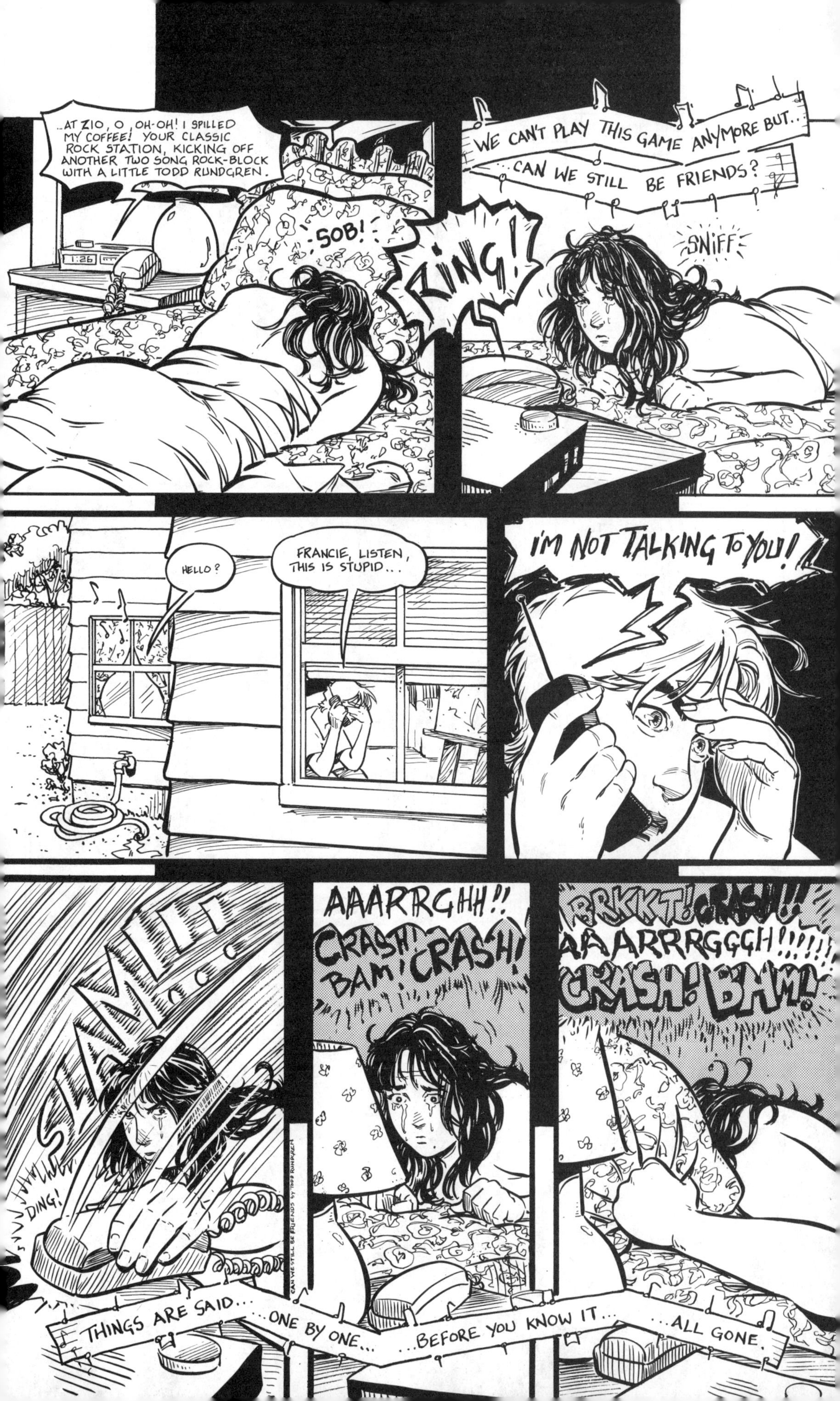

..AT ZIO, O, OH-OH! I SPILLED MY COFFEE! YOUR CLASSIC ROCK STATION, KICKING OFF ANOTHER TWO SONG ROCK-BLOCK WITH A LITTLE TODD RUNDGREN.
1:26
SOB!
RING!
WE CAN'T PLAY THIS GAME ANYMORE BUT...
...CAN WE STILL BE FRIENDS?
SNIFF
HELLO?
FRANCIE, LISTEN, THIS IS STUPID...
I'M NOT TALKING TO YOU!
SLAM!!
DING!
AAARRGHH!!
CRASH! BAM! CRASH!
BRKKT! CRASH!!
AAAARRRGGGH!!!!!
CRASH! BAM!
CAN WE STILL BE FRIENDS BY TODD RUNDGREN
THINGS ARE SAID... ...ONE BY ONE... ...BEFORE YOU KNOW IT... ...ALL GONE.

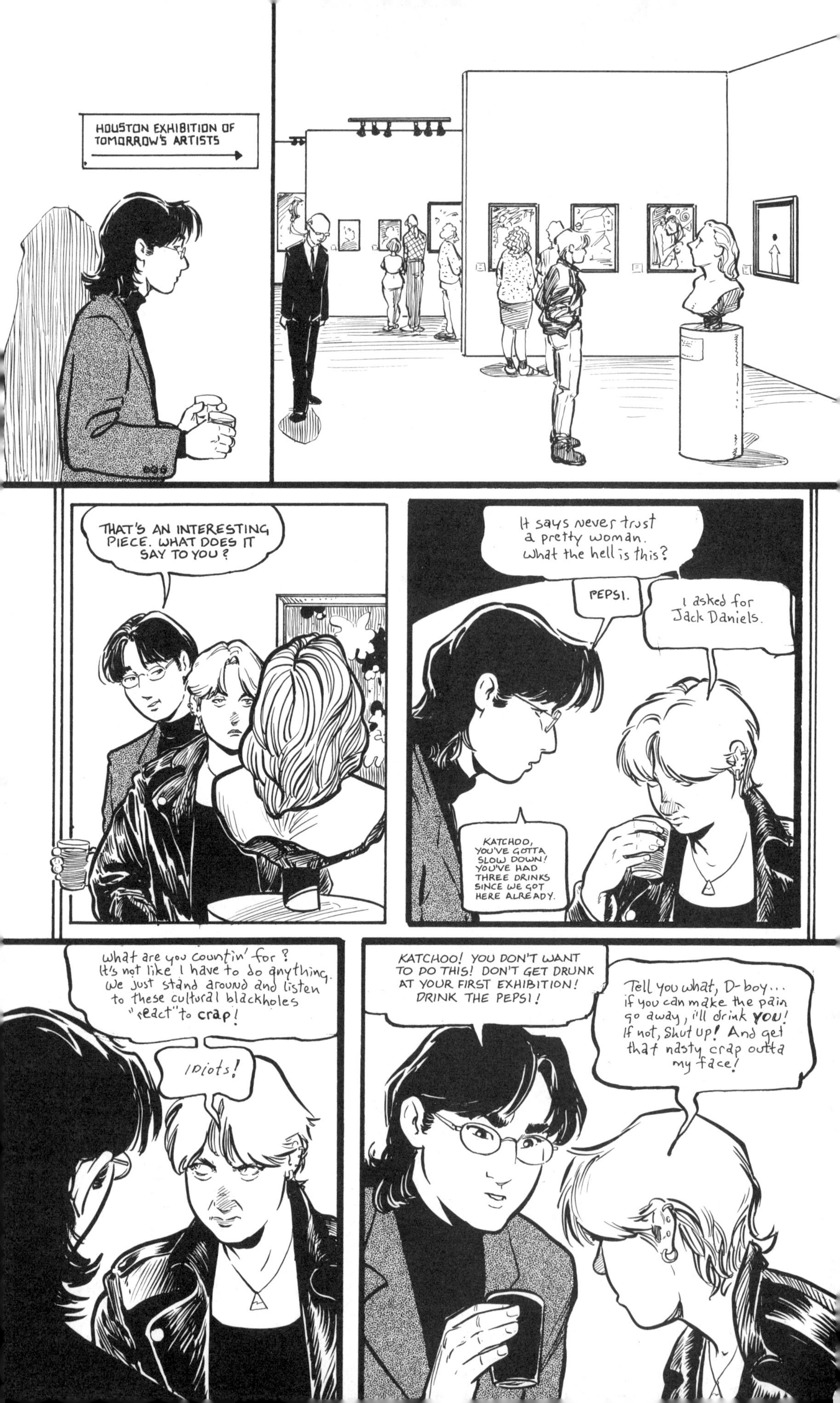
HOUSTON EXHIBITION OF TOMORROW'S ARTISTS
THAT'S AN INTERESTING PIECE. WHAT DOES IT SAY TO YOU?
It says never trust a pretty woman. What the hell is this?
PEPSI.
I asked for Jack Daniels.
KATCHOO, YOU'VE GOTTA SLOW DOWN! YOU'VE HAD THREE DRINKS SINCE WE GOT HERE ALREADY.
What are you countin' for? It's not like I have to do anything. We just stand around and listen to these cultural blackholes "react" to crap!
IDIOTS!
KATCHOO! YOU DON'T WANT TO DO THIS! DON'T GET DRUNK AT YOUR FIRST EXHIBITION! DRINK THE PEPSI!
Tell you what, D-boy... if you can make the pain go away, I'll drink YOU! If not, Shut up! And get that nasty crap outta my face!

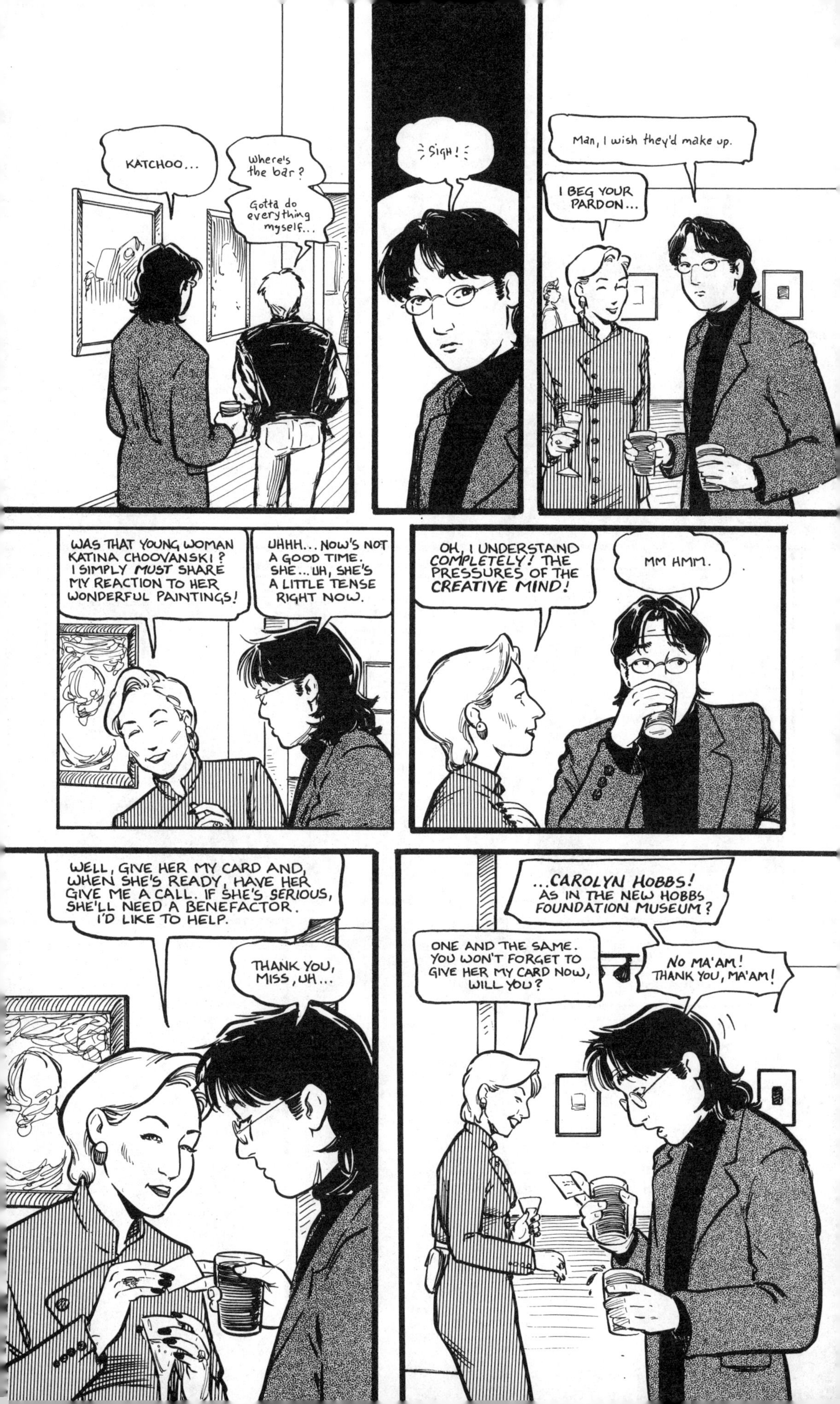

KATCHOO...
Where's the bar?
Gotta do everything myself...
SIGH!
I BEG YOUR PARDON...
Man, I wish they'd make up.
WAS THAT YOUNG WOMAN KATINA CHOOVANSKI? I SIMPLY MUST SHARE MY REACTION TO HER WONDERFUL PAINTINGS!
UHHH... NOW'S NOT A GOOD TIME. SHE... UH, SHE'S A LITTLE TENSE RIGHT NOW.
OH, I UNDERSTAND COMPLETELY! THE PRESSURES OF THE CREATIVE MIND!
MM HMM.
WELL, GIVE HER MY CARD AND, WHEN SHE'S READY, HAVE HER GIVE ME A CALL. IF SHE'S SERIOUS, SHE'LL NEED A BENEFACTOR. I'D LIKE TO HELP.
THANK YOU, MISS, UH...
...CAROLYN HOBBS! AS IN THE NEW HOBBS FOUNDATION MUSEUM?
ONE AND THE SAME. YOU WON'T FORGET TO GIVE HER MY CARD NOW, WILL YOU?
NO MA'AM! THANK YOU, MA'AM!

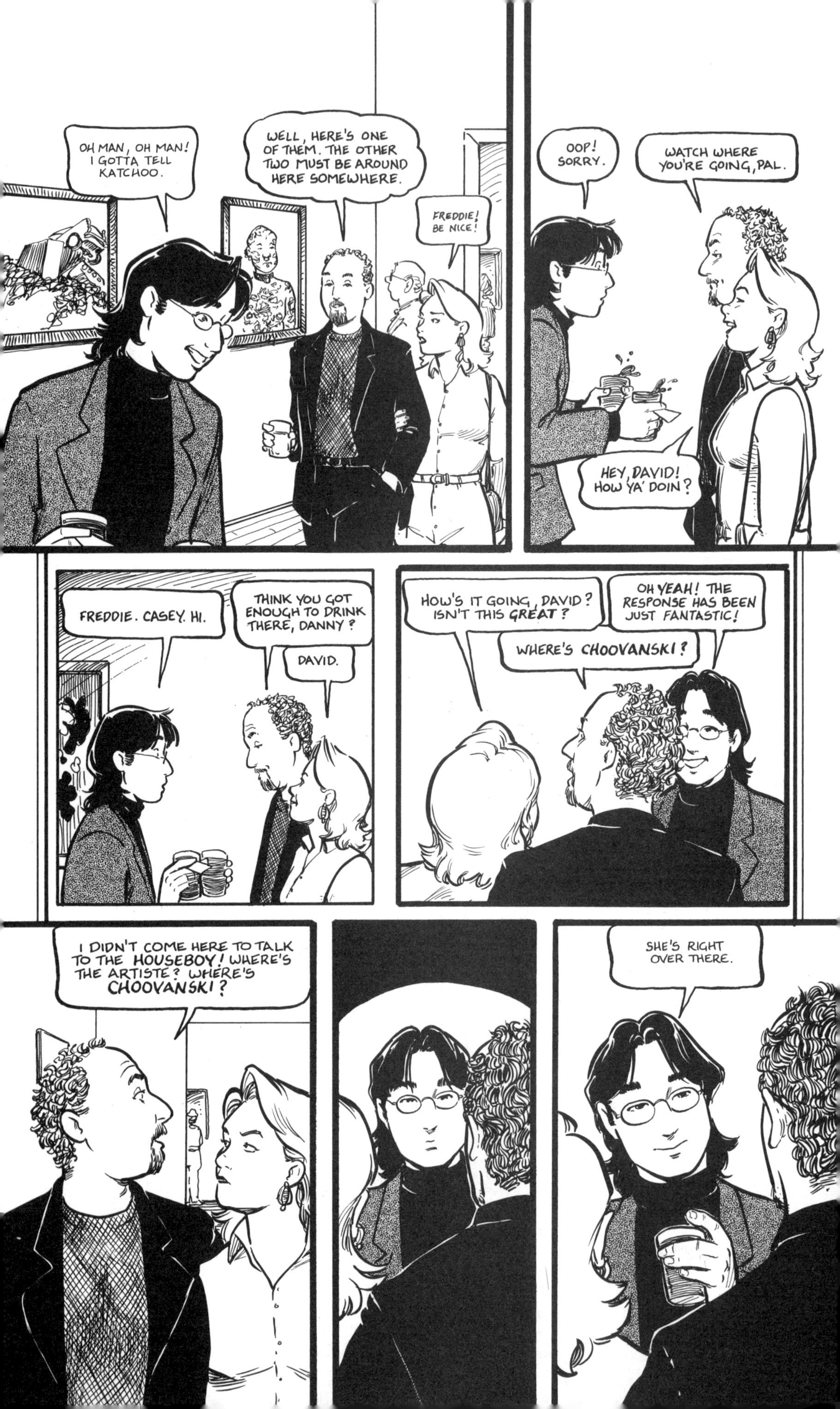

OH MAN, OH MAN! I GOTTA TELL KATCHOO.
WELL, HERE'S ONE OF THEM. THE OTHER TWO MUST BE AROUND HERE SOMEWHERE.
FREDDIE! BE NICE!
OOP! SORRY.
WATCH WHERE YOU'RE GOING, PAL.
HEY, DAVID! HOW YA' DOIN?
FREDDIE. CASEY. HI.
THINK YOU GOT ENOUGH TO DRINK THERE, DANNY?
DAVID.
HOW'S IT GOING, DAVID? ISN'T THIS GREAT?
OH YEAH! THE RESPONSE HAS BEEN JUST FANTASTIC!
WHERE'S CHOOVANSKI?
I DIDN'T COME HERE TO TALK TO THE HOUSEBOY! WHERE'S THE ARTISTE? WHERE'S CHOOVANSKI?
SHE'S RIGHT OVER THERE.

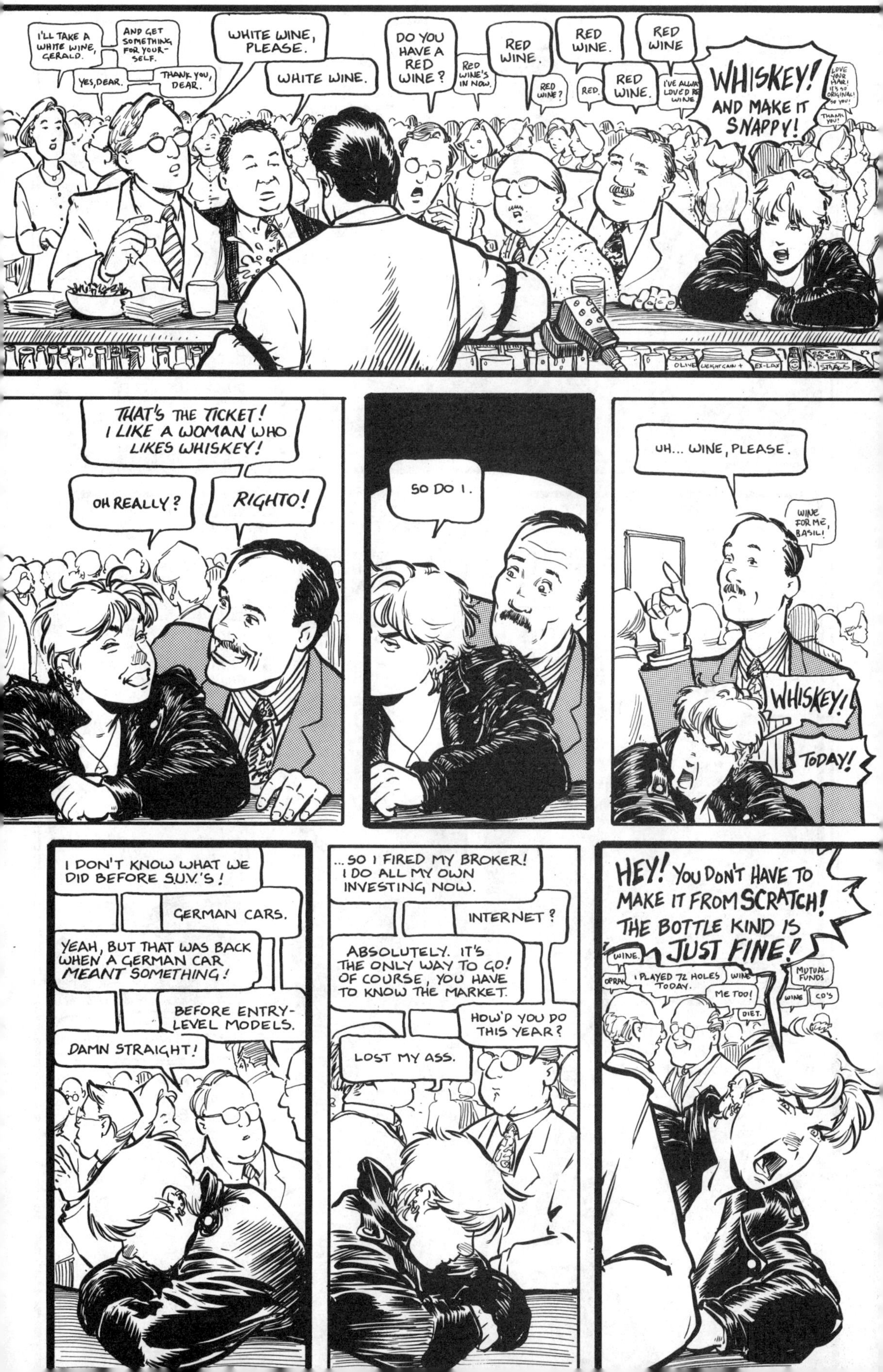
I'LL TAKE A WHITE WINE, GERALD.
YES, DEAR.
AND GET SOMETHING FOR YOURSELF.
THANK YOU, DEAR.
WHITE WINE, PLEASE.
WHITE WINE.
DO YOU HAVE A RED WINE?
RED WINE'S IN NOW.
RED WINE.
RED WINE?
RED WINE.
RED.
RED WINE.
RED WINE
WHISKEY! AND MAKE IT SNAPPY!
LOVE YOUR HAIR! IT'S SO ORIGINAL! SO YOU!
THANK YOU!
OLIVE
EX-LAX
STRAWS
THAT'S THE TICKET! I LIKE A WOMAN WHO LIKES WHISKEY!
OH REALLY?
RIGHTO!
SO DO I.
UH... WINE, PLEASE.
WINE FOR ME, BASIL!
WHISKEY!
TODAY!
I DON'T KNOW WHAT WE DID BEFORE S.U.V.'S!
GERMAN CARS.
YEAH, BUT THAT WAS BACK WHEN A GERMAN CAR MEANT SOMETHING!
BEFORE ENTRY-LEVEL MODELS.
DAMN STRAIGHT!
...SO I FIRED MY BROKER! I DO ALL MY OWN INVESTING NOW.
INTERNET?
ABSOLUTELY. IT'S THE ONLY WAY TO GO! OF COURSE, YOU HAVE TO KNOW THE MARKET.
HOW'D YOU DO THIS YEAR?
LOST MY ASS.
HEY! YOU DON'T HAVE TO MAKE IT FROM SCRATCH! THE BOTTLE KIND IS JUST FINE!
WINE.
I PLAYED 72 HOLES TODAY.
ME TOO!
DIET.
MUTUAL FUNDS
WINE
CD'S

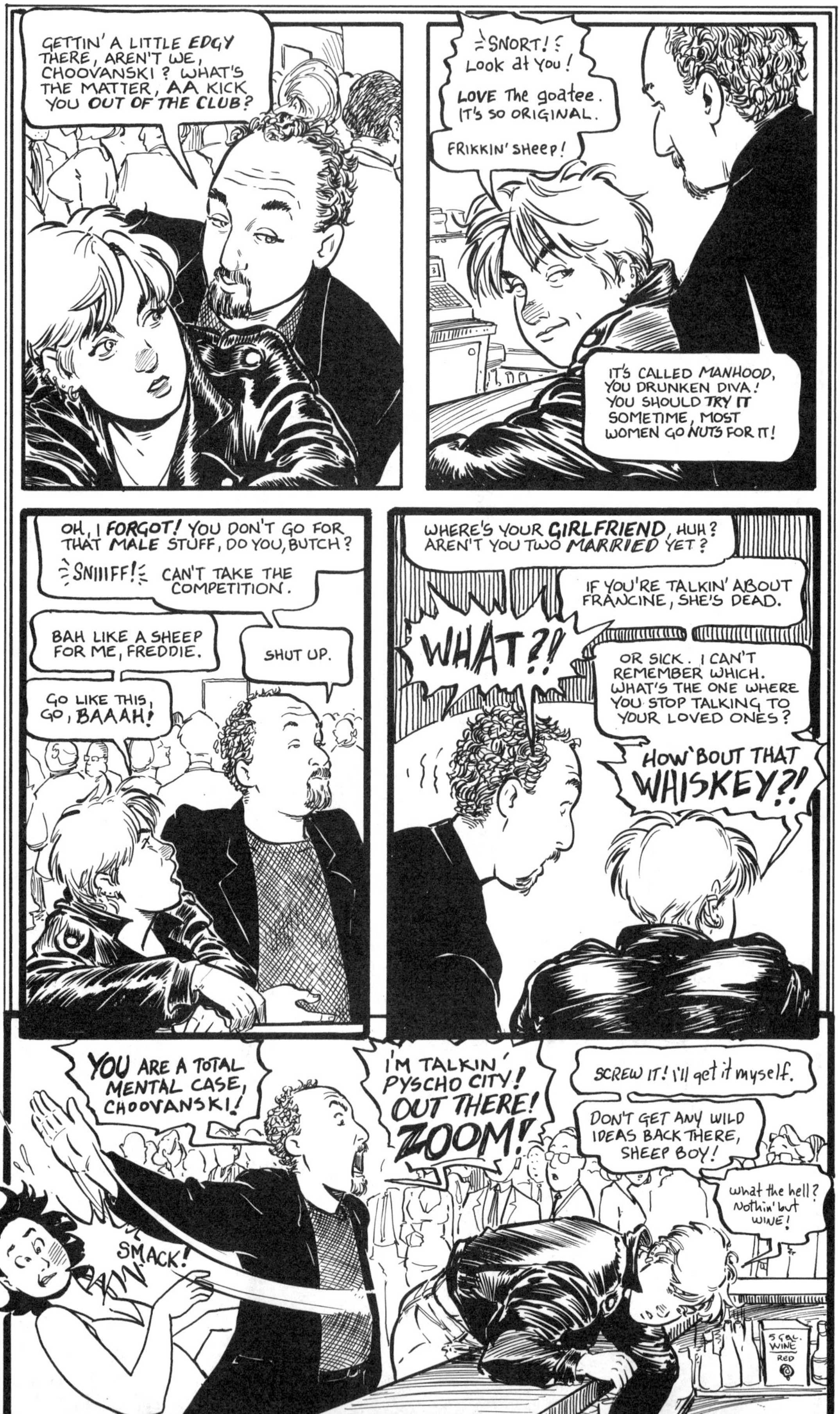
GETTIN' A LITTLE EDGY THERE, AREN'T WE, CHOOVANSKI? WHAT'S THE MATTER, AA KICK YOU OUT OF THE CLUB?
SNORT! Look at you!
LOVE the goatee. IT'S SO ORIGINAL.
FRIKKIN' SHEEP!
IT'S CALLED MANHOOD, YOU DRUNKEN DIVA! YOU SHOULD TRY IT SOMETIME, MOST WOMEN GO NUTS FOR IT!
OH, I FORGOT! YOU DON'T GO FOR THAT MALE STUFF, DO YOU, BUTCH?
SNIIIFF! CAN'T TAKE THE COMPETITION.
BAH LIKE A SHEEP FOR ME, FREDDIE.
SHUT UP.
GO LIKE THIS, GO, BAAAH!
WHERE'S YOUR GIRLFRIEND, HUH? AREN'T YOU TWO MARRIED YET?
IF YOU'RE TALKIN' ABOUT FRANCINE, SHE'S DEAD.
WHAT?!
OR SICK. I CAN'T REMEMBER WHICH. WHAT'S THE ONE WHERE YOU STOP TALKING TO YOUR LOVED ONES?
HOW'BOUT THAT WHISKEY?!
YOU ARE A TOTAL MENTAL CASE, CHOOVANSKI!
I'M TALKIN' PYSCHO CITY! OUT THERE! ZOOM!
SCREW IT! I'll get it myself.
DON'T GET ANY WILD IDEAS BACK THERE, SHEEP BOY!
what the hell? Nothin' but WINE!
SMACK!
5 GAL. WINE RED

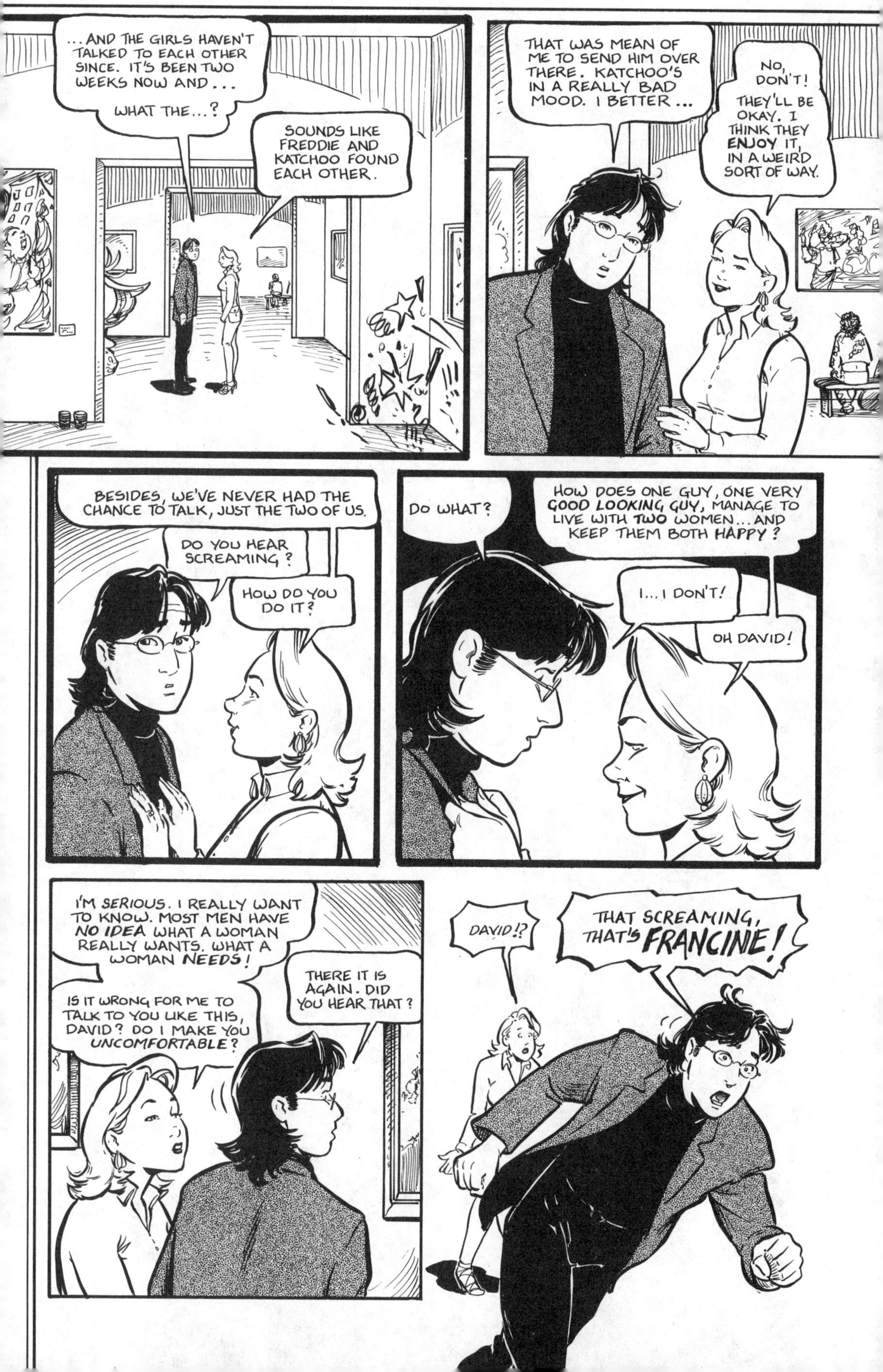

... AND THE GIRLS HAVEN'T TALKED TO EACH OTHER SINCE. IT'S BEEN TWO WEEKS NOW AND ...
WHAT THE ...?
SOUNDS LIKE FREDDIE AND KATCHOO FOUND EACH OTHER.
THAT WAS MEAN OF ME TO SEND HIM OVER THERE. KATCHOO'S IN A REALLY BAD MOOD. I BETTER ...
NO, DON'T! THEY'LL BE OKAY. I THINK THEY ENJOY IT, IN A WEIRD SORT OF WAY.
BESIDES, WE'VE NEVER HAD THE CHANCE TO TALK, JUST THE TWO OF US.
DO YOU HEAR SCREAMING?
HOW DO YOU DO IT?
DO WHAT?
HOW DOES ONE GUY, ONE VERY GOOD LOOKING GUY, MANAGE TO LIVE WITH TWO WOMEN ... AND KEEP THEM BOTH HAPPY?
I ... I DON'T!
OH DAVID!
I'M SERIOUS. I REALLY WANT TO KNOW. MOST MEN HAVE NO IDEA WHAT A WOMAN REALLY WANTS. WHAT A WOMAN NEEDS!
IS IT WRONG FOR ME TO TALK TO YOU LIKE THIS, DAVID? DO I MAKE YOU UNCOMFORTABLE?
THERE IT IS AGAIN. DID YOU HEAR THAT?
DAVID!?
THAT SCREAMING, THAT'S FRANCINE!

"In the end, it's not the words of our enemies we will remember, but the silence of our friends."

-Martin Luther King, Jr.

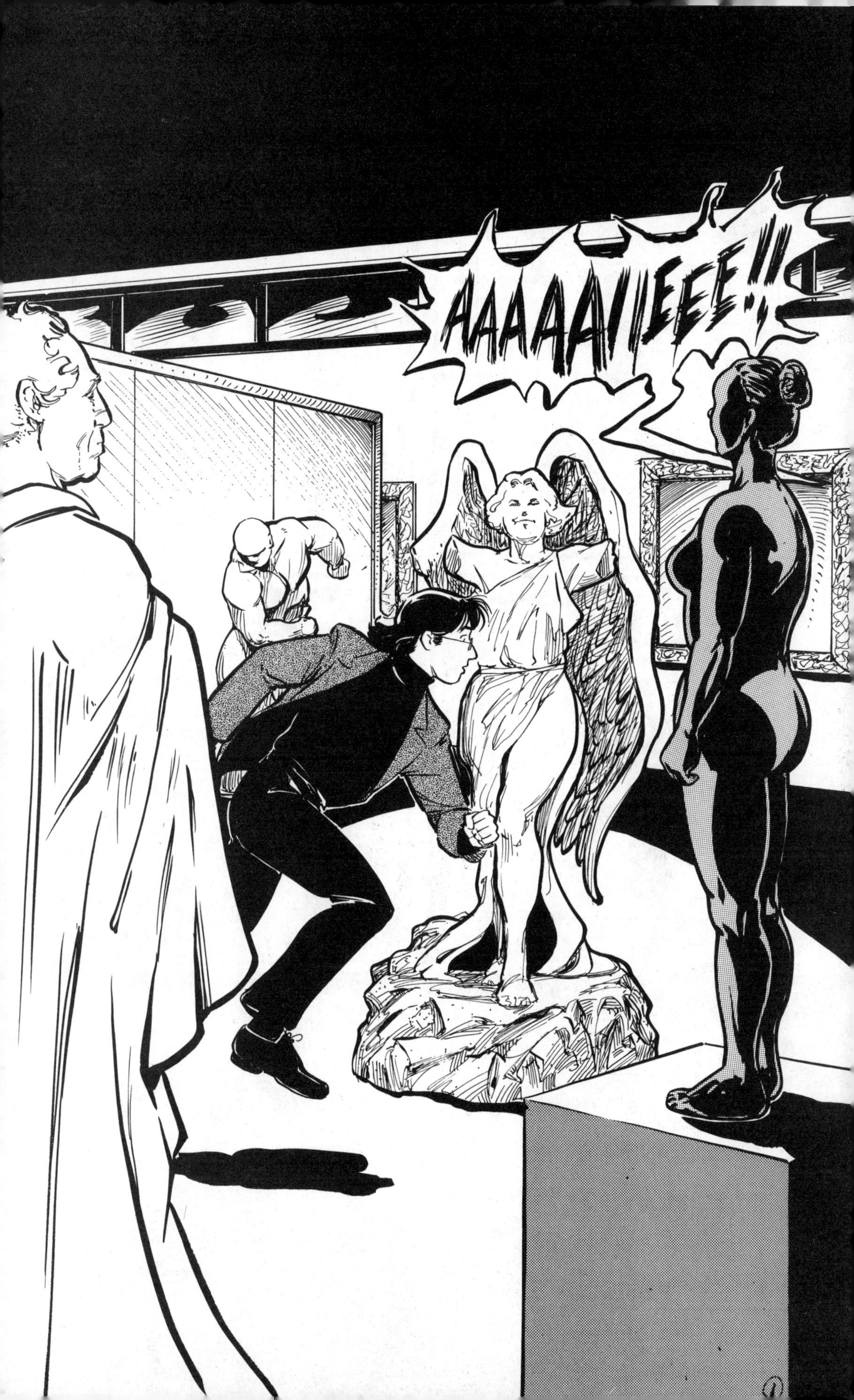
AAAAAIIEEE!!

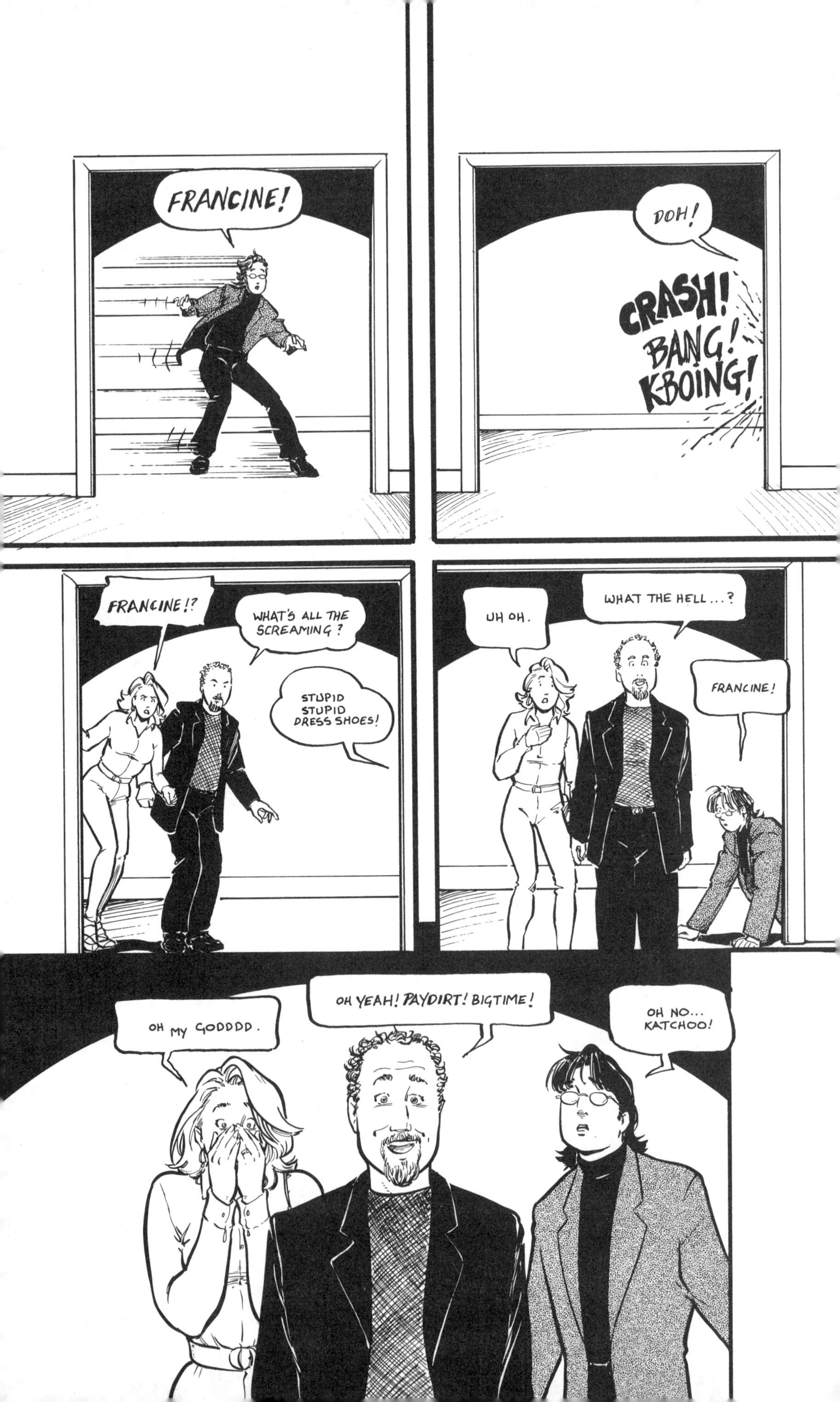
FRANCINE!
DOH!
CRASH! BANG! K-BOING!
FRANCINE!?
WHAT'S ALL THE SCREAMING?
STUPID STUPID DRESS SHOES!
UH OH.
WHAT THE HELL...?
FRANCINE!
OH MY GODDDD.
OH YEAH! PAYDIRT! BIGTIME!
OH NO... KATCHOO!

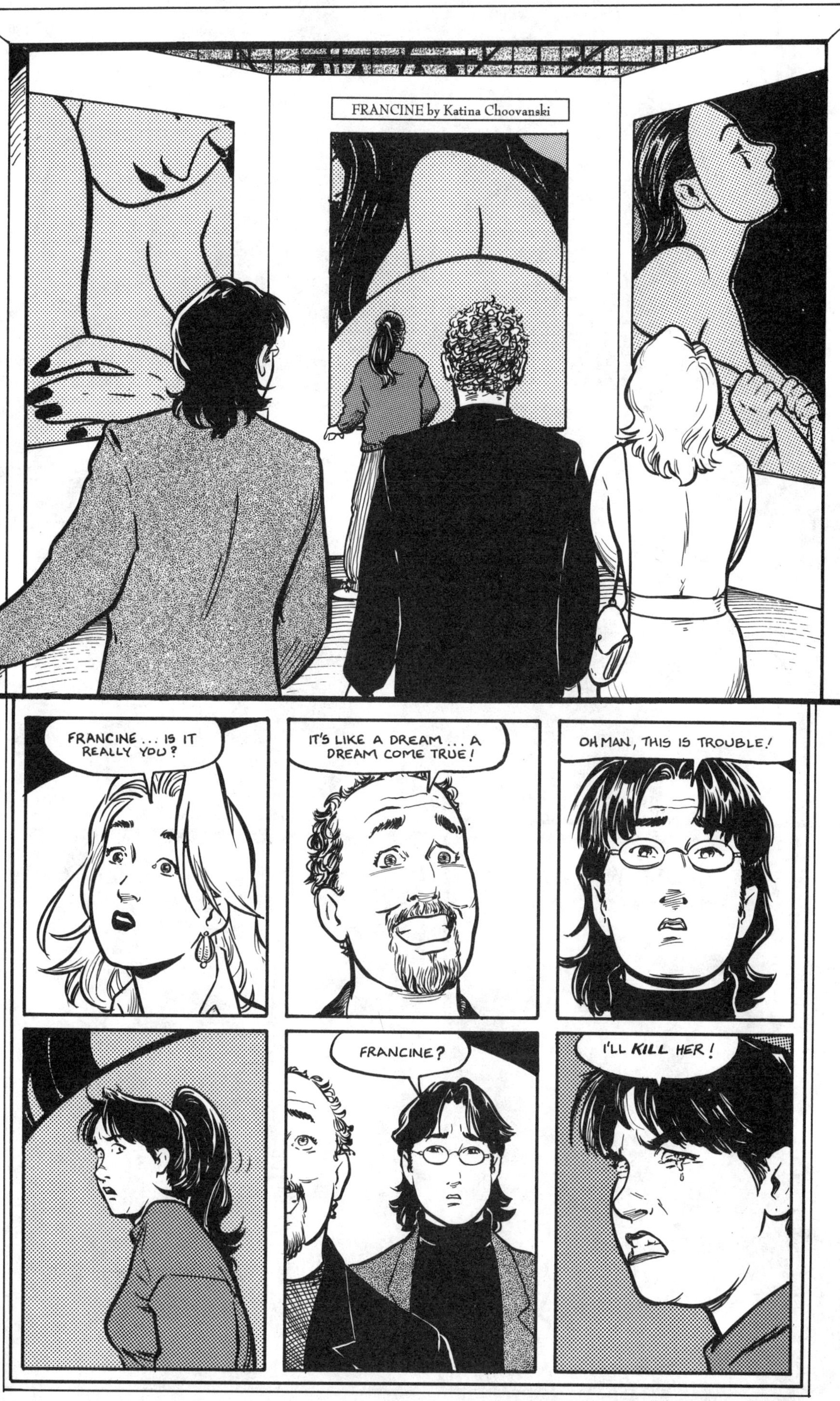
FRANCINE by Katina Choovanski
FRANCINE ... IS IT REALLY YOU?
IT'S LIKE A DREAM ... A DREAM COME TRUE!
OH MAN, THIS IS TROUBLE!
FRANCINE?
I'LL KILL HER!

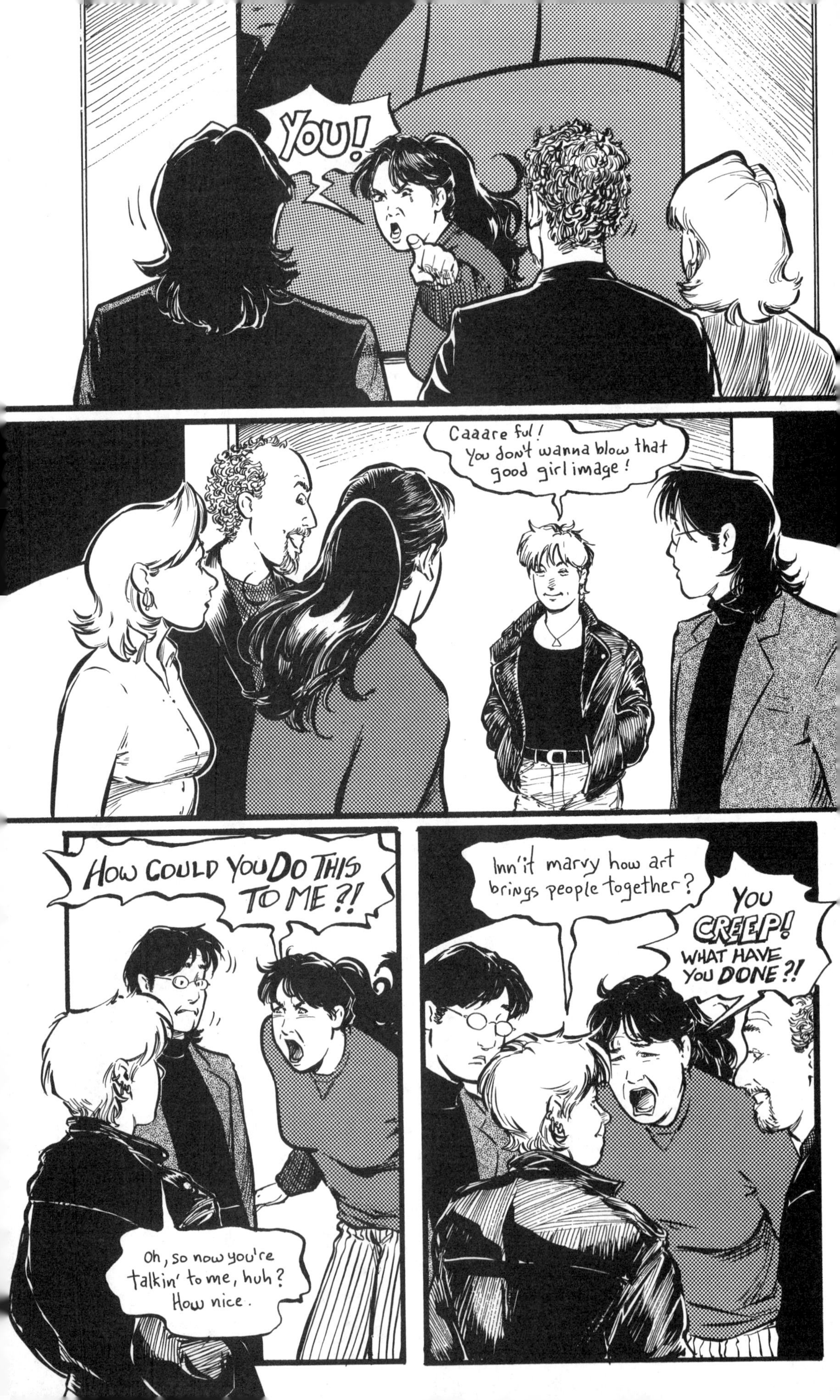
YOU!
Caaare ful! You don't wanna blow that good girl image!
HOW COULD YOU DO THIS TO ME?!
Oh, so now you're talkin' to me, huh? How nice.
Inn'it marvy how art brings people together?
YOU CREEP! WHAT HAVE YOU DONE?!

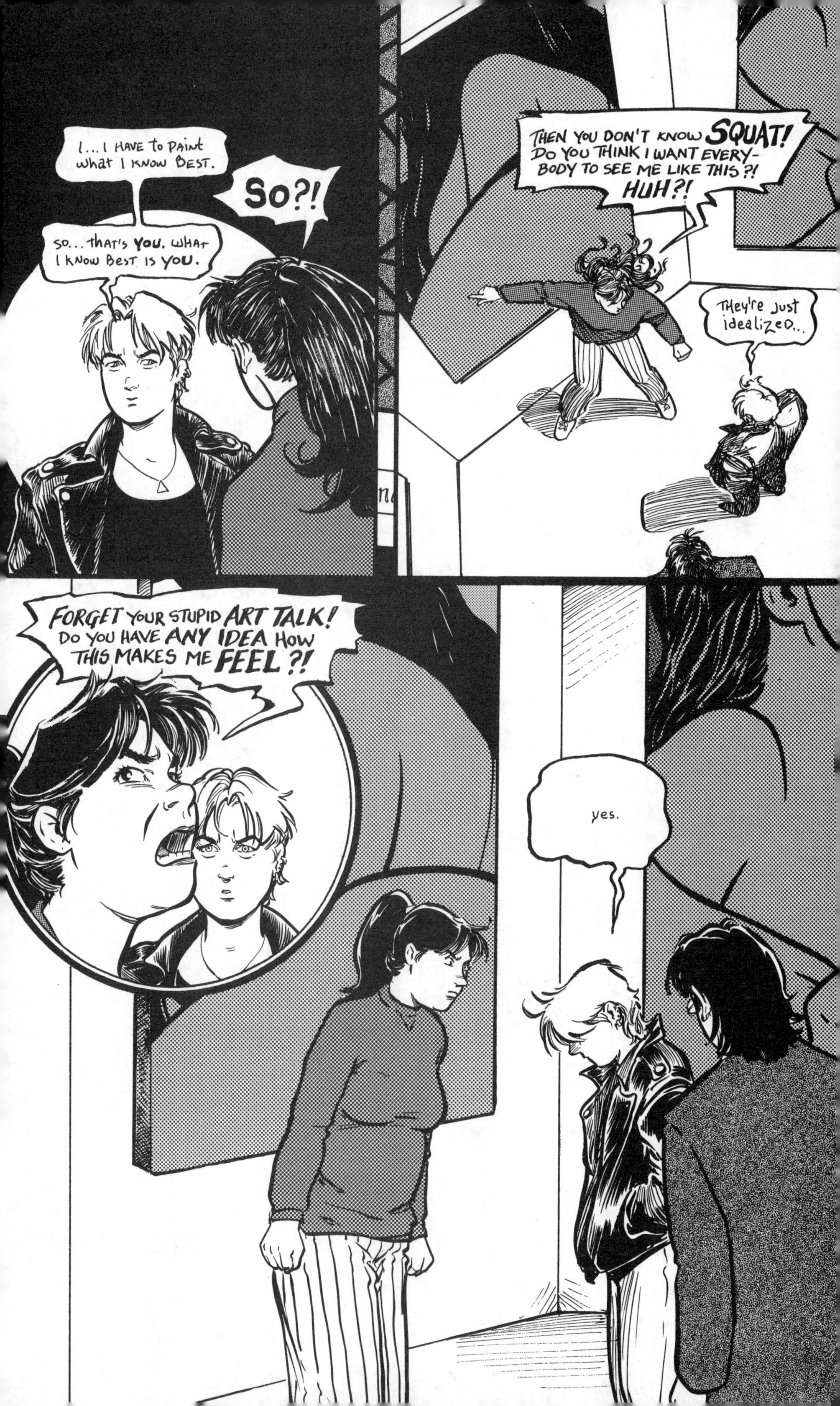

I... I HAVE TO PAINT WHAT I KNOW BEST.
SO?!
SO... THAT'S YOU. WHAT I KNOW BEST IS YOU.
THEN YOU DON'T KNOW SQUAT! DO YOU THINK I WANT EVERY-BODY TO SEE ME LIKE THIS?! HUH?!
THEY'RE JUST IDEALIZED...
FORGET YOUR STUPID ART TALK! DO YOU HAVE ANY IDEA HOW THIS MAKES ME FEEL?!
yes.

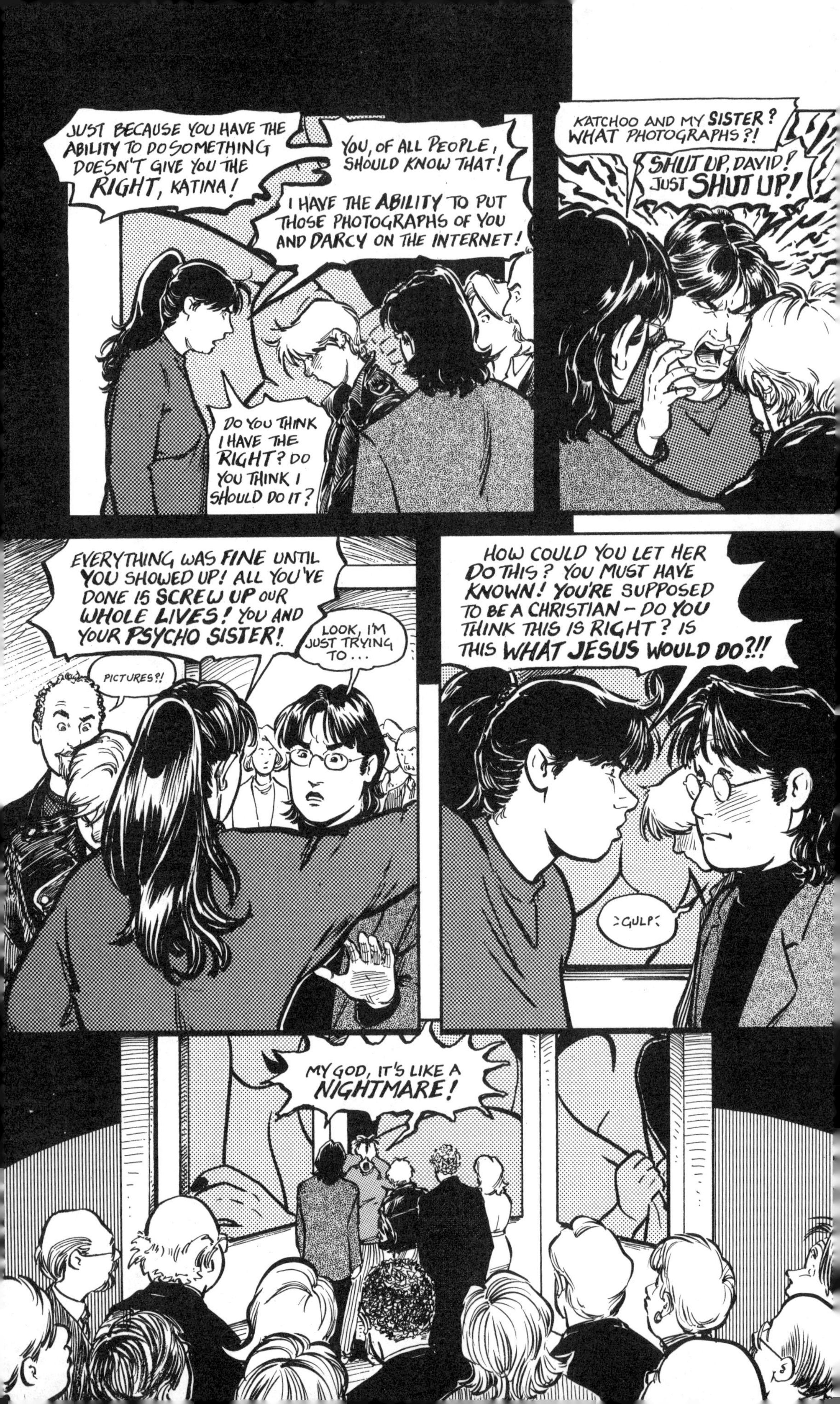
JUST BECAUSE YOU HAVE THE ABILITY TO DO SOMETHING DOESN'T GIVE YOU THE RIGHT, KATINA!
YOU, OF ALL PEOPLE, SHOULD KNOW THAT!
I HAVE THE ABILITY TO PUT THOSE PHOTOGRAPHS OF YOU AND DARCY ON THE INTERNET!
DO YOU THINK I HAVE THE RIGHT? DO YOU THINK I SHOULD DO IT?
KATCHOO AND MY SISTER? WHAT PHOTOGRAPHS?!
SHUT UP, DAVID! JUST SHUT UP!
EVERYTHING WAS FINE UNTIL YOU SHOWED UP! ALL YOU'VE DONE IS SCREW UP OUR WHOLE LIVES! YOU AND YOUR PSYCHO SISTER!
PICTURES?!
LOOK, I'M JUST TRYING TO...
HOW COULD YOU LET HER DO THIS? YOU MUST HAVE KNOWN! YOU'RE SUPPOSED TO BE A CHRISTIAN – DO YOU THINK THIS IS RIGHT? IS THIS WHAT JESUS WOULD DO?!!
GULP
MY GOD, IT'S LIKE A NIGHTMARE!

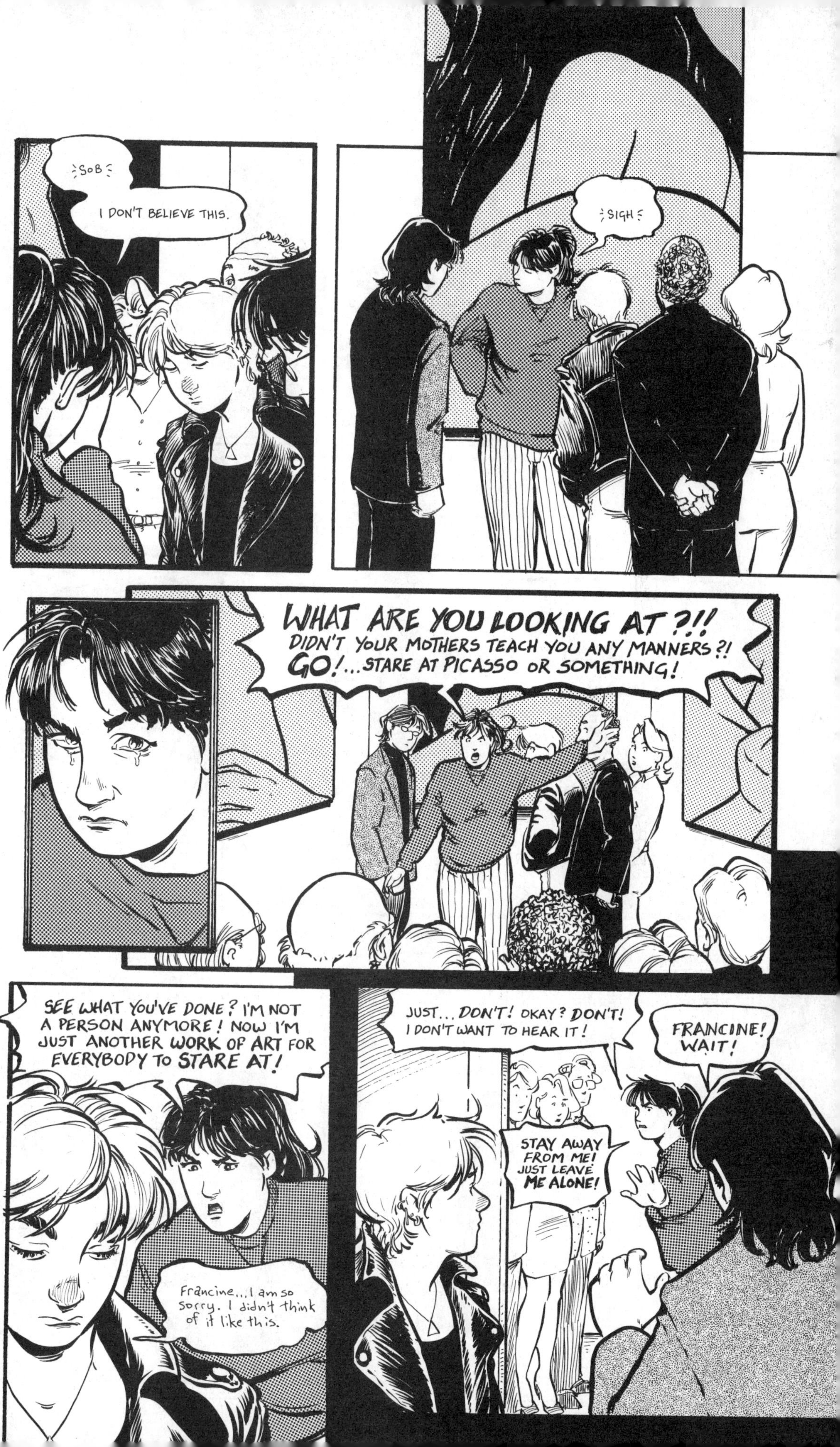
SOB
I DON'T BELIEVE THIS.
SIGH
WHAT ARE YOU LOOKING AT ?!! DIDN'T YOUR MOTHERS TEACH YOU ANY MANNERS ?! GO!... STARE AT PICASSO OR SOMETHING!
SEE WHAT YOU'VE DONE? I'M NOT A PERSON ANYMORE! NOW I'M JUST ANOTHER WORK OF ART FOR EVERYBODY TO STARE AT!
Francine... I am so sorry. I didn't think of it like this.
JUST... DON'T! OKAY? DON'T! I DON'T WANT TO HEAR IT!
FRANCINE! WAIT!
STAY AWAY FROM ME! JUST LEAVE ME ALONE!

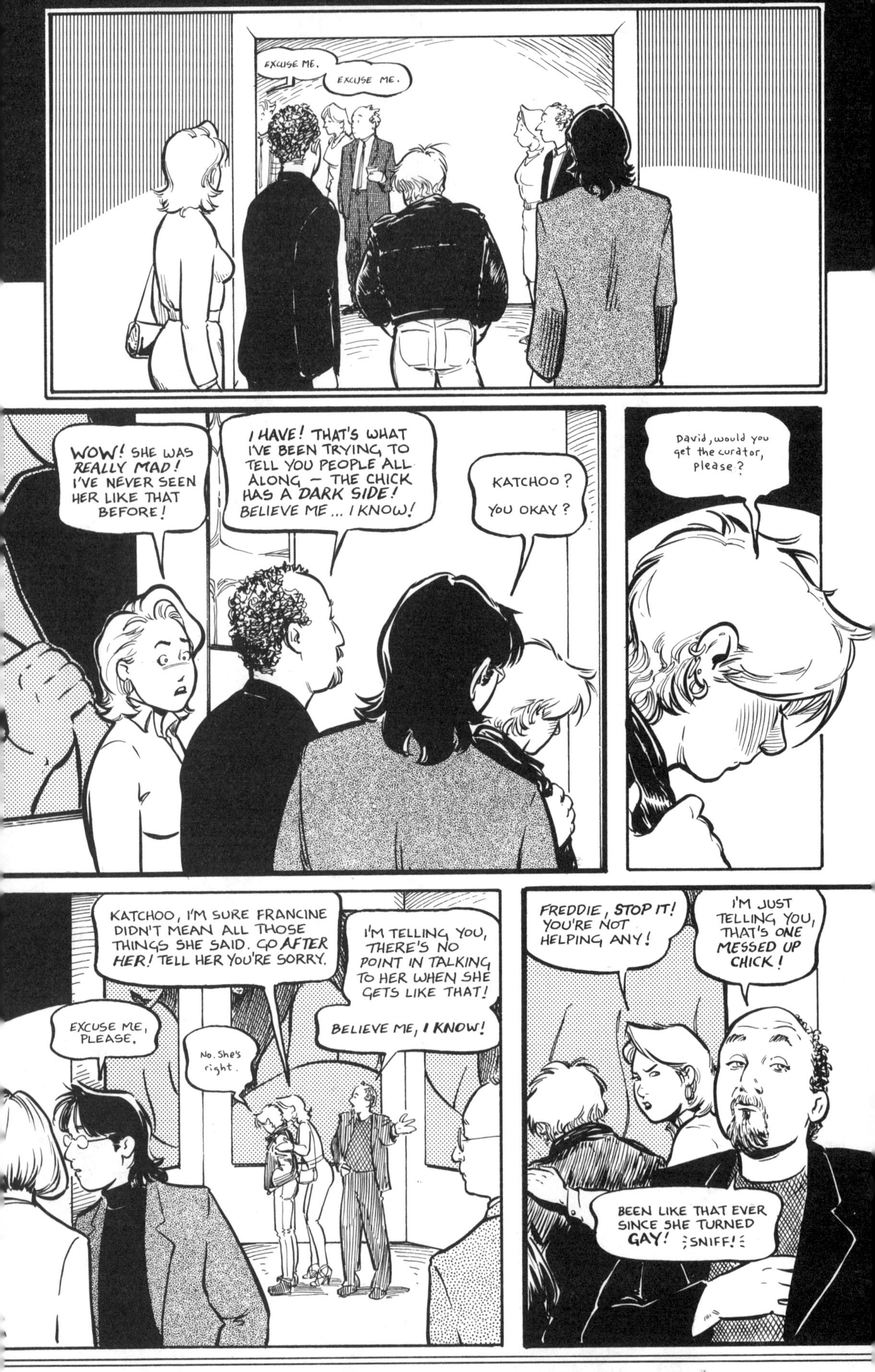
EXCUSE ME.
EXCUSE ME.
WOW! SHE WAS REALLY MAD! I'VE NEVER SEEN HER LIKE THAT BEFORE!
I HAVE! THAT'S WHAT I'VE BEEN TRYING TO TELL YOU PEOPLE ALL ALONG — THE CHICK HAS A DARK SIDE! BELIEVE ME... I KNOW!
KATCHOO?
YOU OKAY?
David, would you get the curator, please?
KATCHOO, I'M SURE FRANCINE DIDN'T MEAN ALL THOSE THINGS SHE SAID. GO AFTER HER! TELL HER YOU'RE SORRY.
I'M TELLING YOU, THERE'S NO POINT IN TALKING TO HER WHEN SHE GETS LIKE THAT!
BELIEVE ME, I KNOW!
EXCUSE ME, PLEASE.
No. She's right.
FREDDIE, STOP IT! YOU'RE NOT HELPING ANY!
I'M JUST TELLING YOU, THAT'S ONE MESSED UP CHICK!
BEEN LIKE THAT EVER SINCE SHE TURNED GAY! SNIFF!

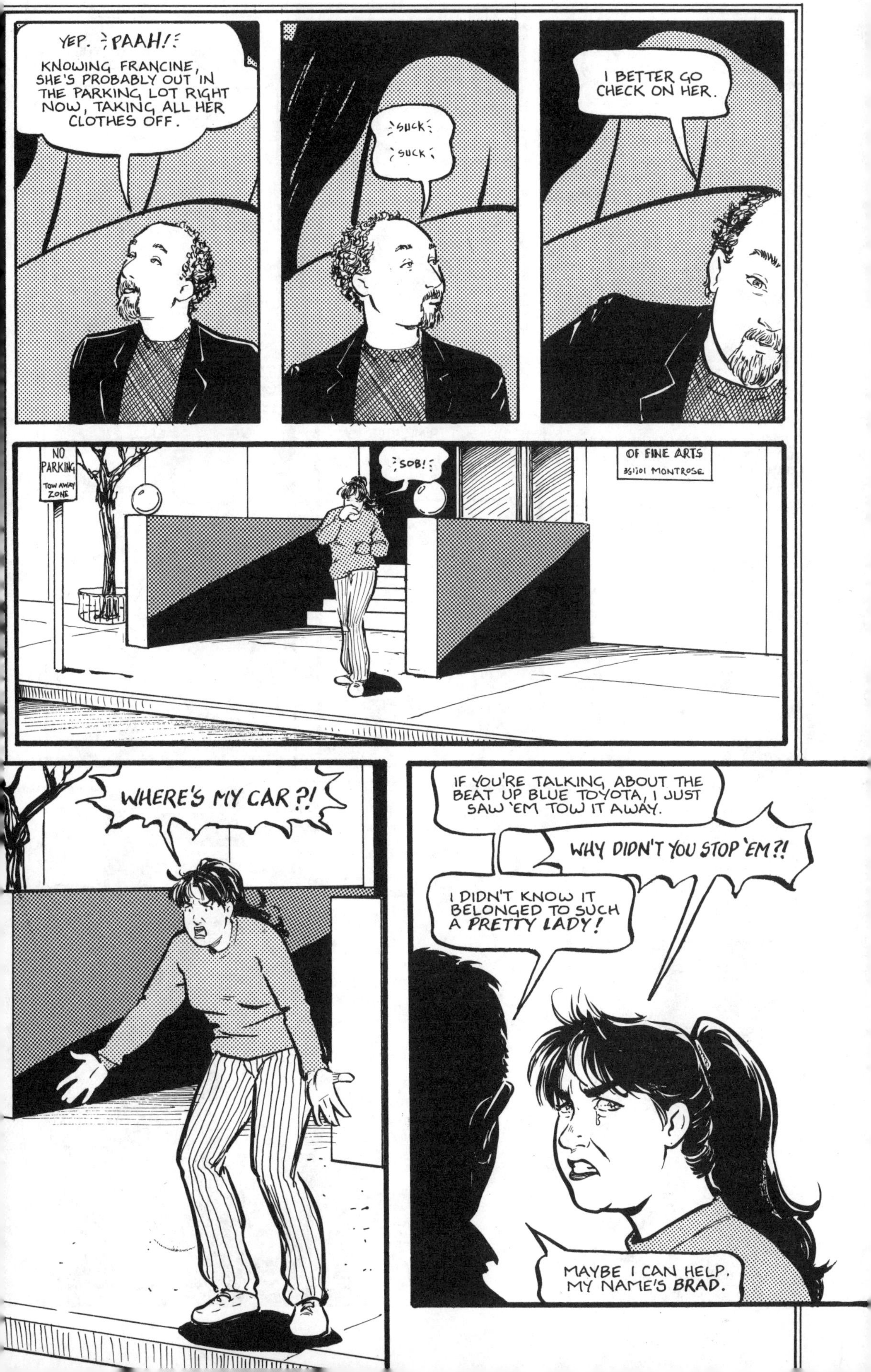
YEP. PAAH!
KNOWING FRANCINE, SHE'S PROBABLY OUT IN THE PARKING LOT RIGHT NOW, TAKING ALL HER CLOTHES OFF.
SUCK
SUCK
I BETTER GO CHECK ON HER.
NO PARKING
TOW AWAY ZONE
SOB!
OF FINE ARTS
MONTROSE
WHERE'S MY CAR?!
IF YOU'RE TALKING ABOUT THE BEAT UP BLUE TOYOTA, I JUST SAW 'EM TOW IT AWAY.
WHY DIDN'T YOU STOP 'EM?!
I DIDN'T KNOW IT BELONGED TO SUCH A PRETTY LADY!
MAYBE I CAN HELP. MY NAME'S BRAD.

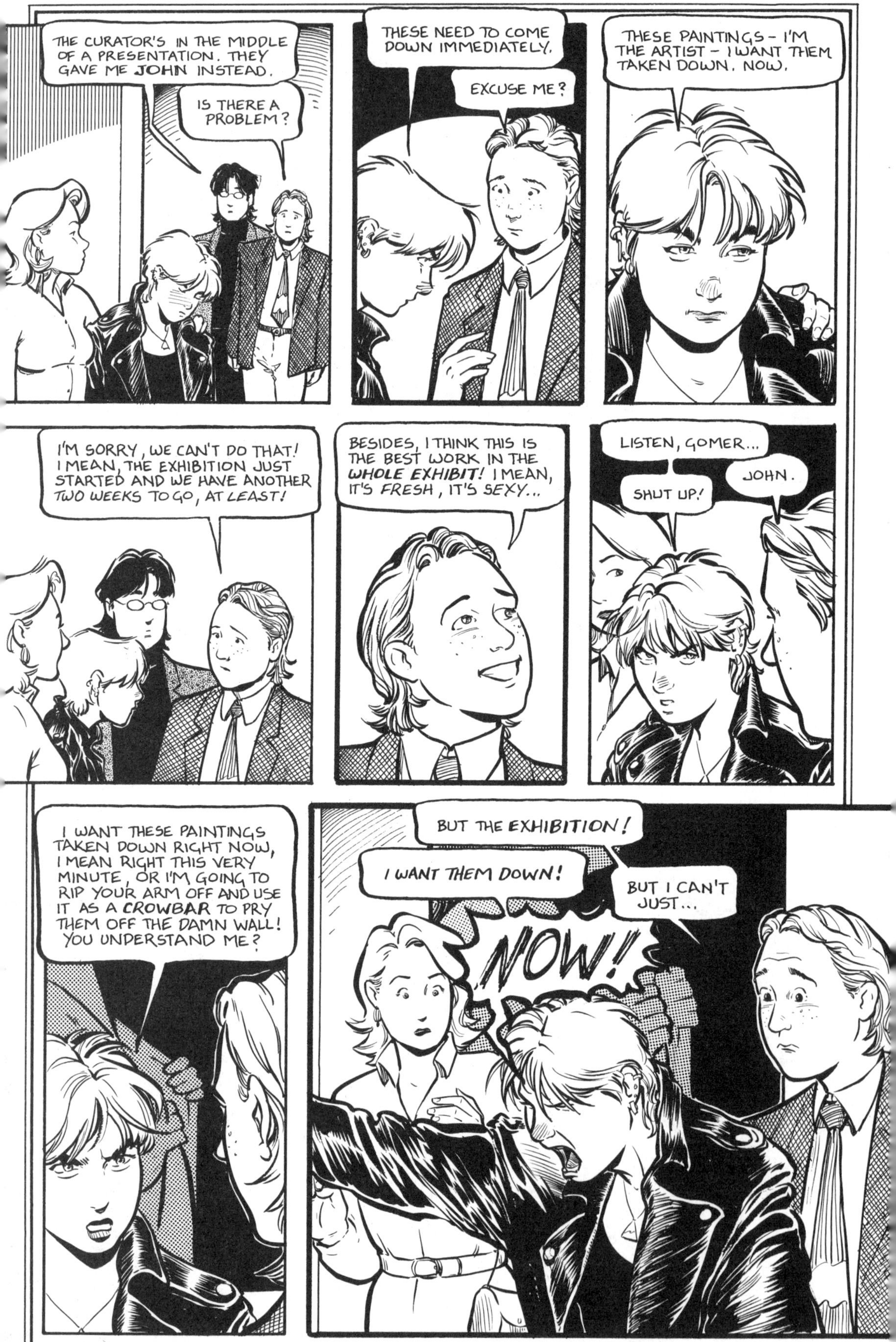

THE CURATOR'S IN THE MIDDLE OF A PRESENTATION. THEY GAVE ME JOHN INSTEAD.
IS THERE A PROBLEM?
THESE NEED TO COME DOWN IMMEDIATELY.
EXCUSE ME?
THESE PAINTINGS - I'M THE ARTIST - I WANT THEM TAKEN DOWN. NOW.
I'M SORRY, WE CAN'T DO THAT! I MEAN, THE EXHIBITION JUST STARTED AND WE HAVE ANOTHER TWO WEEKS TO GO, AT LEAST!
BESIDES, I THINK THIS IS THE BEST WORK IN THE WHOLE EXHIBIT! I MEAN, IT'S FRESH, IT'S SEXY...
LISTEN, GOMER...
JOHN.
SHUT UP!
I WANT THESE PAINTINGS TAKEN DOWN RIGHT NOW, I MEAN RIGHT THIS VERY MINUTE, OR I'M GOING TO RIP YOUR ARM OFF AND USE IT AS A CROWBAR TO PRY THEM OFF THE DAMN WALL! YOU UNDERSTAND ME?
BUT THE EXHIBITION!
I WANT THEM DOWN!
BUT I CAN'T JUST...
NOW!

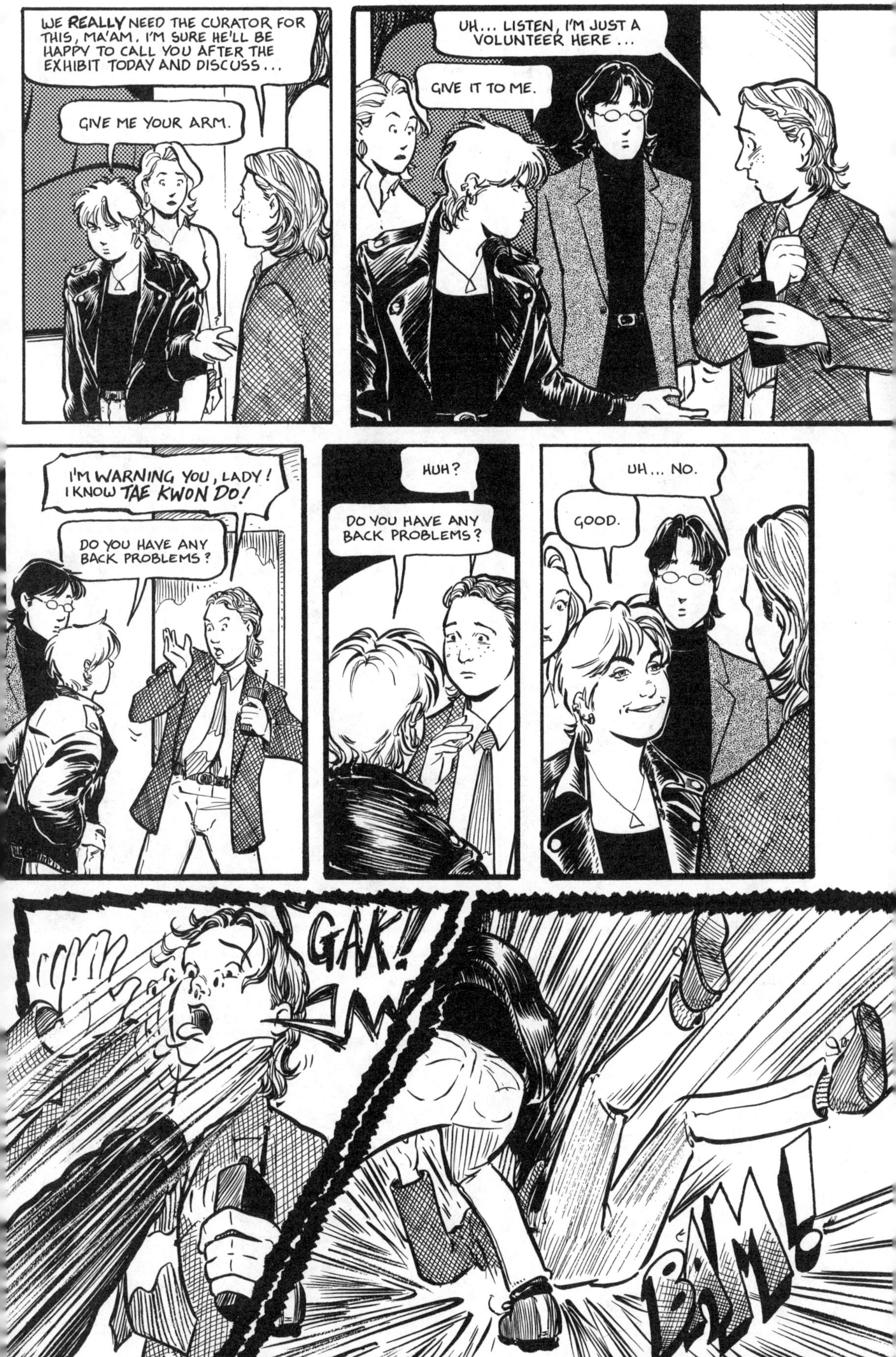
WE REALLY NEED THE CURATOR FOR THIS, MA'AM. I'M SURE HE'LL BE HAPPY TO CALL YOU AFTER THE EXHIBIT TODAY AND DISCUSS...
GIVE ME YOUR ARM.
UH... LISTEN, I'M JUST A VOLUNTEER HERE...
GIVE IT TO ME.
I'M WARNING YOU, LADY! I KNOW TAE KWON DO!
DO YOU HAVE ANY BACK PROBLEMS?
HUH?
DO YOU HAVE ANY BACK PROBLEMS?
UH... NO.
GOOD.
GAK!
BAM!

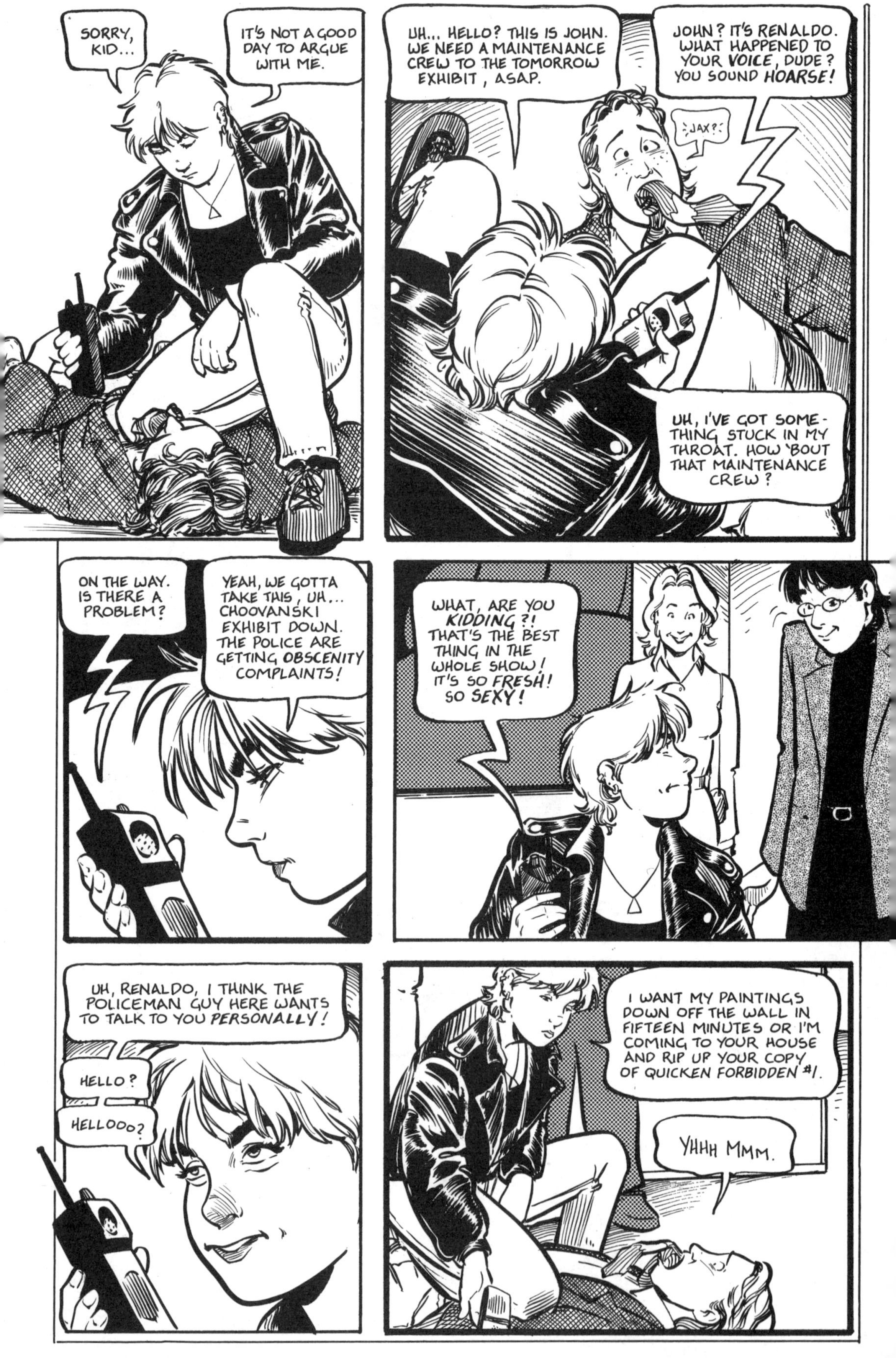
SORRY, KID...
IT'S NOT A GOOD DAY TO ARGUE WITH ME.
UH... HELLO? THIS IS JOHN. WE NEED A MAINTENANCE CREW TO THE TOMORROW EXHIBIT, ASAP.
JOHN? IT'S RENALDO. WHAT HAPPENED TO YOUR VOICE, DUDE? YOU SOUND HOARSE!
JAX?
UH, I'VE GOT SOMETHING STUCK IN MY THROAT. HOW 'BOUT THAT MAINTENANCE CREW?
ON THE WAY. IS THERE A PROBLEM?
YEAH, WE GOTTA TAKE THIS, UH... CHOOVANSKI EXHIBIT DOWN. THE POLICE ARE GETTING OBSCENITY COMPLAINTS!
WHAT, ARE YOU KIDDING?! THAT'S THE BEST THING IN THE WHOLE SHOW! IT'S SO FRESH! SO SEXY!
UH, RENALDO, I THINK THE POLICEMAN GUY HERE WANTS TO TALK TO YOU PERSONALLY!
HELLO?
HELLOOO?
I WANT MY PAINTINGS DOWN OFF THE WALL IN FIFTEEN MINUTES OR I'M COMING TO YOUR HOUSE AND RIP UP YOUR COPY OF QUICKEN FORBIDDEN #1.
YHHH MMM.

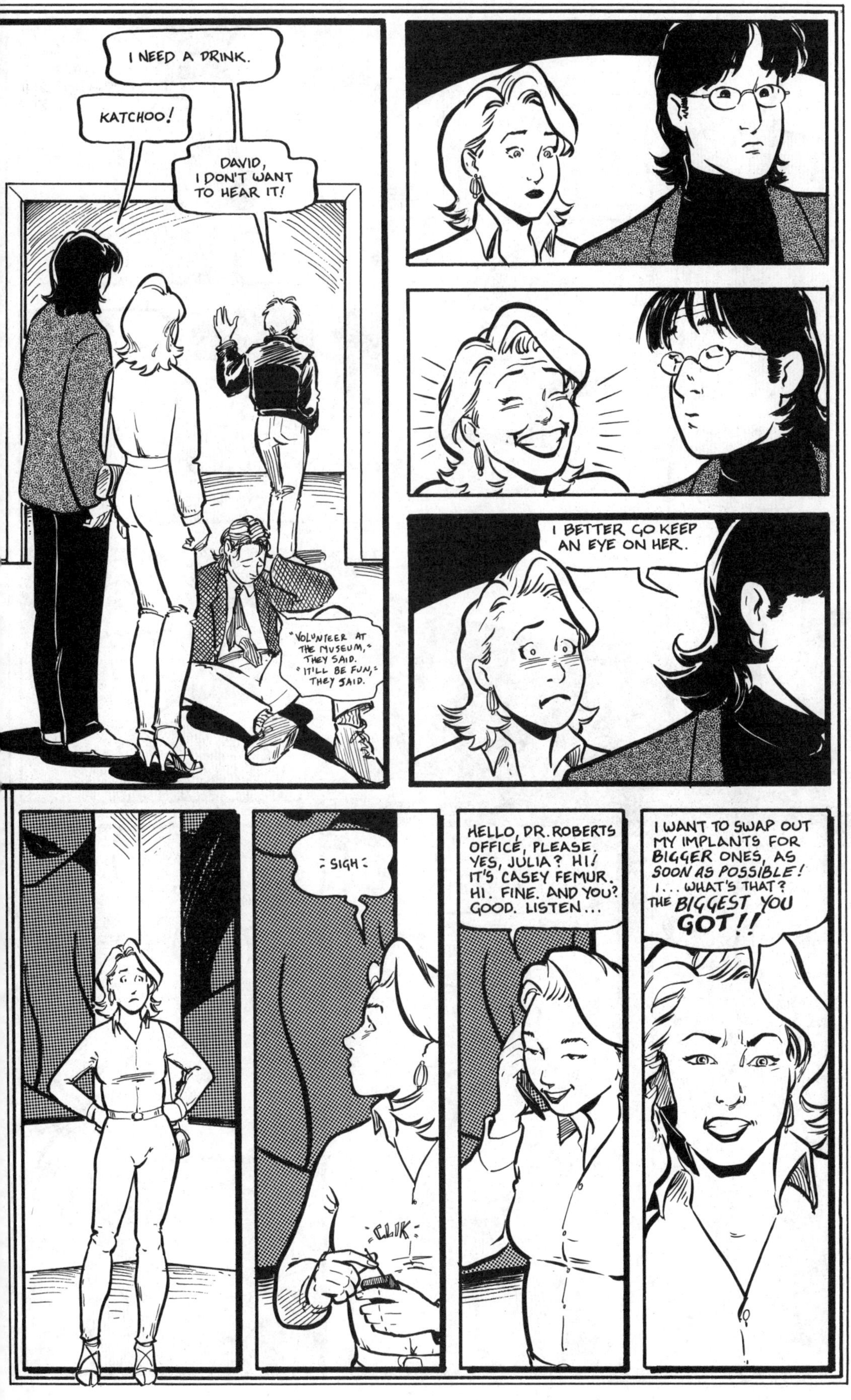
I NEED A DRINK.
KATCHOO!
DAVID, I DON'T WANT TO HEAR IT!
"VOLUNTEER AT THE MUSEUM," THEY SAID. "IT'LL BE FUN," THEY SAID.
I BETTER GO KEEP AN EYE ON HER.
:SIGH:
:CLIK:
HELLO, DR. ROBERTS OFFICE, PLEASE. YES, JULIA? HI! IT'S CASEY FEMUR. HI. FINE. AND YOU? GOOD. LISTEN...
I WANT TO SWAP OUT MY IMPLANTS FOR BIGGER ONES, AS SOON AS POSSIBLE! I... WHAT'S THAT? THE BIGGEST YOU GOT!!

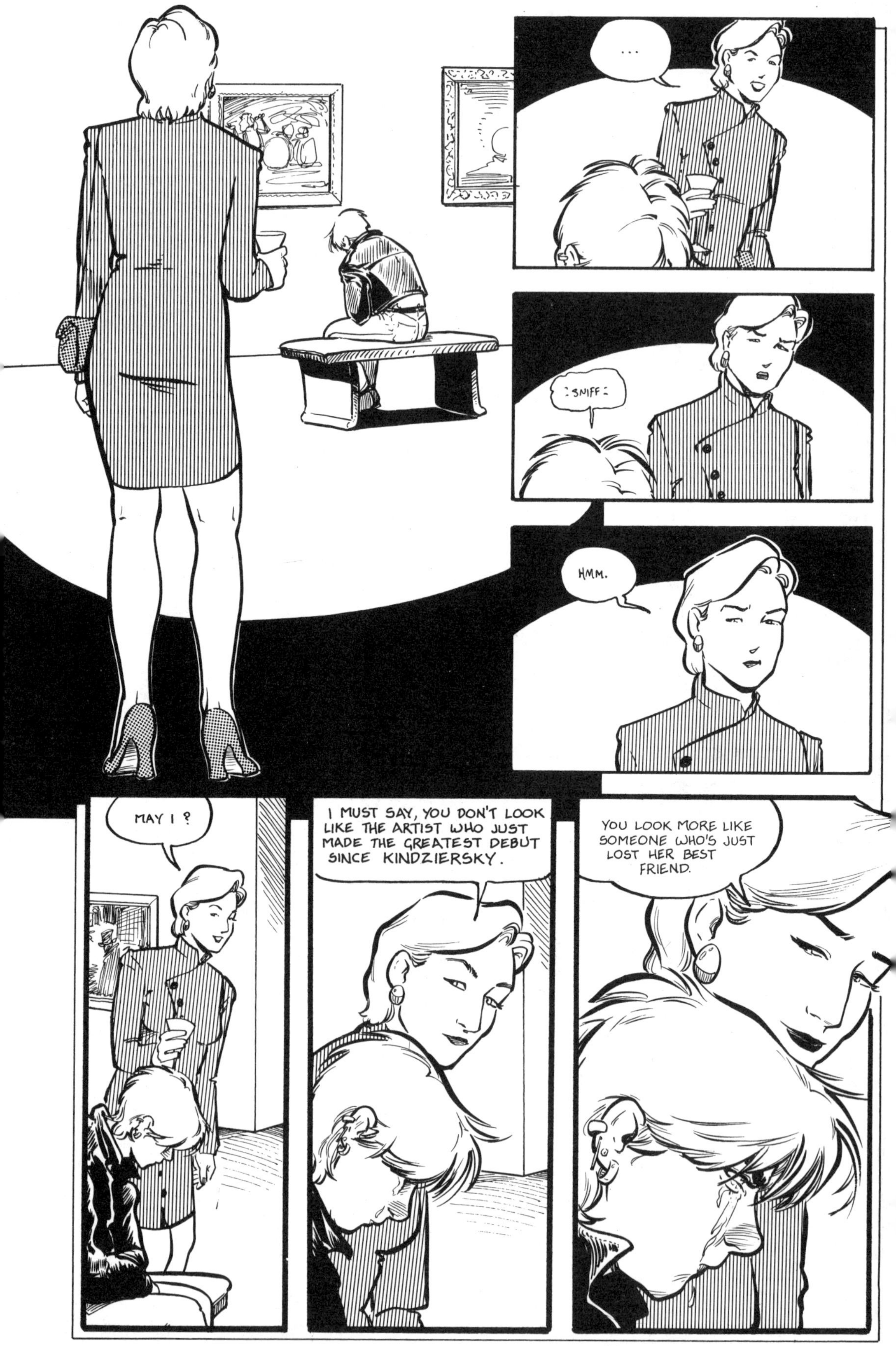
...
: SNIFF :
HMM.
MAY I ?
I MUST SAY, YOU DON'T LOOK LIKE THE ARTIST WHO JUST MADE THE GREATEST DEBUT SINCE KINDZIERSKY.
YOU LOOK MORE LIKE SOMEONE WHO'S JUST LOST HER BEST FRIEND.

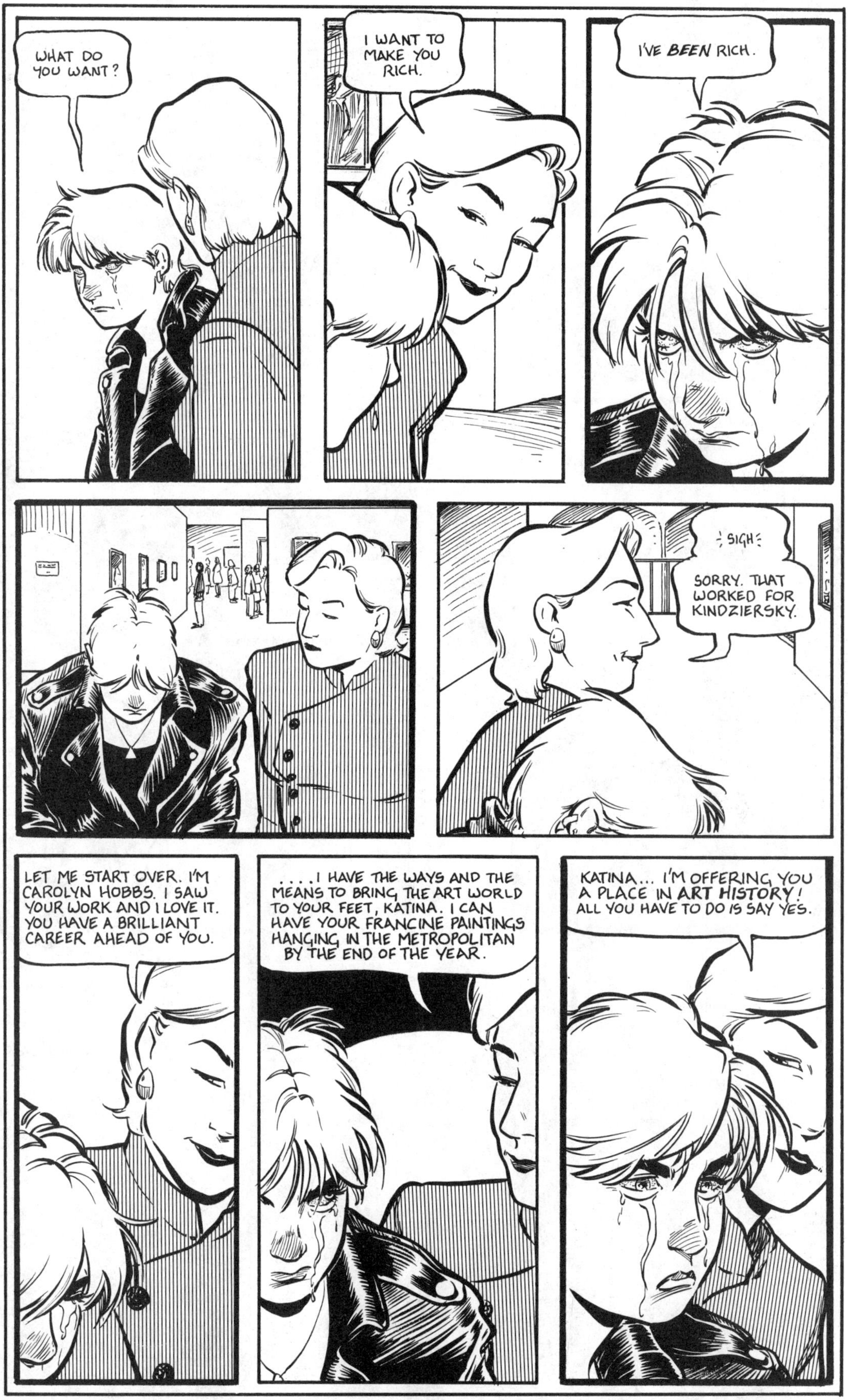
WHAT DO YOU WANT?
I WANT TO MAKE YOU RICH.
I'VE *BEEN* RICH.
SIGH
SORRY. THAT WORKED FOR KINDZIERSKY.
LET ME START OVER. I'M CAROLYN HOBBS. I SAW YOUR WORK AND I LOVE IT. YOU HAVE A BRILLIANT CAREER AHEAD OF YOU.
....I HAVE THE WAYS AND THE MEANS TO BRING THE ART WORLD TO YOUR FEET, KATINA. I CAN HAVE YOUR FRANCINE PAINTINGS HANGING IN THE METROPOLITAN BY THE END OF THE YEAR.
KATINA... I'M OFFERING YOU A PLACE IN **ART HISTORY**! ALL YOU HAVE TO DO IS SAY YES.

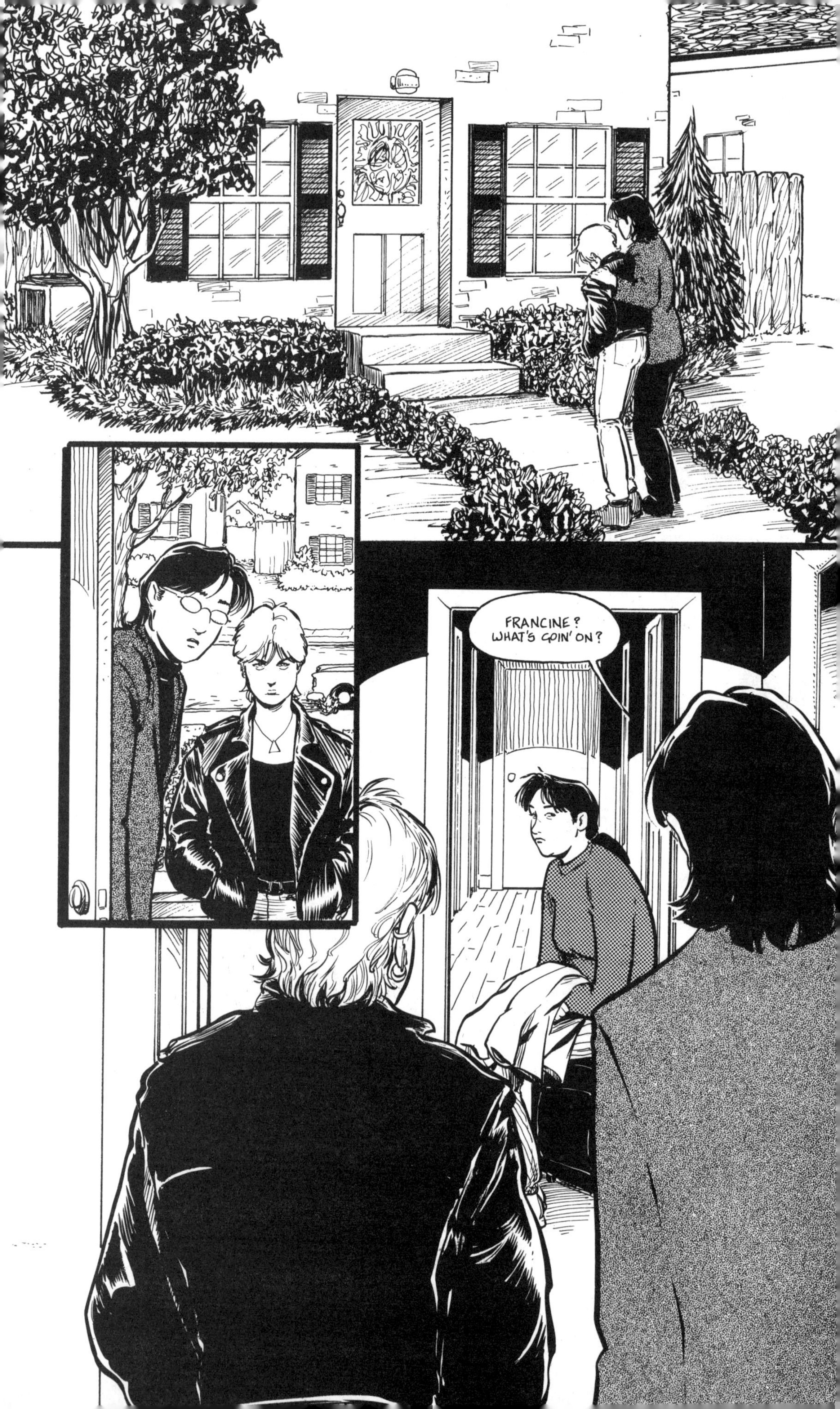
FRANCINE?
WHAT'S GOIN' ON?

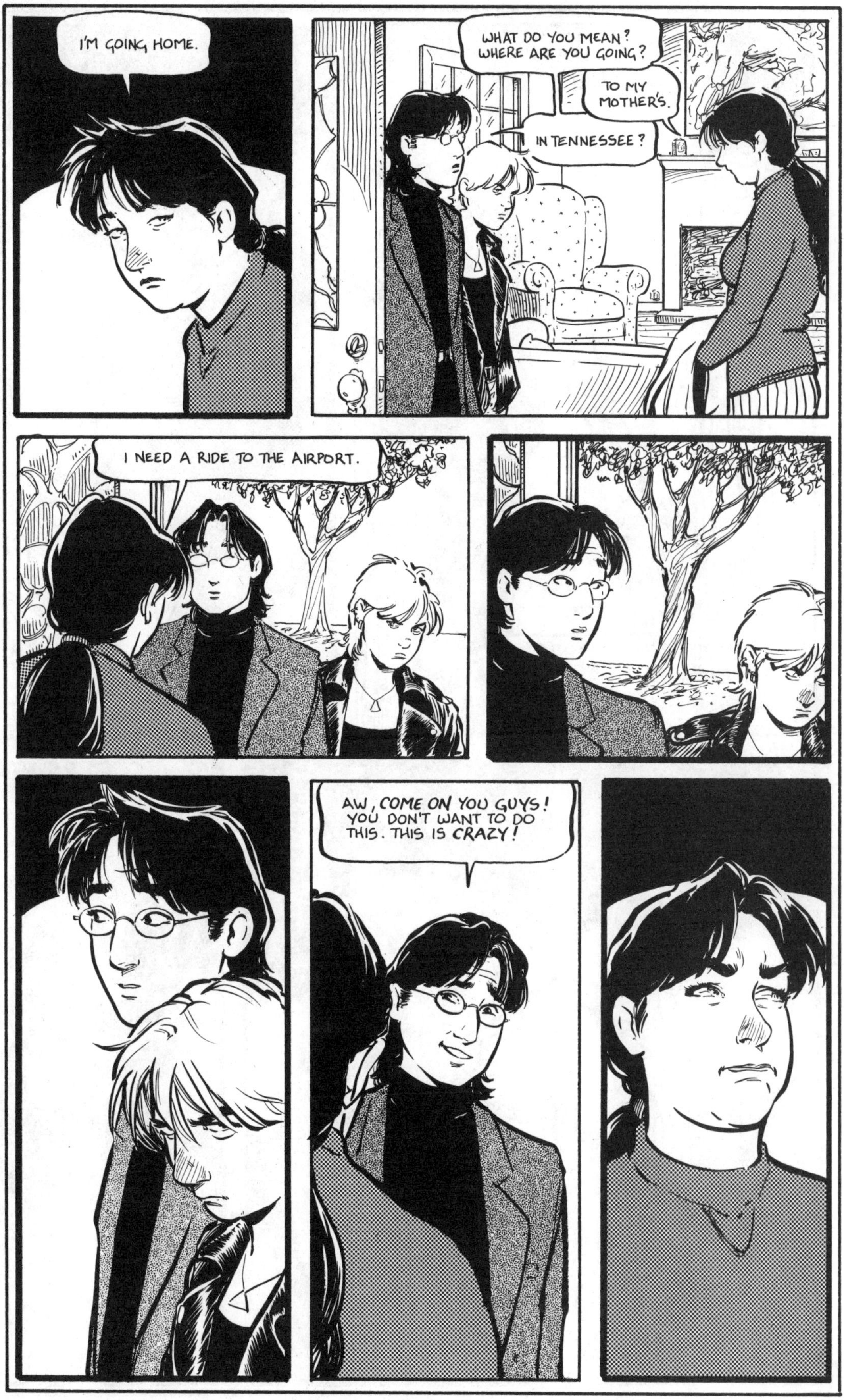
I'M GOING HOME.
WHAT DO YOU MEAN? WHERE ARE YOU GOING?
TO MY MOTHER'S.
IN TENNESSEE?
I NEED A RIDE TO THE AIRPORT.
AW, COME ON YOU GUYS! YOU DON'T WANT TO DO THIS. THIS IS CRAZY!

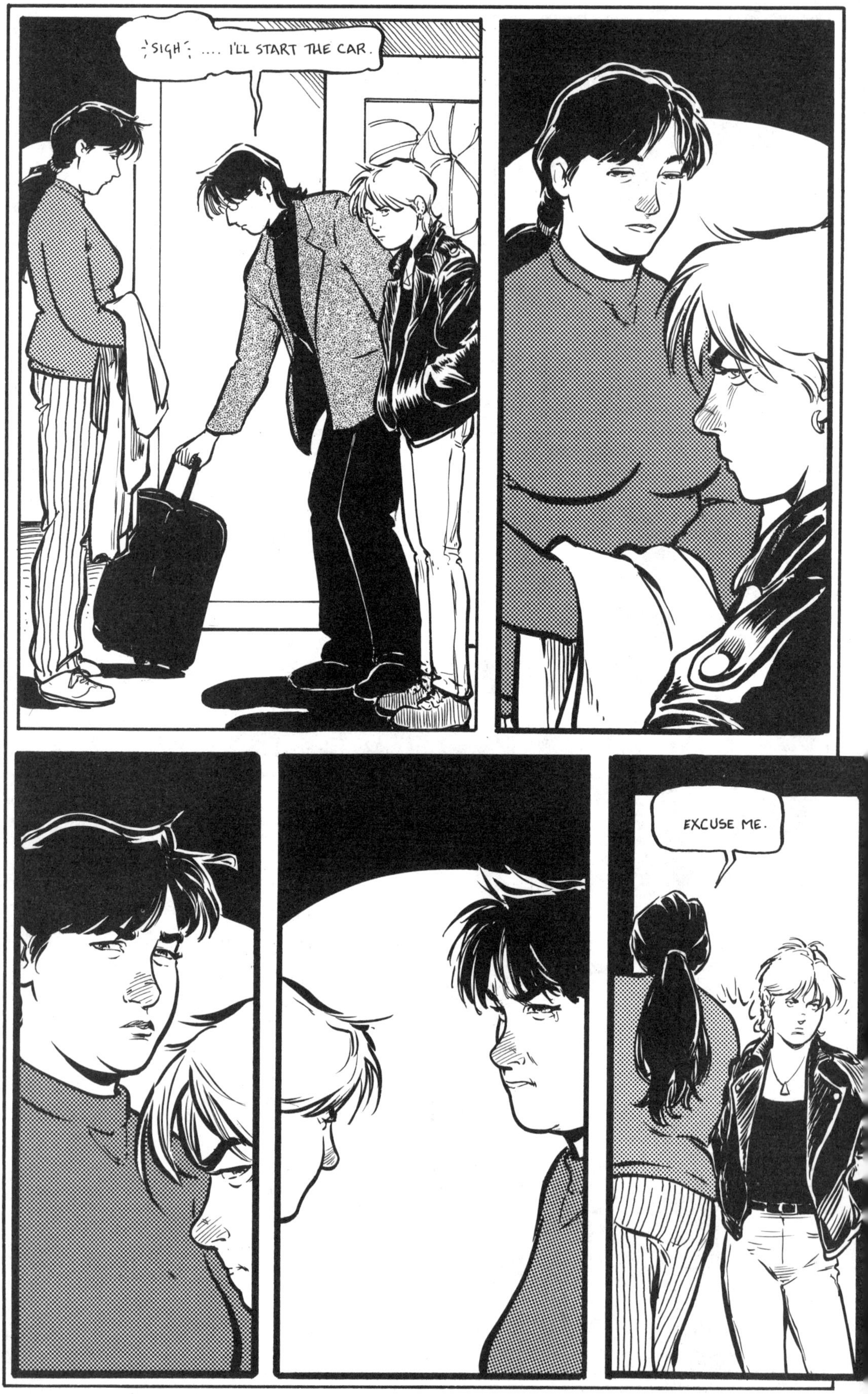
SIGH .... I'LL START THE CAR.
EXCUSE ME.

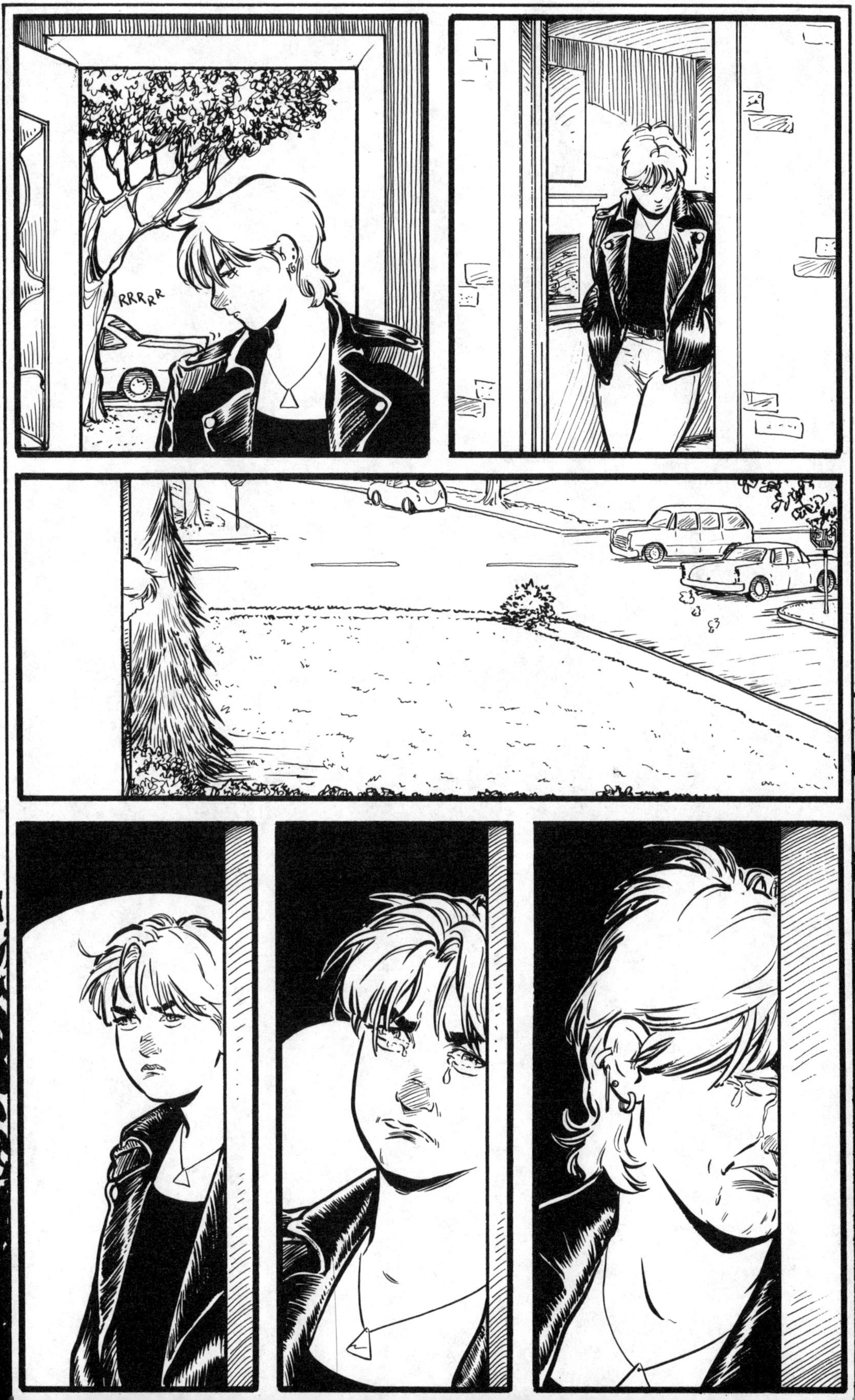
RRRRR

IT'S TOO DARK TODAY
words and music by Griffin Silver

It's too dark today
The sun ain't out and the room's never seemed this way and there's a shadow
Where there's never been before on your pillow
I'm seeing things I never saw in this house alone
It's much too dark today
I been pacing
Or lying around
Don't want to face it
What do you do when you feel this way
When there's years to go and it started today
What can I do to keep from going down
I was thinking of going out but
It's too dark today
Hardly a change from the night to the day
Did you walk out on me or did I send you away
God it's really clear that I can't run things from here
What do you do when you feel this way
When there's years to go and it started today
What can I do to keep from going down
I was thinking of going out but
It's too dark today
It's too dark today
It's too dark today
It's too dark today
It's too dark today
It's too dark today
It's too dark today
It's too dark today
It's too dark today
It's too dark today
It's too dark today
It's too dark today
It's too dark today
It's too dark today
It's too dark today
It's too dark today
It's too dark today
It's too dark today
It's too dark today
It's too dark today
It's too dark today
It's too dark today
It's too dark today
It's too dark today

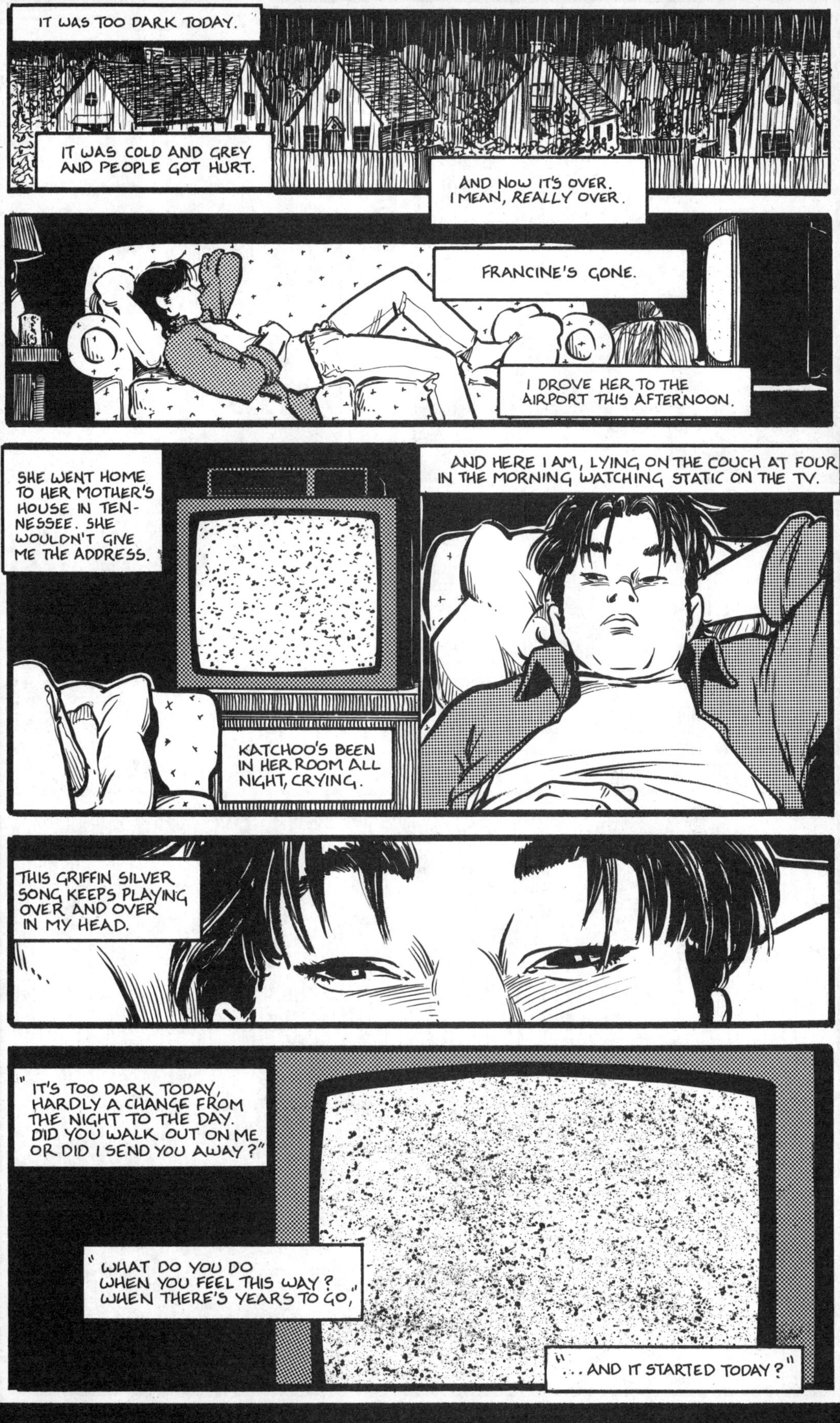

IT WAS TOO DARK TODAY.
IT WAS COLD AND GREY AND PEOPLE GOT HURT.
AND NOW IT'S OVER. I MEAN, REALLY OVER.
FRANCINE'S GONE.
I DROVE HER TO THE AIRPORT THIS AFTERNOON.
SHE WENT HOME TO HER MOTHER'S HOUSE IN TEN-NESSEE. SHE WOULDN'T GIVE ME THE ADDRESS.
AND HERE I AM, LYING ON THE COUCH AT FOUR IN THE MORNING WATCHING STATIC ON THE TV.
KATCHOO'S BEEN IN HER ROOM ALL NIGHT, CRYING.
THIS GRIFFIN SILVER SONG KEEPS PLAYING OVER AND OVER IN MY HEAD.
"IT'S TOO DARK TODAY, HARDLY A CHANGE FROM THE NIGHT TO THE DAY. DID YOU WALK OUT ON ME OR DID I SEND YOU AWAY?"
"WHAT DO YOU DO WHEN YOU FEEL THIS WAY? WHEN THERE'S YEARS TO GO,"
"...AND IT STARTED TODAY?"

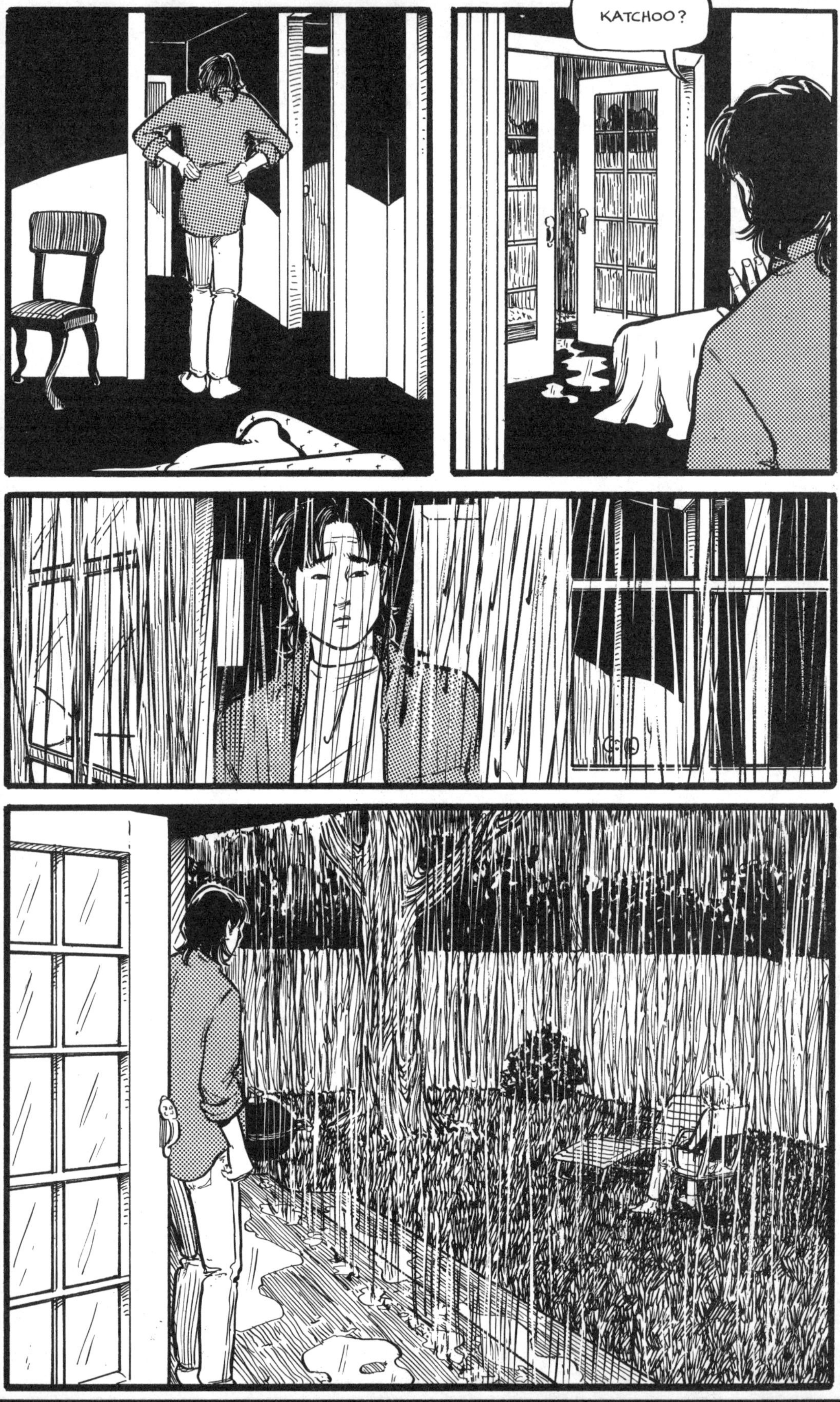
KATCHOO?

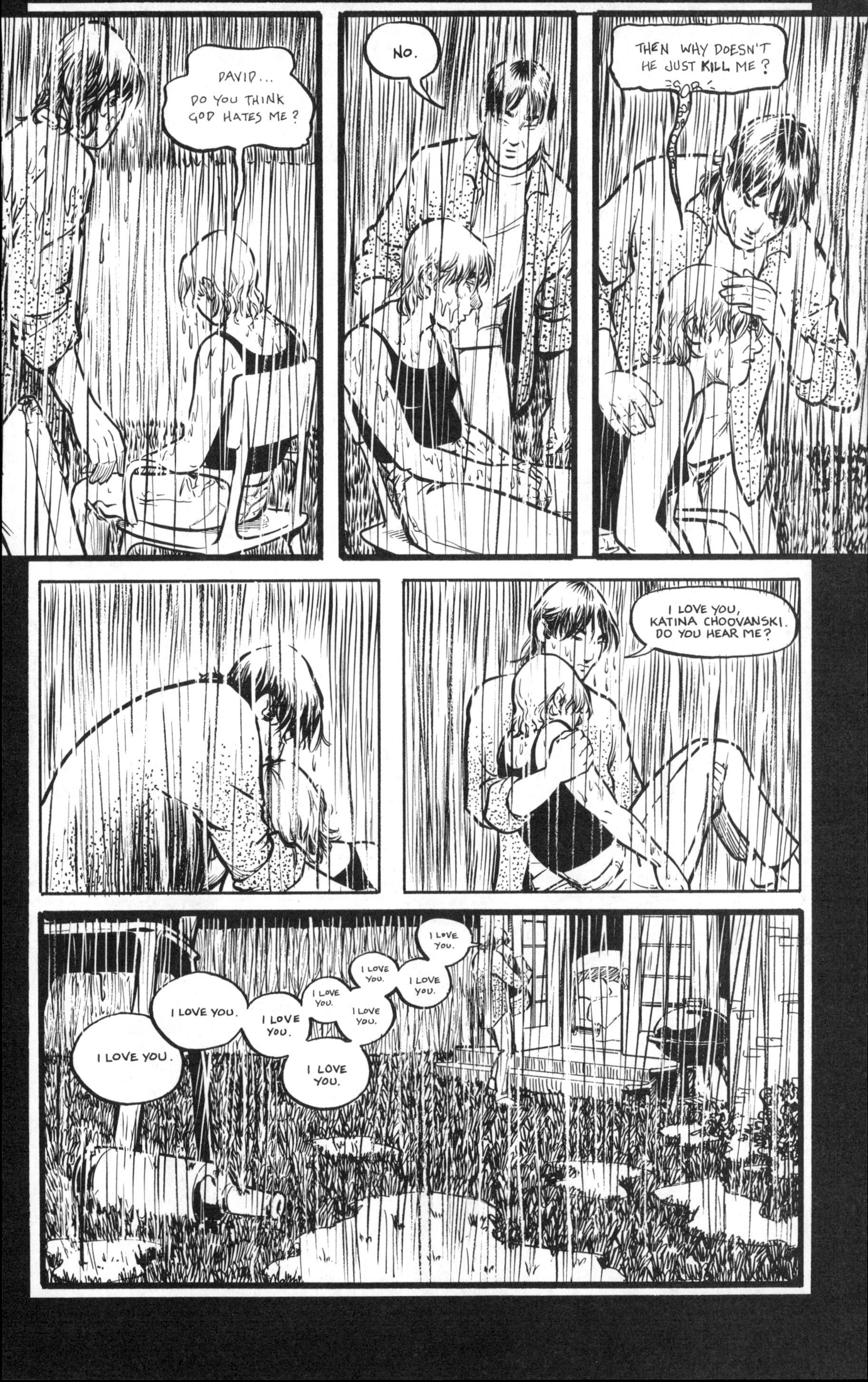
DAVID...
DO YOU THINK GOD HATES ME?
NO.
THEN WHY DOESN'T HE JUST KILL ME?
SOB
I LOVE YOU, KATINA CHOOVANSKI. DO YOU HEAR ME?
I LOVE YOU.
I LOVE YOU.
I LOVE YOU.
I LOVE YOU.
I LOVE YOU.
I LOVE YOU.
I LOVE YOU.
I LOVE YOU.
I LOVE YOU.

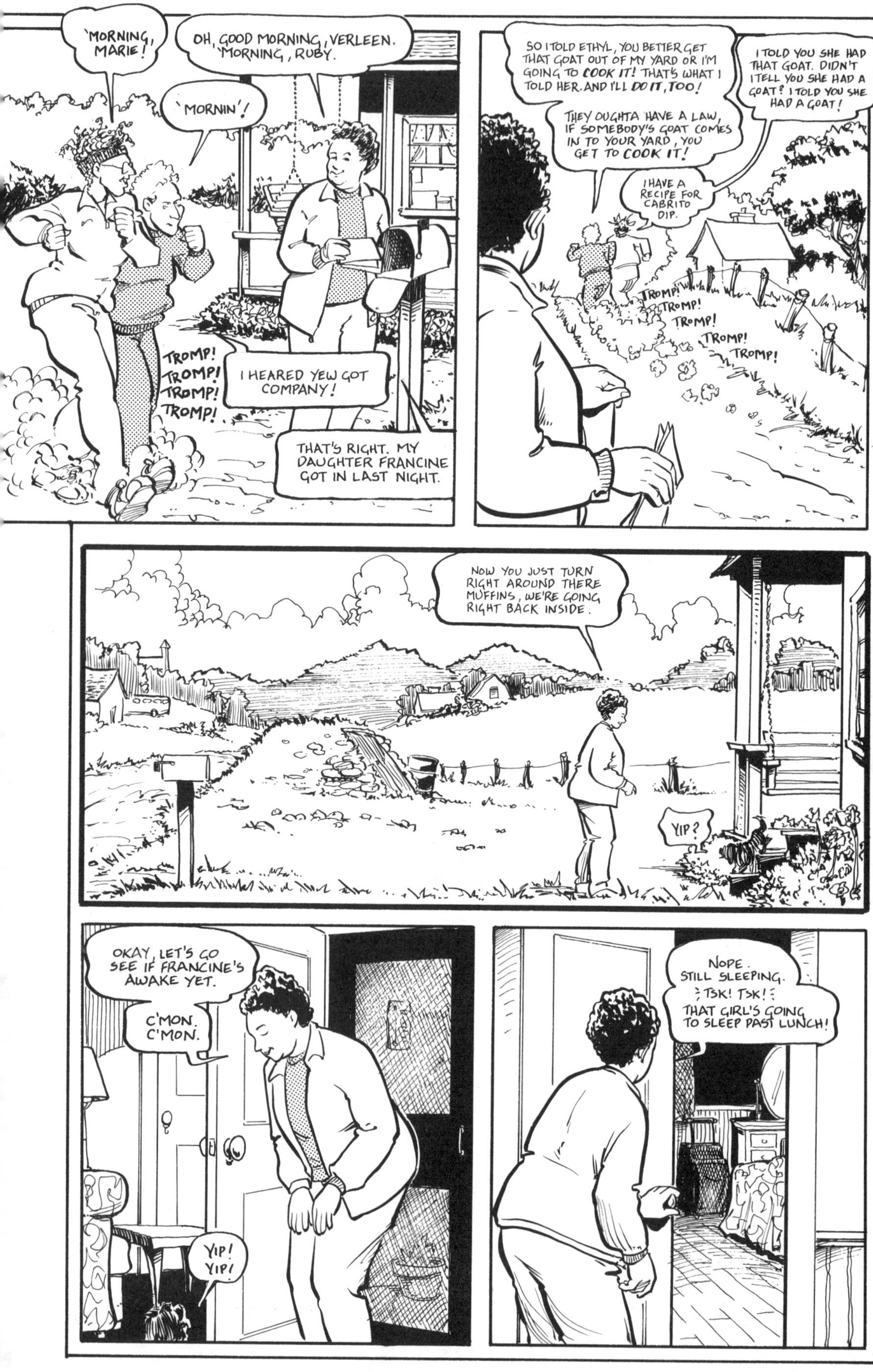

'MORNING, MARIE!
OH, GOOD MORNING, VERLEEN. 'MORNING, RUBY.
'MORNIN'!
TROMP! TROMP! TROMP! TROMP!
I HEARED YEW GOT COMPANY!
THAT'S RIGHT. MY DAUGHTER FRANCINE GOT IN LAST NIGHT.
SO I TOLD ETHYL, YOU BETTER GET THAT GOAT OUT OF MY YARD OR I'M GOING TO COOK IT! THAT'S WHAT I TOLD HER. AND I'LL DO IT, TOO!
THEY OUGHTA HAVE A LAW, IF SOMEBODY'S GOAT COMES IN TO YOUR YARD, YOU GET TO COOK IT!
I TOLD YOU SHE HAD THAT GOAT. DIDN'T I TELL YOU SHE HAD A GOAT? I TOLD YOU SHE HAD A GOAT!
I HAVE A RECIPE FOR CABRITO DIP.
TROMP! TROMP! TROMP! TROMP! TROMP!
NOW YOU JUST TURN RIGHT AROUND THERE MUFFINS, WE'RE GOING RIGHT BACK INSIDE.
YIP?
OKAY, LET'S GO SEE IF FRANCINE'S AWAKE YET.
C'MON. C'MON.
YIP! YIP!
NOPE. STILL SLEEPING.
TSK! TSK!
THAT GIRL'S GOING TO SLEEP PAST LUNCH!

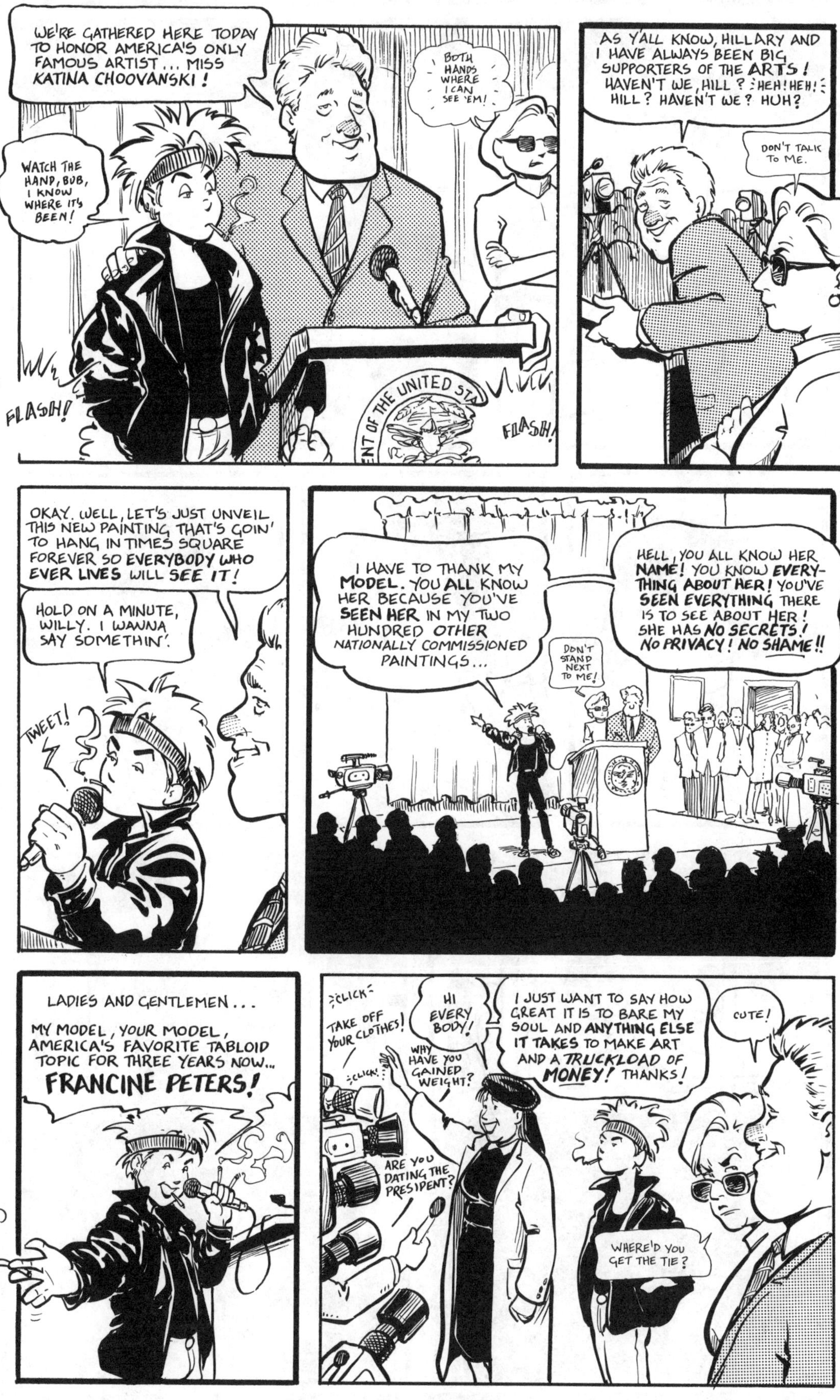
WE'RE GATHERED HERE TODAY TO HONOR AMERICA'S ONLY FAMOUS ARTIST... MISS KATINA CHOOVANSKI!
BOTH HANDS WHERE I CAN SEE 'EM!
WATCH THE HAND, BUB, I KNOW WHERE IT'S BEEN!
FLASH!
FLASH!
AS Y'ALL KNOW, HILLARY AND I HAVE ALWAYS BEEN BIG SUPPORTERS OF THE ARTS! HAVEN'T WE, HILL? HEH! HEH! HILL? HAVEN'T WE? HUH?
DON'T TALK TO ME.
OKAY. WELL, LET'S JUST UNVEIL THIS NEW PAINTING THAT'S GOIN' TO HANG IN TIMES SQUARE FOREVER SO EVERYBODY WHO EVER LIVES WILL SEE IT!
HOLD ON A MINUTE, WILLY. I WANNA SAY SOMETHIN'.
TWEET!
I HAVE TO THANK MY MODEL. YOU ALL KNOW HER BECAUSE YOU'VE SEEN HER IN MY TWO HUNDRED OTHER NATIONALLY COMMISSIONED PAINTINGS...
HELL, YOU ALL KNOW HER NAME! YOU KNOW EVERYTHING ABOUT HER! YOU'VE SEEN EVERYTHING THERE IS TO SEE ABOUT HER! SHE HAS NO SECRETS! NO PRIVACY! NO SHAME!!
DON'T STAND NEXT TO ME!
LADIES AND GENTLEMEN...
MY MODEL, YOUR MODEL, AMERICA'S FAVORITE TABLOID TOPIC FOR THREE YEARS NOW... FRANCINE PETERS!
CLICK
TAKE OFF YOUR CLOTHES!
CLICK!
HI EVERYBODY!
WHY HAVE YOU GAINED WEIGHT?
I JUST WANT TO SAY HOW GREAT IT IS TO BARE MY SOUL AND ANYTHING ELSE IT TAKES TO MAKE ART AND A TRUCKLOAD OF MONEY! THANKS!
CUTE!
ARE YOU DATING THE PRESIDENT?
WHERE'D YOU GET THE TIE?

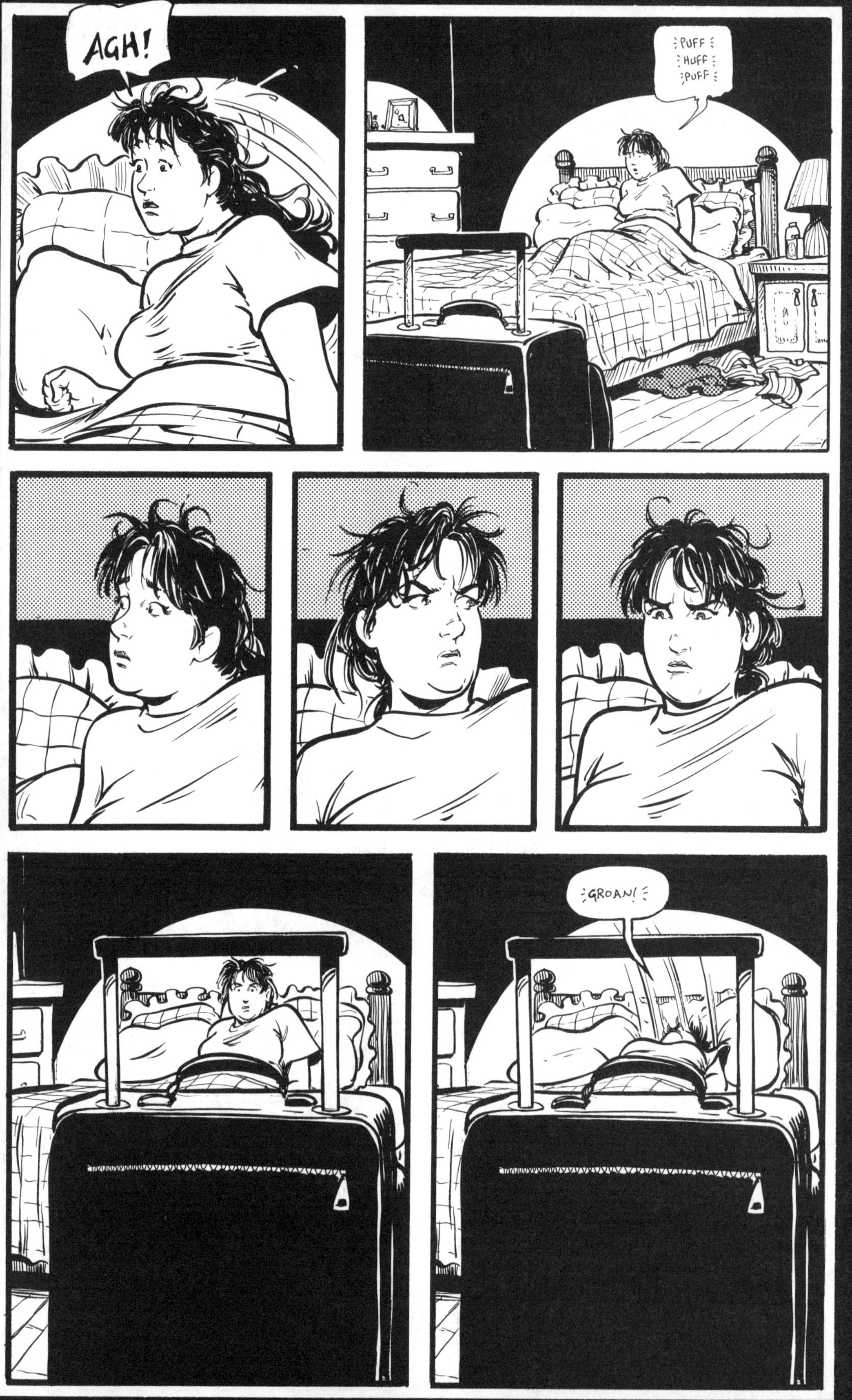
AGH!
PUFF
HUFF
PUFF
GROAN!

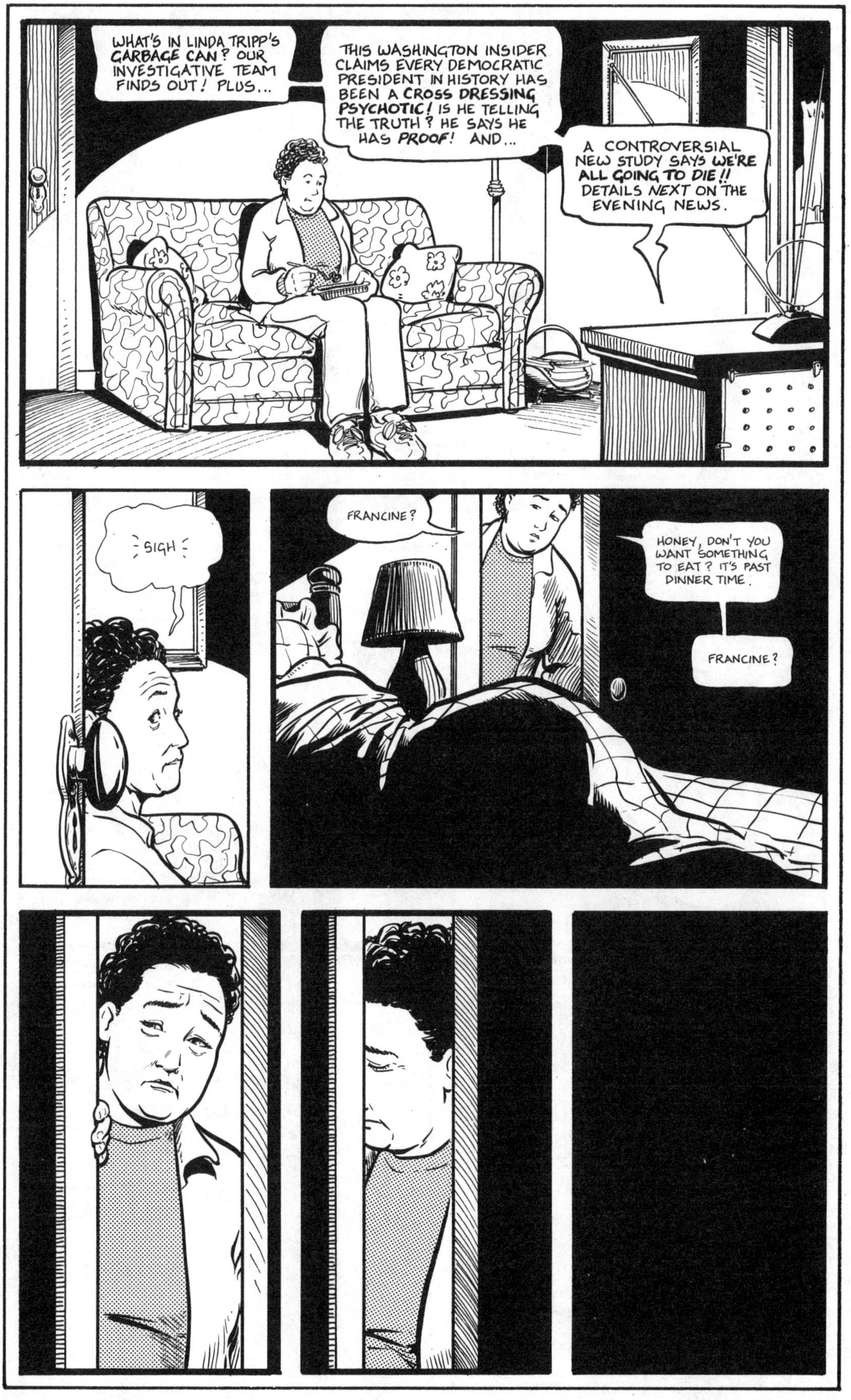

WHAT'S IN LINDA TRIPP'S GARBAGE CAN? OUR INVESTIGATIVE TEAM FINDS OUT! PLUS...
THIS WASHINGTON INSIDER CLAIMS EVERY DEMOCRATIC PRESIDENT IN HISTORY HAS BEEN A CROSS DRESSING PSYCHOTIC! IS HE TELLING THE TRUTH? HE SAYS HE HAS PROOF! AND...
A CONTROVERSIAL NEW STUDY SAYS WE'RE ALL GOING TO DIE!! DETAILS NEXT ON THE EVENING NEWS.
SIGH
FRANCINE?
HONEY, DON'T YOU WANT SOMETHING TO EAT? IT'S PAST DINNER TIME.
FRANCINE?

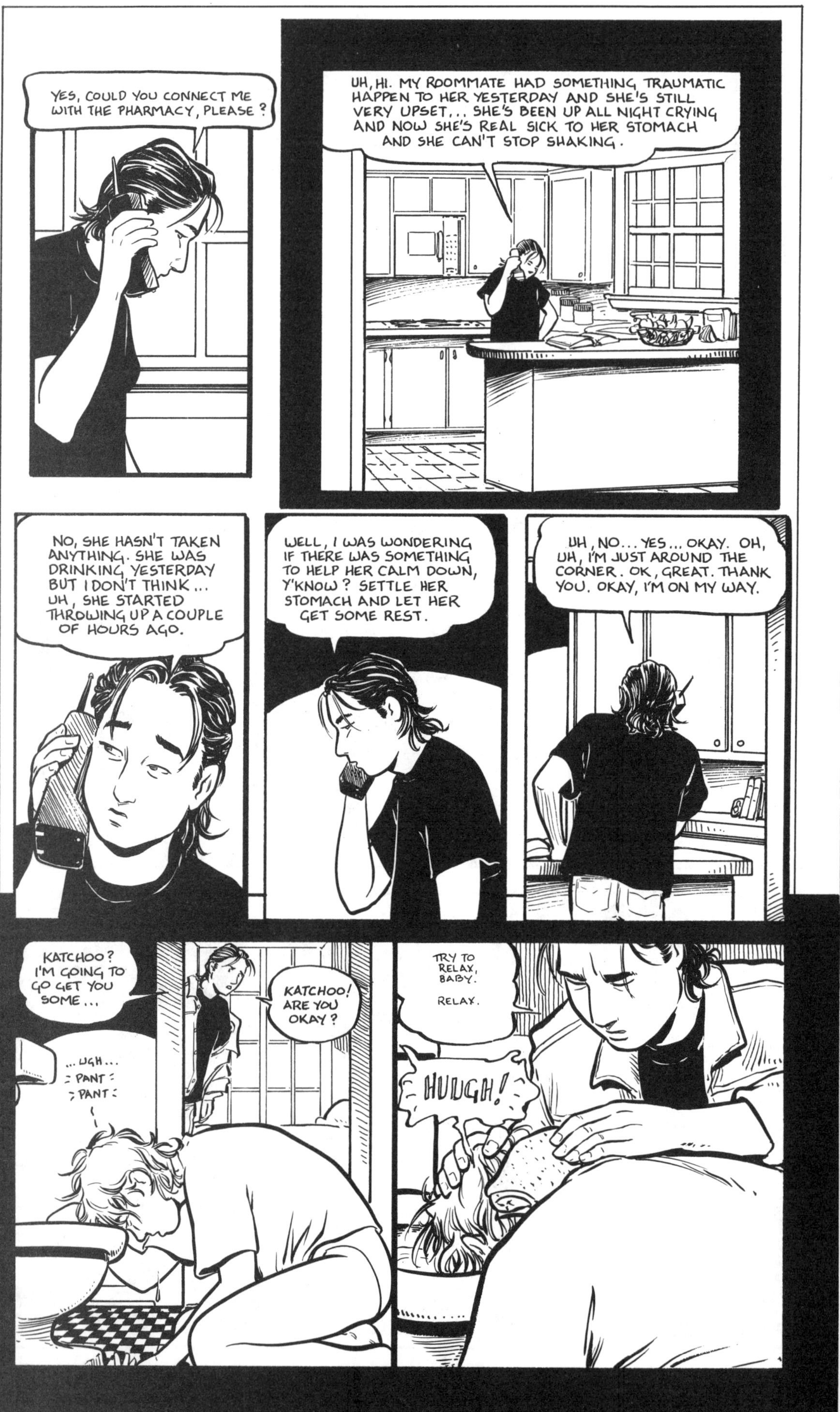
YES, COULD YOU CONNECT ME WITH THE PHARMACY, PLEASE?
UH, HI. MY ROOMMATE HAD SOMETHING TRAUMATIC HAPPEN TO HER YESTERDAY AND SHE'S STILL VERY UPSET... SHE'S BEEN UP ALL NIGHT CRYING AND NOW SHE'S REAL SICK TO HER STOMACH AND SHE CAN'T STOP SHAKING.
NO, SHE HASN'T TAKEN ANYTHING. SHE WAS DRINKING YESTERDAY BUT I DON'T THINK... UH, SHE STARTED THROWING UP A COUPLE OF HOURS AGO.
WELL, I WAS WONDERING IF THERE WAS SOMETHING TO HELP HER CALM DOWN, Y'KNOW? SETTLE HER STOMACH AND LET HER GET SOME REST.
UH, NO... YES... OKAY. OH, UH, I'M JUST AROUND THE CORNER. OK, GREAT. THANK YOU. OKAY, I'M ON MY WAY.
KATCHOO? I'M GOING TO GO GET YOU SOME...
...UGH...
PANT
PANT
KATCHOO! ARE YOU OKAY?
TRY TO RELAX, BABY.
RELAX.
HUUGH!

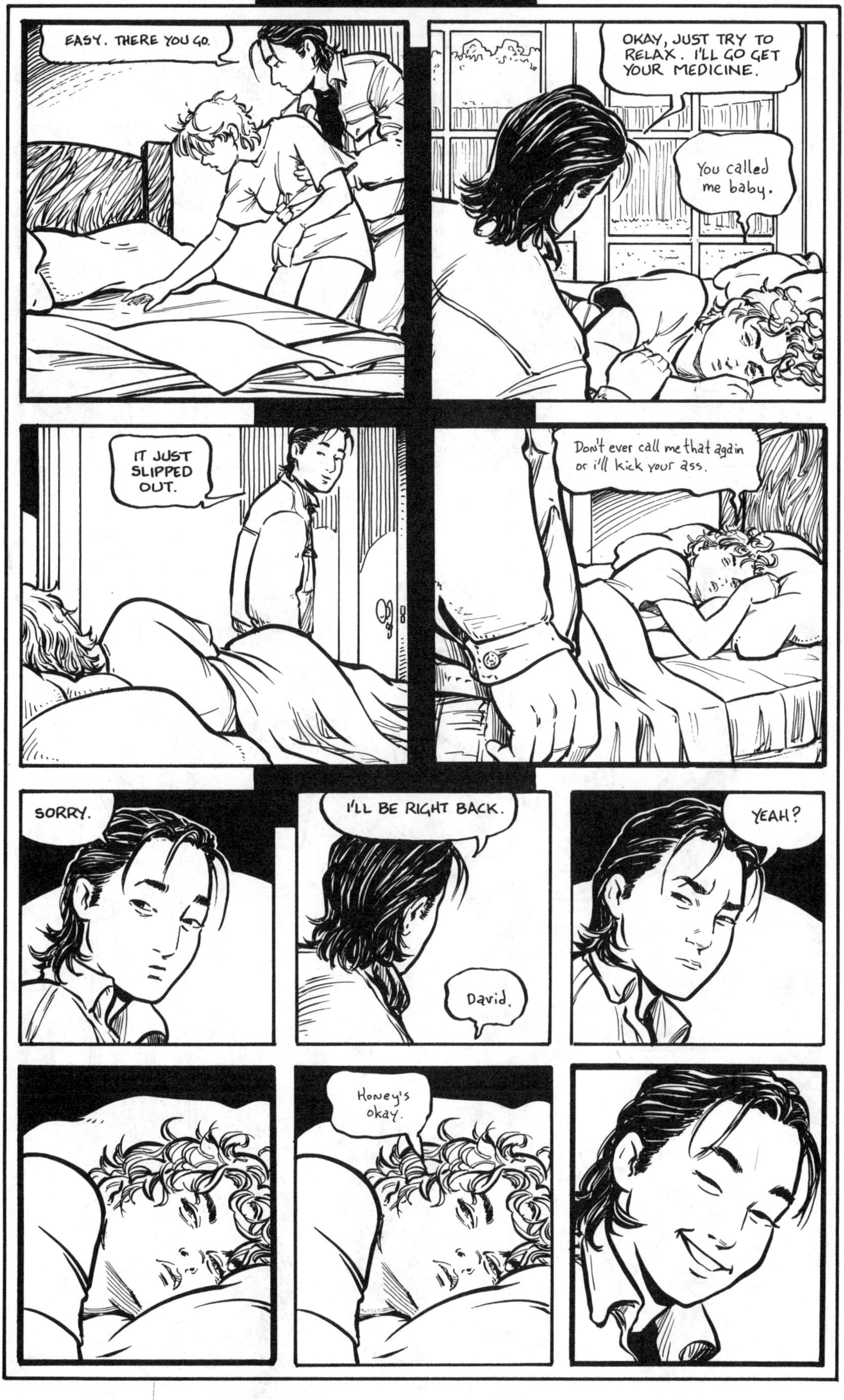
EASY. THERE YOU GO.
OKAY, JUST TRY TO RELAX. I'LL GO GET YOUR MEDICINE.
You called me baby.
IT JUST SLIPPED OUT.
Don't ever call me that again or i'll kick your ass.
SORRY.
I'LL BE RIGHT BACK.
David.
YEAH?
Honey's okay.

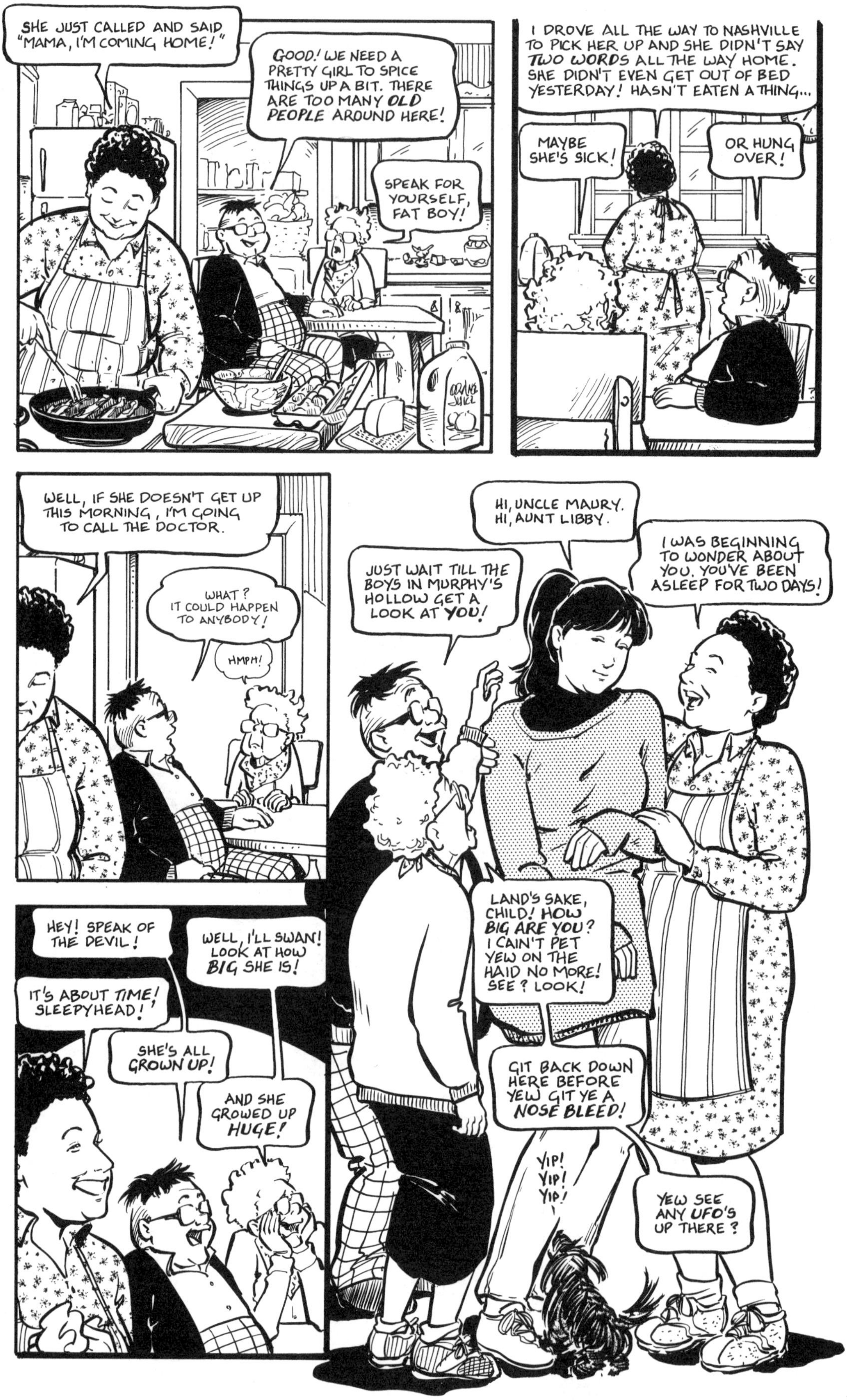
SHE JUST CALLED AND SAID "MAMA, I'M COMING HOME!"
GOOD! WE NEED A PRETTY GIRL TO SPICE THINGS UP A BIT. THERE ARE TOO MANY OLD PEOPLE AROUND HERE!
SPEAK FOR YOURSELF, FAT BOY!
I DROVE ALL THE WAY TO NASHVILLE TO PICK HER UP AND SHE DIDN'T SAY TWO WORDS ALL THE WAY HOME. SHE DIDN'T EVEN GET OUT OF BED YESTERDAY! HASN'T EATEN A THING...
MAYBE SHE'S SICK!
OR HUNG OVER!
WELL, IF SHE DOESN'T GET UP THIS MORNING, I'M GOING TO CALL THE DOCTOR.
WHAT? IT COULD HAPPEN TO ANYBODY!
HMPH!
HEY! SPEAK OF THE DEVIL!
WELL, I'LL SWAN! LOOK AT HOW BIG SHE IS!
IT'S ABOUT TIME! SLEEPYHEAD!
SHE'S ALL GROWN UP!
AND SHE GROWED UP HUGE!
HI, UNCLE MAURY. HI, AUNT LIBBY.
JUST WAIT TILL THE BOYS IN MURPHY'S HOLLOW GET A LOOK AT YOU!
I WAS BEGINNING TO WONDER ABOUT YOU. YOU'VE BEEN ASLEEP FOR TWO DAYS!
LAND'S SAKE, CHILD! HOW BIG ARE YOU? I CAIN'T PET YEW ON THE HAID NO MORE! SEE? LOOK!
GIT BACK DOWN HERE BEFORE YEW GIT YE A NOSE BLEED!
YIP! YIP! YIP!
YEW SEE ANY UFO'S UP THERE?

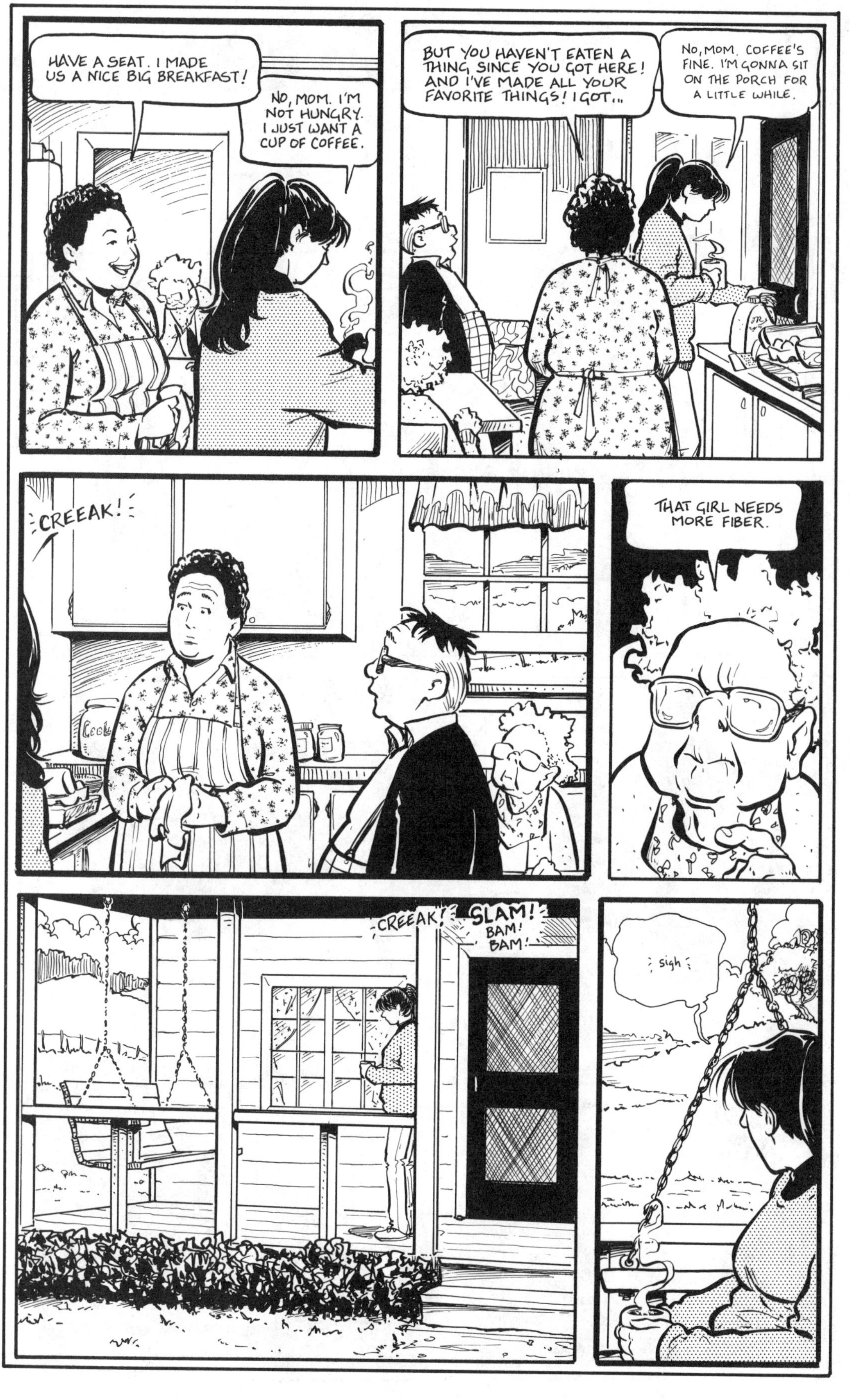

HAVE A SEAT. I MADE US A NICE BIG BREAKFAST!
NO, MOM. I'M NOT HUNGRY. I JUST WANT A CUP OF COFFEE.
BUT YOU HAVEN'T EATEN A THING SINCE YOU GOT HERE! AND I'VE MADE ALL YOUR FAVORITE THINGS! I GOT...
NO, MOM. COFFEE'S FINE. I'M GONNA SIT ON THE PORCH FOR A LITTLE WHILE.
CREEAK!
THAT GIRL NEEDS MORE FIBER.
CREEAK!
SLAM!
BAM!
BAM!
sigh

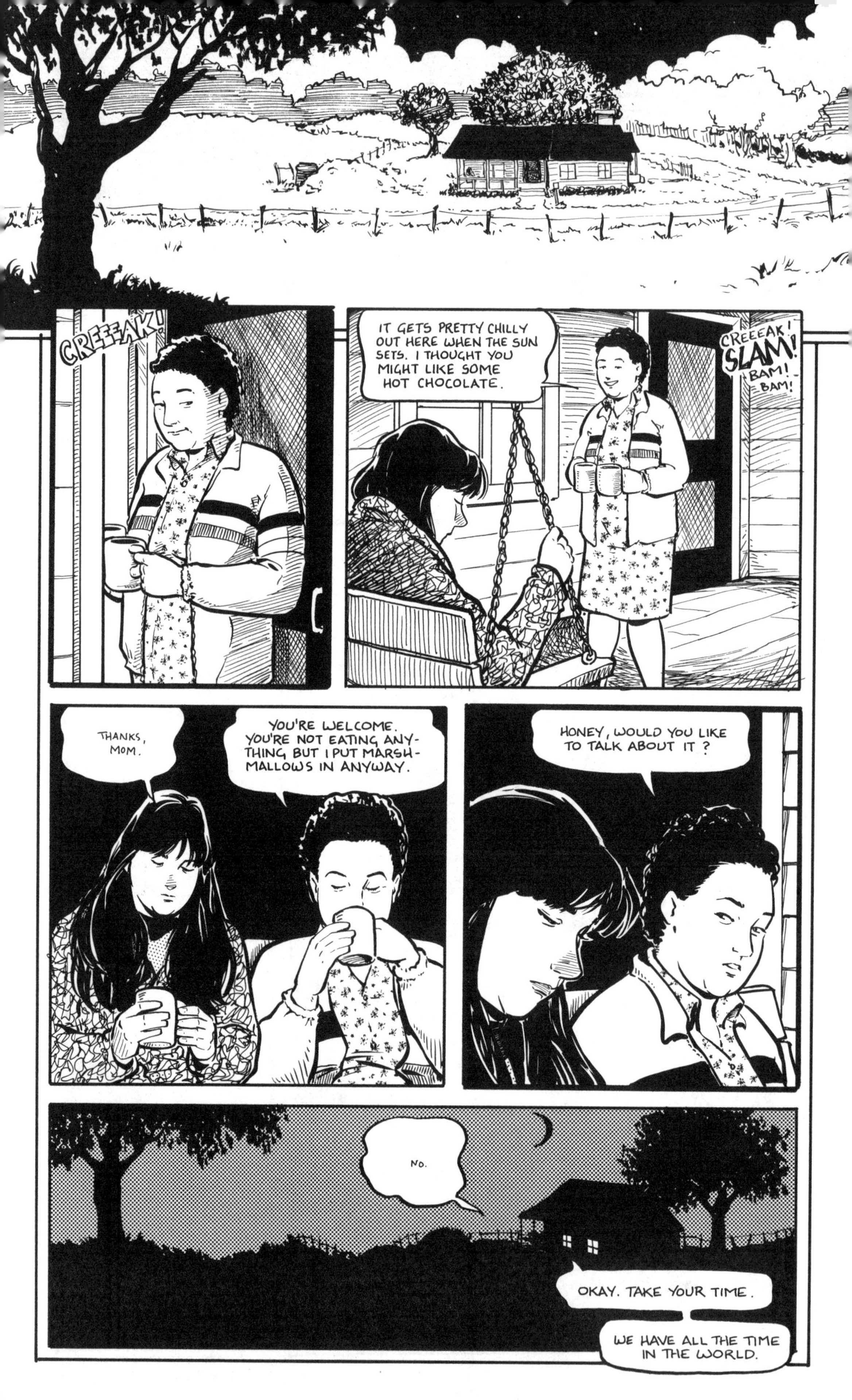
CREEEAK!
IT GETS PRETTY CHILLY OUT HERE WHEN THE SUN SETS. I THOUGHT YOU MIGHT LIKE SOME HOT CHOCOLATE.
CREEEAK! SLAM! BAM! BAM!
THANKS, MOM.
YOU'RE WELCOME. YOU'RE NOT EATING ANYTHING BUT I PUT MARSHMALLOWS IN ANYWAY.
HONEY, WOULD YOU LIKE TO TALK ABOUT IT ?
NO.
OKAY. TAKE YOUR TIME.
WE HAVE ALL THE TIME IN THE WORLD.

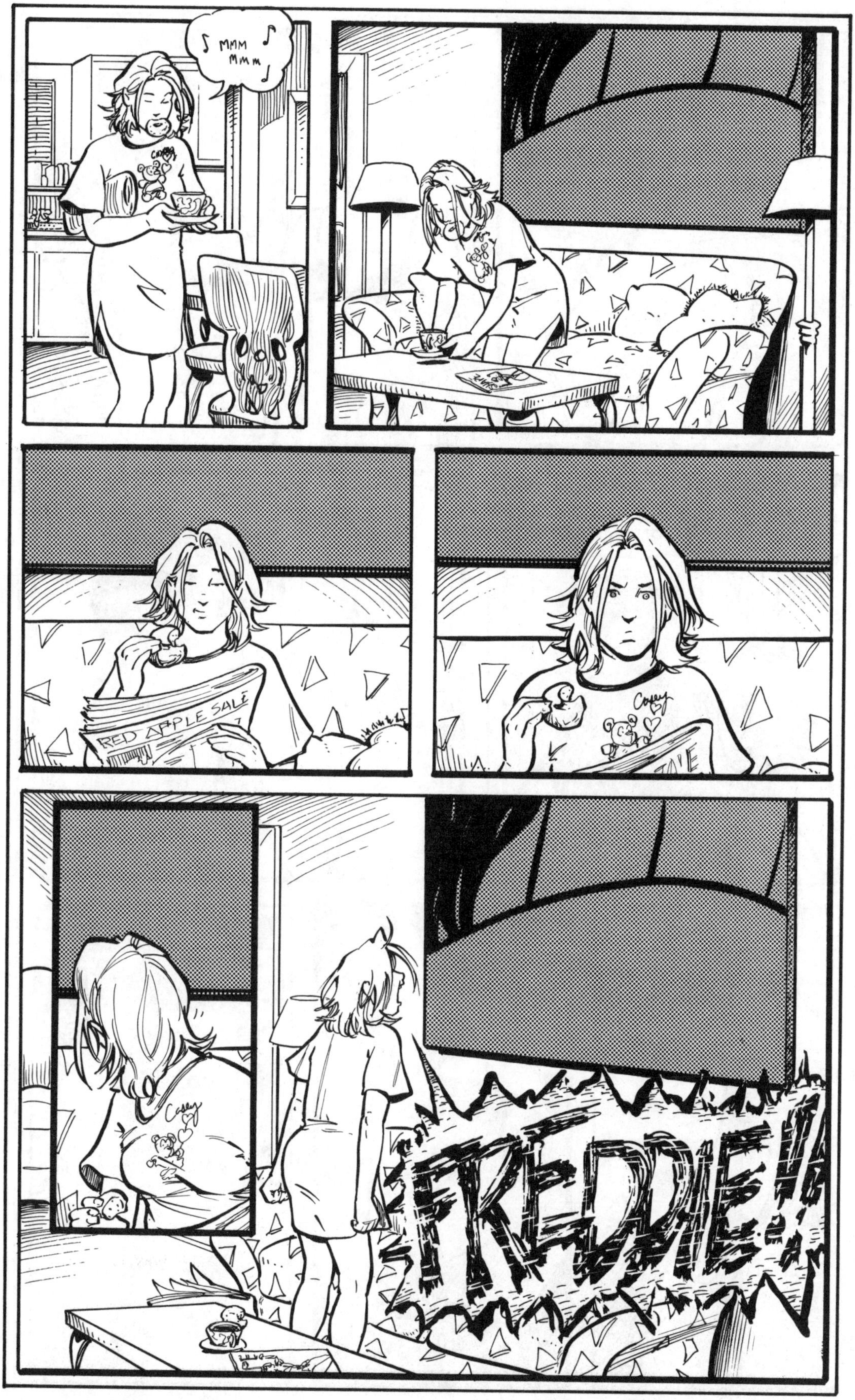
MMM MMM
RED APPLE SALE
FREDDIE!!

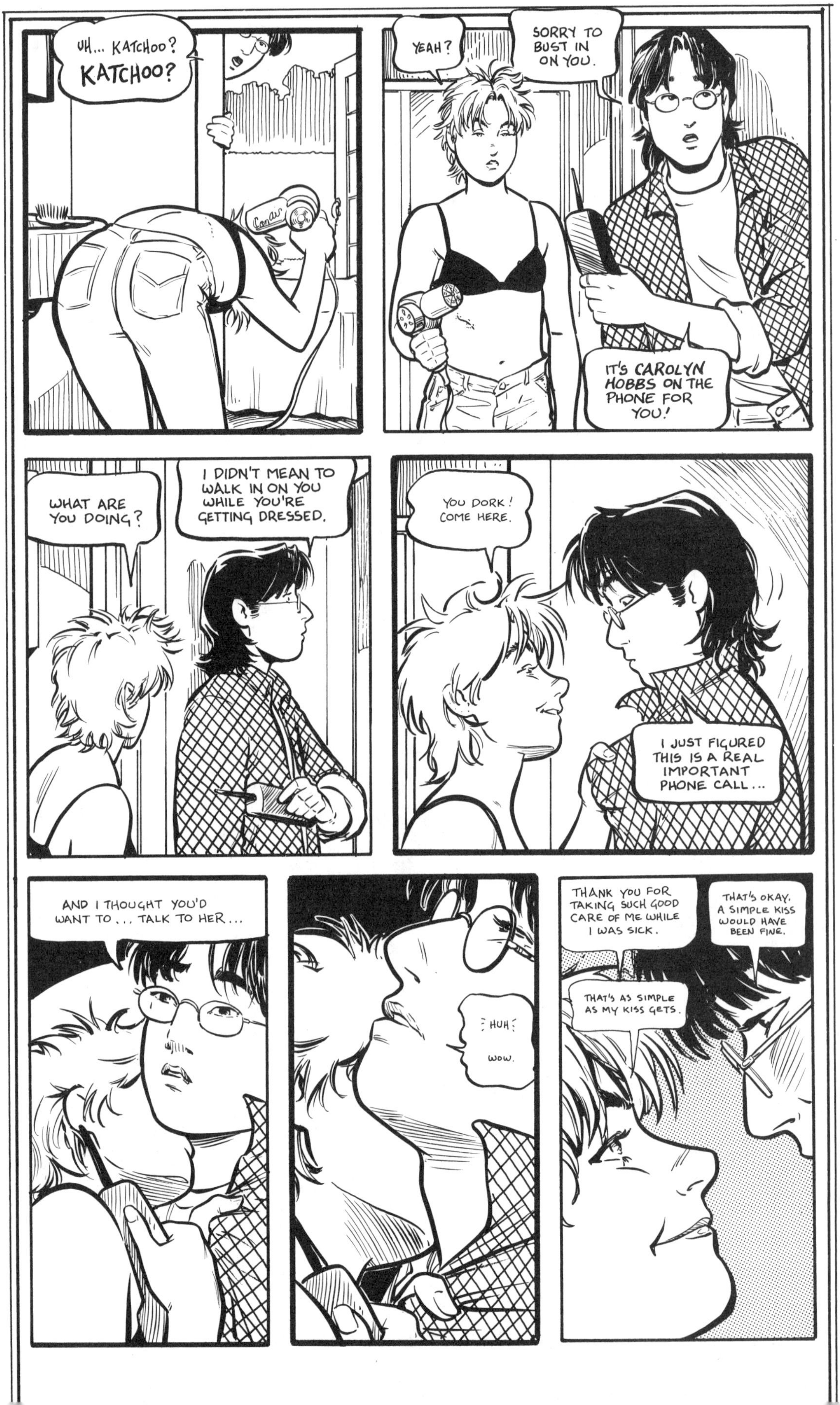
UH... KATCHOO? KATCHOO?
YEAH?
SORRY TO BUST IN ON YOU.
IT'S CAROLYN HOBBS ON THE PHONE FOR YOU!
WHAT ARE YOU DOING?
I DIDN'T MEAN TO WALK IN ON YOU WHILE YOU'RE GETTING DRESSED.
YOU DORK! COME HERE.
I JUST FIGURED THIS IS A REAL IMPORTANT PHONE CALL...
AND I THOUGHT YOU'D WANT TO... TALK TO HER...
HUH
WOW.
THANK YOU FOR TAKING SUCH GOOD CARE OF ME WHILE I WAS SICK.
THAT'S OKAY. A SIMPLE KISS WOULD HAVE BEEN FINE.
THAT'S AS SIMPLE AS MY KISS GETS.

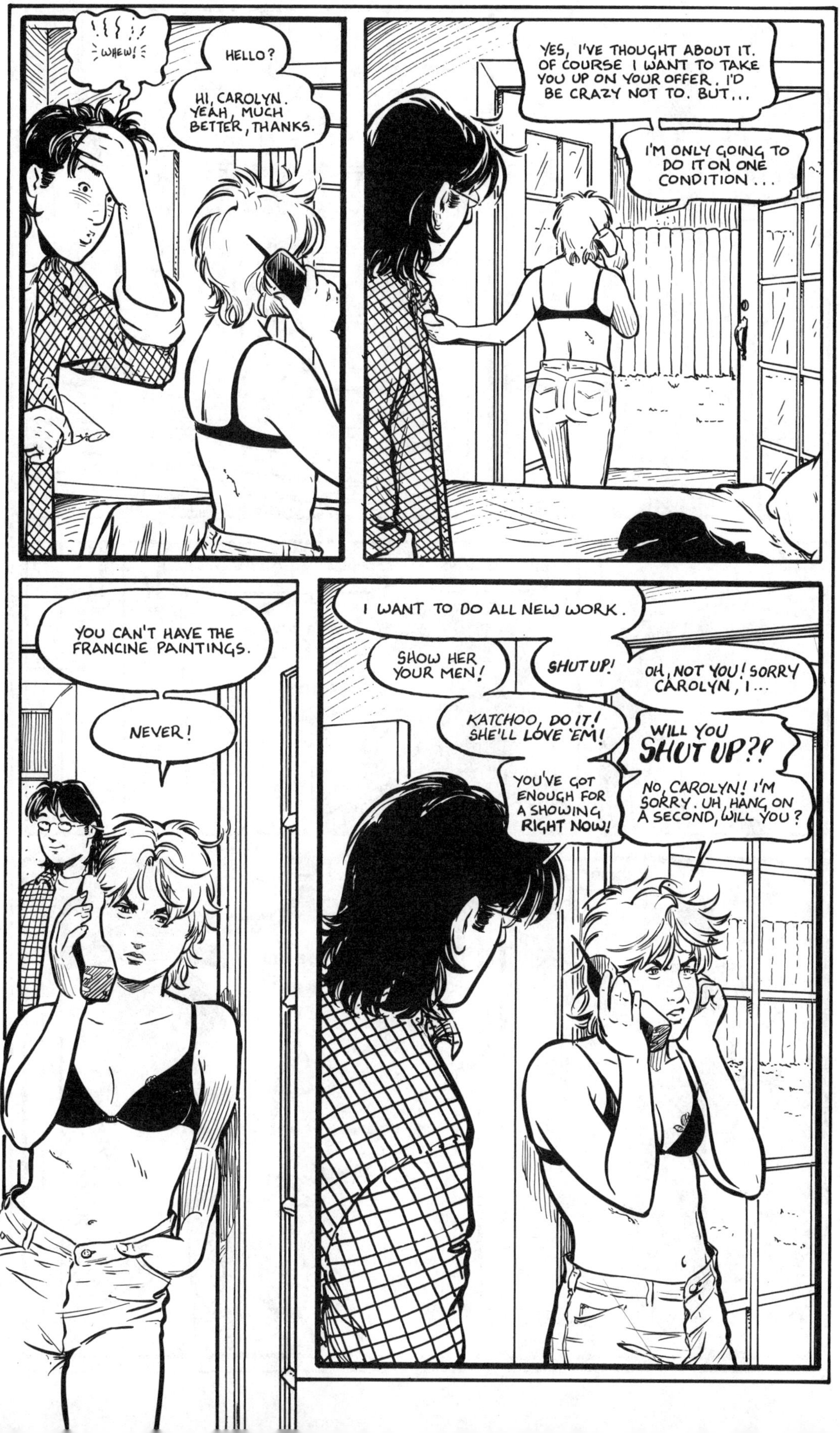
WHEW!
HELLO?
HI, CAROLYN. YEAH, MUCH BETTER, THANKS.
YES, I'VE THOUGHT ABOUT IT. OF COURSE I WANT TO TAKE YOU UP ON YOUR OFFER. I'D BE CRAZY NOT TO. BUT...
I'M ONLY GOING TO DO IT ON ONE CONDITION...
YOU CAN'T HAVE THE FRANCINE PAINTINGS.
NEVER!
I WANT TO DO ALL NEW WORK.
SHOW HER YOUR MEN!
SHUT UP!
OH, NOT YOU! SORRY CAROLYN, I...
KATCHOO, DO IT! SHE'LL LOVE 'EM!
WILL YOU SHUT UP?!
YOU'VE GOT ENOUGH FOR A SHOWING RIGHT NOW!
NO, CAROLYN! I'M SORRY. UH, HANG ON A SECOND, WILL YOU?

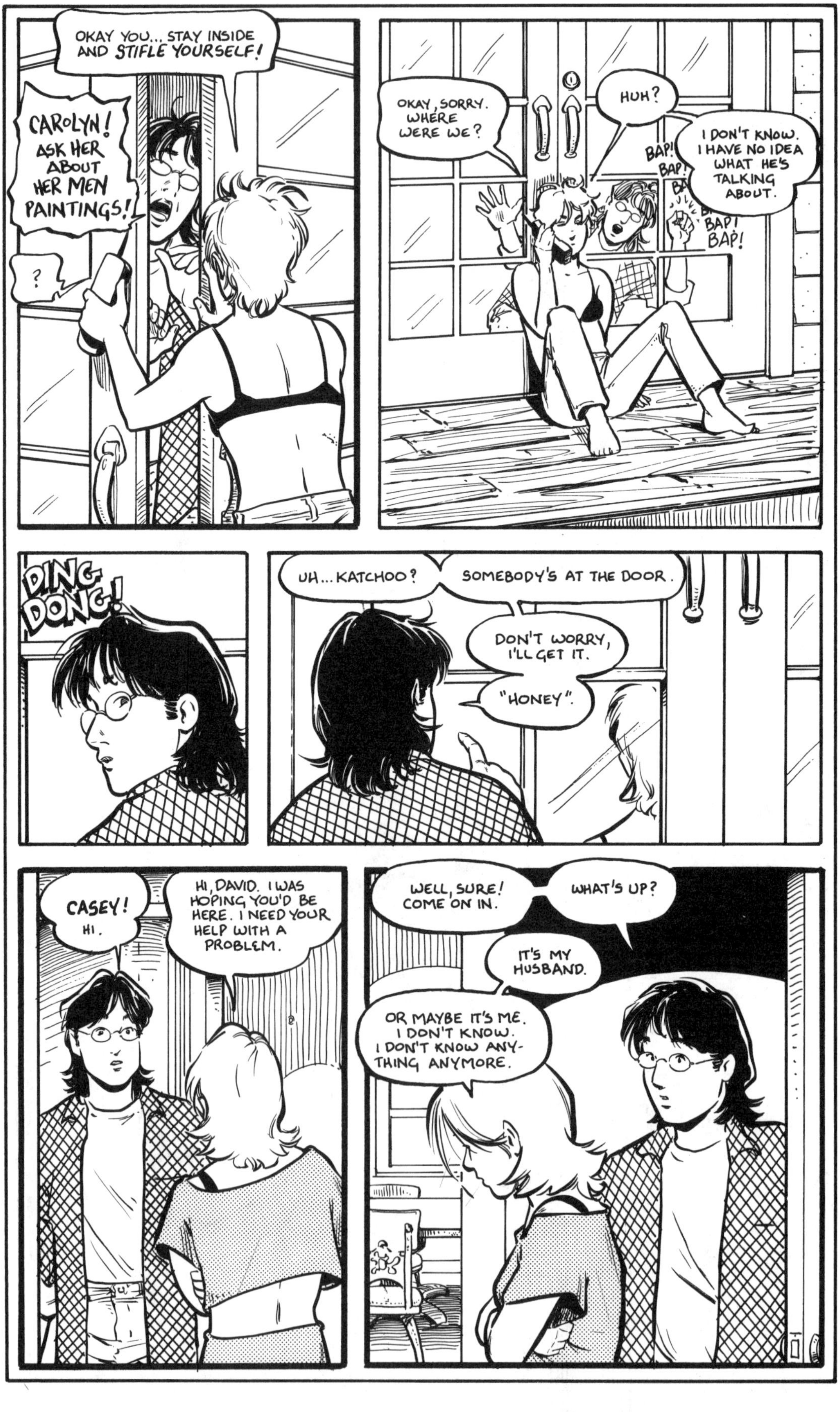

OKAY YOU... STAY INSIDE AND STIFLE YOURSELF!
CAROLYN! ASK HER ABOUT HER MEN PAINTINGS!
?
OKAY, SORRY. WHERE WERE WE?
HUH?
I DON'T KNOW. I HAVE NO IDEA WHAT HE'S TALKING ABOUT.
BAP! BAP! BAP! BAP!
DING DONG!
UH... KATCHOO?
SOMEBODY'S AT THE DOOR.
DON'T WORRY, I'LL GET IT.
"HONEY".
CASEY! HI.
HI, DAVID. I WAS HOPING YOU'D BE HERE. I NEED YOUR HELP WITH A PROBLEM.
WELL, SURE! COME ON IN.
WHAT'S UP?
IT'S MY HUSBAND.
OR MAYBE IT'S ME. I DON'T KNOW. I DON'T KNOW ANY-THING ANYMORE.

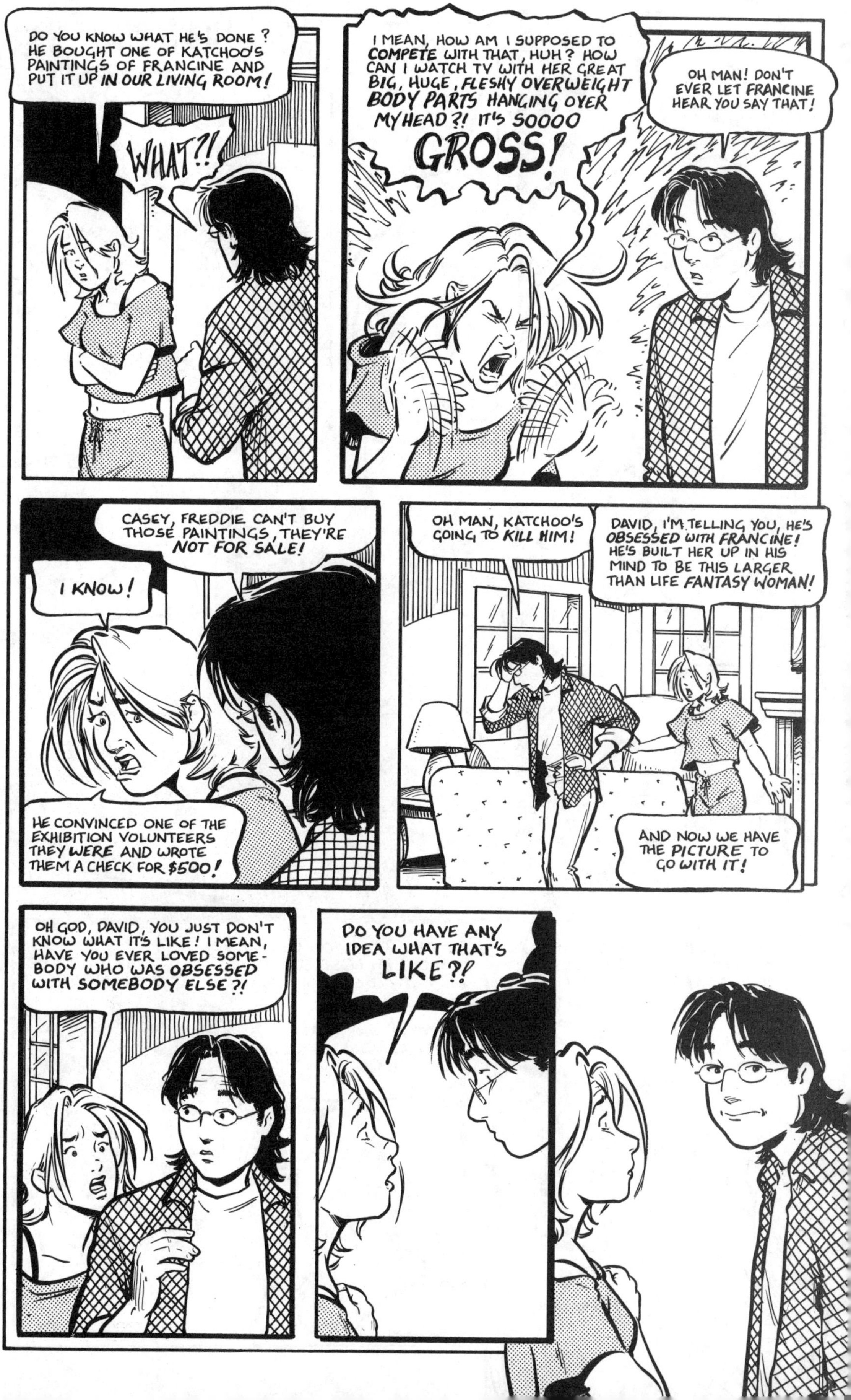

DO YOU KNOW WHAT HE'S DONE? HE BOUGHT ONE OF KATCHOO'S PAINTINGS OF FRANCINE AND PUT IT UP IN OUR LIVING ROOM!
WHAT?!
I MEAN, HOW AM I SUPPOSED TO COMPETE WITH THAT, HUH? HOW CAN I WATCH TV WITH HER GREAT BIG, HUGE, FLESHY OVERWEIGHT BODY PARTS HANGING OVER MY HEAD?! IT'S SOOOO GROSS!
OH MAN! DON'T EVER LET FRANCINE HEAR YOU SAY THAT!
CASEY, FREDDIE CAN'T BUY THOSE PAINTINGS, THEY'RE NOT FOR SALE!
I KNOW!
HE CONVINCED ONE OF THE EXHIBITION VOLUNTEERS THEY WERE AND WROTE THEM A CHECK FOR $500!
OH MAN, KATCHOO'S GOING TO KILL HIM!
DAVID, I'M TELLING YOU, HE'S OBSESSED WITH FRANCINE! HE'S BUILT HER UP IN HIS MIND TO BE THIS LARGER THAN LIFE FANTASY WOMAN!
AND NOW WE HAVE THE PICTURE TO GO WITH IT!
OH GOD, DAVID, YOU JUST DON'T KNOW WHAT IT'S LIKE! I MEAN, HAVE YOU EVER LOVED SOMEBODY WHO WAS OBSESSED WITH SOMEBODY ELSE?!
DO YOU HAVE ANY IDEA WHAT THAT'S LIKE?!

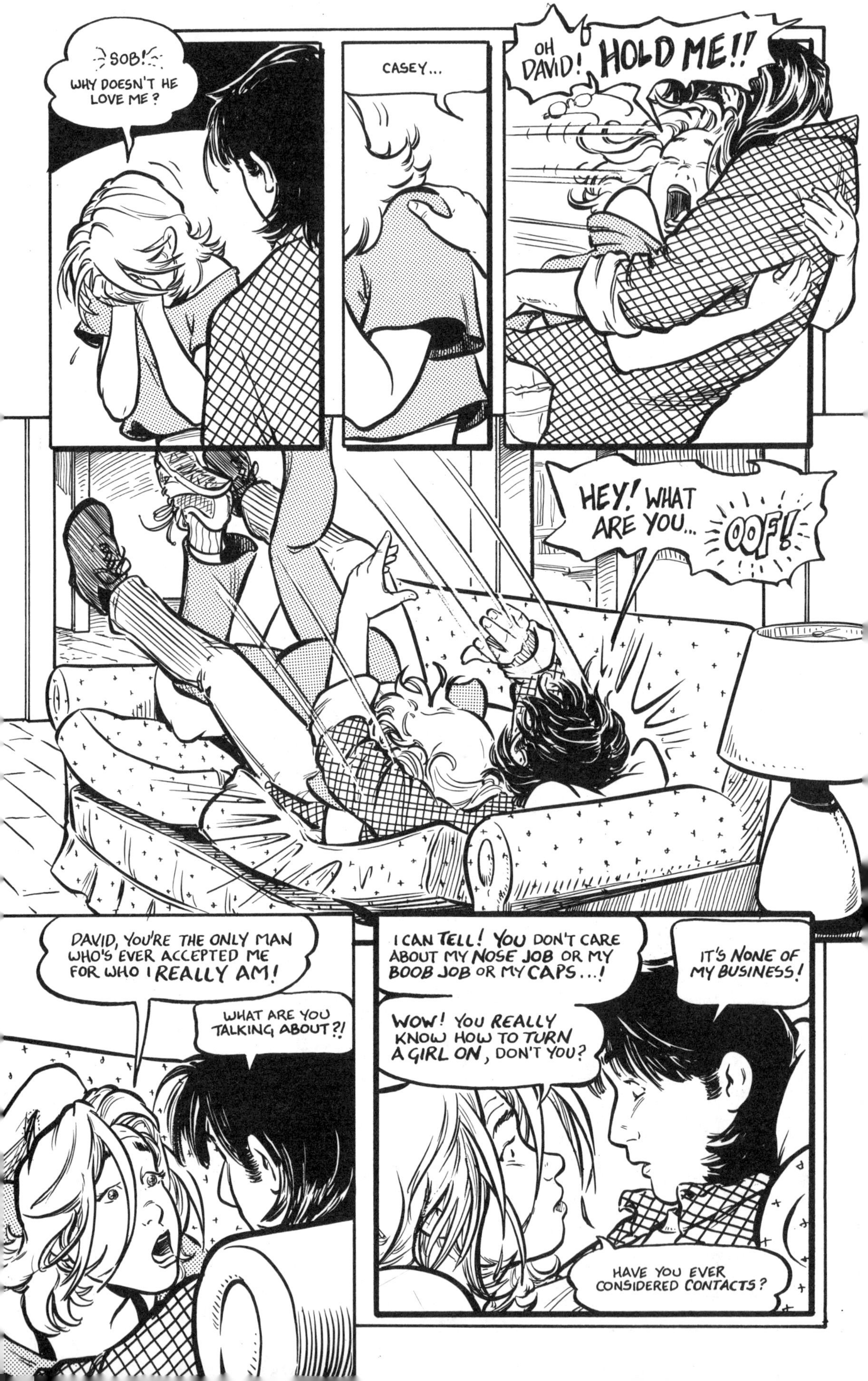
SOB!
WHY DOESN'T HE LOVE ME?
CASEY...
OH DAVID! HOLD ME!!
HEY! WHAT ARE YOU... OOF!
DAVID, YOU'RE THE ONLY MAN WHO'S EVER ACCEPTED ME FOR WHO I REALLY AM!
WHAT ARE YOU TALKING ABOUT?!
I CAN TELL! YOU DON'T CARE ABOUT MY NOSE JOB OR MY BOOB JOB OR MY CAPS...!
IT'S NONE OF MY BUSINESS!
WOW! YOU REALLY KNOW HOW TO TURN A GIRL ON, DON'T YOU?
HAVE YOU EVER CONSIDERED CONTACTS?

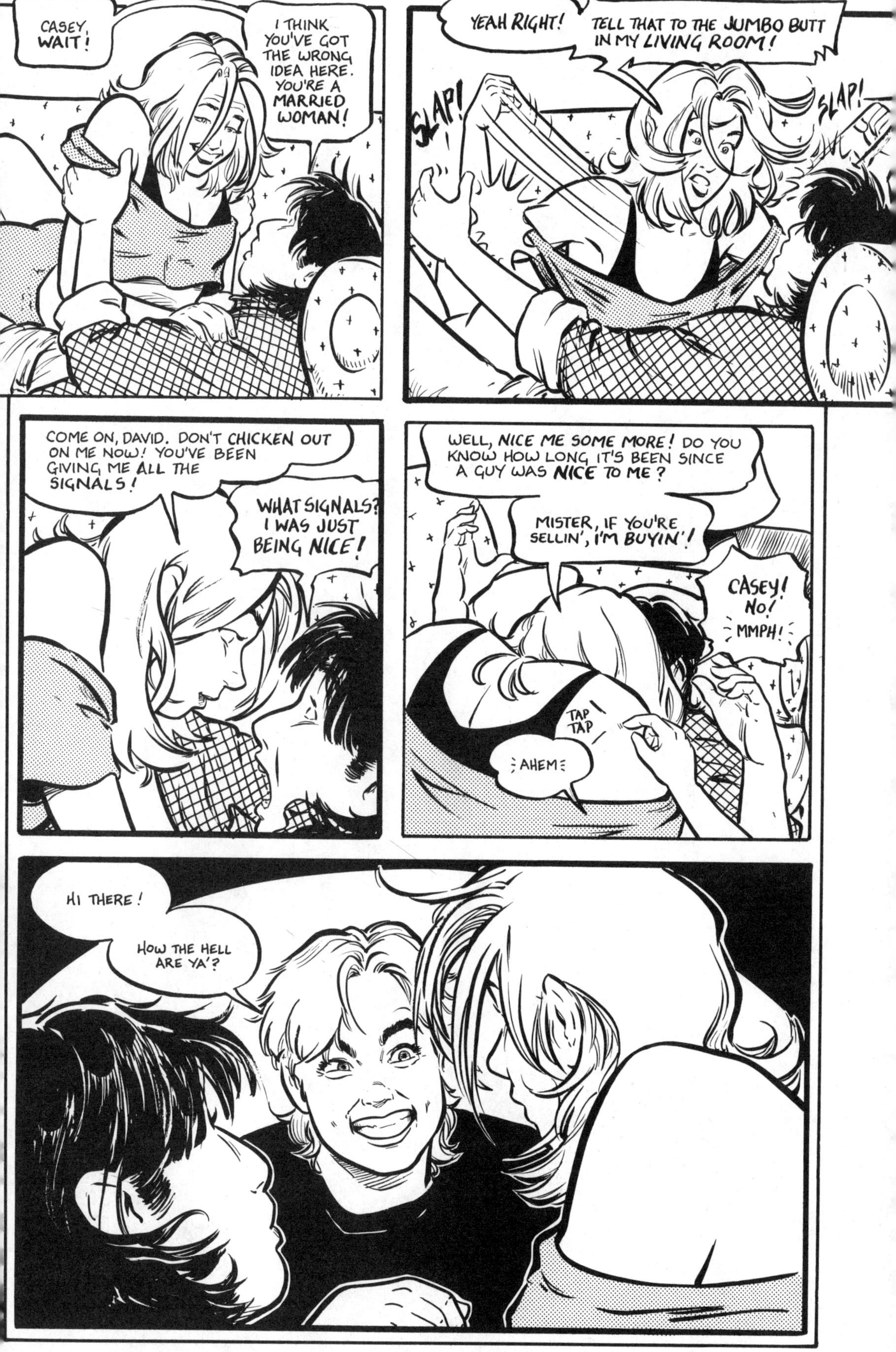

CASEY, WAIT!
I THINK YOU'VE GOT THE WRONG IDEA HERE. YOU'RE A MARRIED WOMAN!
YEAH RIGHT!
TELL THAT TO THE JUMBO BUTT IN MY LIVING ROOM!
SLAP!
SLAP!
COME ON, DAVID. DON'T CHICKEN OUT ON ME NOW! YOU'VE BEEN GIVING ME ALL THE SIGNALS!
WHAT SIGNALS? I WAS JUST BEING NICE!
WELL, NICE ME SOME MORE! DO YOU KNOW HOW LONG IT'S BEEN SINCE A GUY WAS NICE TO ME?
MISTER, IF YOU'RE SELLIN', I'M BUYIN'!
CASEY! NO!
MMPH!
TAP TAP
AHEM
HI THERE!
HOW THE HELL ARE YA'?

I'm not sure God wants us to be happy. I think he wants us to love, and be loved. But we are like children, thinking our toys will make us happy and the whole world is our nursery. Something must drive us out of that nursery and into the lives of others, and that something is suffering.

-C. S. Lewis

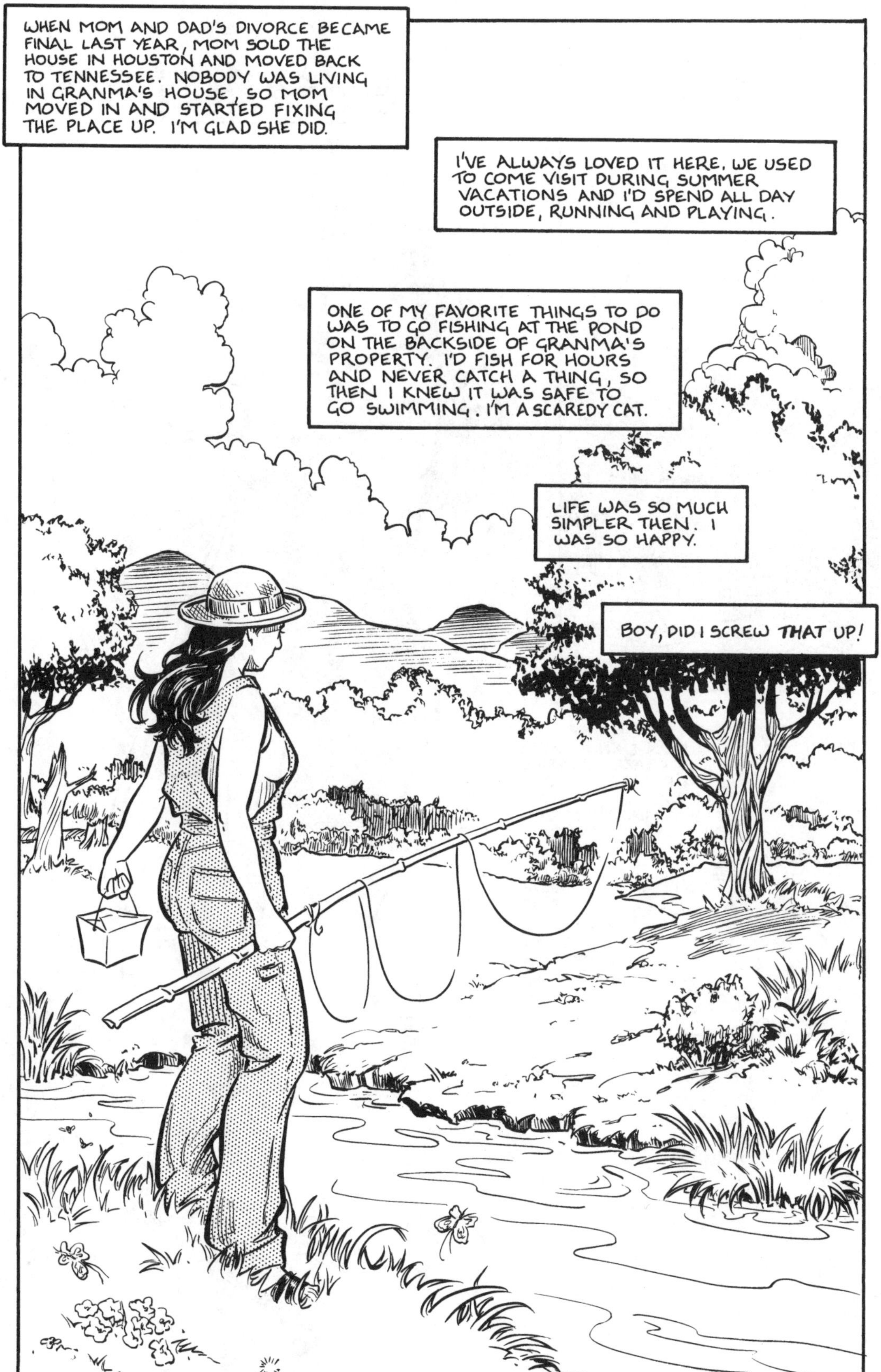

WHEN MOM AND DAD'S DIVORCE BECAME FINAL LAST YEAR, MOM SOLD THE HOUSE IN HOUSTON AND MOVED BACK TO TENNESSEE. NOBODY WAS LIVING IN GRANMA'S HOUSE, SO MOM MOVED IN AND STARTED FIXING THE PLACE UP. I'M GLAD SHE DID.
I'VE ALWAYS LOVED IT HERE. WE USED TO COME VISIT DURING SUMMER VACATIONS AND I'D SPEND ALL DAY OUTSIDE, RUNNING AND PLAYING.
ONE OF MY FAVORITE THINGS TO DO WAS TO GO FISHING AT THE POND ON THE BACKSIDE OF GRANMA'S PROPERTY. I'D FISH FOR HOURS AND NEVER CATCH A THING, SO THEN I KNEW IT WAS SAFE TO GO SWIMMING. I'M A SCAREDY CAT.
LIFE WAS SO MUCH SIMPLER THEN. I WAS SO HAPPY.
BOY, DID I SCREW **THAT** UP!

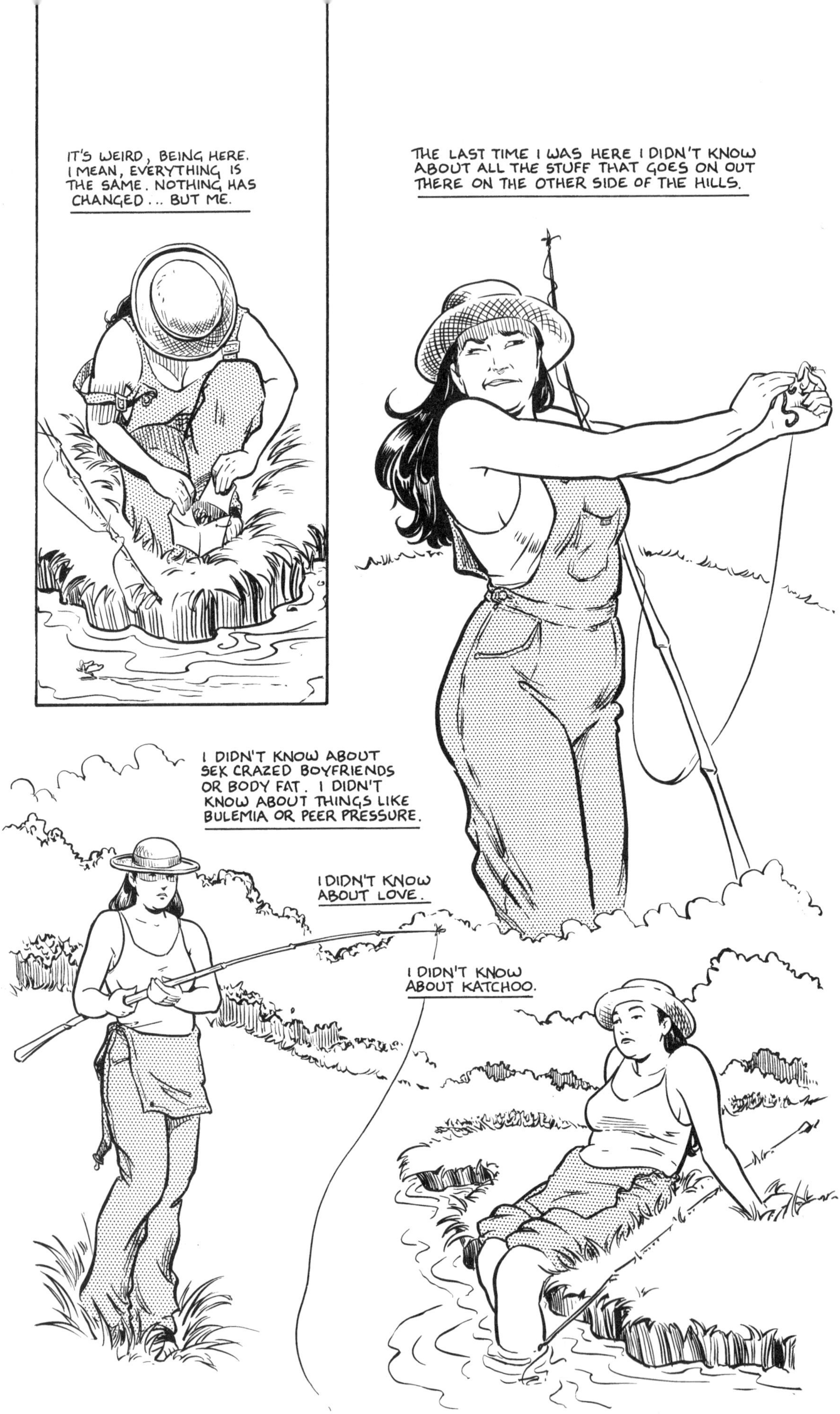
IT'S WEIRD, BEING HERE. I MEAN, EVERYTHING IS THE SAME. NOTHING HAS CHANGED... BUT ME.
THE LAST TIME I WAS HERE I DIDN'T KNOW ABOUT ALL THE STUFF THAT GOES ON OUT THERE ON THE OTHER SIDE OF THE HILLS.
I DIDN'T KNOW ABOUT SEX CRAZED BOYFRIENDS OR BODY FAT. I DIDN'T KNOW ABOUT THINGS LIKE BULEMIA OR PEER PRESSURE.
I DIDN'T KNOW ABOUT LOVE.
I DIDN'T KNOW ABOUT KATCHOO.

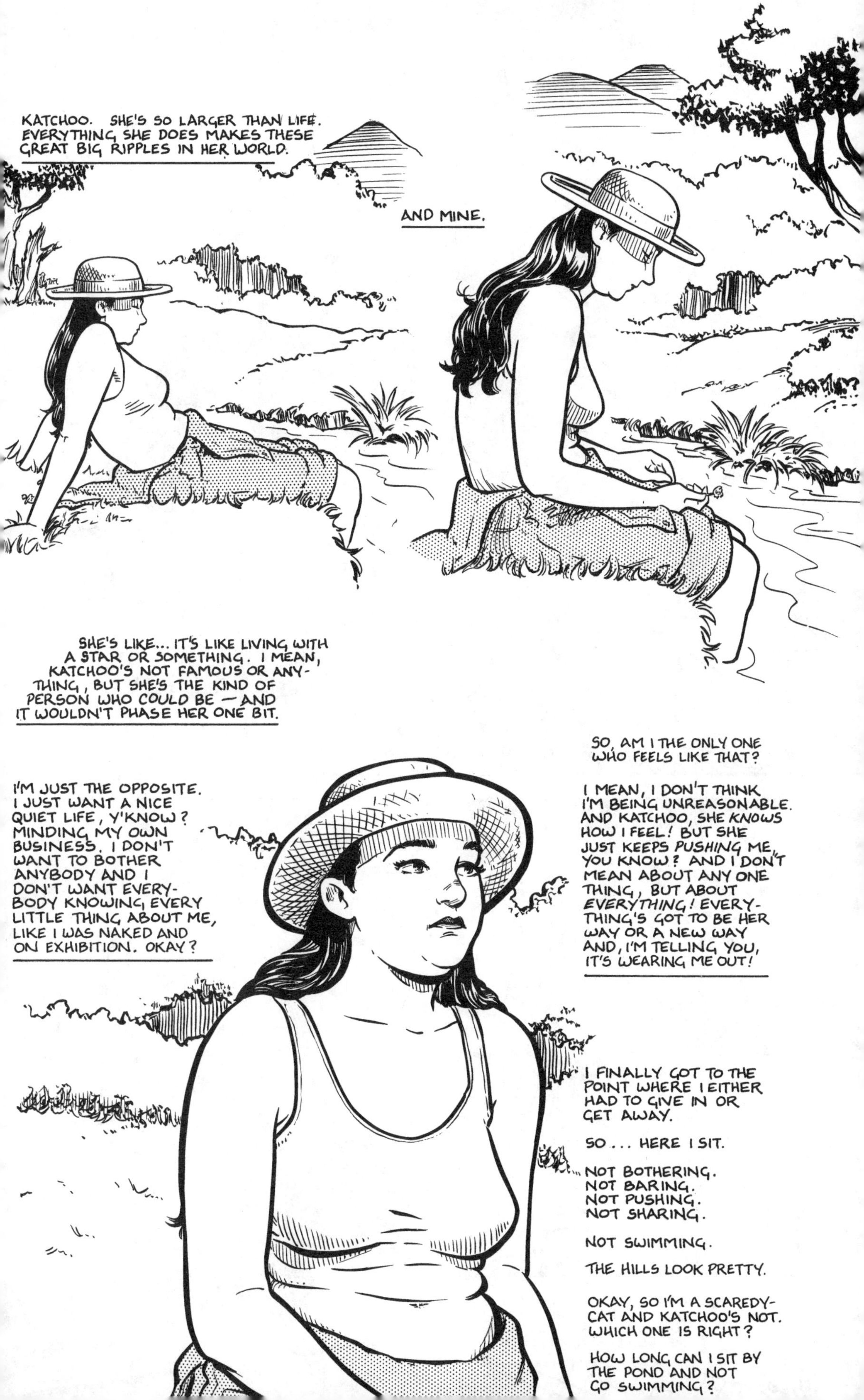
KATCHOO. SHE'S SO LARGER THAN LIFE. EVERYTHING SHE DOES MAKES THESE GREAT BIG RIPPLES IN HER WORLD.
AND MINE.
SHE'S LIKE... IT'S LIKE LIVING WITH A STAR OR SOMETHING. I MEAN, KATCHOO'S NOT FAMOUS OR ANYTHING, BUT SHE'S THE KIND OF PERSON WHO COULD BE — AND IT WOULDN'T PHASE HER ONE BIT.
I'M JUST THE OPPOSITE. I JUST WANT A NICE QUIET LIFE, Y'KNOW? MINDING MY OWN BUSINESS. I DON'T WANT TO BOTHER ANYBODY AND I DON'T WANT EVERYBODY KNOWING EVERY LITTLE THING ABOUT ME, LIKE I WAS NAKED AND ON EXHIBITION. OKAY?
SO, AM I THE ONLY ONE WHO FEELS LIKE THAT?
I MEAN, I DON'T THINK I'M BEING UNREASONABLE. AND KATCHOO, SHE KNOWS HOW I FEEL! BUT SHE JUST KEEPS PUSHING ME, YOU KNOW? AND I DON'T MEAN ABOUT ANY ONE THING, BUT ABOUT EVERYTHING! EVERYTHING'S GOT TO BE HER WAY OR A NEW WAY AND, I'M TELLING YOU, IT'S WEARING ME OUT!
I FINALLY GOT TO THE POINT WHERE I EITHER HAD TO GIVE IN OR GET AWAY.
SO . . . HERE I SIT.
NOT BOTHERING.
NOT BARING.
NOT PUSHING.
NOT SHARING.
NOT SWIMMING.
THE HILLS LOOK PRETTY.
OKAY, SO I'M A SCAREDY-CAT AND KATCHOO'S NOT. WHICH ONE IS RIGHT?
HOW LONG CAN I SIT BY THE POND AND NOT GO SWIMMING?

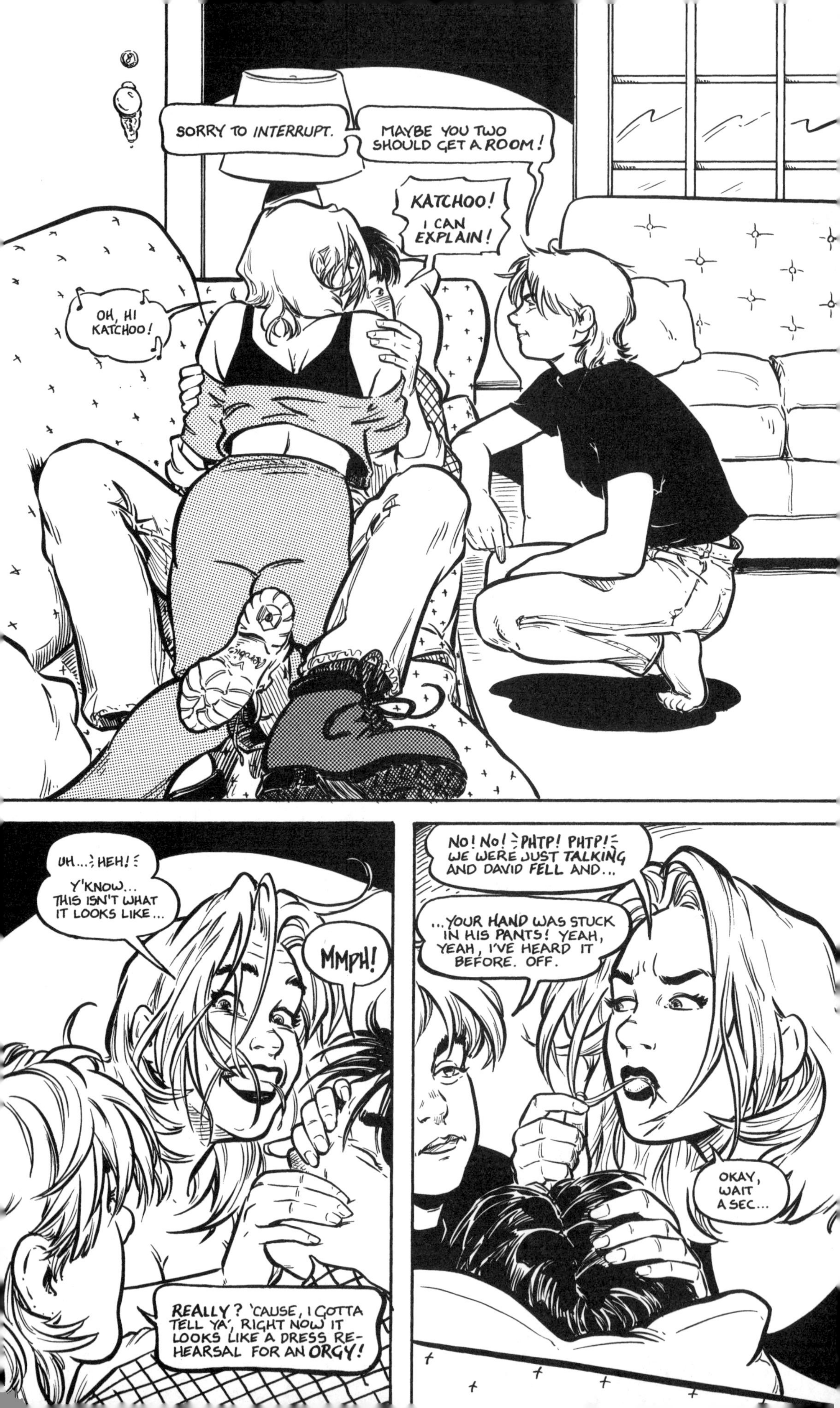
SORRY TO INTERRUPT.
MAYBE YOU TWO SHOULD GET A ROOM!
KATCHOO! I CAN EXPLAIN!
OH, HI KATCHOO!
UH... HEH!
Y'KNOW... THIS ISN'T WHAT IT LOOKS LIKE...
MMPH!
REALLY? 'CAUSE, I GOTTA TELL YA', RIGHT NOW IT LOOKS LIKE A DRESS RE-HEARSAL FOR AN ORGY!
NO! NO! PHTP! PHTP! WE WERE JUST TALKING AND DAVID FELL AND...
...YOUR HAND WAS STUCK IN HIS PANTS! YEAH, YEAH, I'VE HEARD IT BEFORE. OFF.
OKAY, WAIT A SEC...

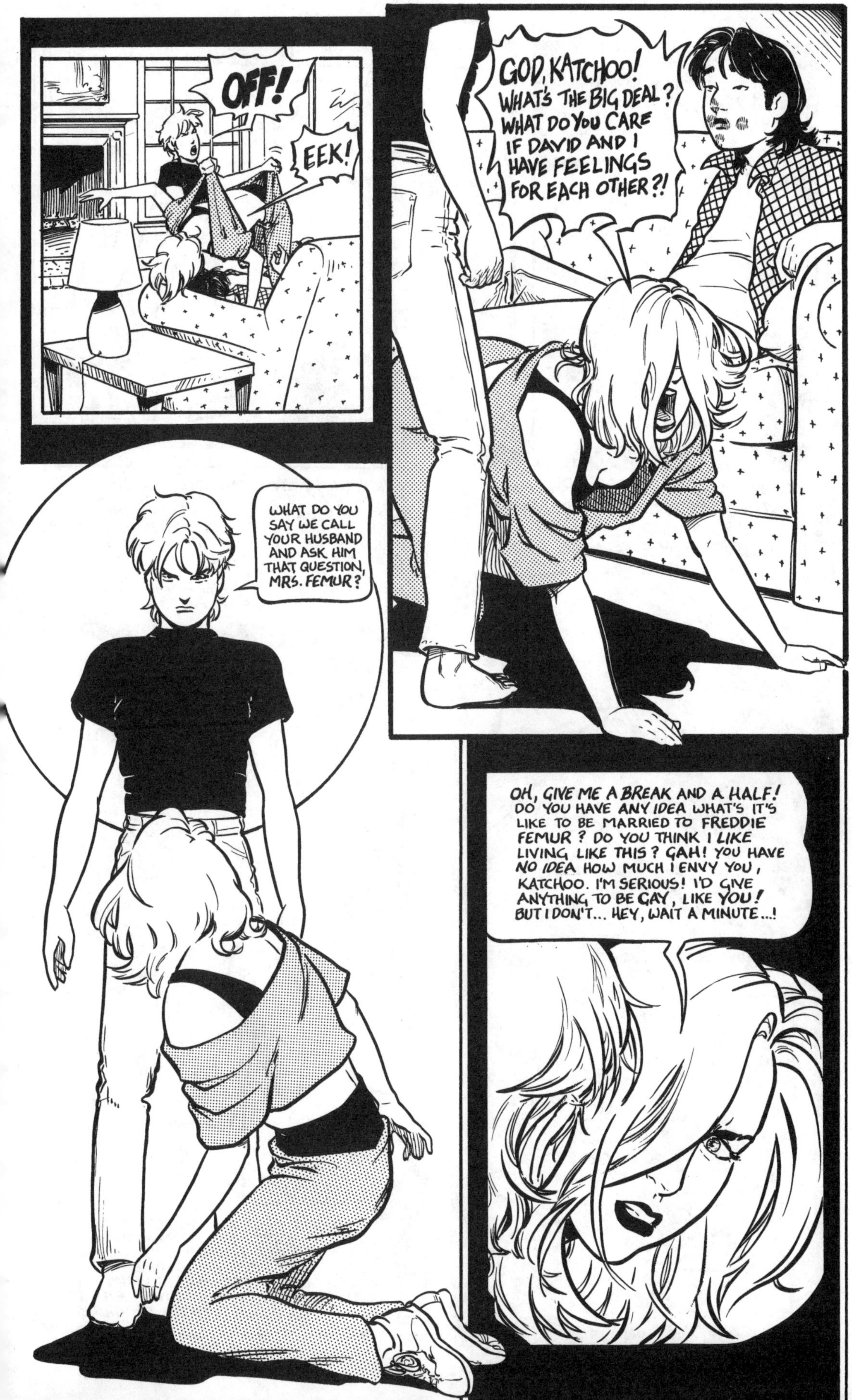
OFF!
EEK!
GOD, KATCHOO! WHAT'S THE BIG DEAL? WHAT DO YOU CARE IF DAVID AND I HAVE FEELINGS FOR EACH OTHER?!
WHAT DO YOU SAY WE CALL YOUR HUSBAND AND ASK HIM THAT QUESTION, MRS. FEMUR?
OH, GIVE ME A BREAK AND A HALF! DO YOU HAVE ANY IDEA WHAT'S IT'S LIKE TO BE MARRIED TO FREDDIE FEMUR? DO YOU THINK I LIKE LIVING LIKE THIS? GAH! YOU HAVE NO IDEA HOW MUCH I ENVY YOU, KATCHOO. I'M SERIOUS! I'D GIVE ANYTHING TO BE GAY, LIKE YOU! BUT I DON'T... HEY, WAIT A MINUTE...!

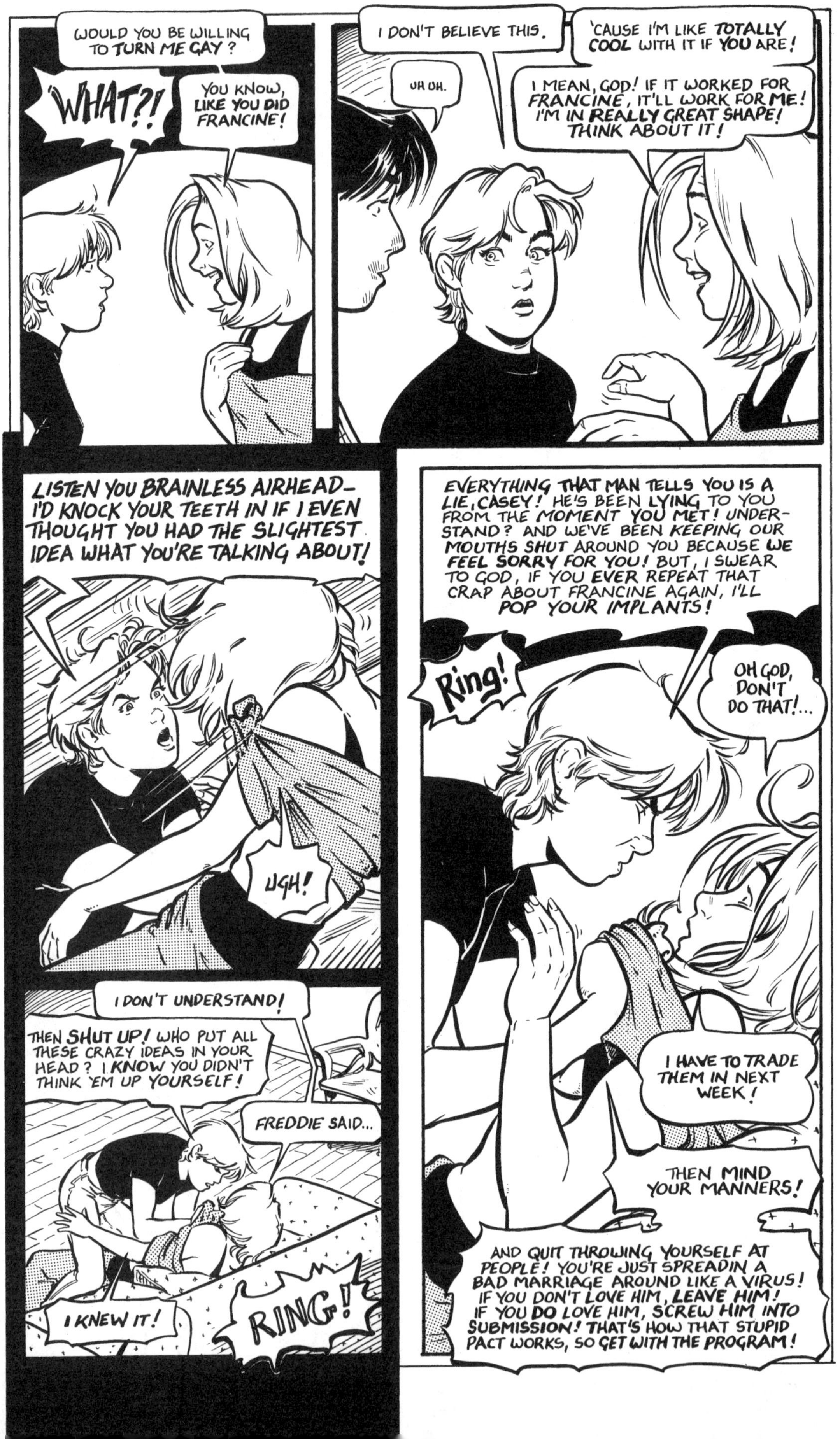

WOULD YOU BE WILLING TO TURN ME GAY?
WHAT?!
YOU KNOW, LIKE YOU DID FRANCINE!
I DON'T BELIEVE THIS.
UH UH.
'CAUSE I'M LIKE TOTALLY COOL WITH IT IF YOU ARE!
I MEAN, GOD! IF IT WORKED FOR FRANCINE, IT'LL WORK FOR ME! I'M IN REALLY GREAT SHAPE! THINK ABOUT IT!
LISTEN YOU BRAINLESS AIRHEAD-- I'D KNOCK YOUR TEETH IN IF I EVEN THOUGHT YOU HAD THE SLIGHTEST IDEA WHAT YOU'RE TALKING ABOUT!
UGH!
I DON'T UNDERSTAND!
THEN SHUT UP! WHO PUT ALL THESE CRAZY IDEAS IN YOUR HEAD? I KNOW YOU DIDN'T THINK 'EM UP YOURSELF!
FREDDIE SAID...
I KNEW IT!
RING!
EVERYTHING THAT MAN TELLS YOU IS A LIE, CASEY! HE'S BEEN LYING TO YOU FROM THE MOMENT YOU MET! UNDERSTAND? AND WE'VE BEEN KEEPING OUR MOUTHS SHUT AROUND YOU BECAUSE WE FEEL SORRY FOR YOU! BUT, I SWEAR TO GOD, IF YOU EVER REPEAT THAT CRAP ABOUT FRANCINE AGAIN, I'LL POP YOUR IMPLANTS!
Ring!
OH GOD, DON'T DO THAT!...
I HAVE TO TRADE THEM IN NEXT WEEK!
THEN MIND YOUR MANNERS!
AND QUIT THROWING YOURSELF AT PEOPLE! YOU'RE JUST SPREADIN A BAD MARRIAGE AROUND LIKE A VIRUS! IF YOU DON'T LOVE HIM, LEAVE HIM! IF YOU DO LOVE HIM, SCREW HIM INTO SUBMISSION! THAT'S HOW THAT STUPID PACT WORKS, SO GET WITH THE PROGRAM!

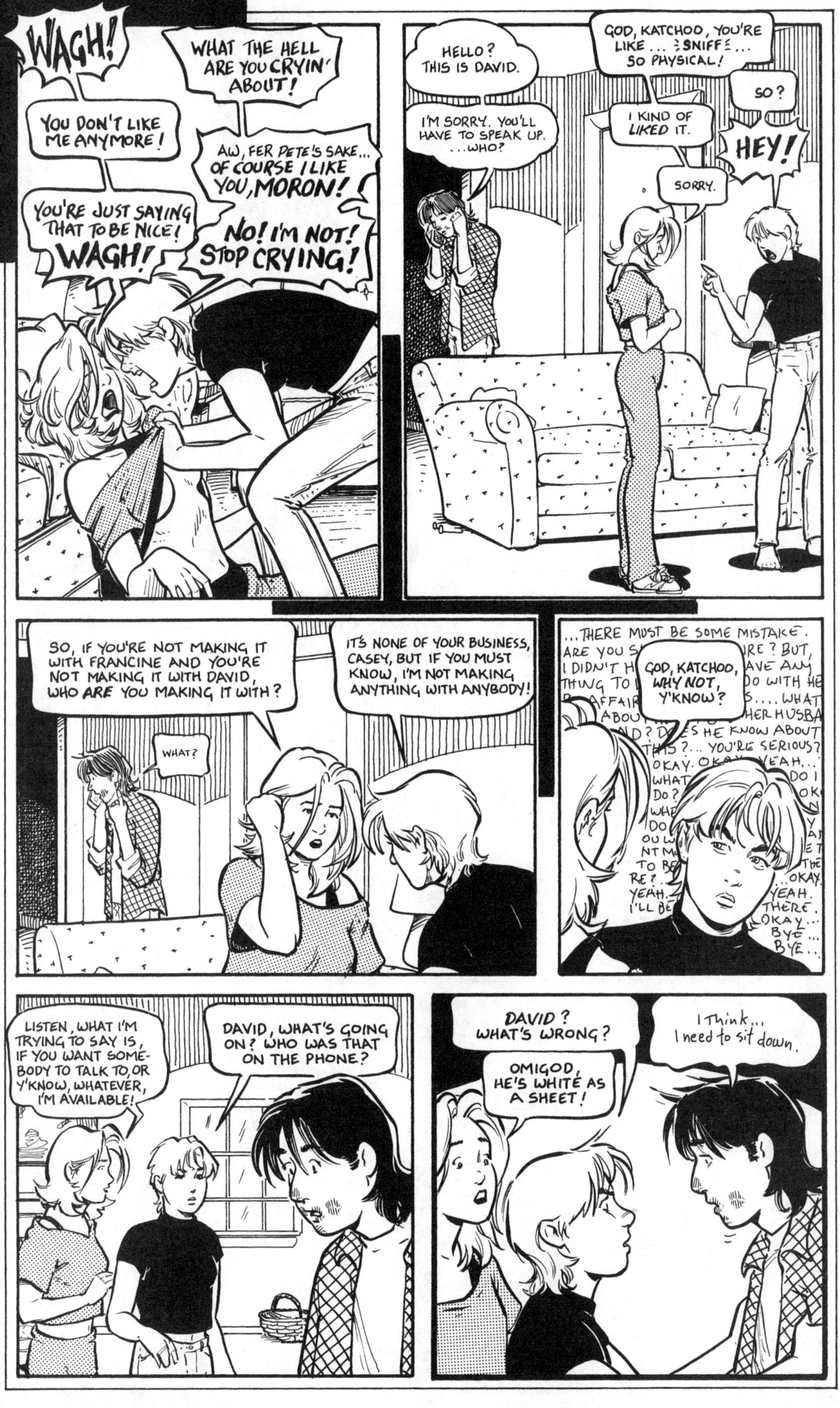
WAGH!
YOU DON'T LIKE ME ANYMORE!
WHAT THE HELL ARE YOU CRYIN' ABOUT!
AW, FER PETE'S SAKE... OF COURSE I LIKE YOU, MORON!
YOU'RE JUST SAYING THAT TO BE NICE! WAGH!
NO! I'M NOT! STOP CRYING!
HELLO? THIS IS DAVID.
I'M SORRY. YOU'LL HAVE TO SPEAK UP. ...WHO?
GOD, KATCHOO, YOU'RE LIKE ... SNIFF ... SO PHYSICAL!
I KIND OF LIKED IT.
SORRY.
SO?
HEY!
SO, IF YOU'RE NOT MAKING IT WITH FRANCINE AND YOU'RE NOT MAKING IT WITH DAVID, WHO ARE YOU MAKING IT WITH?
WHAT?
IT'S NONE OF YOUR BUSINESS, CASEY, BUT IF YOU MUST KNOW, I'M NOT MAKING ANYTHING WITH ANYBODY!
...THERE MUST BE SOME MISTAKE.
GOD, KATCHOO, WHY NOT, Y'KNOW?
OKAY... BYE... BYE...
LISTEN, WHAT I'M TRYING TO SAY IS, IF YOU WANT SOMEBODY TO TALK TO, OR Y'KNOW, WHATEVER, I'M AVAILABLE!
DAVID, WHAT'S GOING ON? WHO WAS THAT ON THE PHONE?
DAVID? WHAT'S WRONG?
OMIGOD, HE'S WHITE AS A SHEET!
I think... I need to sit down.

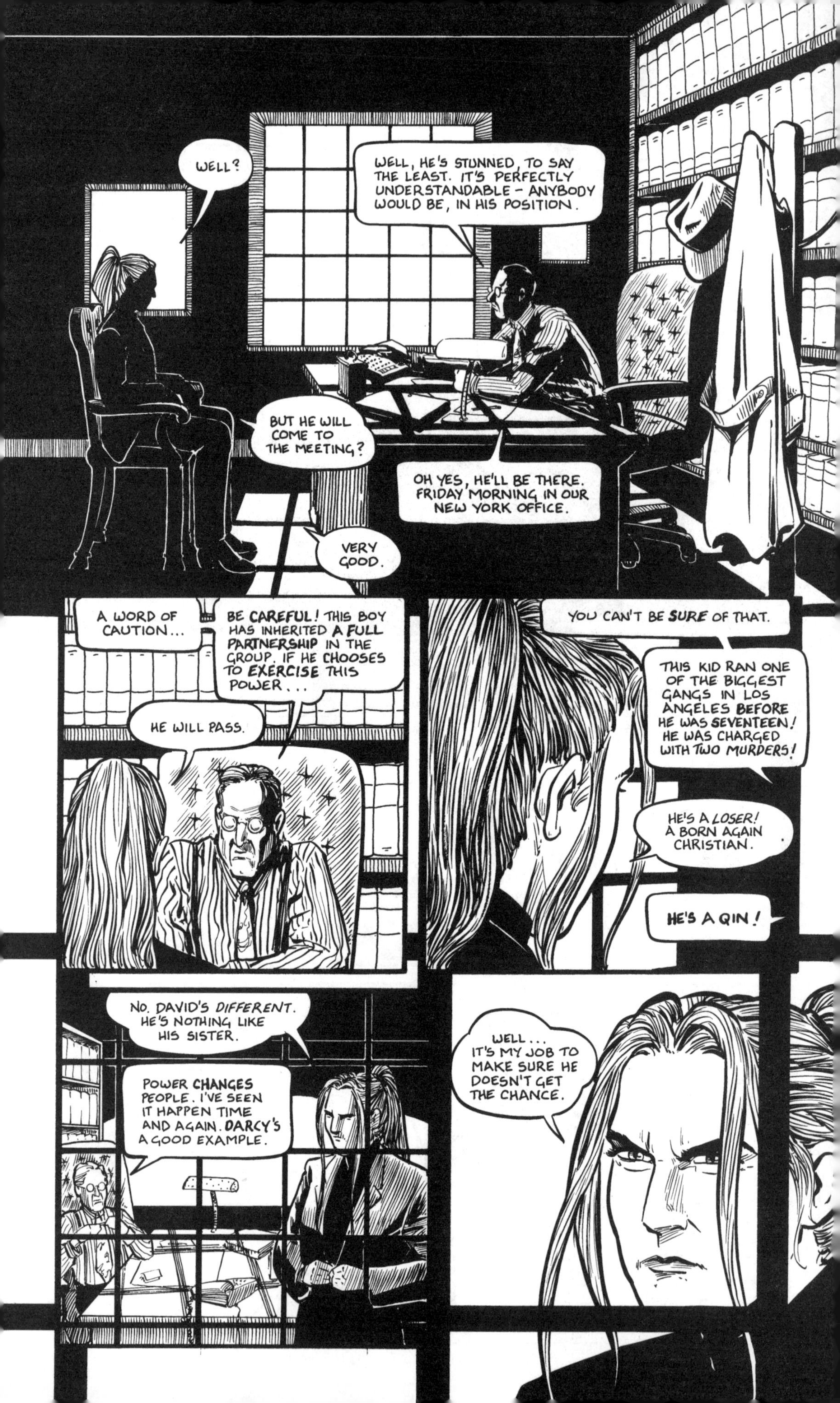
WELL?
WELL, HE'S STUNNED, TO SAY THE LEAST. IT'S PERFECTLY UNDERSTANDABLE - ANYBODY WOULD BE, IN HIS POSITION.
BUT HE WILL COME TO THE MEETING?
OH YES, HE'LL BE THERE. FRIDAY MORNING IN OUR NEW YORK OFFICE.
VERY GOOD.
A WORD OF CAUTION...
BE CAREFUL! THIS BOY HAS INHERITED A FULL PARTNERSHIP IN THE GROUP. IF HE CHOOSES TO EXERCISE THIS POWER...
HE WILL PASS.
YOU CAN'T BE SURE OF THAT.
THIS KID RAN ONE OF THE BIGGEST GANGS IN LOS ANGELES BEFORE HE WAS SEVENTEEN! HE WAS CHARGED WITH TWO MURDERS!
HE'S A LOSER! A BORN AGAIN CHRISTIAN.
HE'S A QIN!
NO. DAVID'S DIFFERENT. HE'S NOTHING LIKE HIS SISTER.
POWER CHANGES PEOPLE. I'VE SEEN IT HAPPEN TIME AND AGAIN. DARCY'S A GOOD EXAMPLE.
WELL... IT'S MY JOB TO MAKE SURE HE DOESN'T GET THE CHANCE.

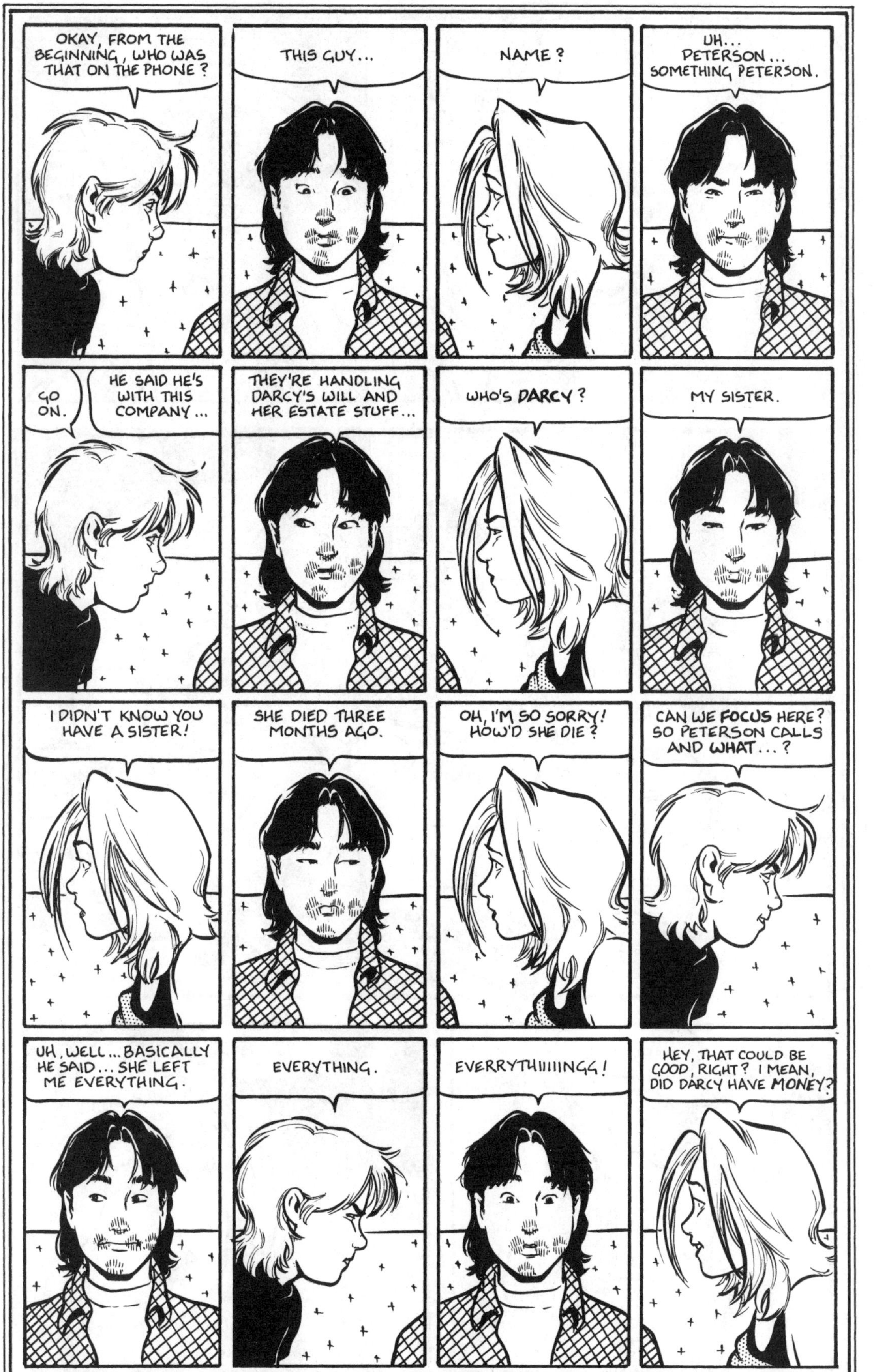
OKAY, FROM THE BEGINNING, WHO WAS THAT ON THE PHONE?
THIS GUY...
NAME?
UH... PETERSON... SOMETHING PETERSON.
GO ON.
HE SAID HE'S WITH THIS COMPANY...
THEY'RE HANDLING DARCY'S WILL AND HER ESTATE STUFF...
WHO'S DARCY?
MY SISTER.
I DIDN'T KNOW YOU HAVE A SISTER!
SHE DIED THREE MONTHS AGO.
OH, I'M SO SORRY! HOW'D SHE DIE?
CAN WE FOCUS HERE? SO PETERSON CALLS AND WHAT...?
UH, WELL... BASICALLY HE SAID... SHE LEFT ME EVERYTHING.
EVERYTHING.
EVERRYTHIIIIINGG!
HEY, THAT COULD BE GOOD, RIGHT? I MEAN, DID DARCY HAVE MONEY?

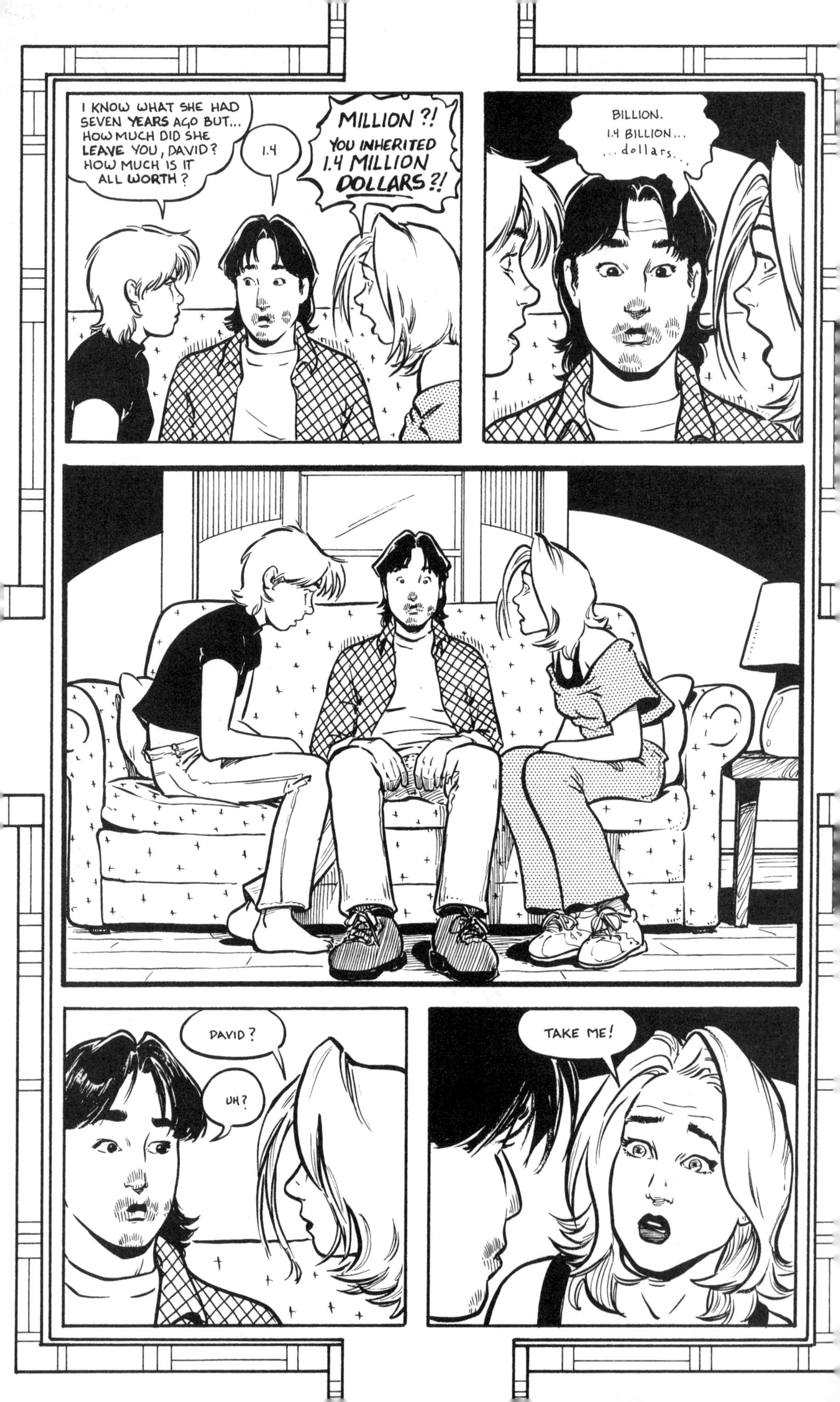

I KNOW WHAT SHE HAD SEVEN YEARS AGO BUT... HOW MUCH DID SHE LEAVE YOU, DAVID? HOW MUCH IS IT ALL WORTH?
1.4
MILLION?! YOU INHERITED 1.4 MILLION DOLLARS?!
BILLION. 1.4 BILLION... ...dollars...
DAVID?
UH?
TAKE ME!

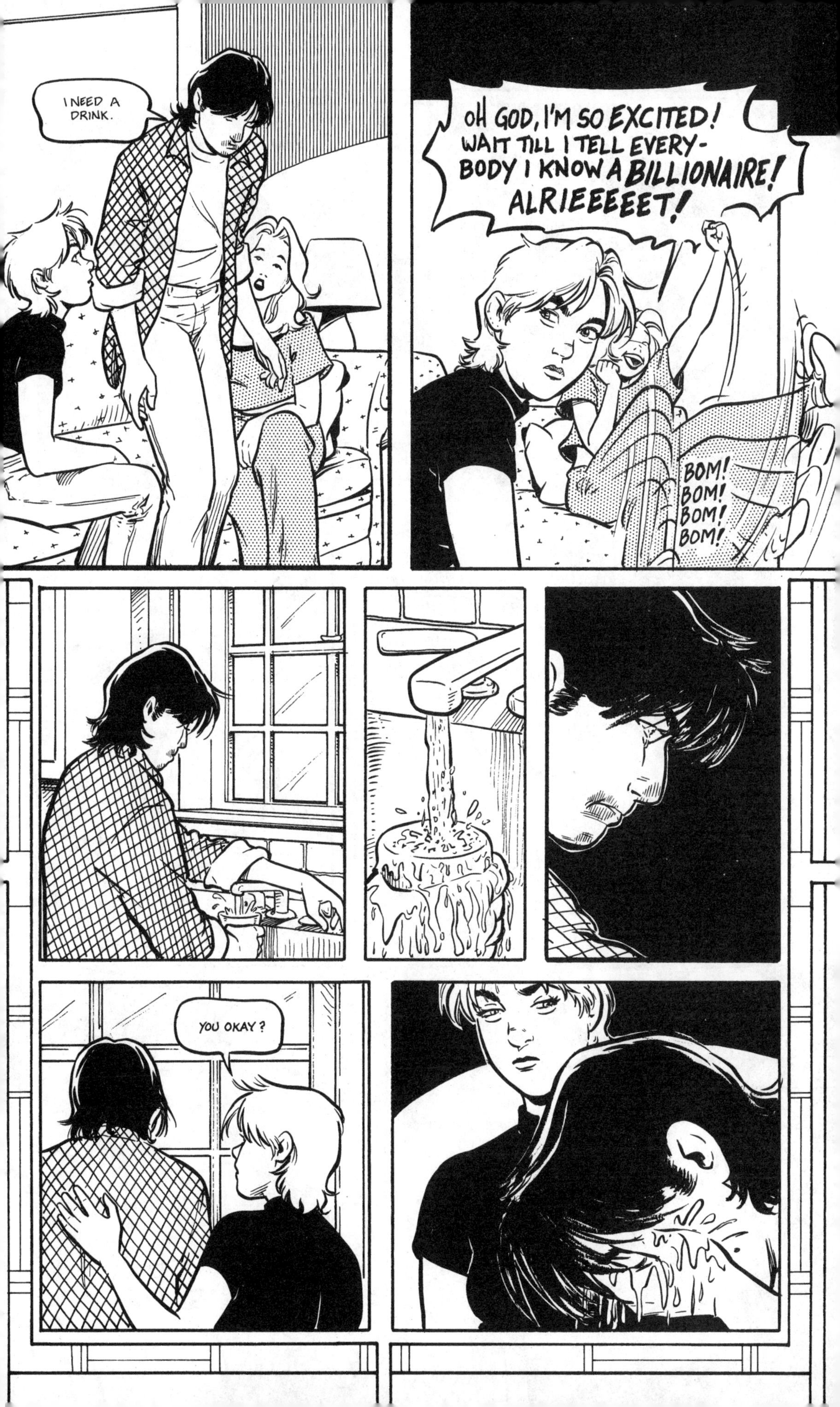
I NEED A DRINK.
OH GOD, I'M SO EXCITED! WAIT TILL I TELL EVERY-BODY I KNOW A BILLIONAIRE! ALRIEEEEEET!
BOM! BOM! BOM! BOM!
YOU OKAY?

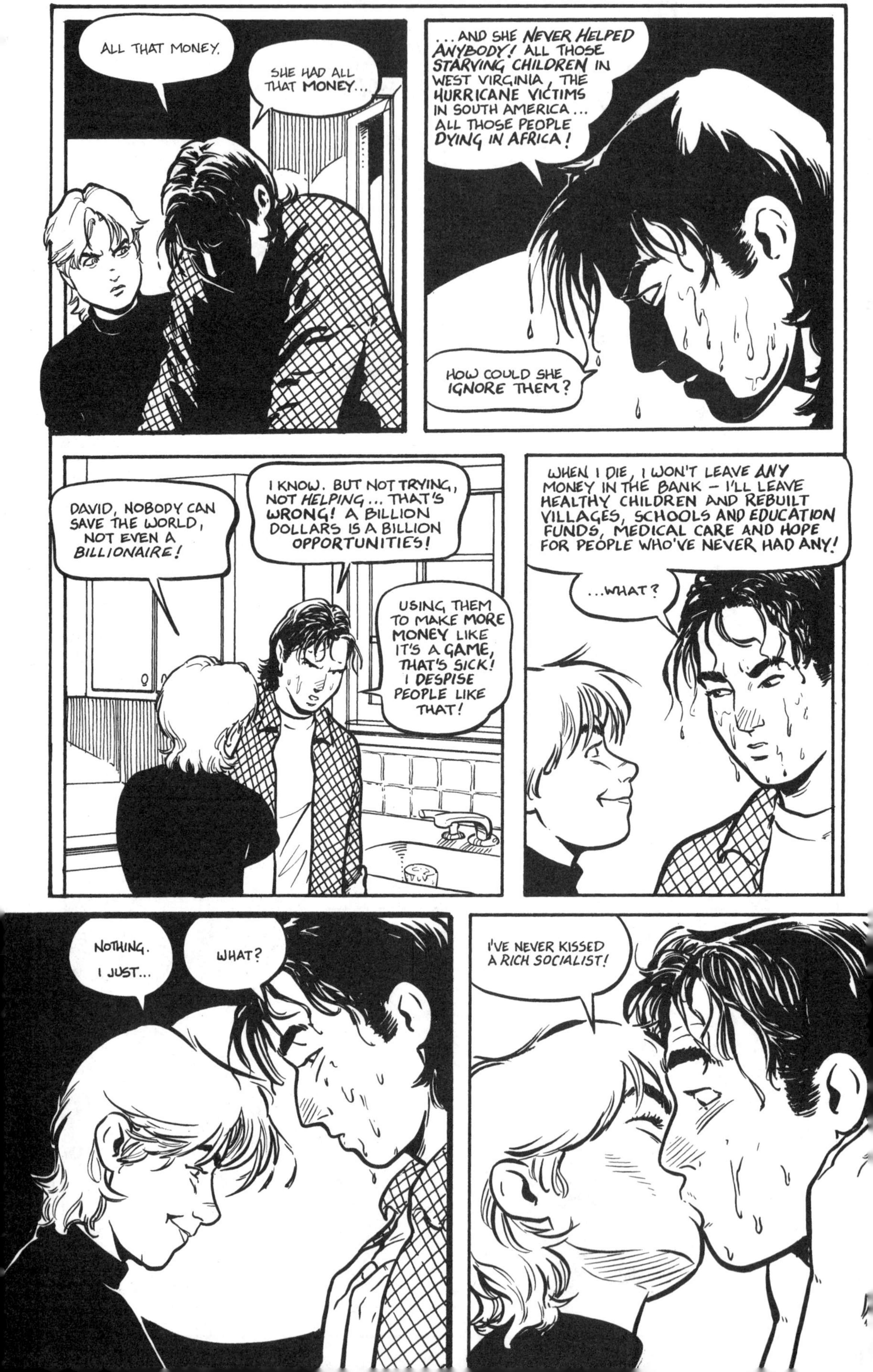
ALL THAT MONEY.
SHE HAD ALL THAT MONEY...
...AND SHE NEVER HELPED ANYBODY! ALL THOSE STARVING CHILDREN IN WEST VIRGINIA, THE HURRICANE VICTIMS IN SOUTH AMERICA... ALL THOSE PEOPLE DYING IN AFRICA!
HOW COULD SHE IGNORE THEM?
DAVID, NOBODY CAN SAVE THE WORLD, NOT EVEN A BILLIONAIRE!
I KNOW. BUT NOT TRYING, NOT HELPING... THAT'S WRONG! A BILLION DOLLARS IS A BILLION OPPORTUNITIES!
USING THEM TO MAKE MORE MONEY LIKE IT'S A GAME, THAT'S SICK! I DESPISE PEOPLE LIKE THAT!
WHEN I DIE, I WON'T LEAVE ANY MONEY IN THE BANK – I'LL LEAVE HEALTHY CHILDREN AND REBUILT VILLAGES, SCHOOLS AND EDUCATION FUNDS, MEDICAL CARE AND HOPE FOR PEOPLE WHO'VE NEVER HAD ANY!
...WHAT?
NOTHING. I JUST...
WHAT?
I'VE NEVER KISSED A RICH SOCIALIST!

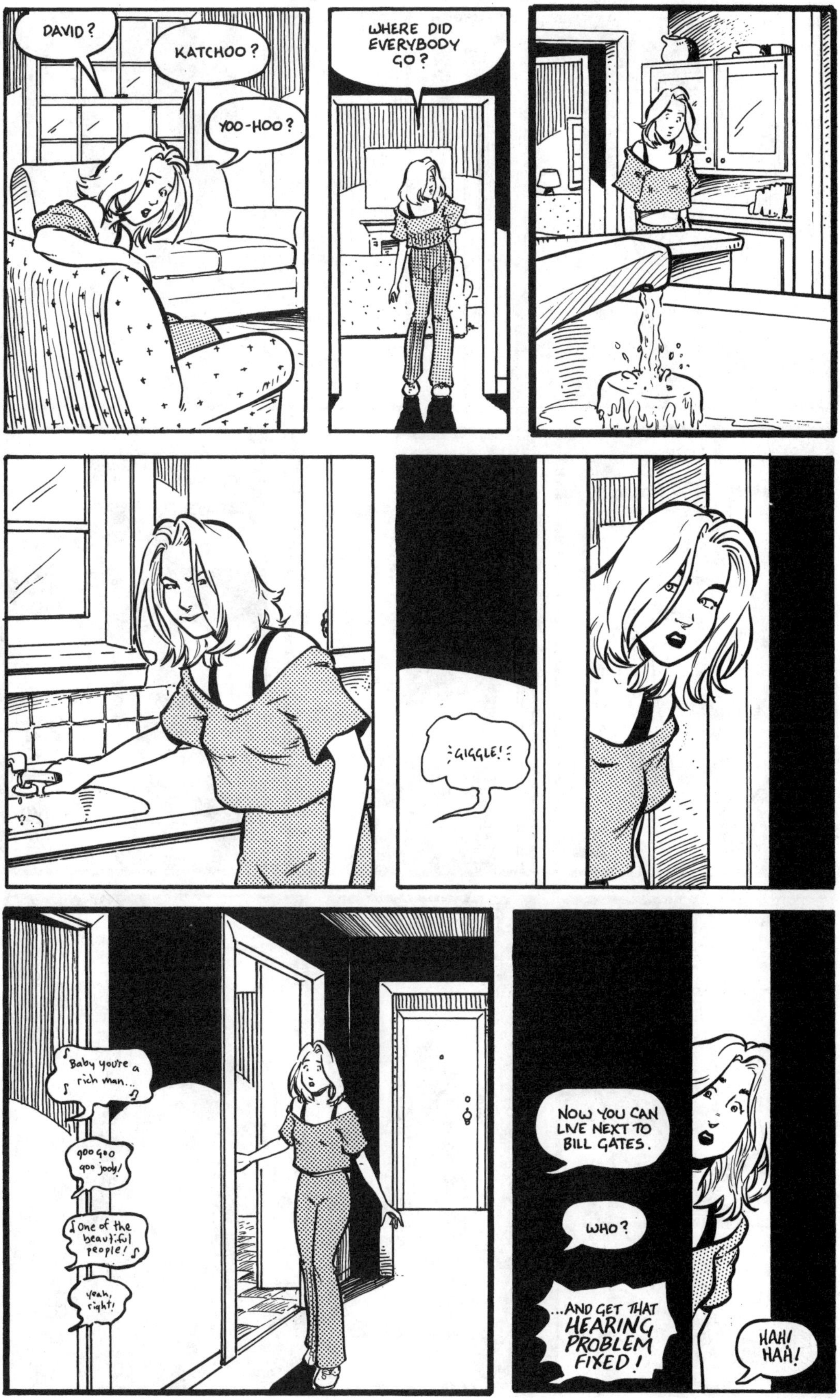
DAVID?
KATCHOO?
YOO-HOO?
WHERE DID EVERYBODY GO?
GIGGLE!
Baby you're a rich man...
goo goo goo jooby!
One of the beautiful people!
Yeah, right!
NOW YOU CAN LIVE NEXT TO BILL GATES.
WHO?
...AND GET THAT HEARING PROBLEM FIXED!
HAH! HAH!

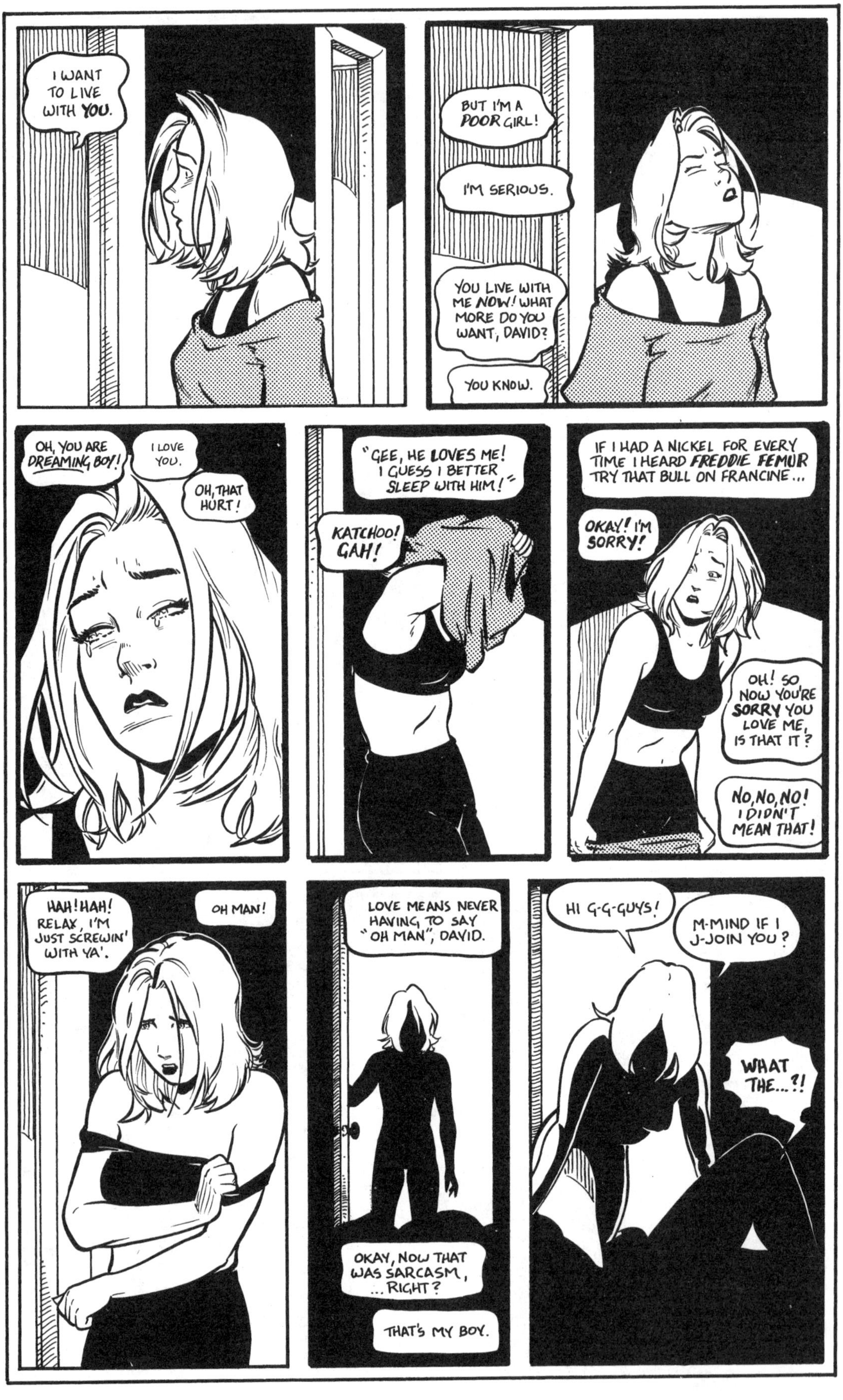
I WANT TO LIVE WITH YOU.
BUT I'M A POOR GIRL!
I'M SERIOUS.
YOU LIVE WITH ME NOW! WHAT MORE DO YOU WANT, DAVID?
YOU KNOW.
OH, YOU ARE DREAMING BOY!
I LOVE YOU.
OH, THAT HURT!
"GEE, HE LOVES ME! I GUESS I BETTER SLEEP WITH HIM!"
KATCHOO! GAH!
IF I HAD A NICKEL FOR EVERY TIME I HEARD FREDDIE FEMUR TRY THAT BULL ON FRANCINE...
OKAY! I'M SORRY!
OH! SO NOW YOU'RE SORRY YOU LOVE ME, IS THAT IT?
NO, NO, NO! I DIDN'T MEAN THAT!
HAH! HAH! RELAX, I'M JUST SCREWIN' WITH YA'.
OH MAN!
LOVE MEANS NEVER HAVING TO SAY "OH MAN", DAVID.
OKAY, NOW THAT WAS SARCASM, ...RIGHT?
THAT'S MY BOY.
HI G-G-GUYS!
M-MIND IF I J-JOIN YOU?
WHAT THE...?!

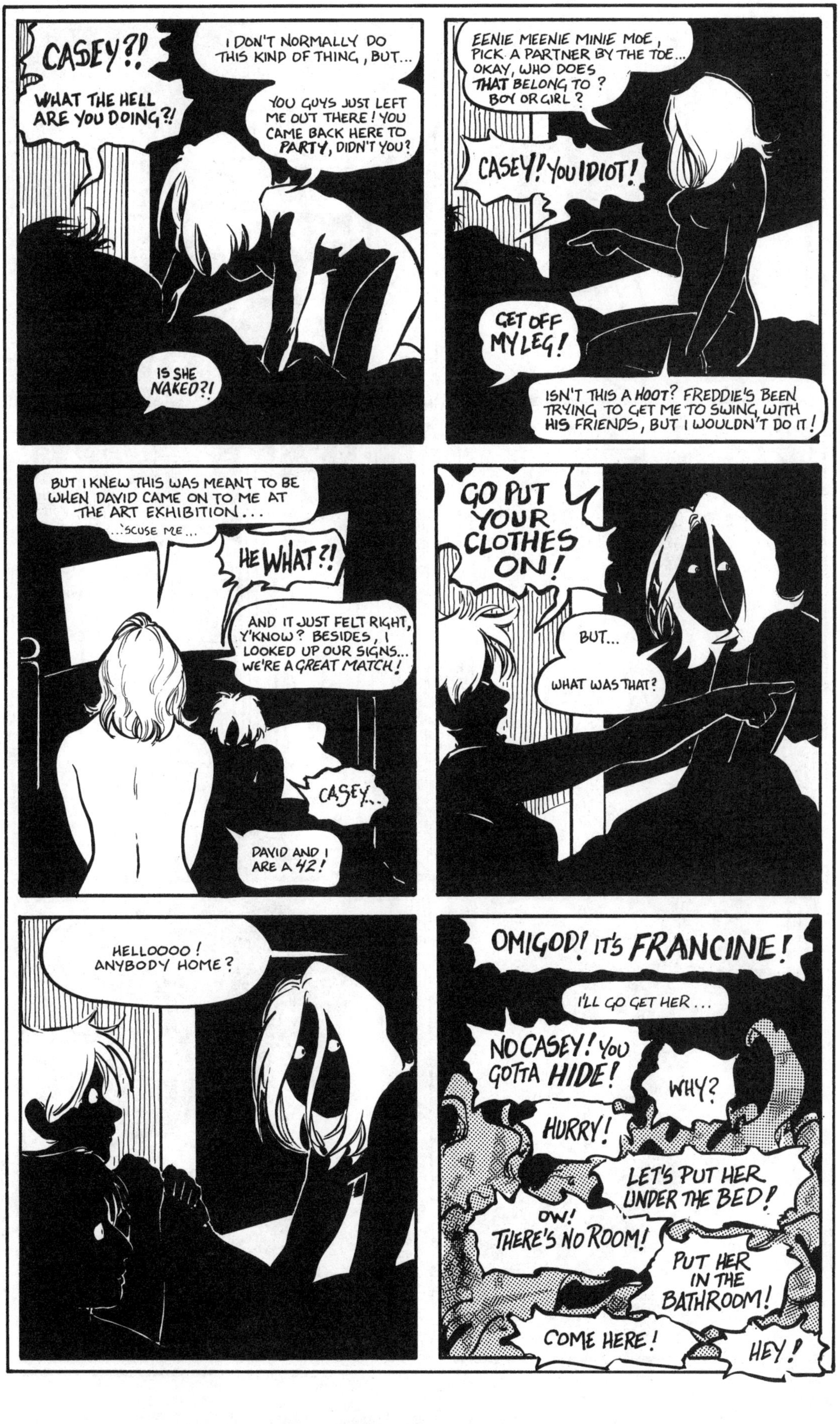
CASEY?!
WHAT THE HELL ARE YOU DOING?!
I DON'T NORMALLY DO THIS KIND OF THING, BUT...
YOU GUYS JUST LEFT ME OUT THERE! YOU CAME BACK HERE TO PARTY, DIDN'T YOU?
IS SHE NAKED?!
EENIE MEENIE MINIE MOE, PICK A PARTNER BY THE TOE... OKAY, WHO DOES THAT BELONG TO? BOY OR GIRL?
CASEY! YOU IDIOT!
GET OFF MY LEG!
ISN'T THIS A HOOT? FREDDIE'S BEEN TRYING TO GET ME TO SWING WITH HIS FRIENDS, BUT I WOULDN'T DO IT!
BUT I KNEW THIS WAS MEANT TO BE WHEN DAVID CAME ON TO ME AT THE ART EXHIBITION...
...'SCUSE ME...
HE WHAT?!
AND IT JUST FELT RIGHT, Y'KNOW? BESIDES, I LOOKED UP OUR SIGNS... WE'RE A GREAT MATCH!
CASEY...
DAVID AND I ARE A 42!
GO PUT YOUR CLOTHES ON!
BUT...
WHAT WAS THAT?
HELLOOOO! ANYBODY HOME?
OMIGOD! IT'S FRANCINE!
I'LL GO GET HER...
NO CASEY! YOU GOTTA HIDE!
WHY?
HURRY!
LET'S PUT HER UNDER THE BED!
OW! THERE'S NO ROOM!
PUT HER IN THE BATHROOM!
COME HERE!
HEY!

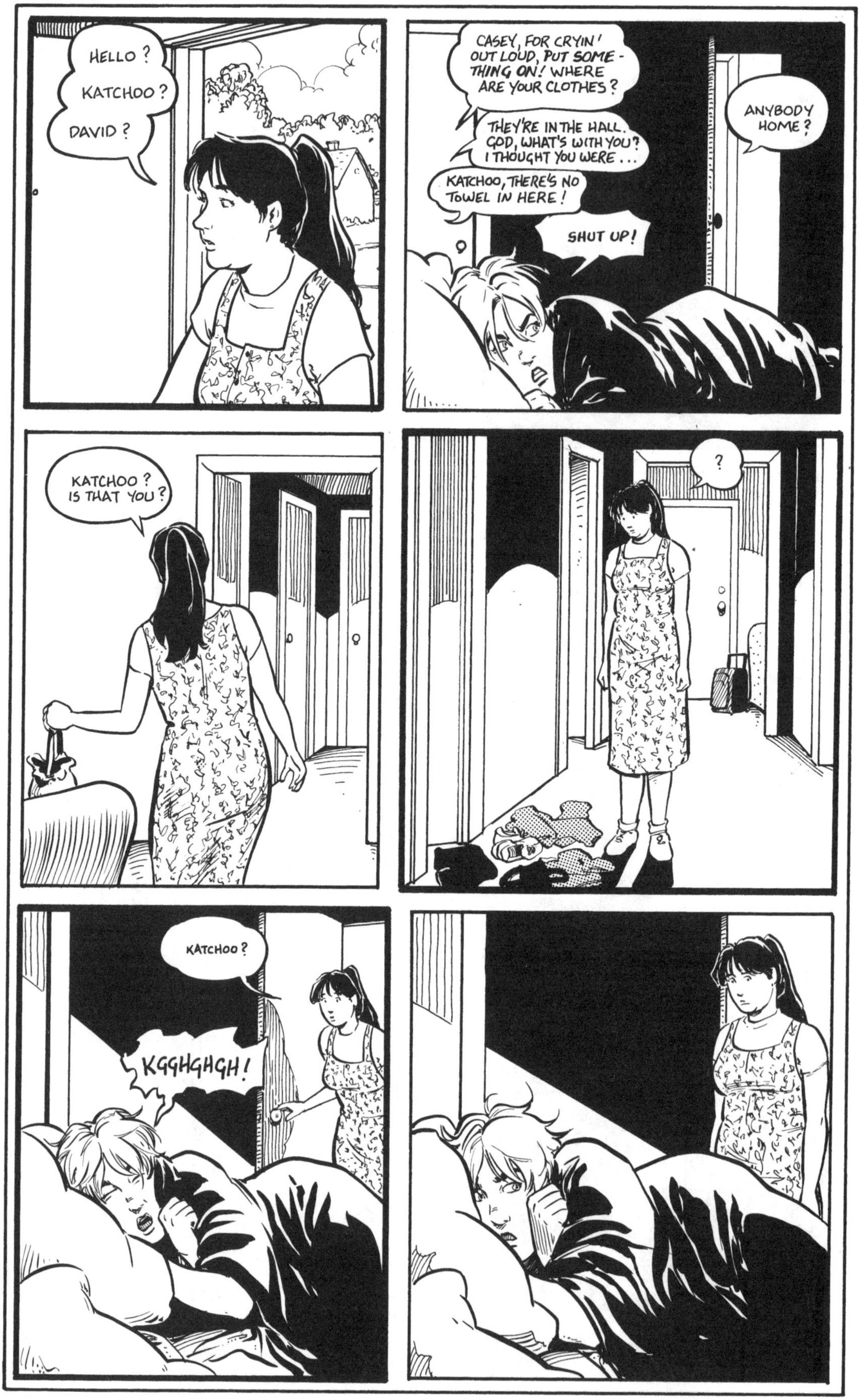
HELLO ?
KATCHOO ?
DAVID ?
CASEY, FOR CRYIN' OUT LOUD, PUT SOME-THING ON! WHERE ARE YOUR CLOTHES ?
THEY'RE IN THE HALL. GOD, WHAT'S WITH YOU? I THOUGHT YOU WERE . . .
KATCHOO, THERE'S NO TOWEL IN HERE !
ANYBODY HOME ?
SHUT UP!
KATCHOO ? IS THAT YOU ?
?
KATCHOO ?
KGGHGHGH !

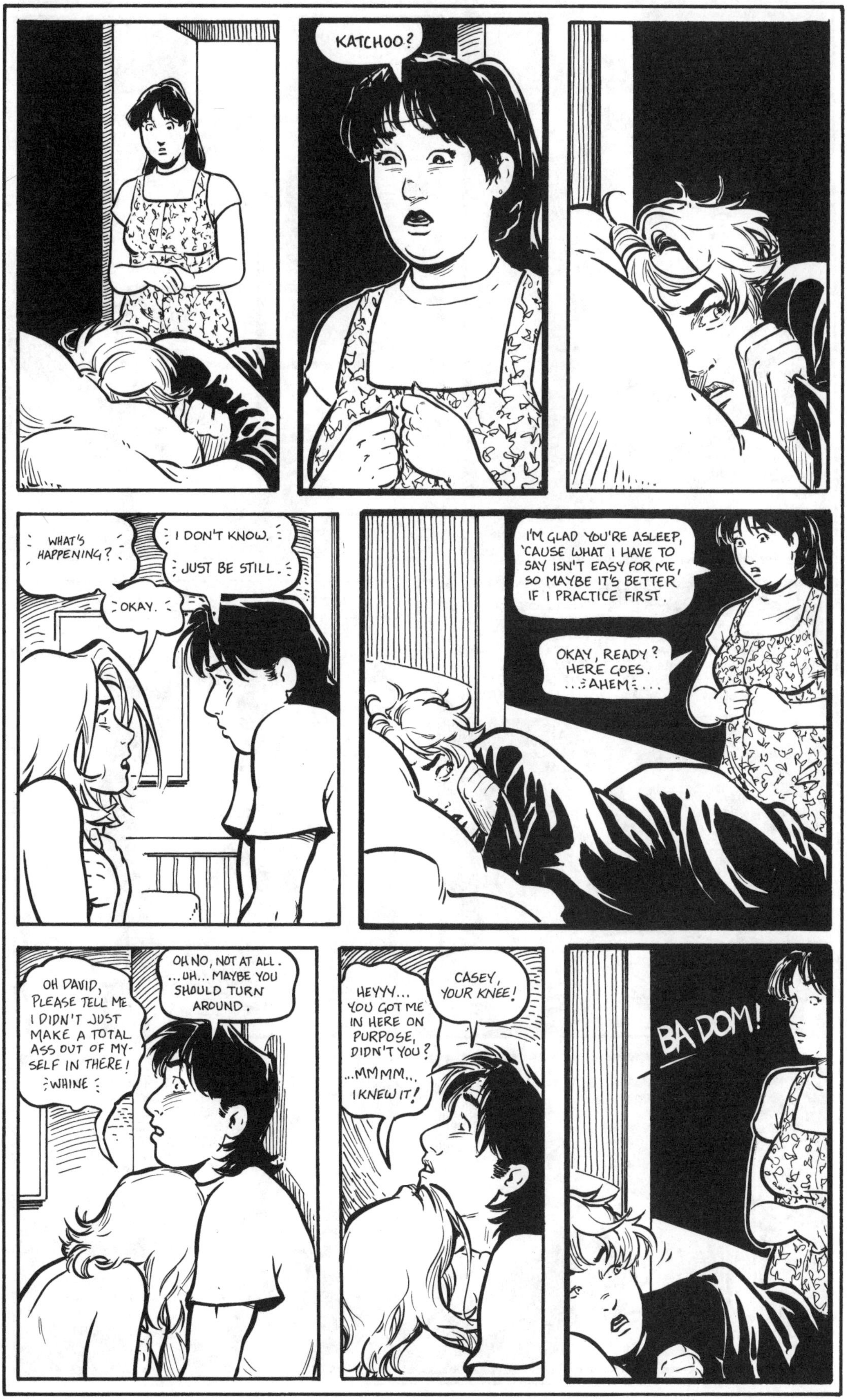
KATCHOO?
WHAT'S HAPPENING?
I DON'T KNOW.
JUST BE STILL.
OKAY.
I'M GLAD YOU'RE ASLEEP, 'CAUSE WHAT I HAVE TO SAY ISN'T EASY FOR ME, SO MAYBE IT'S BETTER IF I PRACTICE FIRST.
OKAY, READY? HERE GOES. ...AHEM...
OH DAVID, PLEASE TELL ME I DIDN'T JUST MAKE A TOTAL ASS OUT OF MY-SELF IN THERE! WHINE
OH NO, NOT AT ALL. ...UH... MAYBE YOU SHOULD TURN AROUND.
HEYYY... YOU GOT ME IN HERE ON PURPOSE, DIDN'T YOU? ...MMMM... I KNEW IT!
CASEY, YOUR KNEE!
BA-DOM!

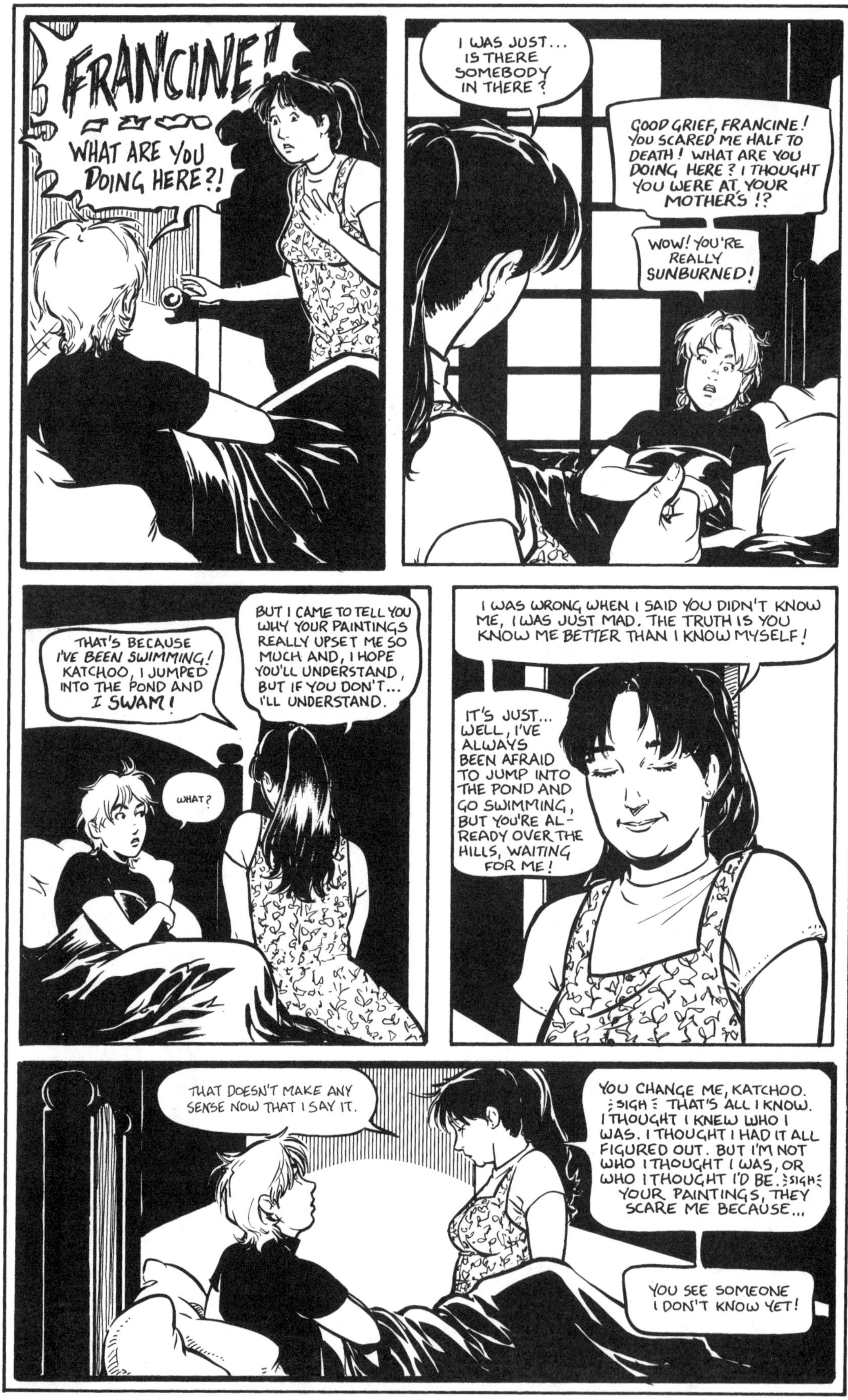
FRANCINE!
WHAT ARE YOU DOING HERE?!
I WAS JUST... IS THERE SOMEBODY IN THERE?
GOOD GRIEF, FRANCINE! YOU SCARED ME HALF TO DEATH! WHAT ARE YOU DOING HERE? I THOUGHT YOU WERE AT YOUR MOTHER'S!?
WOW! YOU'RE REALLY SUNBURNED!
THAT'S BECAUSE I'VE BEEN SWIMMING! KATCHOO, I JUMPED INTO THE POND AND I SWAM!
BUT I CAME TO TELL YOU WHY YOUR PAINTINGS REALLY UPSET ME SO MUCH AND, I HOPE YOU'LL UNDERSTAND, BUT IF YOU DON'T... I'LL UNDERSTAND.
WHAT?
I WAS WRONG WHEN I SAID YOU DIDN'T KNOW ME, I WAS JUST MAD. THE TRUTH IS YOU KNOW ME BETTER THAN I KNOW MYSELF!
IT'S JUST... WELL, I'VE ALWAYS BEEN AFRAID TO JUMP INTO THE POND AND GO SWIMMING, BUT YOU'RE AL-READY OVER THE HILLS, WAITING FOR ME!
THAT DOESN'T MAKE ANY SENSE NOW THAT I SAY IT.
YOU CHANGE ME, KATCHOO. SIGH THAT'S ALL I KNOW. I THOUGHT I KNEW WHO I WAS. I THOUGHT I HAD IT ALL FIGURED OUT. BUT I'M NOT WHO I THOUGHT I WAS, OR WHO I THOUGHT I'D BE. SIGH YOUR PAINTINGS, THEY SCARE ME BECAUSE...
YOU SEE SOMEONE I DON'T KNOW YET!

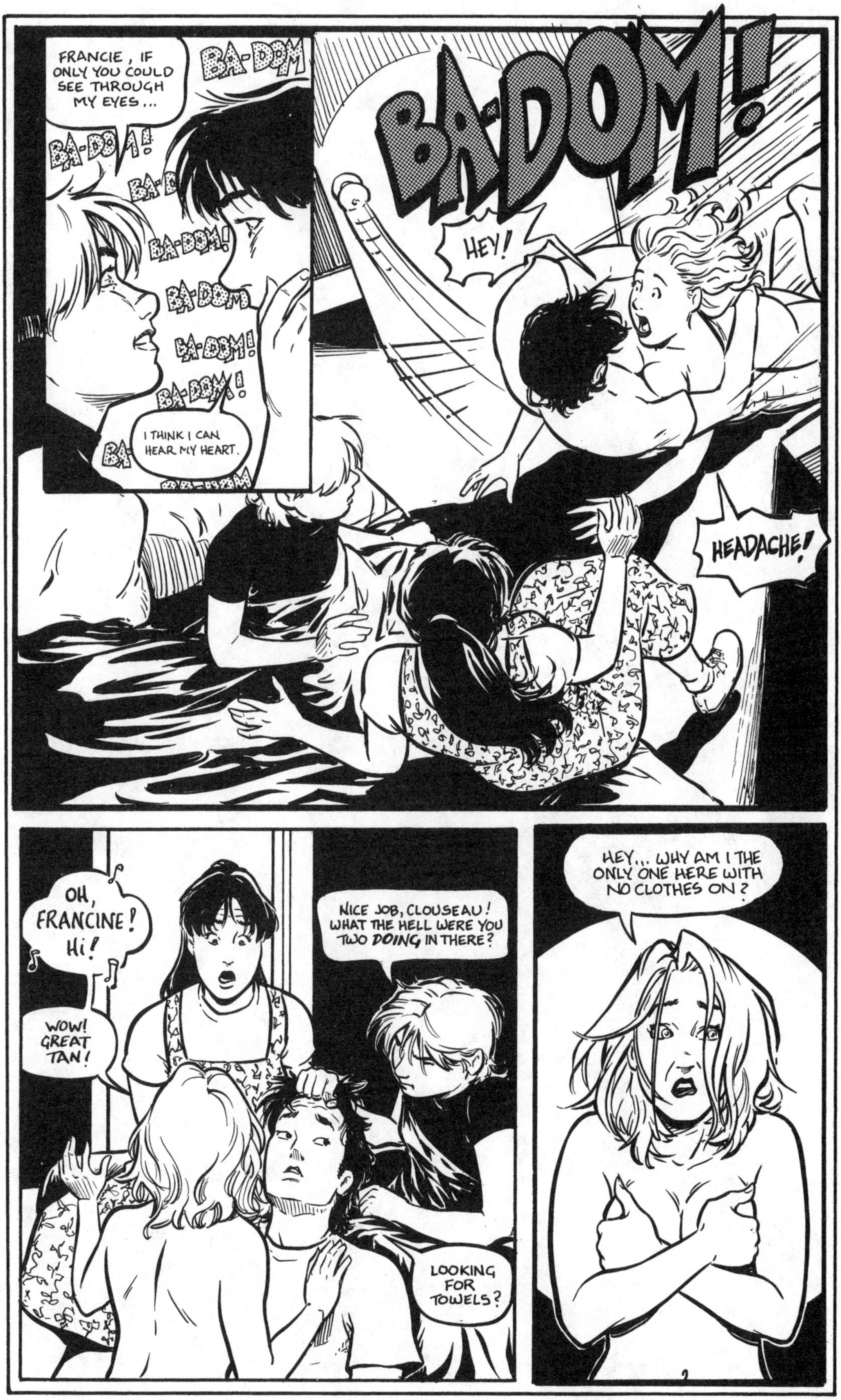

FRANCIE, IF ONLY YOU COULD SEE THROUGH MY EYES...
BA-DOM
BA-DOM!
BA-D
BA-DOM!
BA-DOM
BA-DOM!
BA-DOM!
I THINK I CAN HEAR MY HEART.
BA-DOM!
HEY!
HEADACHE!
OH, FRANCINE! Hi!
WOW! GREAT TAN!
NICE JOB, CLOUSEAU! WHAT THE HELL WERE YOU TWO DOING IN THERE?
LOOKING FOR TOWELS?
HEY... WHY AM I THE ONLY ONE HERE WITH NO CLOTHES ON?

I me mine
I me mine
I me mine
I me mine
I me mine
I me mine
I me mine

I me mine

I me mine

I me mine

I me mine

All through the day
I me mine
I me mine
I me mine
All through the night
I me mine
I me mine
I me mine

-George Harrison

I me mine

I me mine

I me mine

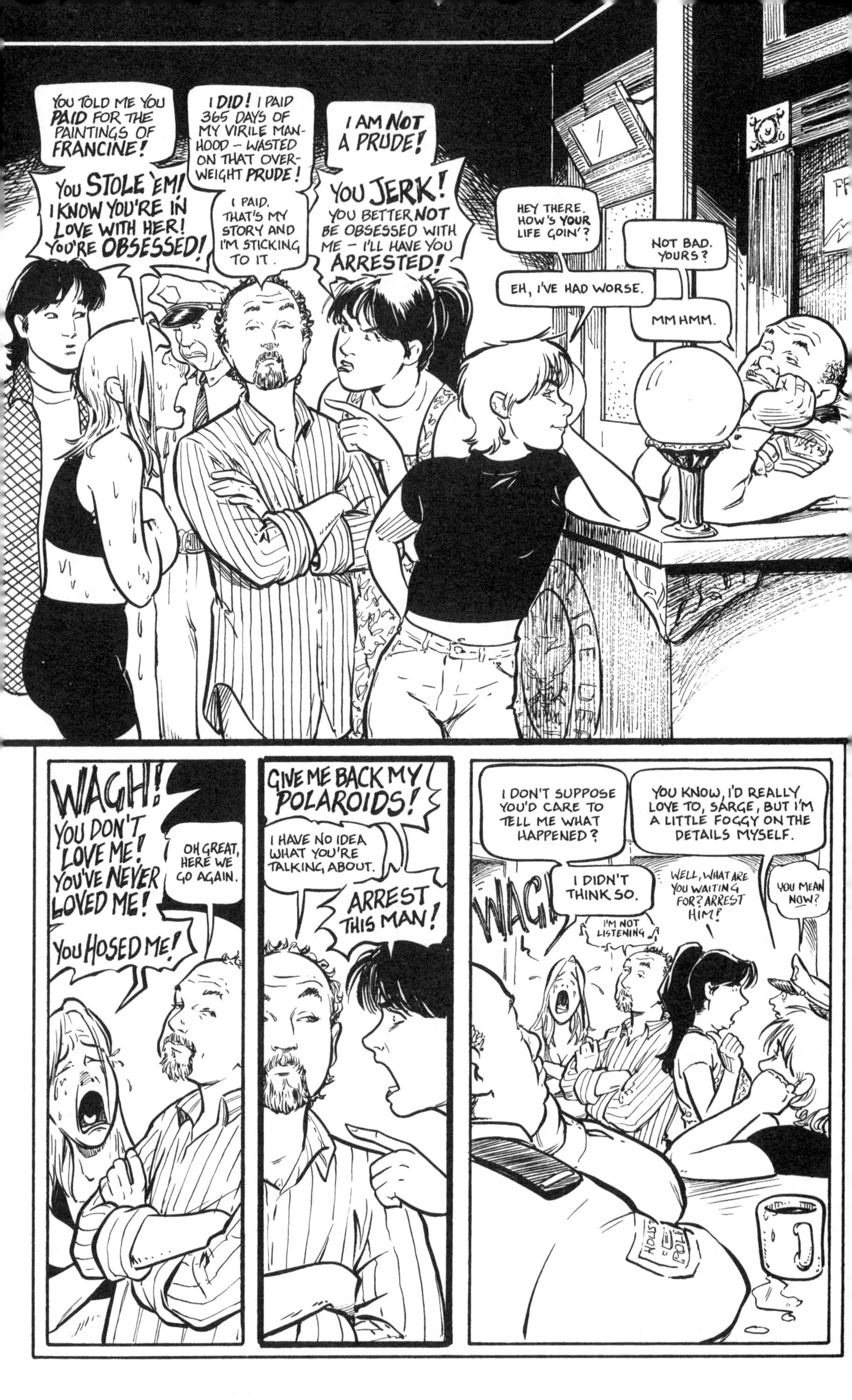

YOU TOLD ME YOU PAID FOR THE PAINTINGS OF FRANCINE!
YOU STOLE 'EM! I KNOW YOU'RE IN LOVE WITH HER! YOU'RE OBSESSED!
I DID! I PAID 365 DAYS OF MY VIRILE MAN-HOOD – WASTED ON THAT OVER-WEIGHT PRUDE!
I PAID. THAT'S MY STORY AND I'M STICKING TO IT.
I AM NOT A PRUDE!
YOU JERK! YOU BETTER NOT BE OBSESSED WITH ME – I'LL HAVE YOU ARRESTED!
HEY THERE. HOW'S YOUR LIFE GOIN'?
NOT BAD. YOURS?
EH, I'VE HAD WORSE.
MMHMM.
WAGH! YOU DON'T LOVE ME! YOU'VE NEVER LOVED ME!
YOU HOSED ME!
OH GREAT, HERE WE GO AGAIN.
GIVE ME BACK MY POLAROIDS!
I HAVE NO IDEA WHAT YOU'RE TALKING ABOUT.
ARREST THIS MAN!
I DON'T SUPPOSE YOU'D CARE TO TELL ME WHAT HAPPENED?
YOU KNOW, I'D REALLY LOVE TO, SARGE, BUT I'M A LITTLE FOGGY ON THE DETAILS MYSELF.
I DIDN'T THINK SO.
WAGH
I'M NOT LISTENING
WELL, WHAT ARE YOU WAITING FOR? ARREST HIM!
YOU MEAN NOW?

PEOPLE! PEOPLE! PLEASE...!

I'VE BEEN STARVING MYSELF TO DEATH BECAUSE YOU SAID YOU DIDN'T LIKE FAT GIRLS!

FRANCINE'S NOT FAT, SHE'S RUBENESQUE!

AND YOU'RE GROTESQUE, YOU CREEP!

OHH.. EVERYTIME SHE SAYS THAT MY HEART SKIPS A BEAT.

ALRIGHT! THAT'S ENOUGH! I WANT SOME ANSWERS HERE OR I'M GOING TO START THROWING PEOPLE IN JAIL!

I THINK I CAN EXPLAIN... I'M AN ATTORNEY...

YEAH, THAT EXPLAINS A LOT!

WAGH!

WANTED

YOU SEE, IT'S LIKE THIS, I WAS SITTING AT HOME, READING MY BIBLE...

THAT'S A DAMN LIE!

WAGH!

I WANT MY PAINTINGS BACK, YOU PIG! AND MY BIKINI! AND MY POLAROIDS!

I BOUGHT THOSE PAINTINGS FAIR AND SQUARE! I HAVE A LEGAL RECEIPT!

THOSE PAINTINGS WEREN'T FOR SALE! YOU STOLE THEM!

QUIET! QUIET!

I AM NOT A CROOK! I'M WELL WITHIN MY LEGAL RIGHTS!

YOU GO GIRL.

WAGH!

POLICE

AD LIB AD NAUSEAM

SIGNORA EL LOOPO

BLAM!

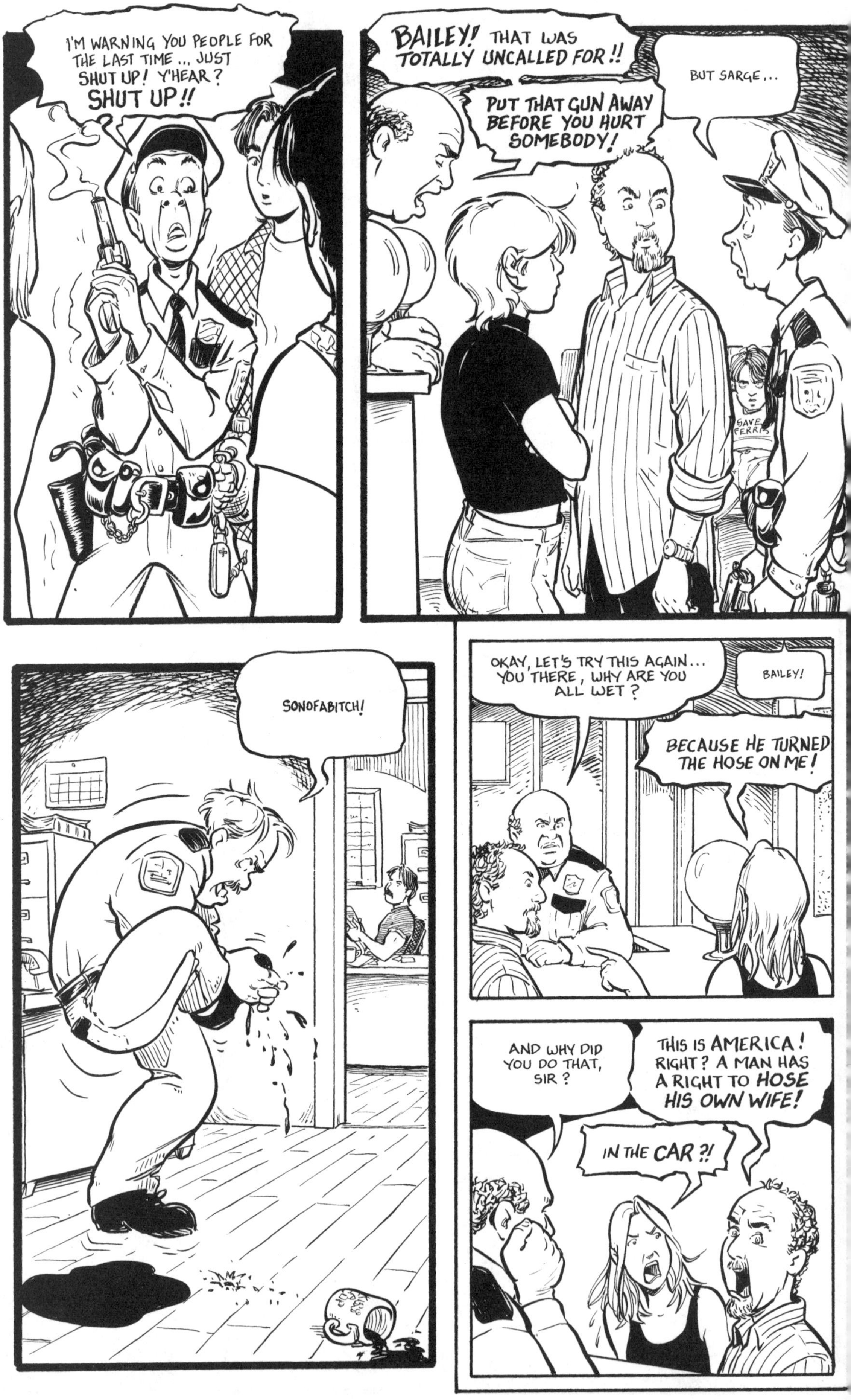
I'M WARNING YOU PEOPLE FOR THE LAST TIME ... JUST SHUT UP! Y'HEAR? SHUT UP!!
BAILEY! THAT WAS TOTALLY UNCALLED FOR!!
PUT THAT GUN AWAY BEFORE YOU HURT SOMEBODY!
BUT SARGE...
SAVE FERRIS
SONOFABITCH!
OKAY, LET'S TRY THIS AGAIN... YOU THERE, WHY ARE YOU ALL WET?
BAILEY!
BECAUSE HE TURNED THE HOSE ON ME!
AND WHY DID YOU DO THAT, SIR?
THIS IS AMERICA! RIGHT? A MAN HAS A RIGHT TO HOSE HIS OWN WIFE!
IN THE CAR?!

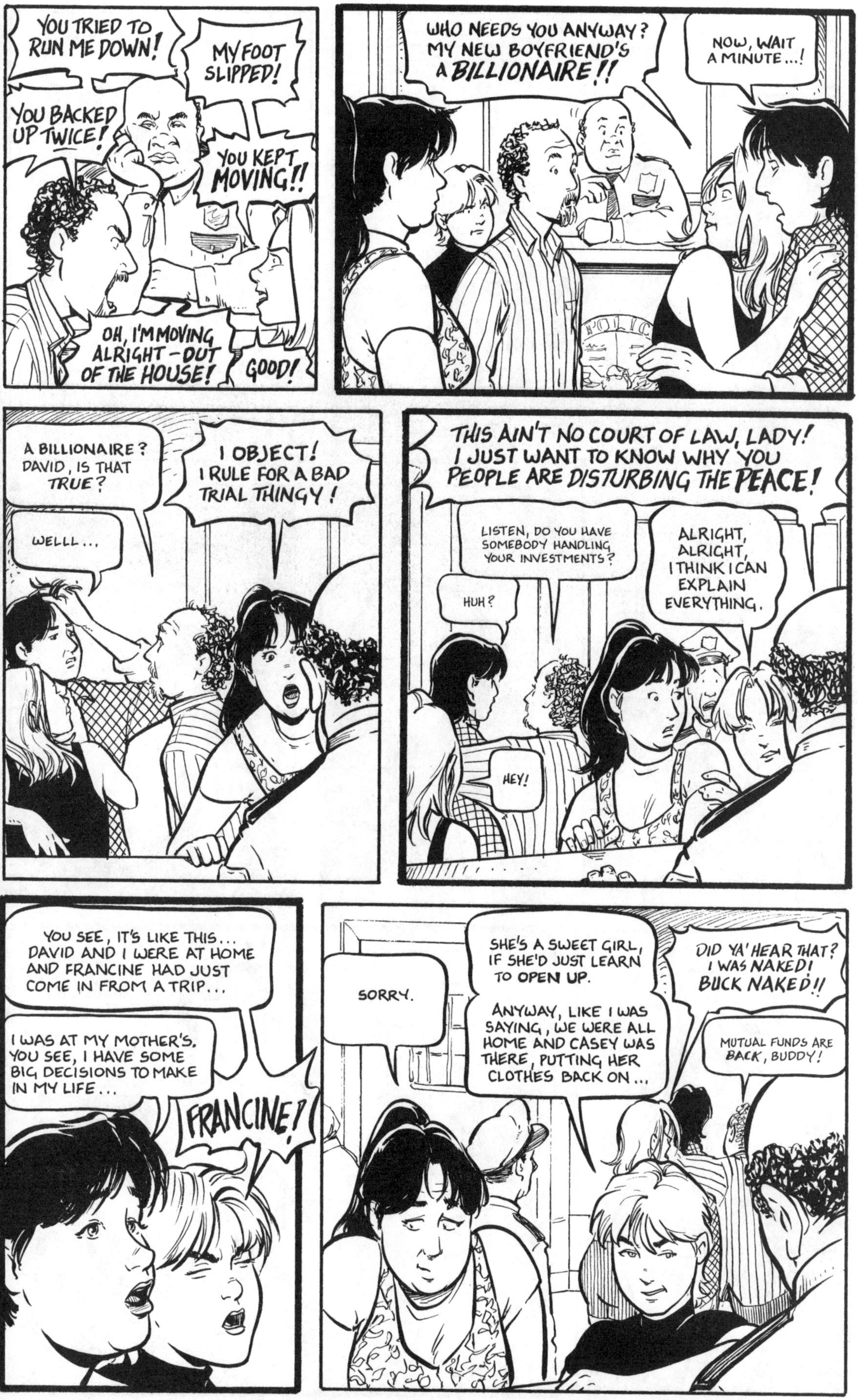

YOU TRIED TO RUN ME DOWN!
MY FOOT SLIPPED!
YOU BACKED UP TWICE!
YOU KEPT MOVING!!
OH, I'M MOVING ALRIGHT—OUT OF THE HOUSE!
GOOD!
WHO NEEDS YOU ANYWAY? MY NEW BOYFRIEND'S A BILLIONAIRE!!
NOW, WAIT A MINUTE...!
A BILLIONAIRE? DAVID, IS THAT TRUE?
I OBJECT! I RULE FOR A BAD TRIAL THINGY!
WELLL...
THIS AIN'T NO COURT OF LAW, LADY! I JUST WANT TO KNOW WHY YOU PEOPLE ARE DISTURBING THE PEACE!
LISTEN, DO YOU HAVE SOMEBODY HANDLING YOUR INVESTMENTS?
ALRIGHT, ALRIGHT, I THINK I CAN EXPLAIN EVERYTHING.
HUH?
HEY!
YOU SEE, IT'S LIKE THIS... DAVID AND I WERE AT HOME AND FRANCINE HAD JUST COME IN FROM A TRIP...
I WAS AT MY MOTHER'S. YOU SEE, I HAVE SOME BIG DECISIONS TO MAKE IN MY LIFE...
FRANCINE!
SORRY.
SHE'S A SWEET GIRL, IF SHE'D JUST LEARN TO OPEN UP.
ANYWAY, LIKE I WAS SAYING, WE WERE ALL HOME AND CASEY WAS THERE, PUTTING HER CLOTHES BACK ON...
DID YA' HEAR THAT? I WAS NAKED! BUCK NAKED!!
MUTUAL FUNDS ARE BACK, BUDDY!

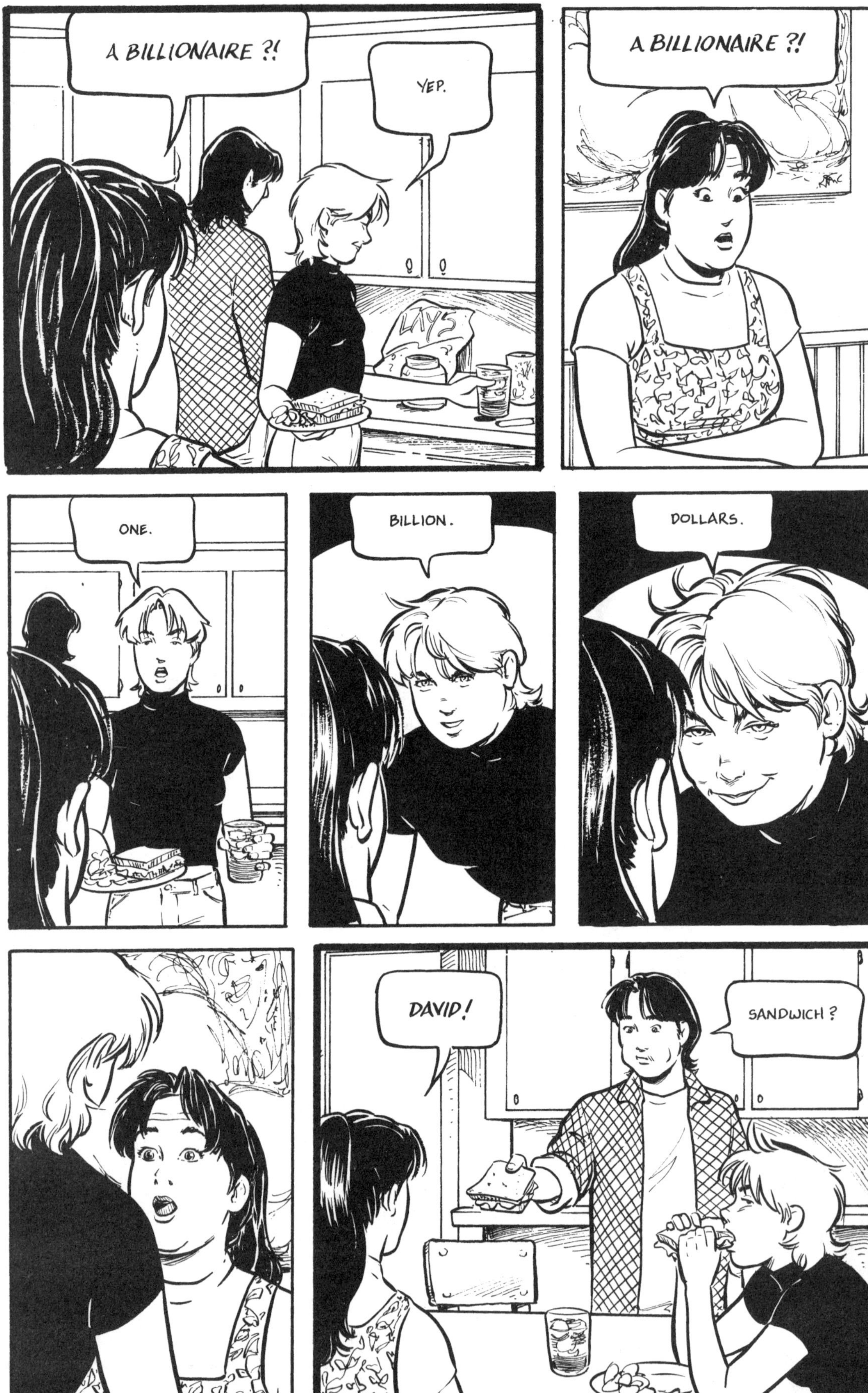
A BILLIONAIRE ?!
YEP.
A BILLIONAIRE ?!
ONE.
BILLION.
DOLLARS.
DAVID!
SANDWICH?

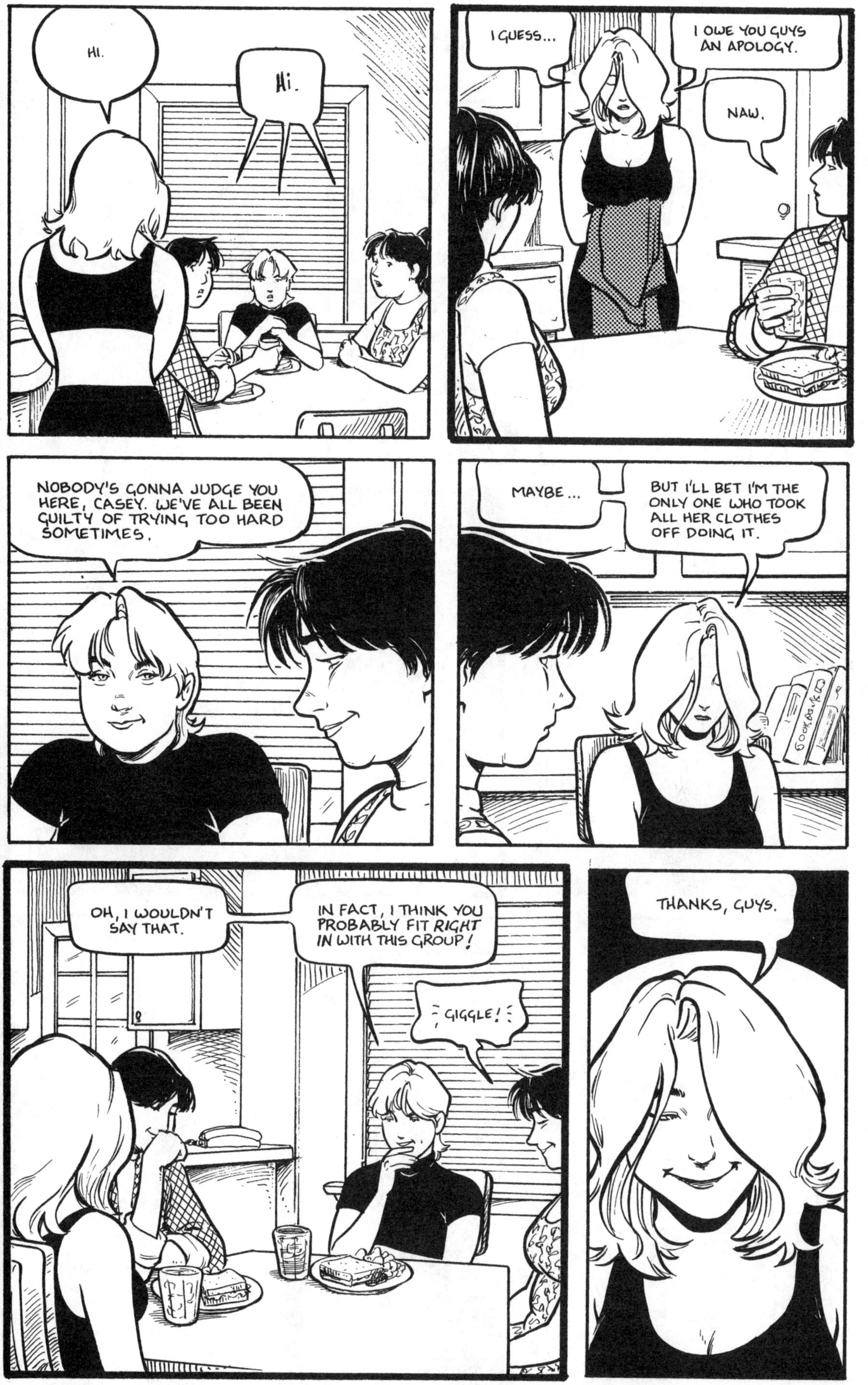
HI.
Hi.
I GUESS...
I OWE YOU GUYS AN APOLOGY.
NAW.
NOBODY'S GONNA JUDGE YOU HERE, CASEY. WE'VE ALL BEEN GUILTY OF TRYING TOO HARD SOMETIMES.
MAYBE...
BUT I'LL BET I'M THE ONLY ONE WHO TOOK ALL HER CLOTHES OFF DOING IT.
OH, I WOULDN'T SAY THAT.
IN FACT, I THINK YOU PROBABLY FIT *RIGHT IN* WITH THIS GROUP!
GIGGLE!
THANKS, GUYS.

CAN I JUST ASK A QUESTION?

WHY WERE DAVID AND CASEY HIDING IN THE BATHROOM WHEN I CAME IN?

I MEAN... ?

OH! WELL, BECAUSE...
...UH....

I DON'T KNOW!

KATCHOO, WHY DID YOU TELL US TO HIDE IN THE BATHROOM?

BECAUSE...

I THOUGHT IT WAS FUNNY.

≀SNORT!≀

"KATCHOO, THERE'S NO TOWELS!"

HA HA! HA HA! HA HA! HA! HA HA! HA HA HA! HA HA! HA HA! HA HA!

AW GEEZ, I CRACK MYSELF UP.

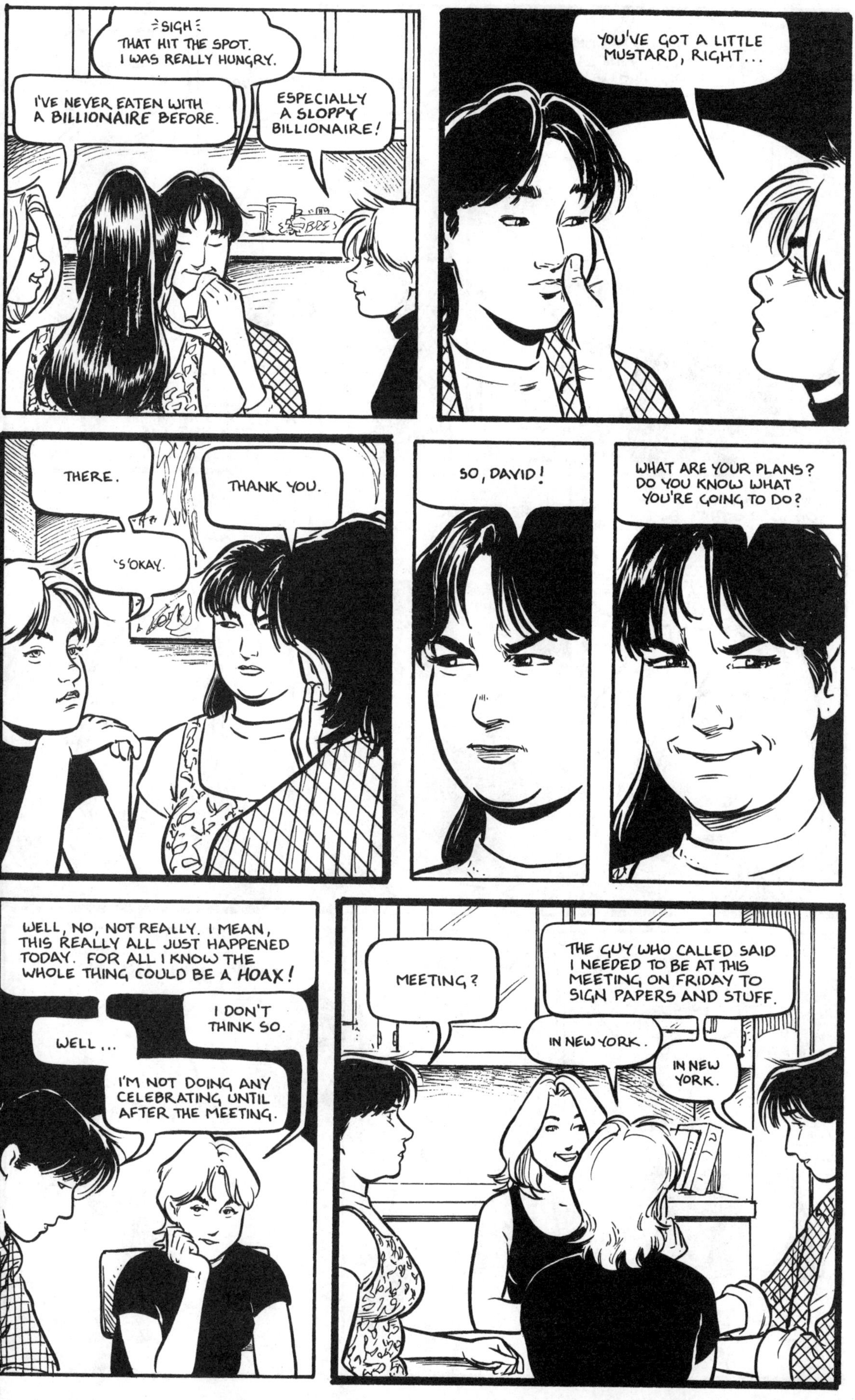

SIGH
THAT HIT THE SPOT. I WAS REALLY HUNGRY.
I'VE NEVER EATEN WITH A BILLIONAIRE BEFORE.
ESPECIALLY A SLOPPY BILLIONAIRE!
YOU'VE GOT A LITTLE MUSTARD, RIGHT...
THERE.
THANK YOU.
'S'OKAY.
SO, DAVID!
WHAT ARE YOUR PLANS? DO YOU KNOW WHAT YOU'RE GOING TO DO?
WELL, NO, NOT REALLY. I MEAN, THIS REALLY ALL JUST HAPPENED TODAY. FOR ALL I KNOW THE WHOLE THING COULD BE A HOAX!
WELL...
I DON'T THINK SO.
I'M NOT DOING ANY CELEBRATING UNTIL AFTER THE MEETING.
MEETING?
THE GUY WHO CALLED SAID I NEEDED TO BE AT THIS MEETING ON FRIDAY TO SIGN PAPERS AND STUFF.
IN NEW YORK.
IN NEW YORK.

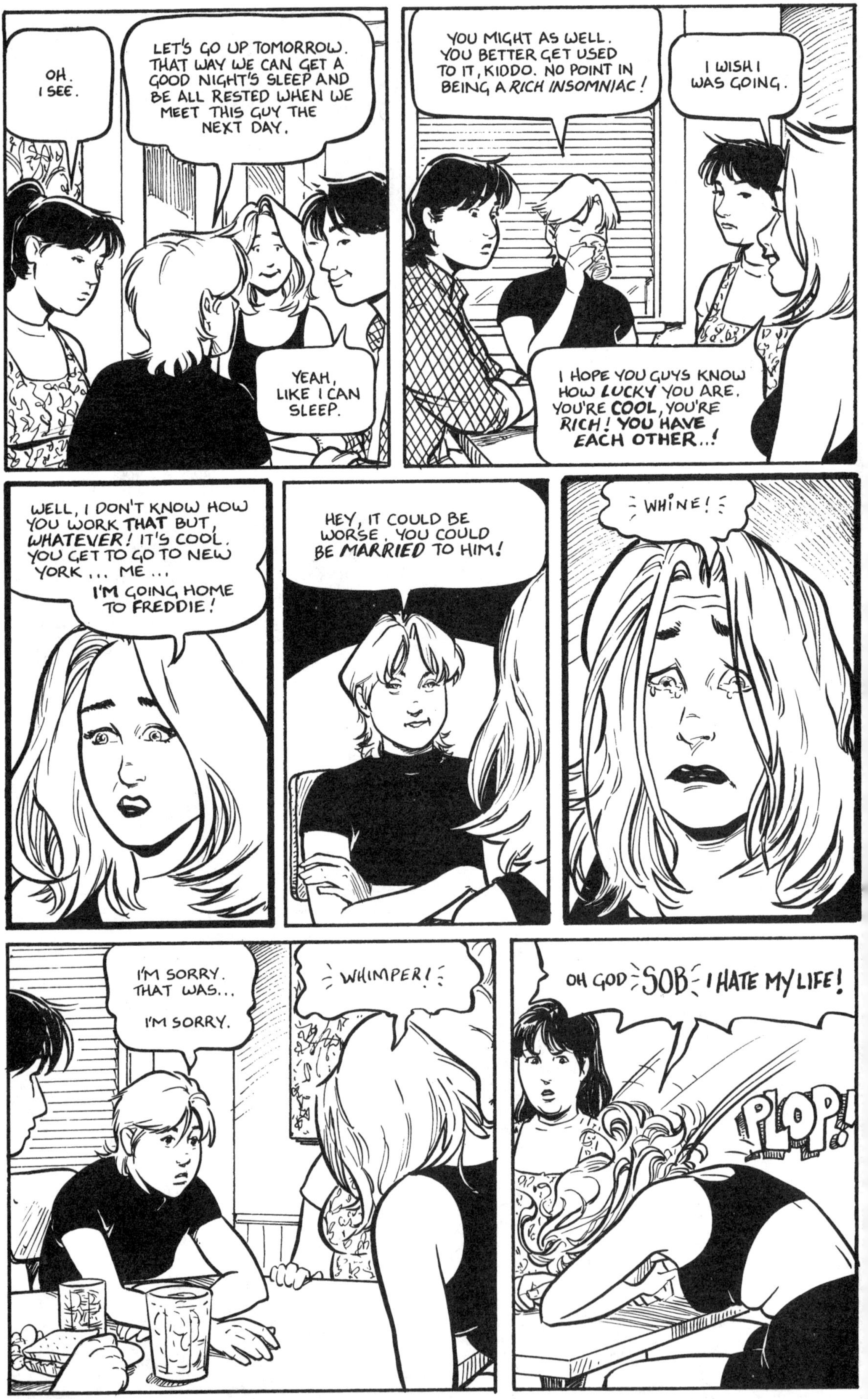

OH. I SEE.
LET'S GO UP TOMORROW. THAT WAY WE CAN GET A GOOD NIGHT'S SLEEP AND BE ALL RESTED WHEN WE MEET THIS GUY THE NEXT DAY.
YEAH, LIKE I CAN SLEEP.
YOU MIGHT AS WELL. YOU BETTER GET USED TO IT, KIDDO. NO POINT IN BEING A RICH INSOMNIAC!
I WISH I WAS GOING.
I HOPE YOU GUYS KNOW HOW LUCKY YOU ARE. YOU'RE COOL, YOU'RE RICH! YOU HAVE EACH OTHER...!
WELL, I DON'T KNOW HOW YOU WORK THAT BUT, WHATEVER! IT'S COOL. YOU GET TO GO TO NEW YORK ... ME ... I'M GOING HOME TO FREDDIE!
HEY, IT COULD BE WORSE. YOU COULD BE MARRIED TO HIM!
WHINE!
I'M SORRY. THAT WAS... I'M SORRY.
WHIMPER!
OH GOD SOB I HATE MY LIFE!
PLOP!

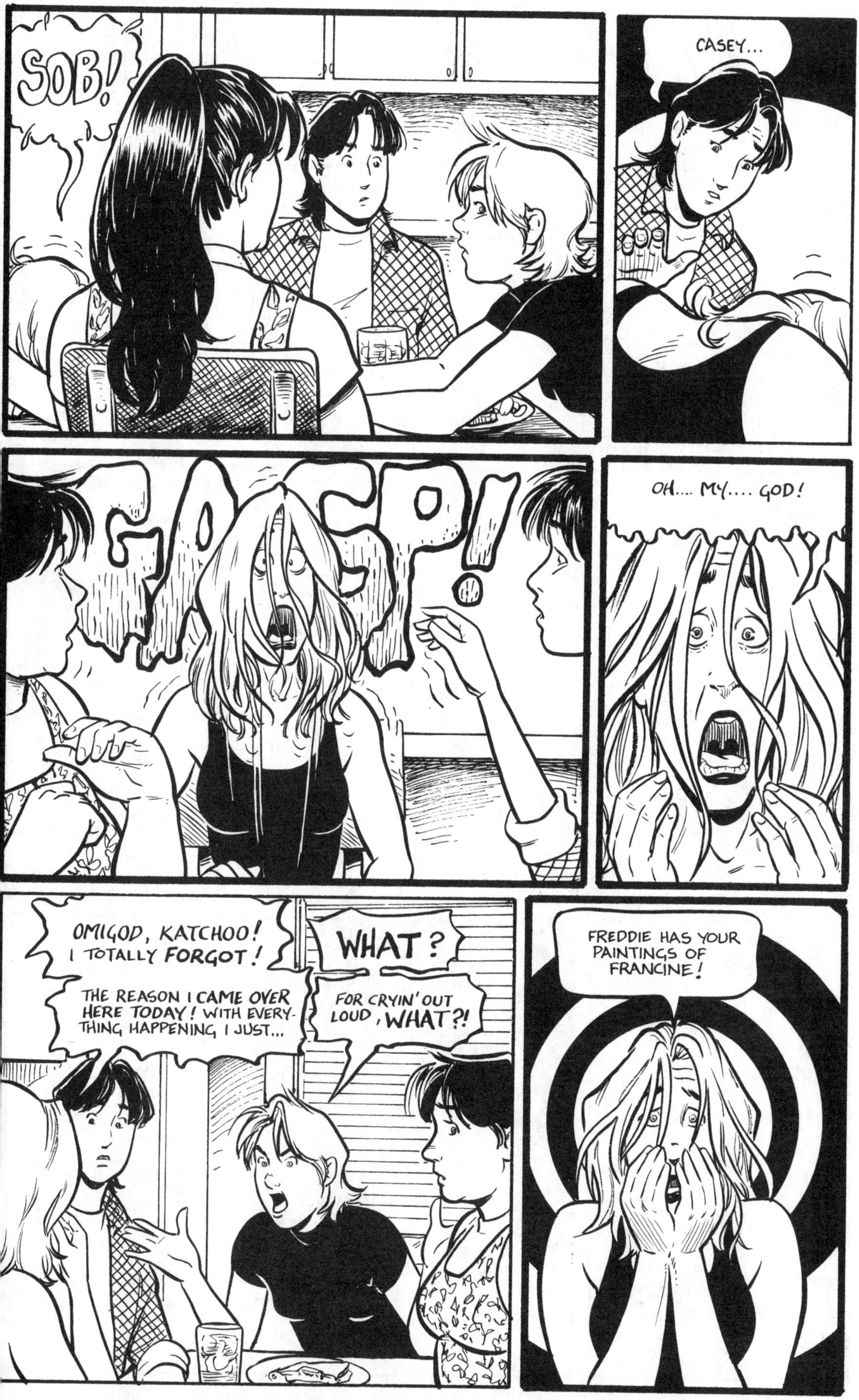
SOB!
CASEY...
GASP!
OH.... MY.... GOD!
OMIGOD, KATCHOO! I TOTALLY FORGOT!
THE REASON I CAME OVER HERE TODAY! WITH EVERYTHING HAPPENING I JUST...
WHAT?
FOR CRYIN' OUT LOUD, WHAT?!
FREDDIE HAS YOUR PAINTINGS OF FRANCINE!

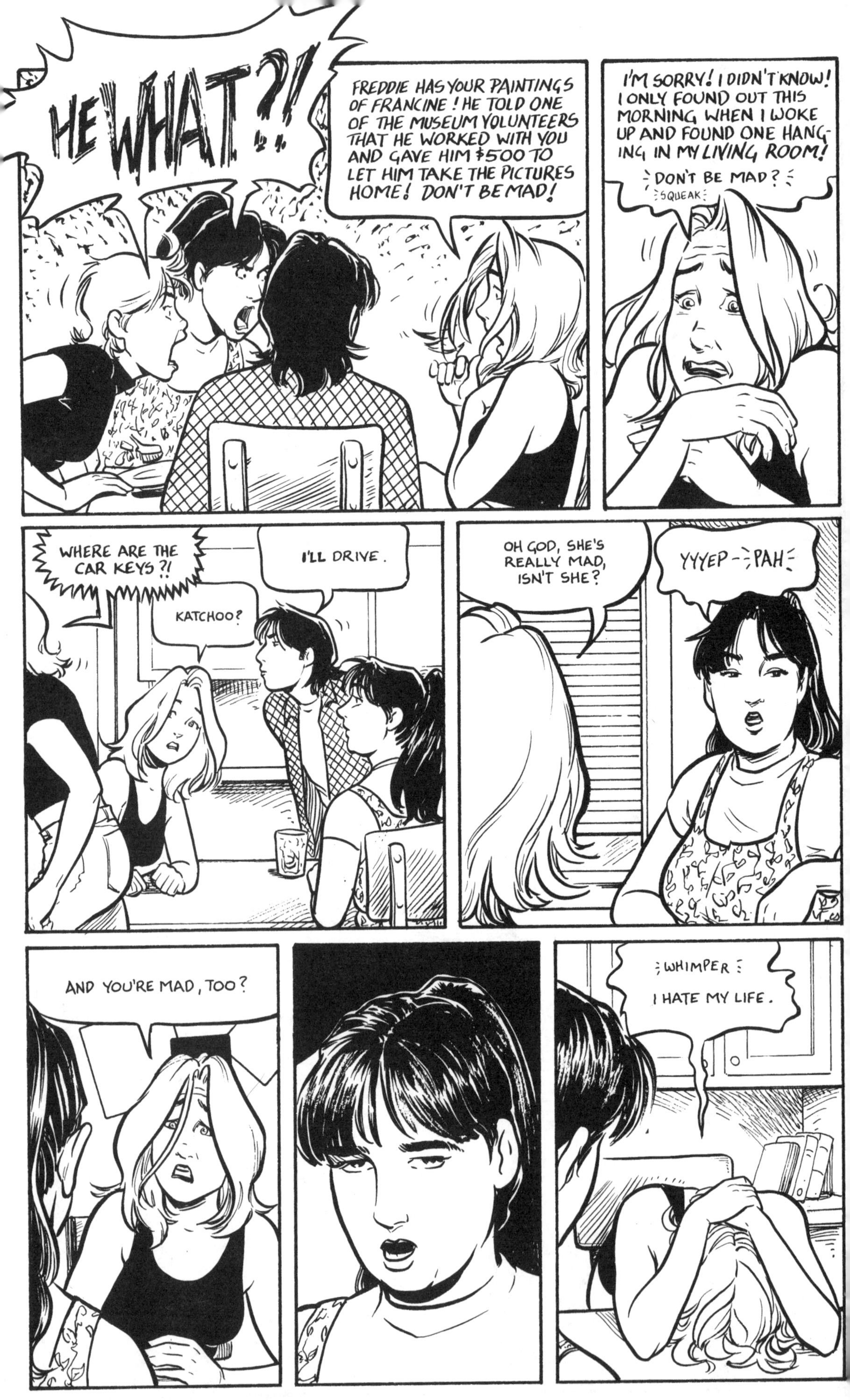
HE WHAT?!
FREDDIE HAS YOUR PAINTINGS OF FRANCINE! HE TOLD ONE OF THE MUSEUM VOLUNTEERS THAT HE WORKED WITH YOU AND GAVE HIM $500 TO LET HIM TAKE THE PICTURES HOME! DON'T BE MAD!
I'M SORRY! I DIDN'T KNOW! I ONLY FOUND OUT THIS MORNING WHEN I WOKE UP AND FOUND ONE HANGING IN MY LIVING ROOM!
DON'T BE MAD?
SQUEAK
WHERE ARE THE CAR KEYS?!
I'LL DRIVE.
KATCHOO?
OH GOD, SHE'S REALLY MAD, ISN'T SHE?
YYYEP — PAH
AND YOU'RE MAD, TOO?
WHIMPER
I HATE MY LIFE.

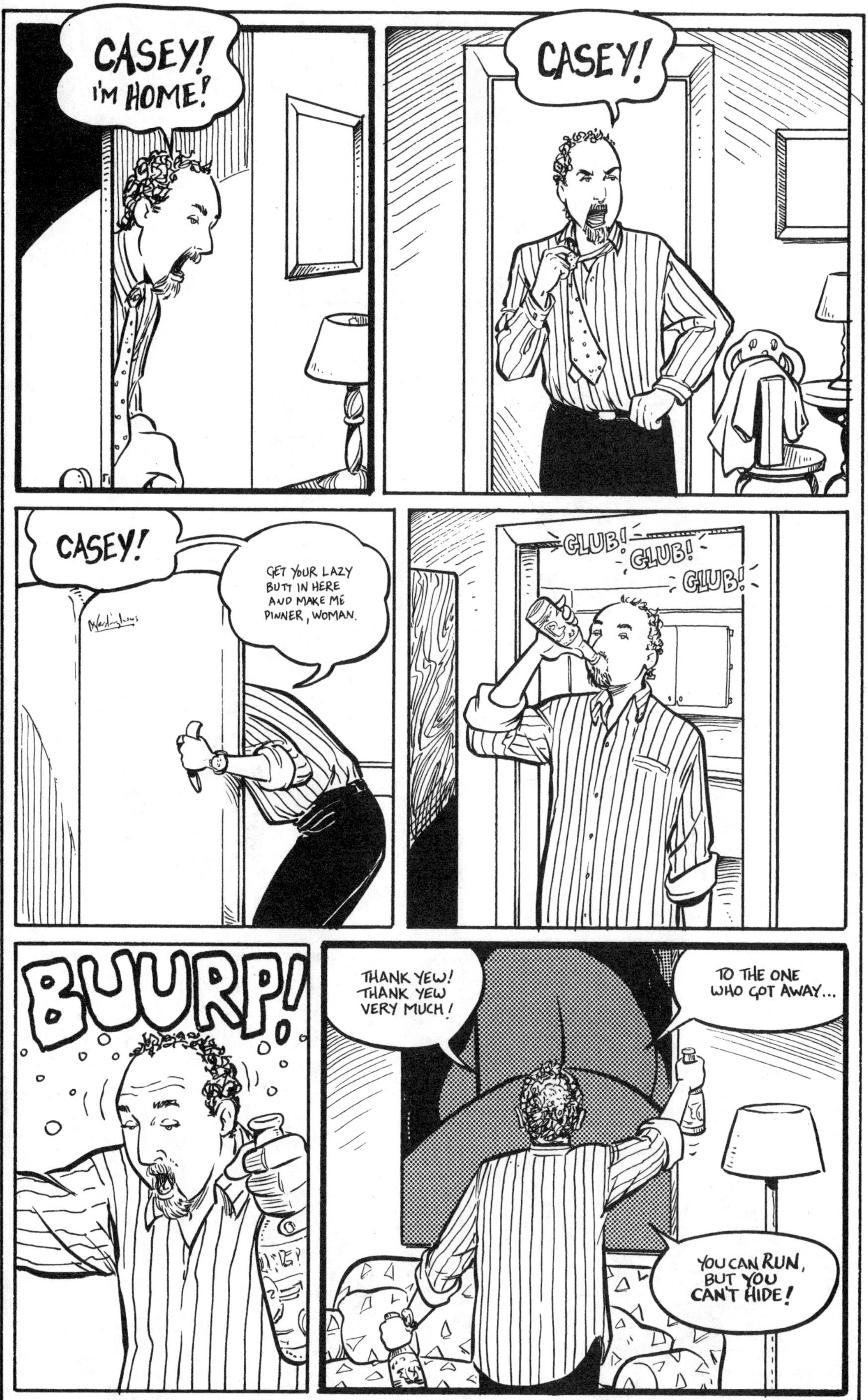

CASEY! I'M HOME!
CASEY!
CASEY!
GET YOUR LAZY BUTT IN HERE AND MAKE ME DINNER, WOMAN.
GLUB! GLUB! GLUB!
BUURP!
THANK YEW! THANK YEW VERY MUCH!
TO THE ONE WHO GOT AWAY...
YOU CAN RUN, BUT YOU CAN'T HIDE!

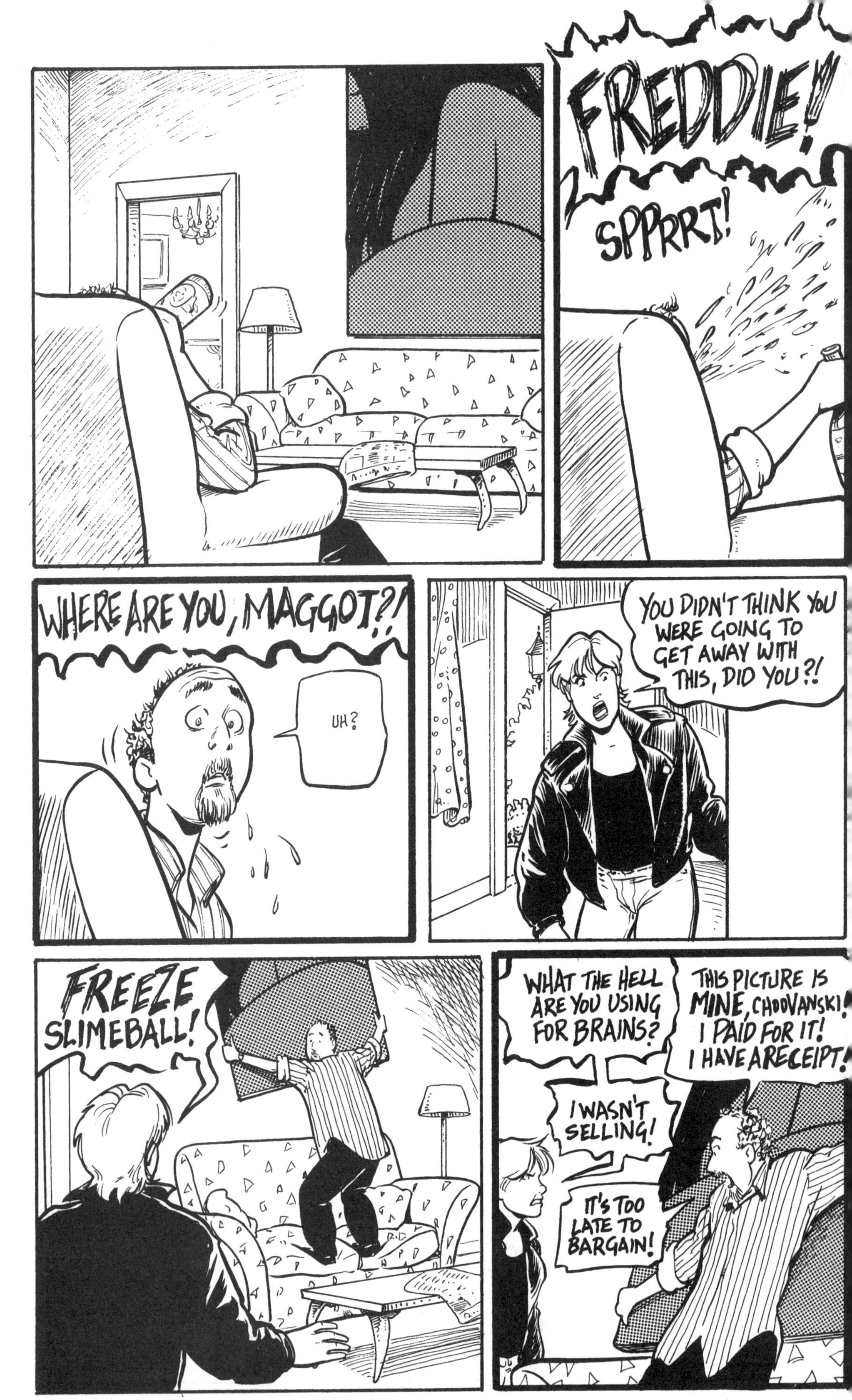
FREDDIE!
SPPRRT!
WHERE ARE YOU, MAGGOT?!
UH?
YOU DIDN'T THINK YOU WERE GOING TO GET AWAY WITH THIS, DID YOU?!
FREEZE SLIMEBALL!
WHAT THE HELL ARE YOU USING FOR BRAINS?
THIS PICTURE IS MINE, CHOOVANSKI! I PAID FOR IT! I HAVE A RECEIPT!
I WASN'T SELLING!
IT'S TOO LATE TO BARGAIN!

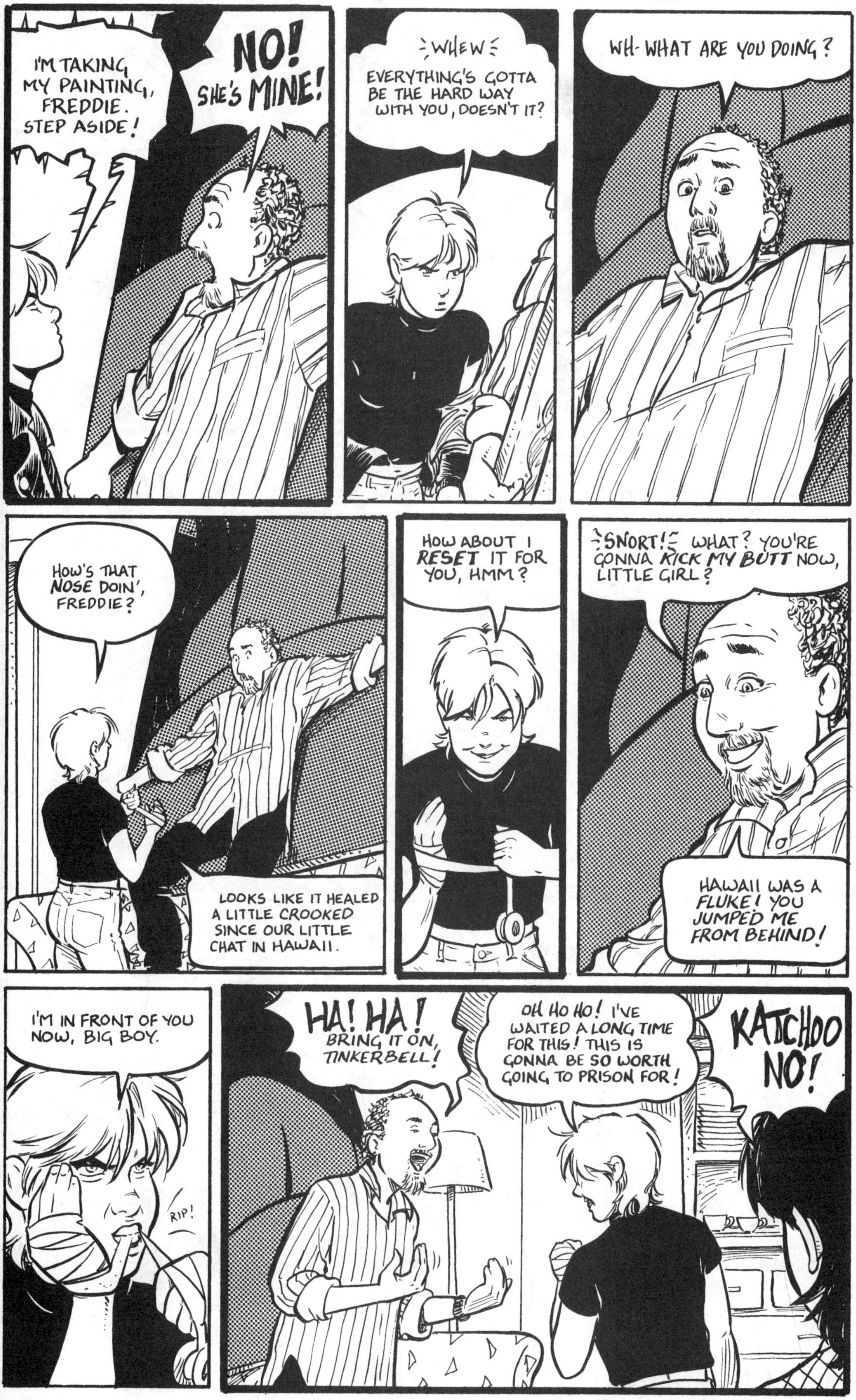

I'M TAKING MY PAINTING, FREDDIE. STEP ASIDE!
NO! SHE'S MINE!
WHEW
EVERYTHING'S GOTTA BE THE HARD WAY WITH YOU, DOESN'T IT?
WH-WHAT ARE YOU DOING?
HOW'S THAT NOSE DOIN', FREDDIE?
LOOKS LIKE IT HEALED A LITTLE CROOKED SINCE OUR LITTLE CHAT IN HAWAII.
HOW ABOUT I RESET IT FOR YOU, HMM?
SNORT! WHAT? YOU'RE GONNA KICK MY BUTT NOW, LITTLE GIRL?
HAWAII WAS A FLUKE! YOU JUMPED ME FROM BEHIND!
I'M IN FRONT OF YOU NOW, BIG BOY.
RIP!
HA! HA! BRING IT ON, TINKERBELL!
OH HO HO! I'VE WAITED A LONG TIME FOR THIS! THIS IS GONNA BE SO WORTH GOING TO PRISON FOR!
KATCHOO NO!

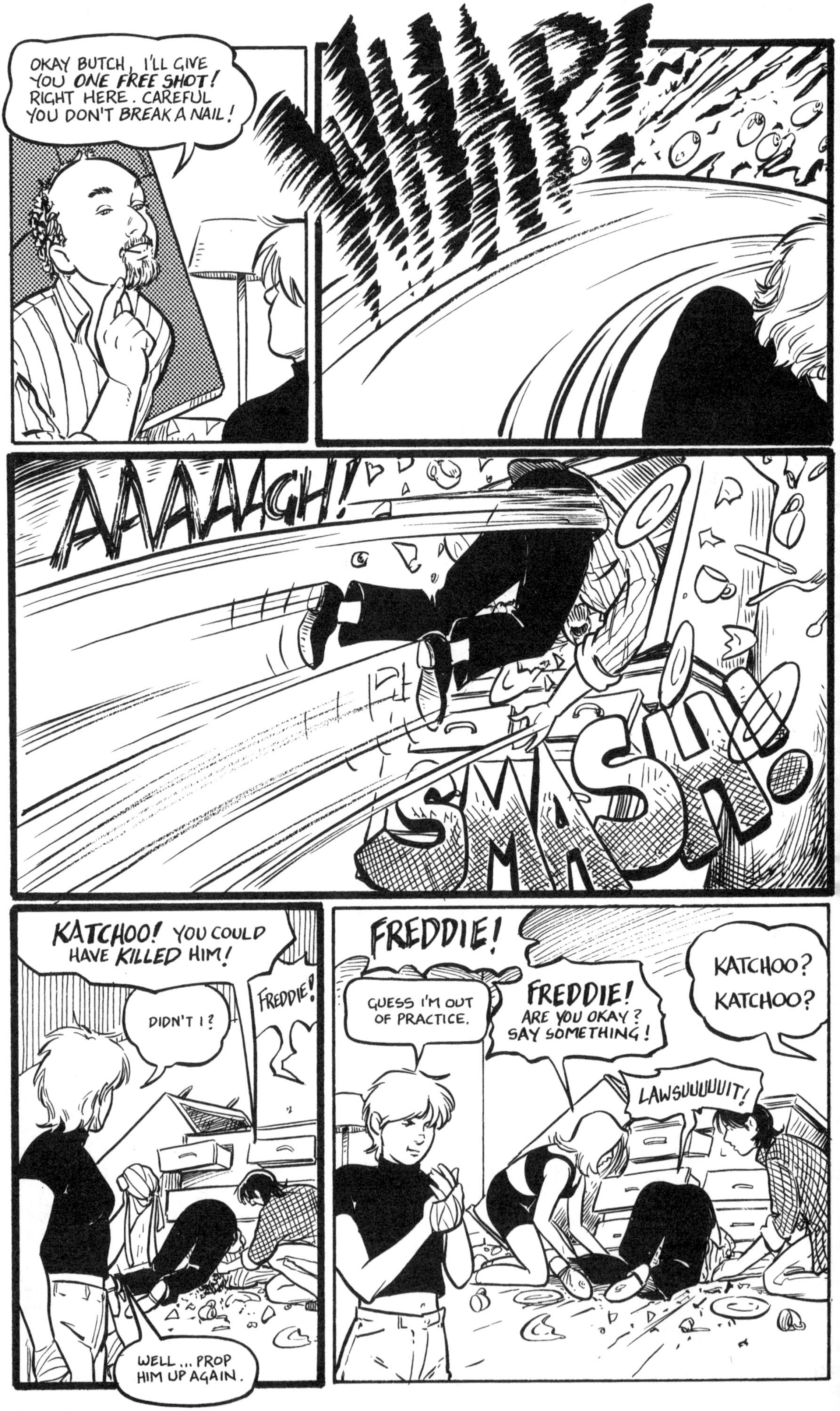
OKAY BUTCH, I'LL GIVE YOU ONE FREE SHOT! RIGHT HERE. CAREFUL YOU DON'T BREAK A NAIL!
WHAP!
AAAAAGH!
SMASH!
KATCHOO! YOU COULD HAVE KILLED HIM!
DIDN'T I?
FREDDIE!
WELL... PROP HIM UP AGAIN.
FREDDIE!
GUESS I'M OUT OF PRACTICE.
FREDDIE! ARE YOU OKAY? SAY SOMETHING!
KATCHOO? KATCHOO?
LAWSUUUUUIT!

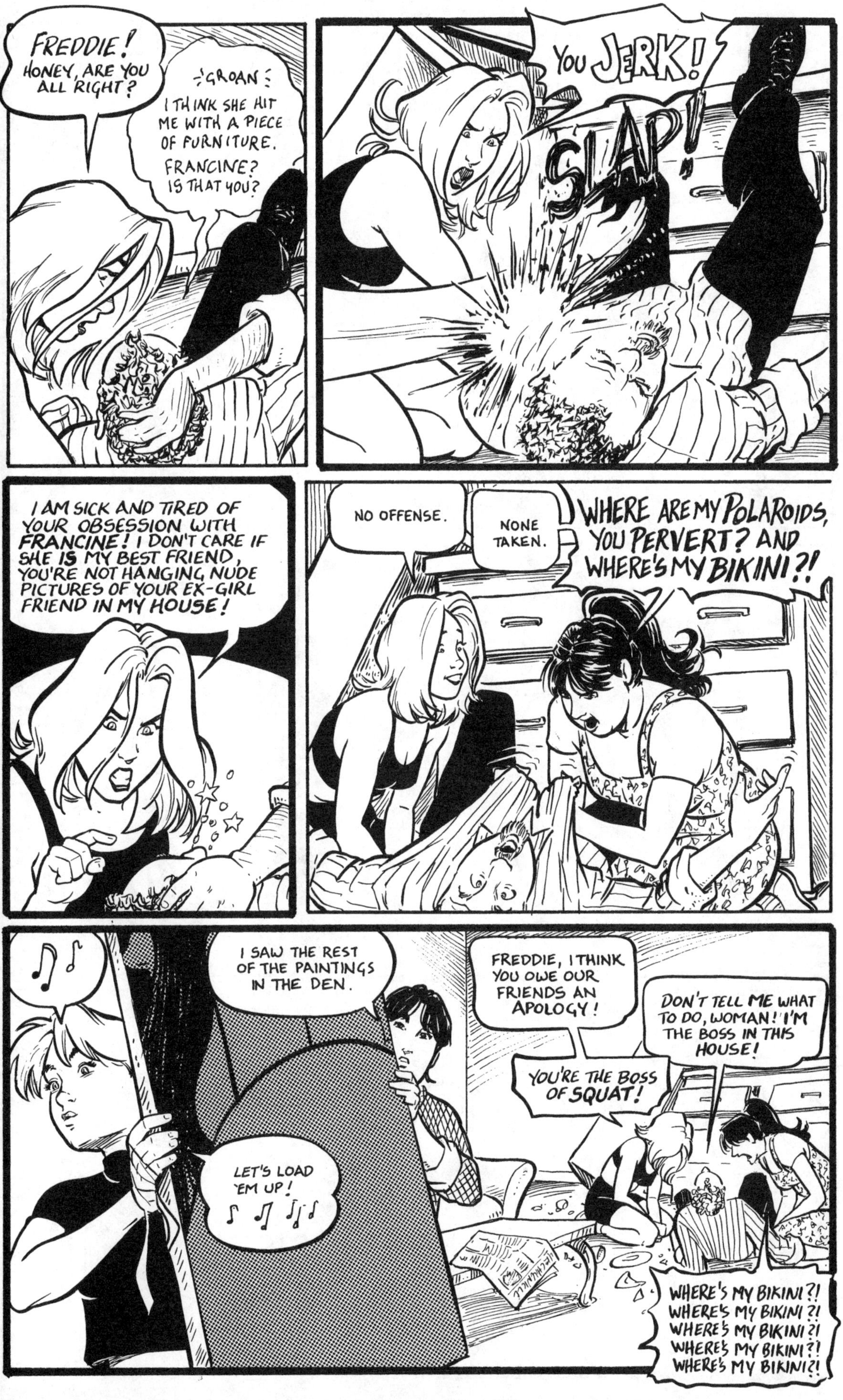
FREDDIE! HONEY, ARE YOU ALL RIGHT?
GROAN
I THINK SHE HIT ME WITH A PIECE OF FURNITURE.
FRANCINE? IS THAT YOU?
YOU JERK!
SLAP!
I AM SICK AND TIRED OF YOUR OBSESSION WITH FRANCINE! I DON'T CARE IF SHE IS MY BEST FRIEND, YOU'RE NOT HANGING NUDE PICTURES OF YOUR EX-GIRL FRIEND IN MY HOUSE!
NO OFFENSE.
NONE TAKEN.
WHERE ARE MY POLAROIDS, YOU PERVERT? AND WHERE'S MY BIKINI?!
I SAW THE REST OF THE PAINTINGS IN THE DEN.
LET'S LOAD 'EM UP!
FREDDIE, I THINK YOU OWE OUR FRIENDS AN APOLOGY!
DON'T TELL ME WHAT TO DO, WOMAN! I'M THE BOSS IN THIS HOUSE!
YOU'RE THE BOSS OF SQUAT!
WHERE'S MY BIKINI?!
WHERE'S MY BIKINI?!
WHERE'S MY BIKINI?!
WHERE'S MY BIKINI?!
WHERE'S MY BIKINI?!

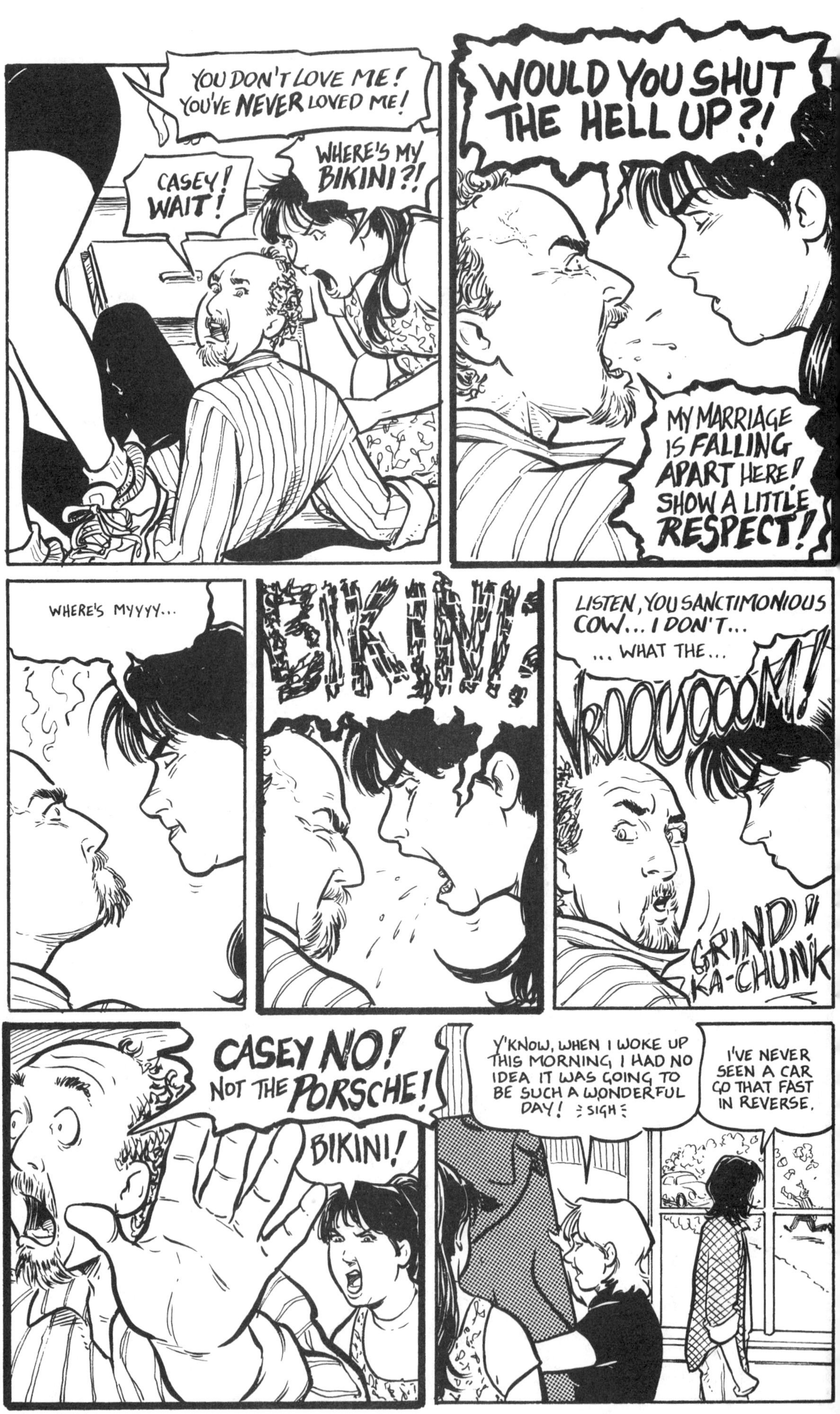
YOU DON'T LOVE ME! YOU'VE NEVER LOVED ME!
CASEY! WAIT!
WHERE'S MY BIKINI?!
WOULD YOU SHUT THE HELL UP?!
MY MARRIAGE IS FALLING APART HERE! SHOW A LITTLE RESPECT!
WHERE'S MYYYY...
BIKINI!
LISTEN, YOU SANCTIMONIOUS COW... I DON'T...
... WHAT THE...
VROOOOOOOM!
GRIND!!
KA-CHUNK
CASEY NO! NOT THE PORSCHE!
BIKINI!
Y'KNOW, WHEN I WOKE UP THIS MORNING, I HAD NO IDEA IT WAS GOING TO BE SUCH A WONDERFUL DAY! SIGH
I'VE NEVER SEEN A CAR GO THAT FAST IN REVERSE.

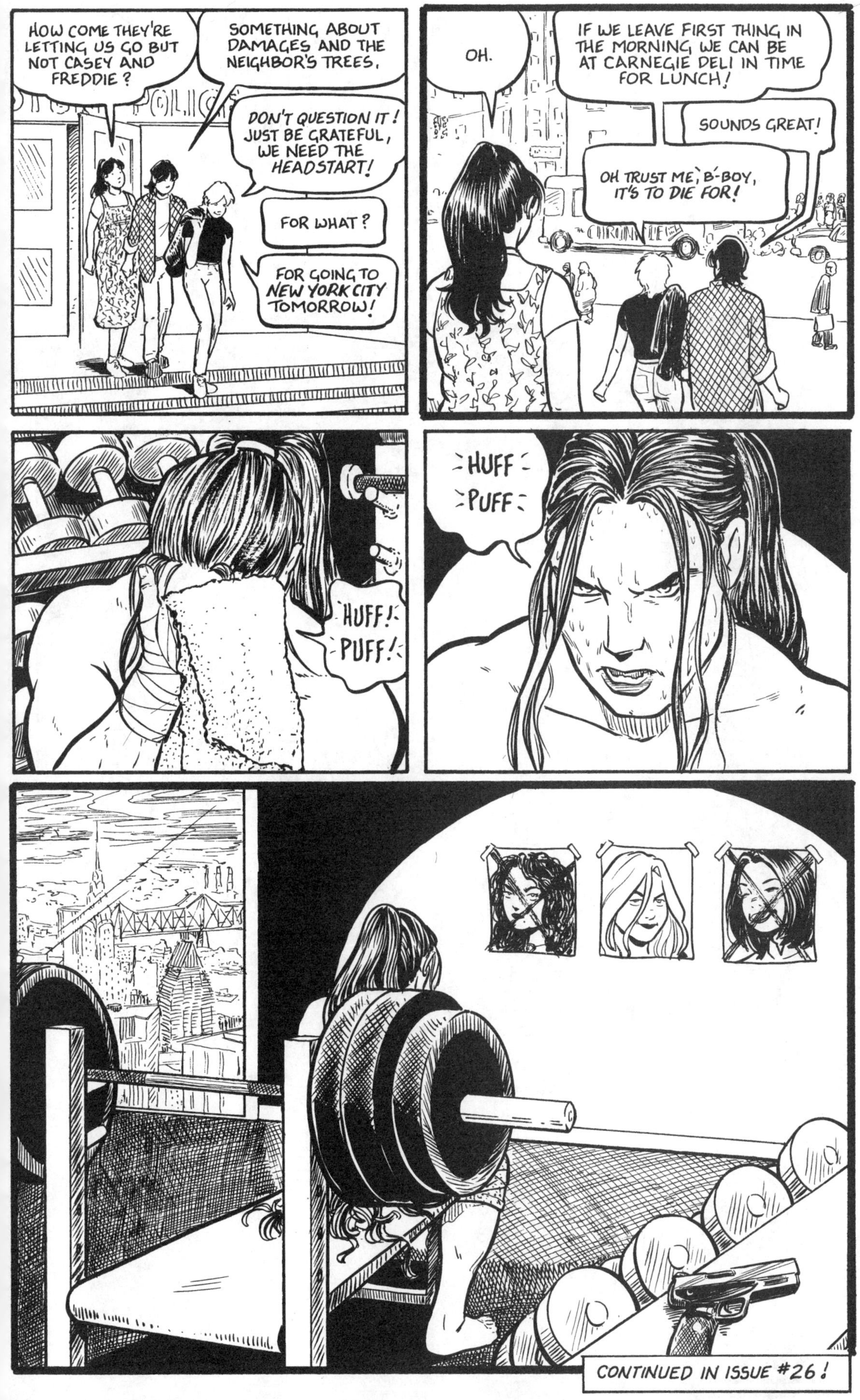

HOW COME THEY'RE LETTING US GO BUT NOT CASEY AND FREDDIE?
SOMETHING ABOUT DAMAGES AND THE NEIGHBOR'S TREES.
DON'T QUESTION IT! JUST BE GRATEFUL, WE NEED THE HEADSTART!
FOR WHAT?
FOR GOING TO NEW YORK CITY TOMORROW!
OH.
IF WE LEAVE FIRST THING IN THE MORNING WE CAN BE AT CARNEGIE DELI IN TIME FOR LUNCH!
SOUNDS GREAT!
OH TRUST ME, B-BOY, IT'S TO DIE FOR!
HUFF! PUFF!
HUFF PUFF
CONTINUED IN ISSUE #26!

TERRY MOORE

STRANGERS IN PARADISE

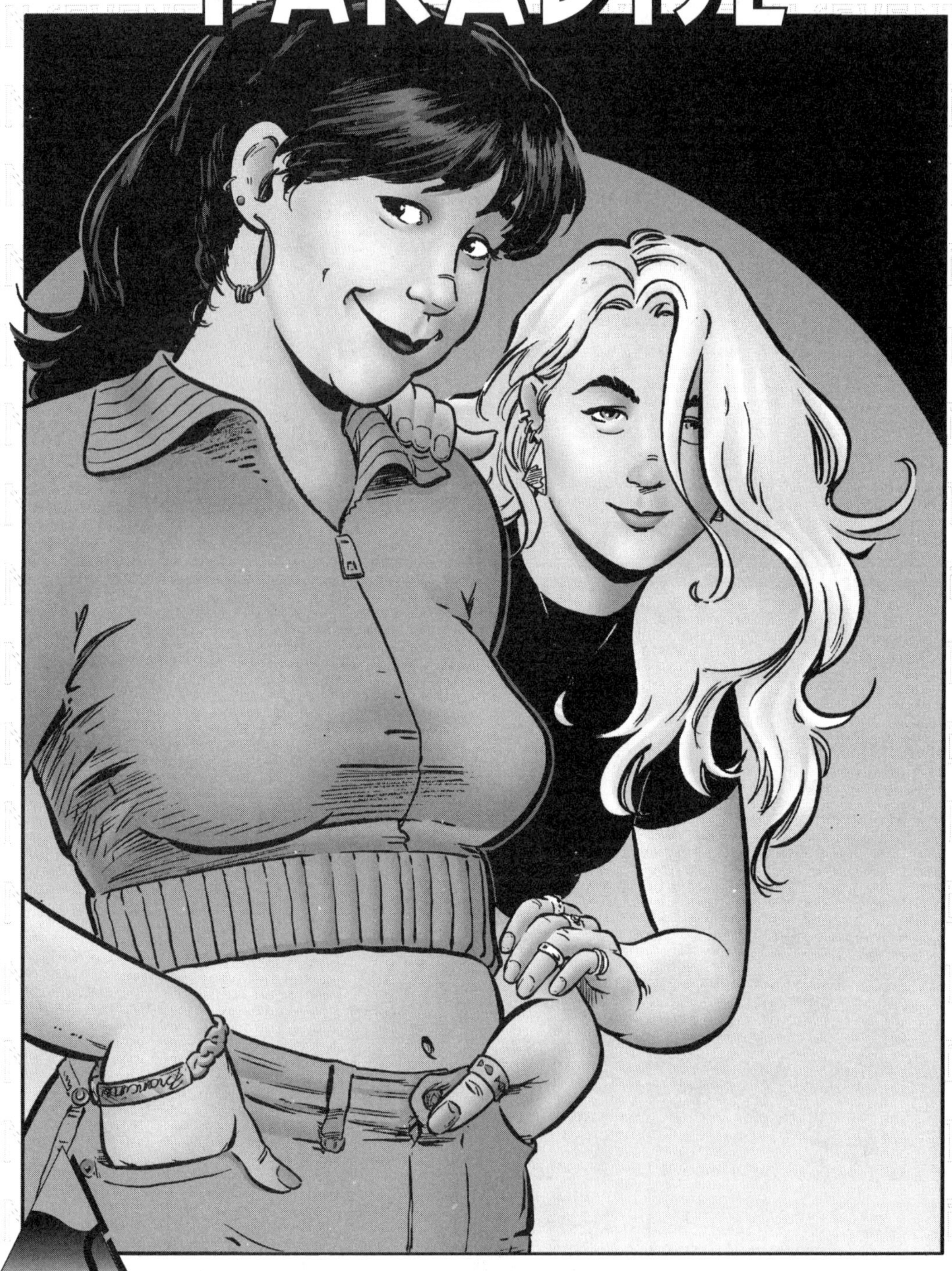

ABSTRACT STUDIO

SEVENTEEN

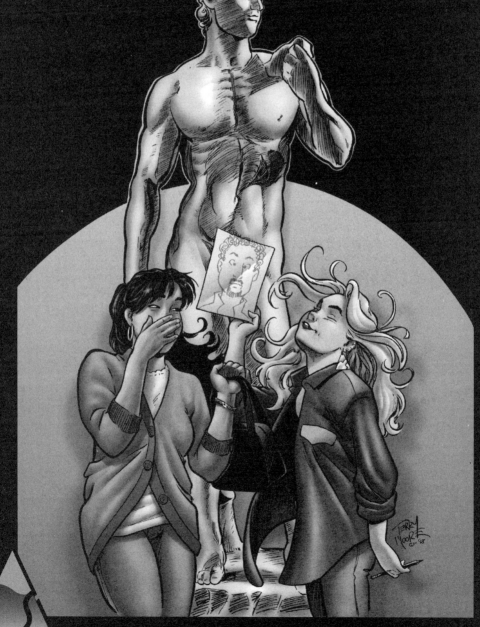

TERRY MOORE

STRANGERS IN PARADISE

ABSTRACT
STUDIO

XVIII

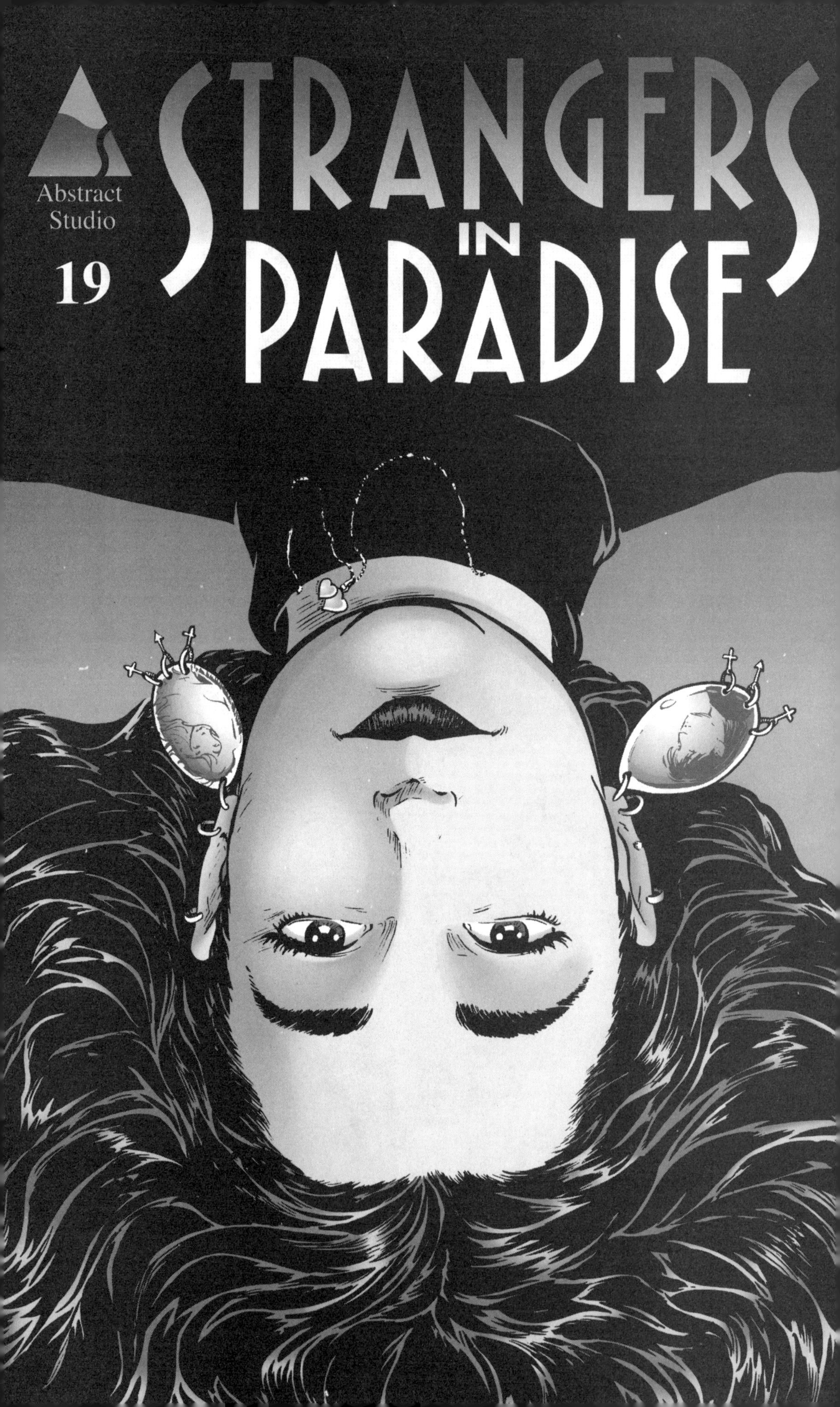
Abstract
Studio
19
STRANGERS
IN
PARADISE

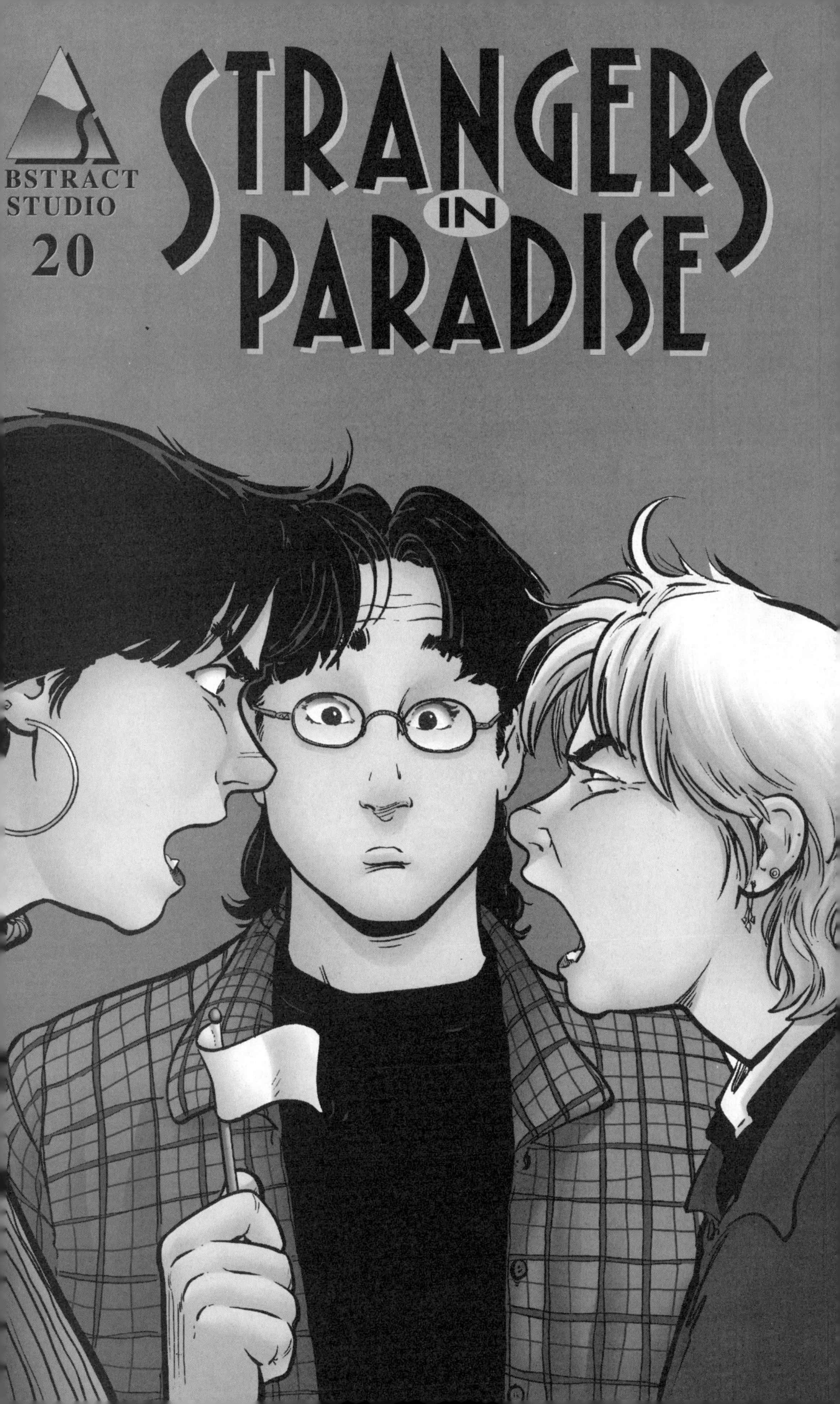
BSTRACT
STUDIO
20
STRANGERS
IN
PARADISE

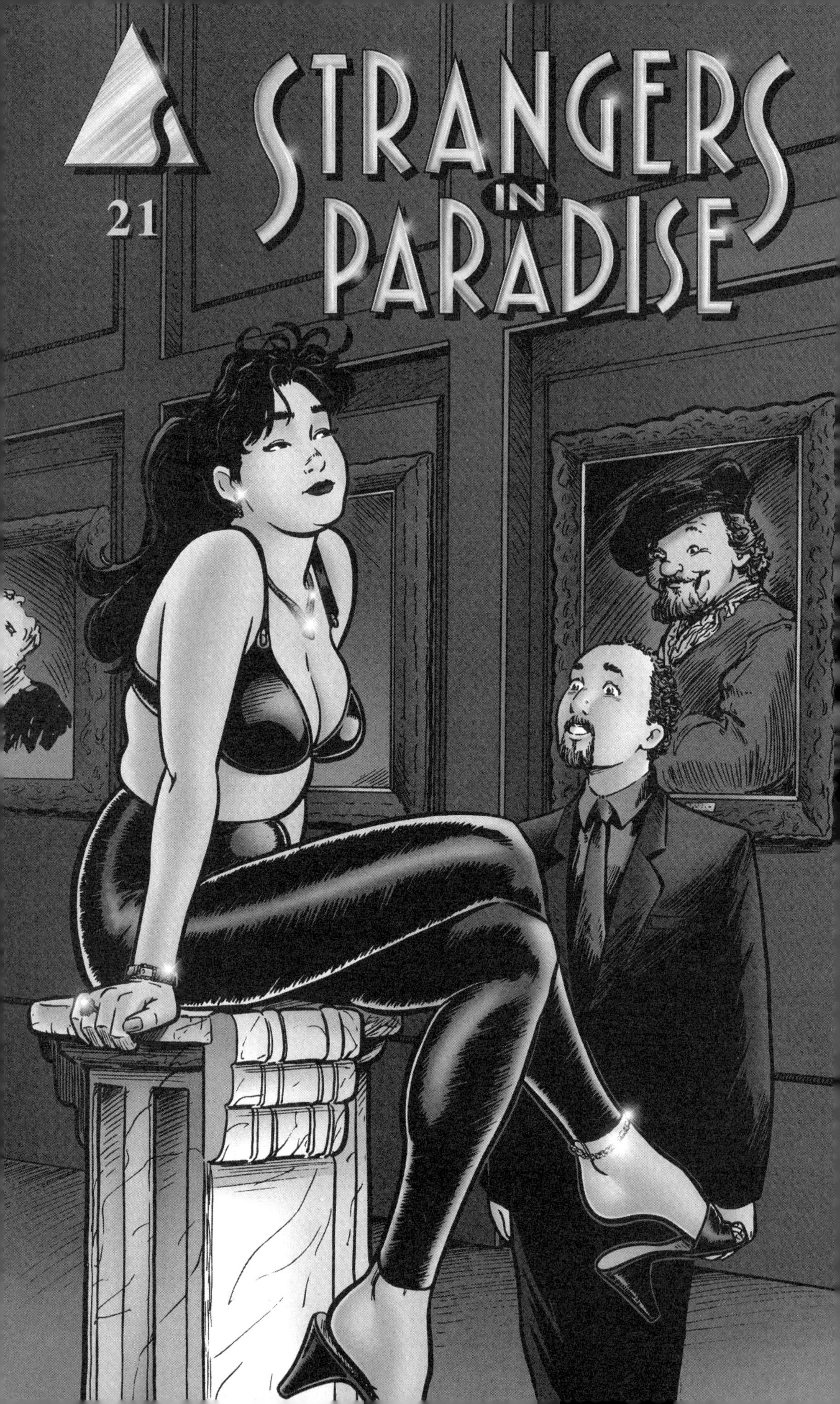
21
STRANGERS IN PARADISE

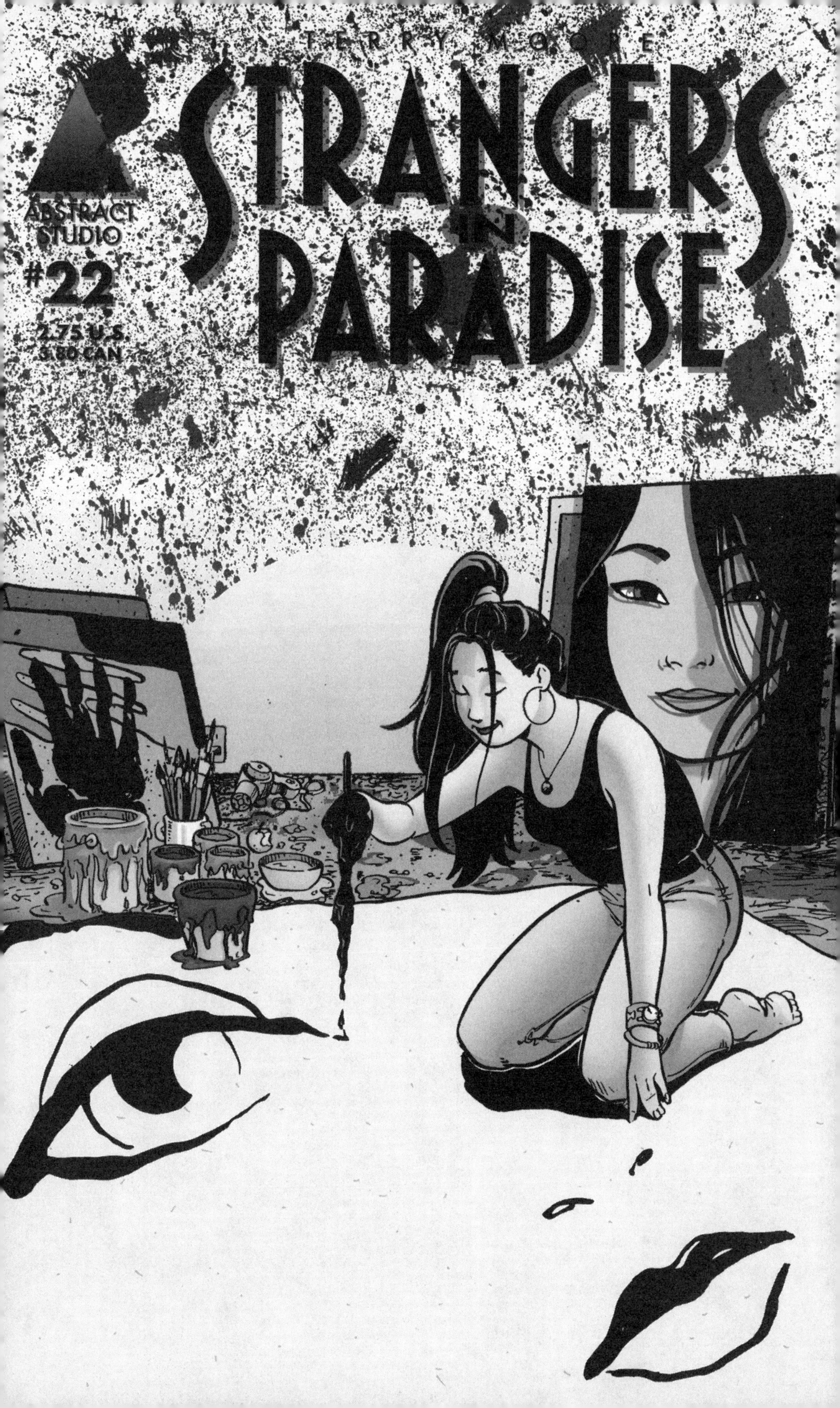
TERRY MOORE
STRANGERS IN PARADISE
ABSTRACT STUDIO
#22
2.75 U.S.
3.80 CAN

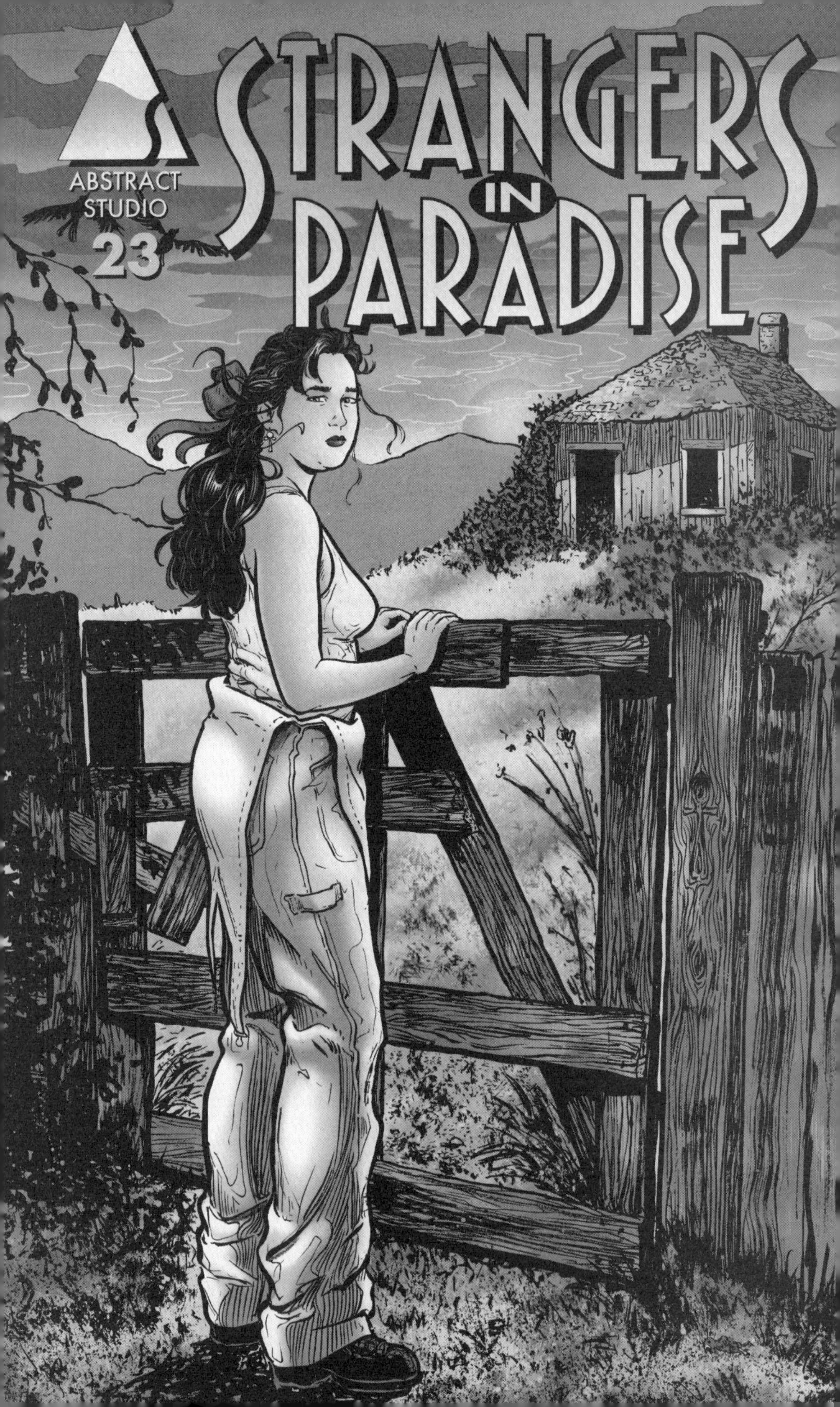
ABSTRACT
STUDIO
23
STRANGERS
IN
PARADISE

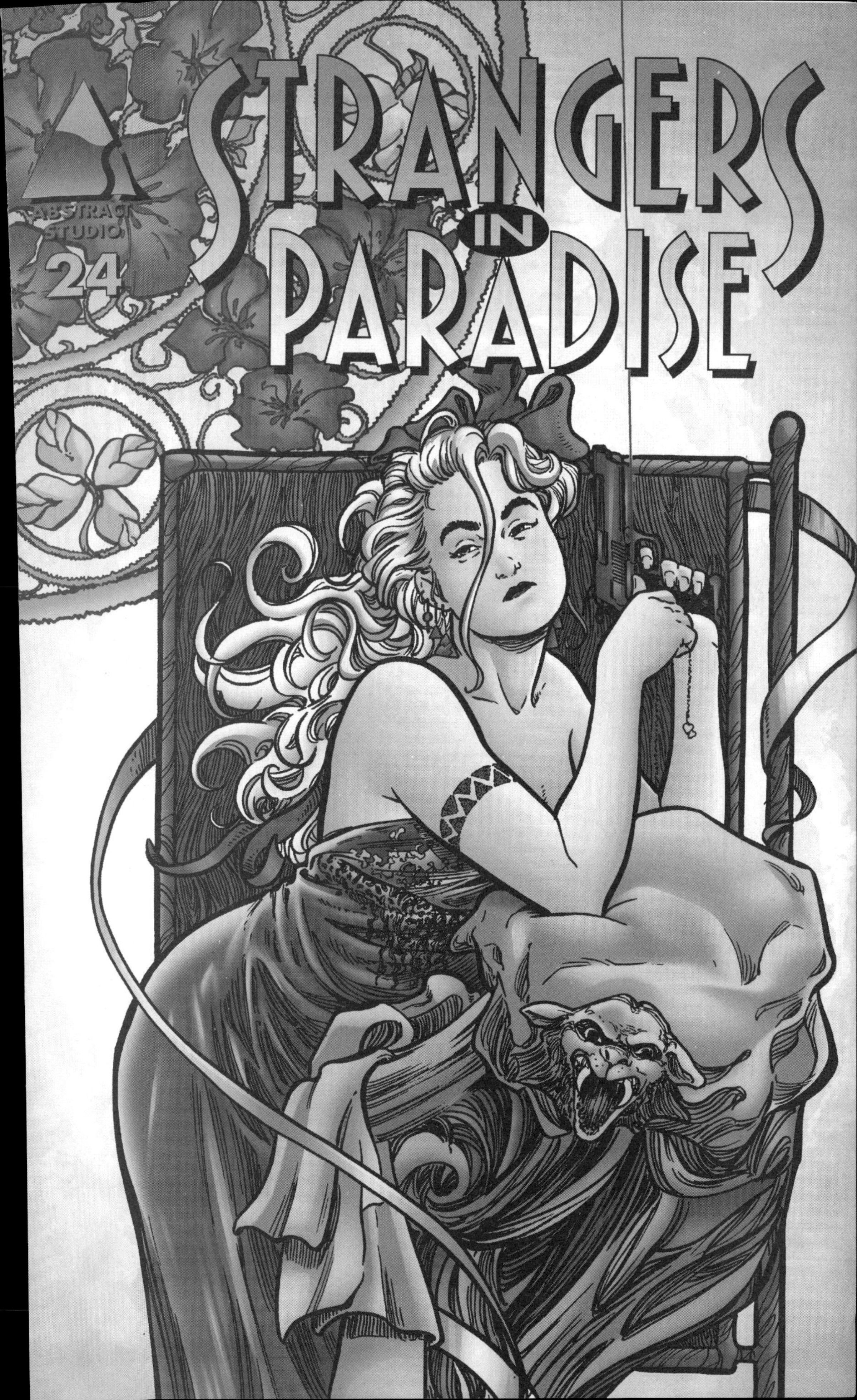

ABSTRACT STUDIO
24
STRANGERS IN PARADISE

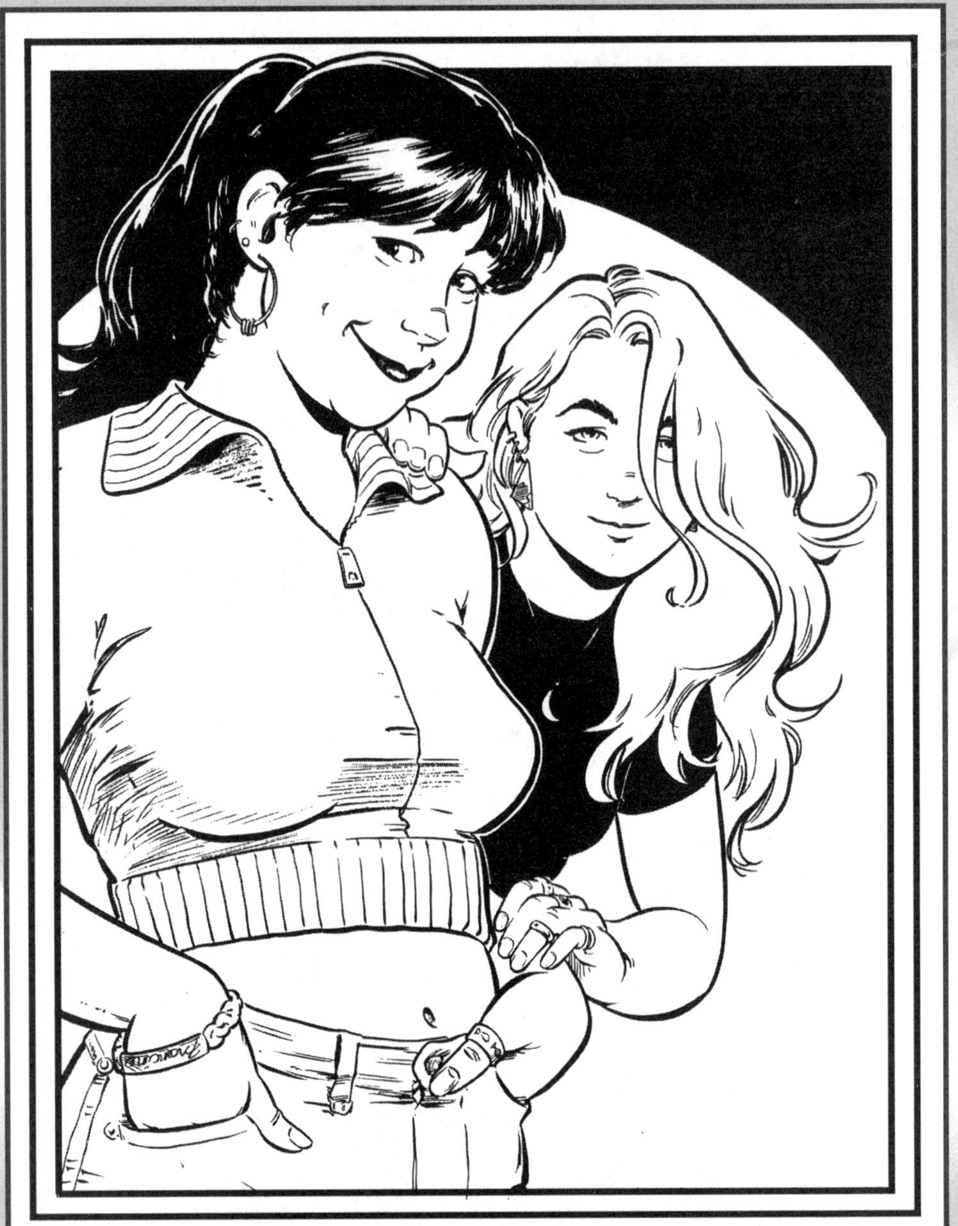

OTHER QUALITY BOOKS IN THE STRANGERS IN PARADISE SERIES:

BOOK 1: THE COLLECTED STRANGERS IN PARADISE
BOOK 2: I DREAM OF YOU
BOOK 3: IT'S A GOOD LIFE
BOOK 4: LOVE ME TENDER
BOOK 5: IMMORTAL ENEMIES
BOOK 6: HIGH SCHOOL
THE COMPLETE STRANGERS IN PARADISE VOLUME ONE
THE COMPLETE STRANGERS IN PARADISE VOLUME TWO

WWW.STRANGERSINPARADISE.COM